Third Edition

RESEARCHING CONSTITUTIONAL LAW

ALBERT P. MELONE
Southern Illinois University Carbondale

WAVELAND

PRESS, INC.

Long Grove, Illinois

Dedicated to John R. Schmidhauser—
a stellar example of a scholar, teacher, and
political practitioner of the post–World War II
generation of American professors
who changed political science
as an academic discipline for the better

For information about this book, contact:
Waveland Press, Inc.
4180 IL Route 83, Suite 101
Long Grove, IL 60047-9580
(847) 634-0081
info@waveland.com
www.waveland.com

Copyright © 2004 by Waveland Press, Inc.

ISBN 1-57766-315-2

All rights reserved. No part of this book may be reproduced, stored in a retrieval system,
or transmitted in any form or by any means without permission in writing from the
publisher.

Printed in the United States of America

7 6 5 4 3 2 1

CONTENTS

3 Why and How to Brief a Case

65

PREFACE

My motivations for writing this book remain the same as when I began work on the first edition in the 1980s. Fundamentally, I have written this book for students in the belief that a central goal of liberal arts education is to help individuals acquire the skills necessary for living an independent life. It is not enough to know the right answers to pre-programmed questions, nor is it sufficient to know what the right questions might be. The ability to study issues outside a structured classroom setting is the training for life that distinguishes the truly educated. *Researching Constitutional Law* reflects the view that all persons living in a democratic polity should possess the tools to research questions that guide how they must live. The law belongs to the people and each member of the political community should know how to investigate questions of law and society.

A focus on constitutional law is particularly appropriate for ordinary citizens because constitutions are statements of principles that guide governments in their internal interactions and the ways governments relate to people. In other words, constitutions are not just lawyers' scribblings on pieces of paper in the manner of a contractual agreement between wary business associates. For good reason, constitution framers intend much more. Because it is their rights and privileges that are fundamentally at stake, it behooves all persons living in the United States to know how to find the law on the Constitution. It is my hope that laypersons, students enrolled in law-related courses, and legal professionals will find this book suitable for their purposes.

As a practical matter, learning to use legal sources equips students with the ability to write intelligent research papers to fulfill course requirements. Instructors everywhere take pleasure in reading and evaluating properly researched and documented student papers. However, despite the best efforts of college curriculum and planning committees, too often instructors are badly disappointed. We hear every excuse ranging from pleas of ignorance about how to accomplish the research and writing to tales of time limitations imposed by the trials of modern life. This book is written in an effort to obviate most student excuses in the knowledge that such a goal is only an ideal. On the bright side, I have been thanked by many students and their instructors who have read and adopted earlier editions of this book. It is because of this positive feedback that I have continued my effort to keep the book current. Happily, students report that they not only learned how to use many important legal research tools and applied those tools to serious social science inquiry but they have used the book as a valuable reference in other courses and professional training.

It became clear to me soon after the publication of the second edition of this text that in short order there would be a need to write a third edition. Between the last years of the twentieth century and the first years of the new millennium, the accessibility of legal materials has accelerated at a breathtaking pace. It seemed that my contemporary students had become computer literate overnight and at the same time overly dependent on Internet sources. It was also evident that publishers of all sorts and libraries around the globe became aware of this revolution and were rushing to fill the demand for such services. Consequently, while I included many Web sites in the second edition of this book I quickly concluded that more were needed. Readers will find in the present edition that I pay considerable attention to electronic sources that facilitate the research process. However, my desire to make this edition useful to the computer-literate audience did not change the basic design of the book. I note many recently published print books and other pertinent works dealing with constitutional law subjects, as was the case for the earlier editions.

I have updated each chapter to include newly available sources both in print and in electronic format. Chapters 1 and 2, which treat primary and secondary sources, have the greatest number of changes. Chapters 3 and 4 have the fewest changes, although I have carefully revised each with an eye for greater clarity. Chapter 5 continues to advise students on writing and documenting sources in a variety of formats, but it now contains a special section on documenting electronic sources. This chapter also references a new appendix that features an example of a research design. With special emphasis on developments in the last few years, I have added to chapter 6 many new summaries of U.S. Supreme Court opinions. The glossary contains new items as well. For the convenience of readers, I have placed in an appendix a copy of the U.S. Constitution. Finally, I have added entries to the already extensive bibliography—especially new books written between 2000 and 2003. This bibliography should serve as a good starting point for locating books on every aspect of American constitutional law, judicial politics, jurisprudence, and related subjects.

As is usually the case in books of this nature, persons other than the author lend a helping hand. I want to gratefully acknowledge three graduate assistants of the Southern Illinois University Carbondale Department of Political Science who aided me along the way. Valerie Teo tracked down newly published books for possible inclusion in the bibliography. She also proofread several chapters and double-checked Web site addresses for me. Alex Ngoma was particularly careful in proofreading some materials relating to this project. That included test bank questions available to instructors adopting this text for classroom use and aiding in one step of the indexing process. Rory Walters was also a great help in running down sources at the Southern Illinois University Law Library; he was particularly helpful with respect to the legal exercises that are part of the Instructor's Manual available to book adopters through the publisher. The secretarial staff of the Southern Illinois University Carbondale Department of Political Science under the supervision of Rhonda Musgrave aided me in this project by performing a variety of tasks that saved me time and reduced my level of frustration.

My son, Peter Melone, a professionally employed computer systems administrator at Computer Services Corporation, read the first two chapters of the book. He offered valuable advice on how to best word instructions on the uses of electronic sources and the acceptable alternative ways to present Web addresses. I am also grateful to my friend and colleague Vincent Lacey for helping me to think about various issues surrounding the use of electronic sites and for his many encouraging words over the years.

As she has done for the previous editions, Laurel Anne Wendt, associate director of the SIU Law Library, helped to locate materials for this edition of the book. She took an active interest in my project and she has for years cheerfully aided my students when they use our university law library. Adria Olmi, formerly the SIUC law reference librarian and now a reference librarian at Aquinas College in Nashville, Tennessee, helped track down many new legal materials and made my task much less time consuming than would have otherwise been the case. She was always accessible and willing to help in locating and understanding new legal source materials.

A special acknowledgment is due Tyson Tanner, a former constitutional law student who is presently enrolled in law school. He has granted permission to reprint as an appendix a slightly modified version of his research design that he wrote as part of a course requirement. His research design serves to supplement my written instructions for writing research designs as a suitable example to follow.

I am grateful to Don Rosso, associate editor at Waveland Press, for the careful production of this manuscript including a first-rate job of copyediting and to publisher Neil Rowe for his continued interest in keeping this book current.

I owe a continuing debt of gratitude to my spouse Peggy for her continuing good cheer and support through it all.

PRIMARY SOURCES
JUDICIAL OPINIONS AND STATUTORY LAW

Introduction

The first two chapters of this book will acquaint students with the primary and secondary sources necessary to locate legal materials for their research. The goal of this first chapter is to familiarize students with the most basic legal materials upon which additional research tools are predicated. I present these materials with a view toward minimizing unnecessary legal jargon, making it possible for students to conduct legal research for undergraduate and graduate assignments. Many examples in this chapter are from the field of constitutional law; however, they are applicable to many law-related undergraduate and graduate courses including administrative law, business law, criminal justice, consumer affairs, legal studies, paralegal studies, and planning law.

The usual starting point for legal research in the United States and other common law countries is the reported opinions of judges and justices. In the civil law countries of western Europe, in contrast, legal analysis begins with statutory laws in the form of elaborate codes, and some continental legal scholars insist that is where all analysis must center, if not end. Statutory law is also important in modern America, but less so. What judges say the law means through their written judicial opinions is the most logical point to begin the search for legal knowledge because judges are empowered to find and interpret legal norms. In fact, judges often create the law. Without their written opinions, it is impossible to cite cases as precedent, and the principle of *stare decisis*—stand by past decisions—has little meaning. With this in mind, understanding where and how to locate the sources of court opinions is fundamentally important.

Many college and university libraries have much of the legal research material discussed in this chapter. Those institutions with law schools naturally will provide the fullest opportunity to conduct legal research. Some readers may discover inadequate library sources; many community libraries, however, have adequate law collections, and many state governments provide law libraries for public use. The Internet is a boon to those with limited hardcopy library facilities. However, it is problematic to conduct legal research and write a scholarly paper by relying exclusively on online resources. Nevertheless, when appropriately utilized, exploring the Internet will save students valuable time and energy. It behooves students to avail themselves of useful sites. Yet, they should understand that not all sites are permanent, and the usefulness of non-subscription sites is limited usually to just a few of the many necessary tasks involved in writing a serious paper. I will describe several of these Web-based non-subscription sites as the topic arises. In addition, several commercial publishers provide online services that are available to attorneys and some libraries. These services are expensive and are not typically available to most readers of this text. Recently, however, many universities and colleges have begun subscribing to less costly services designed for the nonprofessional community. These relatively new services, LexisNexis Academic and Westlaw Campus, are user-friendly. Each provides many resources to undergraduate and graduate students. I will describe these services and their uses at appropriate places in this and the following chapter.

Those already familiar with Web addresses will note that I present the entire URL (Uniform Resource Locator) for each Web address. However, when locating sites it is usually unnecessary to type the HTTP protocol. The World Wide Web designation (www) followed by the remaining server name is quite sufficient to reach most sites. Consequently, in most cases, researchers need not bother with typing the http:// portion of the Web address. I include the full addresses to alert readers to the convention that in referencing Web sites in footnotes, endnotes, and bibliographies, most writing manuals require full addresses as well as additional information that I detail in chapter 5. Also, all readers should understand that the addresses I provide in this and other chapters for various electronic sites are likely to change over time. Consequently, if one cannot find a site based on the addresses that I provide that does not necessarily mean the site itself no longer exists. Rather than giving up, one should try alternative paths to the same source, employing simple word searches and other tools available on your browser. In short, when the need arises go surfing.

Supreme Court Opinions

Because the government, private publishing firms, and Web sites distribute judicial opinions, often there is more than a single citation to the same case: for example, Hill v. Colorado, 530 U.S. 703, 120 S. Ct. 2480, 147 L. Ed. 2d 597 (2000), 2000 LEXIS 4486. We refer to these multiple citations to a single case as *parallel citations*. They function as addresses to find particular judicial opinions in different locations. For the case of *Hill v. Colorado*, the official report is in *United States Reports*.

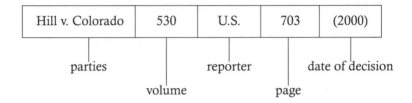

The first entry, 530 U.S. 703, refers to the official government publication *United States Reports* (U.S.). The number preceding the letters U.S. (530) refers to the volume, and the number following U.S. (703) indicates the first page in volume 530 of the *United States Reports* on which *Hill v. Colorado* appears. The citation to the *Supreme Court Reporter* (S. Ct.) is 120 S. Ct. 2480. It indicates that this case is located in volume 120 and begins on page 2480. The third citation, 147 L. Ed. 2d 597 refers to the place in the *United States Supreme Court Reports, Lawyers' Edition* (L. Ed.) where *Hill v. Colorado* may also be located; that is, in volume 147 beginning on page 597. The date in parentheses (2000) is the year the U.S. Supreme Court delivered the opinion in *Hill v. Colorado*. The last parallel citation is to LEXIS, an electronic source that I discuss below. Often researchers have in their possession only the name and date of a court opinion. Consequently, citing the year in which a court delivers an opinion can be a useful piece of information. It is convenient to provide parallel citations because students and instructors often have access to only one set of court reports.

All four of these court reports have one common feature. Each multi-volume set contains the written opinions of the Supreme Court. The *United States Reports* is an official report, whereas the *Supreme Court Reporter*, the *Lawyers' Edition*, and LEXIS are unofficial publications by private firms. Each source has its own special features.

United States Reports (U.S.)

The first ninety volumes of this official report contain the names of the respective court reporter. From 1790 to 1874 the court reporter's name is printed on each volume and is cited, e.g., Marbury v. Madison, 5 U.S. (Cranch) 137 (1803). A list of the full names of the seven reporters follows, along with their name abbreviations as they appear in legal citations, the volume number designations of the *U.S. Reports* to which each contributed, and their corresponding years of service. The designation for the *United States Reports*, changed in 1875, is now by volume number only, beginning with volume 91.

A. J. Dallas (Dall.)	1–4 U.S. (1789–1800)
William Cranch (Cranch)	5–13 U.S. (1801–1815)
Henry Wheaton (Wheat.)	14–25 U.S. (1816–1827)
Richard Peters (Peters)	26–41 U.S. (1828–1842)
Benjamin C. Howard (How.)	42–65 U.S. (1843–1860)
J. S. Black (Black)	66–67 U.S. (1861–1862)
John William Wallace (Wall.)	68–90 U.S. (1863–1874)

In addition to the official opinions of the Supreme Court, the *United States Reports* contains summaries of facts, syllabi, and indexes. Syllabi, sometimes called headnotes, are brief summaries of the important aspects of cases and contain references to the pages of the written opinions containing significant legal points. These features provide a quick reference to the contents of each case and can save valuable research time.

Shortly after the justices of the Supreme Court hand down an opinion, the Government Printing Office releases a *slip opinion*, the first release of the Supreme Court's decision. Most libraries that have the *U.S. Reports* receive slip opinions. They are placed together in advanced sheets as preliminary prints and ultimately the opinions are placed in bound volumes at the end of the Court's term. Unfortunately, preparing and distributing the final bound volumes takes several years, so practicing attorneys and researchers prefer to use the unofficial reports available through private publishing houses.

When citing a U.S. Supreme Court opinion, legal authorities prefer the official report (U.S.) alone without parallel citations, e.g., California v. Acevedo, 500 U.S. 565 (1991); Taylor v. Doe, 54 U.S. (13 How.) 287 (1851). When referencing a case in the body of a written text along with any form of legal citation (parallel or not), the case name should appear in ordinary typeface. For example, one might write: "The Supreme Court decision in California v. Acevedo, 500 U.S. 565 (1991) held that police in a search extending only to a container within an automobile may search the container without a warrant where they have probable cause to believe that it holds contraband or evidence. . . ." Note that in such instances one should not underline or italicize case names. The same rule applies when a case name with citation appears in a footnote, endnote, or bibliographic entry. However, if the writer provides only the name of the case or the case name and date of the opinion without other citation information (volume number, reporter system, and page number), then one should italicize the case name; e.g., "*California v. Acevedo* (1991) or simply *Acevedo* stands for the proposition that there is no difference. . . ." Incidentally, writers should underline the word when the italic function is unavailable. Today, however, all modern word-processing programs are equipped with the italic function. Writers should use it.

United States Supreme Court Reports, Lawyers' Edition (L. Ed.)

United States Supreme Court Reports, Lawyers' Edition was formerly published under the imprint of the Lawyers Cooperative Publishing Company and the Bancroft-Whitney Company. It is now published by LEXIS Law Publishing and is also available on CD-ROM. It contains all Supreme Court decisions in two series and includes accompanying tables of parallel references to the official *United States Reports*. In addition to the opinions rendered in the official reports, the *Lawyers' Edition* contains features valuable to the practicing attorney and student researcher, including summaries of each case with headnotes (syllabi), and abbreviated versions of the briefs of counsel with annotations discussing important legal developments reported in the official cases. For example, the case of Nixon v. Administrator of General Services, 53 L. Ed. 2d 867 (1976) gave rise to an annotation on Bills of Attainder. The twenty-nine-page essay at the back of the volume provides a thorough and current treatment of the topic. Beginning with volume 32 of the *Second Series*, each volume contains pocket supplements placed inside the back cover. This service provides brief summaries of holdings from later Supreme Court decisions that refer to decisions published in the in-hand *L. Ed. 2d* volume. In this way, it is possible for researchers to learn how later courts treated a case they had just read.

A useful *Desk Book* that accompanies the *Lawyers' Edition, Second Series*, contains a table of cases for those instances when the researcher knows only the case name without the benefit of a volume number, page number, and reporter name. By looking up the case name, the researcher can find parallel legal citations as well as other references keyed to other *Lawyers' Edition, Second Series* material. This annual supplement also contains a table of justices of the Supreme Court, a table of federal laws, rules and regulations cited and construed, and an index to cases and annotations arranged alphabetically by subject matter. Also, see *Later Case Service and Citation Service*. This two-volume set with annual supplements updates annotations found in the *Lawyers' Edition, Second Series*. The publisher has also made available a *Quick Case Table with Annotation References,* a one-volume reference to all headnoted cases decided by the Supreme Court.

When the Supreme Court is in session, the *Lawyers' Edition* is kept current with the twice-monthly publication of advance sheets containing the most recent decisions of the Supreme Court with various research aids furnished by the editors. Together with other LEXIS Law Publishing products, the *Lawyers' Edition* is an outstanding research tool.

Supreme Court Reporter (S. Ct.)

The *Supreme Court Reporter*, issued by the West Group, is an unofficial law reporter containing many of the same features as the *Lawyers' Edition*. For example, headnotes and other references correlate with other West publications. The editors of this reporter also supplement the bound volumes with semimonthly advance sheets when the Supreme Court is in session. The Court's opinions are first placed in temporary volumes before final publication, making it convenient to access decisions.

Unfortunately, in contrast to the *Lawyers' Edition*, the *Supreme Court Reporter* offers one major disadvantage; it begins with the Supreme Court's 1882 term and therefore it does not contain the cases reported in volumes 1–105 of the official *United States Reports*. Nonetheless, the *Supreme Court Reporter* remains a useful reference. It is especially useful when researchers employ it with other products that employ the West Key Number System® (discussed in chapter 2). Occasionally, *Supreme Court Reporter* volumes contain essays of interest to those judicial scholars concerned with more than Court opinions. One such instance is "The Supreme Court's New Rules—Model 1995," by Bennett Baskey and Eugene Gressman (116 S. Ct. 11 (1995)).

Non-Subscription Internet Sources for Supreme Court Opinions

The Legal Information Institute provides all Supreme Court opinions since May 1990 and contains a collection of over 600 historically important decisions. It is available on CD-ROM but is also available without charge at http://www.supct.law.cornell.edu.

The Internet allows researchers to access Supreme Court opinions almost immediately after the justices render their decisions. Depending on the Court term, it is possible to access cases by term, topic, or party name. This service also provides the Court calendar for the current term, the current schedule of oral arguments, biographies of current and former justices, Supreme Court rules, and information about the Court's jurisdiction, organization, and authority. Students also will find a brief glossary of terms, intended for the use of non-lawyers.

Researchers can search and view the full text of 7,407 Supreme Court decisions from volumes 300 to 422 of the *U.S. Reports* (1937–1975) at http://www.fedworld.gov/supcourt. The site allows the researcher to search by case name or keyword. For cases beginning in 1893, see http://www.findlaw.com. The United States Supreme Court now has its official Internet site at http://www.supremecourtus.gov. It includes recent opinions, links to Web sites with Supreme Court opinions, and other features, including the Court calendar, that serious Court watchers pay close attention to.

Other notable Web sites accessible at no cost to users that contain U.S. Supreme Court opinions are http://www.access.gpo.gov/su_docs/supcrt/index.html and http://www.oyez.nwu.edu. The first is the work of the GPO Access User Support Team of the U.S. Government Printing Office. The Oyez site is an ambitious project led by Professor Jerry Goldman of the political science department at Northwestern University. Curious students may wish to consult legal search engines to locate new sites containing Court opinions as they emerge. The Southern Illinois University School of

Law maintains a current list of useful legal search engines at http://www.law.siu.edu/lawlib/general/search.htm. This site includes an unusually good discussion of how Internet search engines function, a tutorial on how to use them, and a description of the major extant search engines.

Access to Court Opinions
through Subscription Services

Many law offices, universities, and colleges now subscribe to online services that are extremely useful for locating, reading, and printing U.S. Supreme Court opinions. These same sources also allow researchers to access a host of opinions of federal and state jurisdictions and other useful research materials and tools that I shall describe as each topic arises. These commercial systems make available a wide variety of legal research materials heretofore available only in print format found on library shelves in brick-and-mortar buildings. They shorten the time attorneys and researchers must spend researching legal issues.

Today, there are two widely used services in use in law offices and law libraries: LexisNexis and Westlaw. Reed Elsevier sells LexisNexis to subscribers and Westlaw is owned by West, which in turn is owned by Thomson Publishing. Each information system has a different database, and each employs user input commands along with key names, concepts, terms, words, cases, authors, courts, judges, and so on. Within minutes, the service prints out the desired information. The clear attraction of these services is the reduction in the time and pain associated with long hours in the library. However, one cannot intelligently use computer services without a preexisting understanding of the organization and functions of law research materials. For this reason, many law schools do not permit first-year law students to use these systems until they have become familiar with a wide array of legal concepts and the physical law library itself. Then, usually during the second semester of study, trained law librarians instruct law students on the use of LexisNexis and/or Westlaw. In any event, to use these higher-powered subscription services one must consult a trained law librarian or have access to an institution or law office that subscribes to one of them.

In addition, however, the providers of LexisNexis and Westlaw have created online legal research tools designed specifically for undergraduate and graduate students without formal legal training. LexisNexis Academic (sometimes called Academic Universe) and Westlaw Campus are sold on a subscription basis to institutions of higher learning at considerably less cost per user than those designed for the professional legal community. Importantly, they avoid legal jargon in favor of an ordinary-language approach with the view of making legal materials available to students of political science, criminal justice, business, economics, and related academic fields.

LexisNexis Academic

In addition to legal materials, this service accesses news and wire services, business and market information, medical news, congressional information, statistical data, and other reference information. Students seeking to find a particular U.S. Supreme Court opinion should first access the *LexisNexis Academic Menu Page* and then under *Academic Search Forms* they should click on *Legal Research*. There you will find six broad categories of basic legal research including: secondary literature, case law, codes & regulations, international legal materials, patent research, and career information. Within the case law section, click on either the *Get a Case* or *Federal Case Law* subsections. Either choice will allow one to find the sought Supreme Court opinion. For example, under the *Get a Case* option researchers are prompted to type in the name of the parties (e.g., *Hill v. Colorado*) or the legal citation (e.g., 530 U.S. 703) to be followed by activating the search button. Within a few seconds, the full opinion appears. This retrieval system contains a number of helpful hints for completing a successful search of pertinent cases, including footnotes and what professional legal researchers call star pagination—references to particular page numbers that correspond to print sources such as the *U.S. Reports*. Researchers using LexisNexis Academic to read and reference court opinions should cite LEXIS; e.g., Hill v. Colorado, 2000 U.S. LEXIS 4486. The number 2000 is the date of decision, U.S. LEXIS is the reporter, and 4486 is the electronic page number where the opinion first appears. Alternatively, through the employment of the star pagination system, researchers may cite the exact page number(s) from the print report where Court opinion writers reference particular words, phrases, or ideas.

Westlaw Campus

West, the legal publishing giant, also has made a product designed for the undergraduate and graduate student audience available to colleges and universities. Like LexisNexis Academic, Westlaw Campus uses natural language relatively free from legal jargon so that college students may access the law without prior legal knowledge. It contains published and unpublished judicial opinions from all federal and state courts. But this service contains much more, making practically the entire West publication system available online to nonprofessionals. These products include, for example, legal codes, encyclopedia materials, legal periodicals, and digest functions that I will discuss later in this and the next chapter. For now, let us concentrate on finding U.S. Supreme Court opinions.

When attempting to retrieve any information from Westlaw Campus students should enter requests at the *Search Center*. Researchers have three search options: *Search For*, *Select Database(s)*, and *Find a Document*. All three allow students to retrieve a case but the simplest method is the last option, *Find a Document*. Researchers are presented with two desirable options. First, insert the legal citation (e.g., 120 S. Ct. 2480) or the name of the parties—in our case, *Hill v. Colorado*. Simply click on the *Go* button and within seconds, the full Supreme Court opinion appears. As with West's *Supreme Court Reporter,* the cases feature several editorial enhancements including paragraph-length summaries of the facts and the main legal issues in a case, sentence-length summaries of each legal issue discussed in the case, and the powerful West Key Number System® that I discuss in chapter 2. Because the West reporter system is in electronic format, cite to the Supreme Court Reporter; e.g., Hill v. Colorado, 120 S. Ct. 2480 (2000).

Although a uniform standard for citing court opinions from the Internet is yet to be achieved, I suggest that researchers list the case name, the report citation, year of decision, and Internet address; for example, Hill v. Colorado, 530 U.S. 703 (2000), available at http://www. Lexis-Nexis.com/universe/ form/academic/s.

Briefs Filed with the U.S. Supreme Court

Supreme Court rules require legal counsel to present written arguments called briefs to support their cases. Attorneys file such briefs, which vary from ten or twenty pages to several hundred pages, with the explicit intent of convincing justices how they should decide the case. Briefs contain detailed legal justifications with appropriate citations to existing precedents and extra-legal materials in support of client interests.

Supreme Court justices are free to reject any or all of the arguments found in the written briefs. Careful reading of briefs and opinions written by justices, however, show that justices often rely on briefs for arguments in support of a given position. Interested third parties may also file amicus curiae briefs with the Court to provide material, information, and arguments to assist decision making.

Researchers use briefs to gain a greater understanding of the issues and possible outcomes of cases than they would receive from only reading Court opinions. Because legal counsel commonly present a wide range of ideas, lines of legal reasoning, and social and political justifications in writing, even when they appear contradictory, briefs of counsel are particularly useful when exploring such addenda. If the researcher is conducting an in-depth study of a particular case, then a careful reading of the submitted briefs will add much to comprehension of the case. In addition, it is interesting to note whether the Court accepts, rejects, or ignores the arguments contained in the briefs.

The following citation is an example of how to reference one of the several sources where Supreme Court arguments and briefs can be found: Appellant's Brief at 112, Roe v. Wade, 410 U.S. 113 (1973), in vol. 75, *Landmark and Arguments of the Supreme Court of the United States: Constitutional Law.* A discussion of these sources follows. See chapter 5 for additional illustrations.

Landmark Briefs and Arguments of the Supreme Court of the United States: Constitutional Law

Before the middle of the nineteenth century, oral argument was the principal form of advocacy. In 1849, the Supreme Court ruled that counsel could not be heard at oral argument unless they first filed a formal written brief. As a result, briefs are not uniformly available for many early cases of the Supreme Court. However, the editors of *Landmark Briefs and Arguments of the Supreme Court of the United States* have made a significant contribution by locating existing documents including notes and summaries of oral arguments held by the National Archives and private sources.

Landmark Briefs and Arguments of the Supreme Court of the United States: Constitutional Law is edited by Philip Kurland and Gerard Casper, published by University Publications of America, and available at many law libraries. The first eighty volumes of this impressive work first appeared in 1978; by 2002, the set numbered 303 volumes and will continue to grow as additional landmark cases are handed down by the high court. Notable examples of cases contained in this set include *McCulloch v. Maryland* (1819) in volume 1, *Carter v. Carter Coal Co.* (1936) in volume 32, *Baker v. Carr* (1962) in volume 56, *Garcia v. San Antonio Metropolitan Transit Authority* (1984) in volume 159, *Reno v. American Civil Liberties Union* (1997) in volume 261, and in volume 303, *Federal Election Commission v. Colorado Republican Federal Campaign Committee* (2001).

U.S. Supreme Court Records and Briefs

Unfortunately, the Kurland and Casper work only contains briefs and oral arguments of landmark decisions. To satisfy research needs about less notable decisions, several publishers have made *U.S. Supreme Court Records and Briefs* available on microfilm and microfiche, beginning with cases decided in 1832 and extending to the present day. This work contains materials pertinent to each Supreme Court opinion. The following publishers were associated at one time or another with the production of these materials: Congressional Information Service (CIS), Scholarly Resources, Information Handling Services, Microcard Editions Services, and the United States Printing Office. Ask your law librarian to determine whether briefs related to your specific research interest are available in microtext format. If a law library has all or some of these materials, hard-copy indexes probably will be on hand as well. Suitable for recent cases, the Findlaw Web site contains in electronic format briefs of counsel of opinions filed before the U.S. Supreme Court beginning in 1999. The site is located at http://supreme.lp.findlaw.com/ supreme_court/briefs/index.html.

The Oyez Project: U.S. Supreme Court Multimedia Database

When it is finished, the Oyez Project at Northwestern University will contain the oral arguments of more than 500 cases decided by the Supreme

Court since 1955. It employs RealAudio technology so that researchers may stream files directly to their computers, enabling them to hear for themselves the audio of actual oral arguments before the Supreme Court. To access this technology, download and install on your computer the free version of *RealPlayer8 (Basic)* or its successor versions when available. Some audio materials available through Oyez require downloading and installing *QuickTime*. The site also contains the full text of Supreme Court opinions and lower court opinions, as well as biographical sketches and photographs of the justices. One can find Oyez at http://www.oyez.nwu.edu or http://www.oyez.org/oyez/frontpage. Also, Findlaw.com posts transcripts and links to other sites, and some news organizations, including CNN.com, PBS.org, and C-Span.org, have in the past posted oral arguments for particularly controversial cases such as the Supreme Court argument that resulted in George W. Bush winning the 2000 presidential election over Albert Gore, and the University of Michigan affirmative action dispute argued in 2003.

A similar project is *May It Please the Court*, edited by Peter Irons and Stephanie Guitton and published in 1993 by the New Press, New York. It contains audiotapes of twenty-three landmark cases as argued before the Supreme Court. It includes the actual voices of the attorneys and justices in oral argument.

LexisNexis and Findlaw

Briefs recently filed before the U.S. Supreme Court from October 1979 forward are accessible online through LexisNexis. If one has access to LexisNexis Academic, click on *Federal Case Law*. Then click the cursor at the *Source List* under the bold heading *Court*. Select *Supreme Court Briefs*. There you will find the briefs of the actual parties and briefs filed by interested parties in the form of amicus curiae briefs. Also, since the 1999 term of the Supreme Court, Findlaw.com has made briefs of counsel available online at http://supreme.findlaw.com/Supreme_Court/resources.html.

Lower Federal Court Reports

Until recently, social scientists placed almost exclusive emphasis on the decisions of the U.S. Supreme Court. There is a growing awareness, however, that preoccupation with the high court unduly constricts our view of how the entire judicial system operates. Besides setting the stage for Supreme Court determination of issues, federal district courts and courts of appeal deal with issues that, for one reason or another, the Supreme Court never adjudicates. Because such decisions may have far-reaching policy implications for the political system at large, they should not be ignored. Students must be aware of developments in the inferior federal courts and should be familiar with the reporter system for federal cases.

Federal Cases (F. Cas.)

Before 1880, opinions of the federal district courts and the circuit courts of appeal were scattered through a variety of reports. In 1880, this situation was remedied when the West Publishing Company reprinted all previously reported federal cases in a thirty-one volume set entitled *Federal Cases*. Although cases are usually reported in chronological order, *Federal Cases* is an exception—cases are arranged alphabetically by the name of the case.[1] The following is a sample citation: United States v. Burr, 25 F. Cas. 1 (C.C.D. Kent. 1806) (No. 14,692).

Federal Reporter (F.), (F. 2d), (F. 3d)

Today, 13 courts adjudicate appeals from the 94 U.S. district courts. The United States Courts of Appeal also hear appeals from federal administrative agencies and other specialized courts such as the Court of International Trade and the U.S. Federal Claims Court. The map below displays the geographical jurisdiction of the eleven numbered circuits and the two un-numbered circuits (the U.S. Court of Appeals for the Federal Circuit and the U.S. Court of Appeals for the District of Columbia). It also lists the specialized courts to which disappointed litigants may appeal their cases.

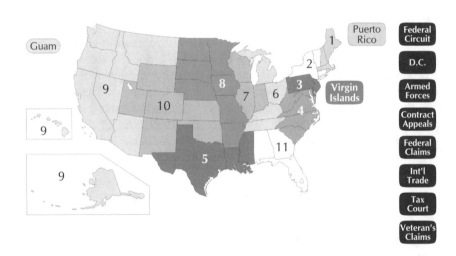

The *Federal Reporter*, also published by West, contains decisions of federal courts with appellate jurisdiction other than the U.S. Supreme Court delivered since 1880. The *Federal Reporter* also contains decisions of specialized federal courts having original and appellate jurisdiction. The opinions of the following courts are reported:

- U.S. Court of Appeals (1891–present)
- U.S. Circuit Courts (1880–1911)

- Commerce Court of the U.S. (1911–1913)
- U.S. District Courts (1880–1932)
- U.S. Court of Claims (1929–1932 and 1960–1982)
- U.S. Court of Customs and Patent Appeals (1929–1982)
- U.S. Emergency Court of Appeals (1943–1961)
- Temporary Emergency Court of Appeals (1972–1993)[2]

Sample citations for decisions of the thirteen judicial bodies that comprise the United States Court of Appeals are: Kadala v. Amoco Oil Co., 820 F. 2d 1355 (4th Cir. 1987); United States v. Smith, 40 F. 3d 933 (8th Cir. 1994).

The Internet is of limited use in locating opinions of the U.S. Court of Appeals because to date very few years of opinions have been placed on the Web. The Internet Legal Resource guide at http://www.ilrg.com reports most federal courts including all circuit courts, and many state supreme and appellate courts maintain their own Internet sites with databases containing their opinions. Because, however, these databases are not comprehensive, researchers will find only relatively recent opinions. For example, researchers may find decisions of the Federal Circuit from 1995 forward at http://www.fedcir.gov/#opinion.

The task is made easy for those researchers with access to LexisNexis or Westlaw because these subscription services contain a complete listing of opinions of the U.S. Courts of Appeal. College students with access to LexisNexis Academic or Westlaw Campus also are able to avail themselves of the complete opinions of this court system. Follow the analogous instructions for locating opinions as one does for U.S. Supreme Court opinions. By the way, West has a separate service called WestDoc. It operates independently from Westlaw and Westlaw Campus. For a fee, one may retrieve state and federal cases and law review articles through WestDoc.

Federal Appendix

Until recently, thousands of federal appeals court opinions have gone unreported because of a lack of publication. Consequently, appeal courts at the federal and state levels render decisions seemingly without precedential value. However, the electronic age has made it possible to post these heretofore unpublished opinions and lawyers may find them useful in building their legal arguments. Yet, some federal circuits have prohibited citation to or reliance upon their unpublished opinions; this has become a cause of much debate within legal circles. Some circuits permit the citation of unpublished opinions as binding opinion, but the rules of other circuits allow citation of unpublished opinions as possessing "persuasive" value only. In this context, the semantically odd practice of publishing "unpublished" opinions of the federal circuit courts began in September 2001.[3] By the time this book is published, the *Federal Appendix* produced by West will contain most of the "unpublished" opinions of nearly all of the federal circuit courts. In addition, it will contain all of the usual editorial aides of the wider West reporting system including headnotes, key numbers, and so on. West suggests that opinions appearing in these volumes should be cited, for example, as: Perkins v. Nelson, 53 Fed. Appx. 893 (10th Cir. 2002). These print opinions also are available electronically through Westlaw, and accessible online through Westlaw Campus.

Federal Supplement (F. Supp.), (F. Supp. 2d)

There is a minimum of one court with original federal jurisdiction in all fifty states, the District of Columbia, Puerto Rico, Guam, the Virgin Islands, and the Northern Mariana Islands. These courts also have local jurisdiction in Guam, the Virgin Islands, and the Northern Mariana Islands. For U.S. District Court opinions before 1932, it is necessary to consult the *Federal Reporter* (1880–1932) and *Federal Cases* (1789–1880). Comprising 999 volumes, *Federal Supplement* contains U.S. District Court decisions for the current era (1932–1998). *Federal Supplement, Second Series* began in 1998 and will continue until a third series begins publication.

The *Federal Supplement* also contains decisions since 1980 of the United States Court of International Trade (formerly named the United States Customs Court), decisions of the Judicial Panel on Multi-District Litigation (1968–present), the U.S Customs Court (1954–1980), and the U.S. Court of Claims (1932–1960).[4] Following are sample citations for United States District Court opinions: Republic of Philippines v. Marcos, 665 F. Supp. 793 (N.D. Cal 1987); Delahanty v. Hinckley, 686 F. Supp. 920 (D.D.C. 1986).

A few reporters publish opinions of federal courts that are unlikely to receive much attention from constitutional law students. First released in 1982, the *United States Claims Court Reporter* contains opinions and speaking orders for the new United States Claims Court and opinions of the U.S. Courts of Appeals and the Supreme Court for cases on appeal from the U.S. Claims Court. *Federal Rules Decisions* reports cases involving U.S. District Court opinions interpreting the federal rules of civil and criminal procedure that are not found in the *Federal Supplement*. The *Military Justice Reporter* contains decisions of the United States Court of Military Appeals and the Army, Navy, Air Force, and Coast Guard Courts of Military Review. Finally, on occasion one may find use for the self-explanatory *Bankruptcy Reporter*. Opinions published in these reporters should be cited as suggested in each volume by the publisher, West.

LexisNexis Academic and Westlaw Campus contain all reported case law of the U.S. District Courts from 1789 to the present day. Those without access to either a law library or university subscription services may want to try various legal search engines with a growing inventory of district court case law. I suggest Findlaw at http://www.findlaw.com and MegaLaw at http://www.megalaw.com.

State Court Reporters

The American federal system presupposes that the majority of human relations are governed by the states. Indeed, most legal activity takes place at state and local levels of government. Although some federal court cases are first processed through state judicial systems, state courts also are important centers for policy making independent of the federal judiciary. Some state court systems are perceived as trail blazers and often are cited as authority in other American courts. Therefore, a working knowledge of state court reporters is a prerequisite for comprehending policy making in the entire judicial system.

Almost one-half of the states publish their own official court reports. Some have elected to report only opinions of the highest state court while others report all appellate courts and some publish only decisions of trial courts.[5] As part of its National Reporter System, West has made state appellate decisions for all the states available, as well as trial court opinions for some states. It divides the nation into seven geographical regions. See table 1 for a listing of each regional reporter with the states covered and a sample citation for each regional entry.

Probably reflecting case volume and market considerations, West also produces three state-specific reporters. First released in 1887, the *New York Supplement* reports all opinions of the New York Court of Appeals, all decisions of the Appellate Division of the Supreme Court, and all opinions of the lower courts of record. In 1960, the *California Reporter* made its debut, reporting all decisions of the California Supreme Court and the California District Courts of Appeal. *Illinois Decisions* contains opinions of the Illinois Supreme Court and the Illinois appellate courts from 1976 forward.

All West law products contain attractive reference features not found in official government reports. Most important is the West Key Number System® (discussed in detail in chapter 2). All West publications are coordinated to provide an interlocking research network. Mastering this system is not particularly difficult and the payoffs are worth the effort.

Once again, LexisNexis Academic and Westlaw Campus contain a large number of cases dating back to the early nineteenth century. The online free services of the Legal Information Institute of Cornell University Law School provide relatively recent state appellate court cases for all 50 states. It is available at http://www.law.cornell.edu/states/index.html. The Findlaw Web site also contains recent cases from all 50 state jurisdictions at http://www.findlaw.com/casecode/index.html#statelaw. Unlike LexisNexis Academic and Westlaw Campus these non-subscription sources contain only some state appellate court opinions commencing in a variety of years; for example, available opinions for Alabama begin in 1998 but for California, researchers may locate opinions dating from 1934.

Table 1   National Reporter System

Reporter	States Covered and Sample Citation
North Western Reporter 1879–1940 (1st series) 1940–present (2nd series)	Iowa, Michigan, Minnesota, Nebraska, North Dakota, South Dakota, Wisconsin. Nelson v. Nelson Cattle Co., 513 N.W. 2d 900 (S.D. 1994).
Pacific Reporter 1883–1931 (1st series) 1931–2000 (2d series) 2000–present (3d series)	Alaska, Arizona, California, Colorado, Hawaii, Idaho, Kansas, Montana, Nevada, New Mexico, Oklahoma, Oregon, Utah, Washington, Wyoming. Buffalo v. State, 901 P. 2d 647 (Nev. 1995).
Atlantic Reporter 1885–1938 (1st series) 1938–present (2d series)	Connecticut, Delaware, Maine, Maryland, New Hampshire, New Jersey, Pennsylvania, Rhode Island, Vermont, District of Columbia Municipal Court of Appeals. Armstead v. State, 673 A. 2d 221 (Md. 1996).
North Eastern Reporter 1885–1936 (1st series) 1936–present (2d series)	Illinois, Indiana, Massachusetts, New York, Ohio. People v. Godina, 584 N.E. 2d 523 (Ill. App.3 Dist. 1991).
South Eastern Reporter 1887–1939 (1st series) 1939–present (2d series)	Georgia, North Carolina, South Carolina, Virginia, West Virginia. State of North Carolina v. Robinson, 409 S.E. 2d 288 (N.C. 1991).
Southern Reporter 1887–1940 (1st series) 1940–present (2d series)	Alabama, Florida, Louisiana, Mississippi. McDonald v. Holmes, 595 So. 2d 434 (Miss. 1992).
South Western Reporter 1886–1940 (1st series) 1940–1999 (2d series) 1999–present (3d series)	Arkansas, Kentucky, Missouri, Tennessee, Texas, Indian Territory (1896–1907). Rodriguez v. State, 93 S.W. 3d 60 (Tex.Crim.App. 2002).

American Law Reports (A.L.R.)

American Law Reports does not neatly fit the description of a court reporter. It contains judicial decisions, but its primary function extends beyond the reporting of court opinions. It is best employed as an excellent annotation elaborating on important judicial opinions.

Once a Lawyers Cooperative and Bancroft-Whitney publication but now acquired by West, *American Law Reports*, in fact, is a highly selective case reporter. The editors choose for inclusion those cases that illustrate important legal developments. An impartial treatment of the law relevant to the particular case follows each judicial opinion. Each annotation includes a detailed treatise on the specific legal topic that discusses the inception, development, and contemporary applicability of the law relating to the reported judicial opinions.

First published in 1919, *American Law Reports* is now in its sixth series. The first series covers the period from 1919 to 1948 and contains 175 volumes. The second series *(A.L.R. 2d)* deals with legal topics from 1948 to 1965 and appears in one hundred volumes. Also in one hundred volumes, the third series *(A.L.R. 3d)* contains both state and federal topics from 1965 to 1969, but from 1969 to 1979, it treats only state law topics. Introduced in 1980, the ninety-volume fourth series *(A.L.R. 4th)* covers state topics only. The fifth series *(A.L.R. 5th)* also covers state topics only, from 1992 to date. The sixth series *(A.L.R. Fed.)* reports only federal law topics from 1969 to date and is the most useful series for those conducting research on contemporary federal law issues and constitutional law matters. However, it is unwise to ignore the other series, especially when one's research entails historical analysis.

Until 1986, the research process was complicated by the existence of several indexes for each *A.L.R.* series. As a result, researchers often were compelled to consult more than one index and sometimes all of them to be certain they had discovered pertinent cases and annotations. This awkward situation was remedied by the publication of a multi-volume *Index to Annotations*, which provides a unified treatment of annotations to most of the *A.L.R.* system. The comprehensive A–Z index is arranged around significant words and facts.

Each constitutional law topic follows a similar format. First, headnotes, abbreviated briefs of counsel, and the court opinion follow the summary of the court decision. An annotation written by a legal expert explains the opinion of the court. Readers also are provided with information about related legal matters. Finally, the article indicates the location of additional analyses with references to commercially available publications and law review articles. These materials are also available through Westlaw Campus.

The *A.L.R.* series can save researchers considerable time and effort. However, for those interested in locating a large body of cases, the West National Reporter System is probably the superior tool. While the *A.L.R.* editors provide an excellent treatment for selected cases, the West National Reporter System publications provide more cases without elaborate editorial annotations. A sample citation for an *American Law Reports* annotation is Marjorie A. Shields, "What Are 'Navigable Waters' Subject to Federal Water Pollution Control Act" (33 U.S.C.A.) §§ 1251 et. seq., 160 A.L.R. Fed. (2000), p. 585.

Keeping Current on Case Law

Persons interested in legal topics should be aware of recent developments in constitutional law. However, keeping abreast of recent developments involves a concentrated and comprehensive effort. The Web sites indicated above are easy to use and provide an eminently practical tool to read U.S. Supreme Court decisions just hours after the decision is handed down.

Then, too, newspapers and other media are sources for current information about legal developments. For example, *The New York Times* and a growing number of leading newspapers often print the entire text or at least substantial parts of important Supreme Court opinions, but these are the exceptions. Most newspapers print summaries provided by news services and often edited by local newspapers reflecting space and cost considerations. The result is sometimes misleading information. The different electronic media, although they employ highly qualified personnel, often present misleading coverage due primarily to the short time allocated for such coverage, and often they confuse dictum pronouncements for rules of law.

Because news stories are not always accurate presentations of the action that occurs in courtrooms, it pays to read a court decision yourself. Unfortunately, it may take weeks or months to obtain official print copies of contemporary court decisions. In addition to consulting Internet sites already discussed, serious students should be aware of *United States Law Week* and *West's Federal Case News*.

U.S. Law Week (U.S.L.W.)

U.S. Law Week, a publication of the Bureau of National Affairs, is a weekly loose-leaf service designed to keep readers current. Its general features include a summary and analysis of new law and leading court cases of the preceding week, new court decisions (reported earlier than any of the court reporters), full text of federal statutes of general interest, and a general news section providing readers with advance notice of developments in pending or proposed legislation, administrative regulations, and litigation.

U.S. Law Week is divided into two parts: general and Supreme Court. The special binder devoted to the Supreme Court includes among its features:

- full text and digests of Court opinions;
- Supreme Court docket information;
- orders granting or denying appellate review;
- summaries of significant oral argument; and
- summer issues, usually in July and August, that analyze the work of the Court during the preceding term.

Both the general and Supreme Court sections include a topical descriptive index and a table of cases that are easy to use. The following are sample citations to a case read and to a story in *U.S. Law Week*: Wilson v. Layne, 67 U.S.L.W. 4322 (May 25, 1999); "Employee Benefits Class Actions," 70 U.S.L.W. 2723 (May 21, 2002).

U.S. Law Week is more than a valuable aid in keeping current on Supreme Court decisions, however. The oral argument feature is particularly useful in gaining insight into the nature of judicial argument. Because justices regularly interrupt attorneys during oral argument with questions and comments that Court observers interpret as clues to probable patterns of judicial voting and case outcomes, oral arguments can reveal conflicts and problems the Court may have with the respective case. While presentations of oral arguments here are not transcripts of proceedings but well-done summaries composed by editors, they are faithful renditions nonetheless. If a researcher wants to read the unvarnished record, he or she should consult *The Complete Oral Arguments of the Supreme Court.* First issued with the 1953 Supreme Court term and continued to the present, full transcripts of existing oral arguments are available on microfiche. A helpful loose-leaf index is available at most law libraries. Kurland and Casper's *Landmark Briefs and Arguments of the Supreme Court of the United States: Constitutional Law* also contains transcripts of oral arguments, as do other sources mentioned earlier in this chapter.

West's Federal Case News

West's Federal Case News is a weekly pamphlet that is helpful for those who wish to keep up with current developments. This service summarizes the latest federal cases even before they are published in regular advance sheets. It also contains selected state cases of current national interest. Each federal court jurisdiction, including the U.S. Supreme Court, is in a different section. By reading several paragraphs, one can decide quickly whether a newly decided case is worthy of further attention. Besides summaries of federal cases, it also contains summaries of leading cases from state courts and congressional and administrative highlights.

Statutory Law and Codification

The ordinary and usual function of U.S. courts, including the Supreme Court, is to interpret legislative acts and administrative regulations. Typically, jurists do not assume that acts of Congress or executive actions or orders are inconsistent with the Constitution. Usually, petitioners ask judges and justices to determine what statutes mean and whether they have been applied properly by government officials. As a fundamental principle of judicial self-restraint, judges and justices will first endeavor to dispose of matters on statutory grounds. Failing such a disposition, judges and justices will then decide whether the statute or administrative regulation in question is inconsistent with the Constitution and therefore null and void under the doctrine of judicial review. Consequently, what the words of a statute really mean is a matter of central importance in judicial decision making.

In ascertaining the meaning of legislative statutes, jurists employ two basic approaches. First, if the words are clear and unambiguous, judges apply their meaning. This is called the plain-meaning rule. Hence the literal wording of legislation is terribly important and both legislative actors and legal professionals carefully debate and even quibble over the meaning of words. Often, however, the meaning of the words found in statutory law is not clear and unambiguous. Indeed, as a result of the necessary give and take of legislative politics, words are left deliberately vague and uncertain with the tacit understanding that the uncertainty will be authoritatively resolved later in the judicial arena. When this occurs, judges find themselves delving into the intention of the lawmakers. Moreover, when judges do so they often study not only the words of statutes but also the reasons for the legislation, and sometimes the motives of those involved in the legislative process. This can be a very dicey matter because it is common for attorneys and judges to find more than a single intention and sometimes even contradictory intentions for why legislators enacted particular statutory provisions into law. Judges then feel forced to make a decision based upon unclear and uncertain evidence about what legislators really meant when they voted for a particular bill to become law.[6]

Thus, questions involving the meaning of federal law often become intellectual excursions in the complex world of the intentions and motives of legislators. A way to ascertain such matters is to consult the legislative histories of bills and enacted laws. In the case of the U.S. Congress, there are three particularly pertinent sources for ascertaining legislative intent: committee reports, committee hearings, and congressional debates.

When a committee of Congress recommends passage of a bill to its parent body, it submits a report explaining why members support passage by the full chamber. Because committee members are responsible for studying the bill in question these reports are usually regarded as most pertinent by judges when ascertaining legislative intent.

Often congressional committees conduct hearings about proposed legislation. Interested parties and experts often testify before legislative committees so that legislators are able to consider the pros and cons of proposed legislation. Consequently, when available, judges may consult committee reports to help them and others to determine why legislation laid before them for interpretation was enacted in the first place. Lastly, debate on the floor of the House of Representatives and the Senate concerning the fate of legislation can be mined by judges, advocates, and scholars to determine how members of Congress understand what the proposed law means and why particular members voted for or against the bill. Government depository libraries contain these documents. These materials are official government publications indexed and collated by official and commercial publishers. Librarians specially trained in government documents can guide students through the maze of complex source material.

Thankfully, in recent decades new publications that are easy to use are readily available, including the *Congressional Index Service (CIS)*, available at most college libraries and online through LexisNexis Academic. Go first to *Legal Research* under the *Academic Search* forms and under *Search for Other Information* click on *Congressional*. This procedure will produce a fresh page called *Congressional Search Forms*. Here researchers will find the *CIS Index* that contains references to and abstracts of congressional publications and legislative histories from 1970 to the present. One may also click on *Publications* for the full text of congressional reports, documents, committee prints, bills, and the *Congressional Record*. The *Congressional Search Forms* page contains a place to track the progress and text of bills and a separate location for Web sites about the American political process including the site for the U.S. House of Representatives (http://www.house.gov) and the U.S. Senate (http://www.senate.gov).

There is available at many libraries a loose-leaf service called the *Congressional Index* published by the Commerce Clearing House. Students also find the various publications of Congressional Quarterly, including the *Congressional Quarterly Weekly Report* and the *Congressional Quarterly Almanac*, very readable and useful. As already mentioned, the U.S. House of Representatives and the U.S. Senate, through the Library of Congress, have made available online indexes on the status of current legislation, including a Web site at http://www.thomas.loc.gov.

When investigating constitutional rights guaranteed by the member states of the national union, state and municipal codes are useful. For example, the Illinois School Code contains within one volume all the statutory rules governing the operations of the state's complicated school system. These prescriptions and proscriptions include due process rights, such as those pertinent to school-board personnel hearings. These state and municipal codes are analogous in form to the various federal codes, so only codes dealing with federal law will be considered here.

Presently, there are three widely available federal codes: *The United States Code, 2000 Edition (U.S.C.)* is the official statement of the law. The *United States Code Service (U.S.C.S.)* and the *United States Code Annotated (U.S.C.A.)* are products of private companies, and both possess features not available in the official *United States Code*.

United States Code (U.S.C.)

Every six years Congress orders the publication of a new edition of the official code for the laws of the United States, with cumulative supplements available for the intervening years. The *United States Code* arranges U.S. laws under 50 separate titles, for example, Title 2, the Congress; Title 18, Crimes and Criminal Procedure; and Title 49, Transportation. These 50 titles are further subdivided into subtitles, parts, chapters, subchapters, and sections. The extensive multi-volume *General Index* to the *U.S. Code* permits researchers to locate the statutory law in codified form quickly. A sample citation for the *United States Code* is: Fraud and Related Activity in Connection with Identification Documents and Information, 18 U.S.C. § 1028 (2000).

The Web site of Cornell University Law School maintains an up-to-date version of the U.S. Code at http://www4.law.cornell.edu/uscode. It contains an update feature that integrates the services of the U.S. House of Representatives so that one may locate changes in statutory law appropriate to each code title and section. One may also want to search the World Wide Web for the *U.S. Code Gopher*; this service contains alternative sites and specialized information about the Code.

United States Code Service (U.S.C.S.)

The *United States Code Service* is more user-friendly than the official code. Among its many features are the exact language from the *Statutes at Large*, legislative histories, annotations of interpretive case law, and references to pertinent law review articles. Users have available to them a four-volume *General Index* accompanied by a paperback *Later Case and Statutory Service*. This set also contains an excellent five-volume annotation of the U.S. Constitution. Supplements inserted at the back of each volume keep the entire set current.

Editors have arranged *U.S.C.S.* exactly as the official *U.S.C.* For example, the codification of law dealing with federal crimes and criminal procedure is in Title 18 of both the official *U.S.C.* and the unofficial *U.S.C.S.* Because most students are too unfamiliar with the various official titles to turn directly to the code when beginning their research, it is advisable to consult the *General Index* first. If the researcher knows the popular name of a law—for example, the Religious Freedom Restoration Act—then consult the special volume index with popular names.

What makes *U.S.C.S.* particularly useful are its extensive research aids. It contains the text of the statutory law, makes reference to amendments, and features a complete research guide. For example, it directs readers to related discussions in the legal encyclopedia *American Jurisprudence 2d*. Its many annotations contain discussions about how the law has been construed by judicial bodies. An attractive feature is its bibliographic reference to law review articles on various topics.

For students of constitutional law, the five volumes containing the Constitution's articles and amendments provide an extensive research guide. These volumes contain many of the same research aids as exist for the code. Under the Nineteenth Amendment, for instance, one finds the exact wording of the constitutional provision, cross-references, a research guide, annotated references to court cases, and statutory law. In addition, there are interpretative notes and references to germane law review articles.

U.S.C.S also contains volumes on court rules including, for example, the Federal Rules of Civil Procedure, the Federal Rules of Criminal Procedure, the Rules of the U.S. Supreme Court, the Rules of the Courts of Appeal, and the Administrative Rules of Procedure. The editors of this set have devoted an entire volume to international agreements. Students assigned the task of writing a paper on particular constitutional provisions will find the special features of this product valuable. Sample citations are: Disclosure of Federal Campaign Funds: Definitions, 2 U.S.C.S. § 431 (LexisNexis Academic, 2003); Disclosure of Federal Campaign Funds: Definitions, 2 U.S.C.S. § 431 (LexisNexis Academic through P.L. 108-30, May 29, 2003). The later citation form is recommended when there is a need to inform readers of the very latest status of legislation.

Access to this particular code service is also available online through LexisNexis Academic. Go first to *Legal Research* under *Academic Search* forms and under *Codes & Regulations* click on *Federal Code*. Use the help screen for further instructions.

United States Code Annotated (U.S.C.A.)

The *United States Code Annotated (U.S.C.A.)*, published by West, features pertinent statutory law with annotations to judicial interpretations and collateral references to many other West products. This fine set also contains an annual multi-volume *General Index* in paperback and a ten-volume treatment covering the provisions of the U.S. Constitution. The editors help researchers find the latest decisions impacting constitutional law by supplementing each hardcover volume with accompanying paperback updates. As with *U.S.C.S.*, the best way to research a statutory topic employing *U.S.C.A.* is to consult the *General Index* or the popular name table found in the last volume of the *General Index* (U to Z).

Students interested in bringing their research up to date should consult the pocket supplements placed at the back of each volume. Students also should inspect the *Supplementary Pamphlet* for each title when made available by the publisher. Finally, when it is important to treat a subject in a current fashion, consult the last published pamphlet of the *U.S. Code Congressional and Administrative News*. It cumulates the changes in U.S. statutory law since the last publication of the *U.S.C.A.* pocket supplements and the latest *Supplementary Pamphlet*. A sample citation is: Health Insurance: Contracting Authority, 5 U.S.C.A. § 8902(b) (West Group 2002 Supp. Pamph.).

Westlaw Campus contains the same complete *U.S.C.A.* as it appears in hardcover. As does LexisNexis Academic, this service contains each statute in the *U.S.C.A.*, abstracts, and references to published court opinions of judges that specifically interpret each statute. If one is investigating the statutory law of one or all fifty states, Westlaw Campus is a welcomed time-saving research tool.

State Codes

Findlaw.com has made state codes available at http://www.findlaw.com/casecode/index.html#statelaw. Also, researchers may glean considerable information about state governments and their various departments and agencies by perusing http://www.statelocalgov.net.

Administrative Agency Reporting

Whether it is the protection of the physical environment from air pollution, the payment of Social Security benefits, or the issuance of marriage licenses, governmental administrative agencies possess considerable authority in regulating most aspects of life. Administrative law consists of the norms that create and govern public bureaucracies, the rules and regulations made by these entities, and the judicial review exercised by courts that define and limit agency discretion.[7]

Administrative rules and regulations do not appear in court reports. However, these materials are accessible and available through the U.S. government and private publishing companies. Two government publications with which students need to be familiar are the *Federal Register* and the *Code of Federal Regulations*.

Federal Register

Since 1936 all federal administrative rules and regulations have been published daily (except Saturday, Sunday, and legal holidays) in the *Federal Register*. Ordering materials chronologically, the *Federal Register* contains newly adopted rules and regulations, notice of proposed regulations and rules, dates of administrative hearings, and decisions of administrative bodies. It also contains presidential executive orders and proclamations. It is indexed monthly, quarterly, and annually. Many college and university libraries are government depository libraries, meaning that these institutions receive from the government the *Federal Register* and other official documents including official congressional documents. Those who do not have access to a government depository library may access the *Federal Register* online at http://www.gpoaccess.gov/fr. Alternatively, LexisNexis Academic users may access the *Federal Register* by going first to *Legal Research* under *Academic Search* forms. Then under *Codes & Regulations*, click on *Federal Regulations*. Use the help screen for further instructions. The *Federal Register* is also available through Westlaw Campus. A sample citation for *Federal Register* items is: Approval and Promulgation of Implementation Plans, 68 Fed.Reg. 37,742 (2003).

Code of Federal Regulations (C.F.R.)

Because the *Federal Register* is arranged chronologically and not by subject matter, it is practically impossible to use it to ascertain rules and regulations by subject matter or agency. The *Code of Federal Regulations* (*C.F.R.*), arranged under fifty separate titles and published annually in pamphlet form, solves this problem. Revised each year, *C.F.R.* enables the researcher to learn which rules and regulations are currently in force. *C.F.R.* also contains an easy-to-use annual index accompanied by monthly updates.

When attempting to update rules and regulations, one should use the *Code of Federal Regulations* together with the daily *Federal Register*. After consulting the annual *C.F.R.* index, look at the monthly cumulative issue entitled *LSA: List of CFR Sections Affected*. This procedure will provide the researcher with an up-to-date account for the year and month. Because rules and regulations are altered and promulgated daily, it is necessary to find the latest possible changes. These can be found by turning to the most recent daily issue of the *Federal Register* and examining the section titled "Cumulative List of Parts Affected." This research procedure will yield a complete and current understanding of agency rules and regulations. A sample citation for the *Code of Federal Regulations* is: Protection of Environment-Compliance Assurance Monitoring, 40 C.F.R. § 64 (2003).

Though not typically available to non-subscribers, the LexisNexis and Westlaw online services and various CD-ROMs contain federal administrative materials. But because LexisNexis Academic and Westlaw Campus are now widely available to college students, the full text of the *Code of Federal Regulations* is easily accessible by computer. Users of LexisNexis Academic may access the *CFR* by going first to *Legal Research* under *Academic Search* forms and under *Codes & Regulations* clicking *Federal Regulations*. This site contains not only federal regulations, but also includes agency opinions and official opinions of the U.S. Attorney General and of the Office of Legal Counsel. Westlaw Campus also has a search procedure for administrative regulations.

The U.S. Printing Office maintains a subscription-free Internet site for the general public at http://www.access.gpo.gov. It contains a complete database for the *Federal Register* from 1995 forward, and one that is more difficult to use for the 1994 *Federal Register* (volume 59). This site also contains the *Code of Federal Regulations* (1996 forward). Also useful to researchers are the *Weekly Compilation of Presidential Documents*, the *United States Government Manual*, congressional bills (1993 forward), congressional hearings (1997 forward), *Congressional Record* (1994 forward), *Congressional Record Index* (1983 forward), and congressional reports on legislation (1995 forward). One will also find public laws beginning in 1995 at this Web site. One may also find the *Code of Federal Regulations* through the Legal Information Institute site of Cornell University Law School at http://cfr.law.cornell.edu/cfr.

Primary Historical Documents

As previously discussed, much constitutional adjudication entails the search for the meaning of words because statutory and constitutional language is often unclear and ambiguous. Some provisions of the Constitution contain relatively clear meanings such as the terms of office for members of Congress and for the president. On the other hand, many provisions are vague, requiring jurists to assign meanings to them as controversies arise. For example, the meaning of such terms as "establishment of religion," "commerce among the states," "executive power," "due process of law," "unreasonable search and seizure," and "cruel and unusual punishment" require interpretation because the words are not amenable to exactly similar interpretations by ordinary users of the English language.

There is considerable debate about the extent to which Supreme Court justices can and should adhere to the strict meaning of the words written in the basic document and to the intentions of those that penned and ratified the Constitution and its amendments. So-called interpretivists insist that when jurists base their judicial opinions on factors other than the plain words of the Constitution or the framers' intentions, they are guilty of substituting their personal values for those of the Constitution's writers. Interpretivists argue that if the Constitution is to be amended, it should be accomplished through the normal amending processes found in the basic document's fifth article.

Advocates of noninterpretivism, on the other hand, do not deny the utility of attempting to ascertain the plain meaning of constitutional words and phrases and the intentions of the constitutional framers. However, they insist that often it is not possible to ascertain meanings in ways supposed by interpretivists. Moreover, they maintain that the Constitution must be read not as a rulebook, but rather it should be viewed as a set of principles because it must be made a useful guide in the contemporary world. Noninterpretivists insist the Constitution is a living document and not a dead letter; as the world changes, our understanding of what the Constitution means must be adjusted to meet the needs of the age.

In the search for constitutional meaning, judges and justices consult not only the Constitution itself but also original historical documents that may shed light on the legal issues at hand.[8] The remaining pages of this chapter are devoted to annotations of some of the most important available historical documents that may be used to ascertain the meaning and intentions of the framers of the Constitution. These sources, listed alphabetically by author, are sometimes cited in Supreme Court opinions or in scholarly tracts of one sort or another.

Bailyn, Bernard, ed. *Debates on the Constitution*. 2 vols. New York: The Library of America, 1993.

This handsome set contains a complete history of the debates over the ratification of the Constitution. It includes speeches, newspaper articles, pamphlets, and private letters of famous and not-so-famous members of the founding generation of Americans. The materials are presented in chronological order.

Cogan, Neil H. *Contexts of the Constitution: A Documentary Collection on Principles of American Constitutional Law*. New York: Foundation Press, 1999.

This recent volume contains a chapter on primary texts that includes such important documents as the Northwest Ordinance and the New Jersey and Virginia Plans. The remaining six chapters divide original documents and texts by principles of constitutionalism, republicanism, democracy, structure, federalism, equality, and rights. Considerable attention is given to the Federalist and Antifederalist Papers.

Elliot, Jonathan. *Elliot's Debates*. 5 vols. Philadelphia: J. B. Lippincott, 1836, 1937.

These volumes contain a collection of the debates and proceedings that took place in the various state conventions that ratified the Constitution in 1787. The volumes are useful when trying to understand what those who ratified the Constitution might have had in mind, as opposed to those who drafted it. Also contained in the volumes is the *Journal of the Federal Convention* and other documents and letters of interest. This multivolume set is commonly employed by serious scholars.

Farrand, Max, ed. *The Records of the Federal Convention of 1787*. 4 vols. New Haven, CT: Yale University Press, 1986.

This four-volume set contains the daily records of the Constitutional Convention, providing researchers with the ability to trace the origin and development of particular clauses. The index found in volume 4 includes references for all clauses that were finally adopted by the delegates. Farrand's compilation is widely respected.

Ketcham, Ralph, ed. *The Antifederalist Papers and the Constitutional Convention Debates*. New York: New American Library, 1986.

The celebration of the bicentennial of the U.S. Constitution gave rise to renewed interest in the debates surrounding its ratification. Although the *Federalist Papers* are well known to students and scholars, the ideas and writings of ratification opponents are not. This publication contains the complete texts of the Antifederalist writings and the Constitutional Convention debates. It also contains a table correlating the arguments of the Federalists and the Antifederalists by numbered papers.

Kurland, Philip B. and Ralph Lerner, eds. *The Founders' Constitution.* 5 vols. Chicago: University of Chicago Press, 1987.

This set is useful for analyzing the Constitution and the first twelve amendments, section by section and clause by clause. The editors provide relevant records of the federal convention, letters and commentary of the framers, scholarly commentary, and court cases interpreting each constitutional provision.

Lloyd, Gordon and Margie Lloyd, eds. *The Essential Bill of Rights: Original Arguments and Fundamental Documents.* Lanham, MD: University Press of America, 1998.

This volume contains landmark documents pertaining to the traditions and arguments behind the establishment of the Bill of Rights. For example, it contains a copy of the Magna Carta, selections from John Locke's *Second Treatise on Government*, the congressional history of the Bill of Rights, and so on.

Madison, James. *Notes of Debates in the Federal Convention of 1787 Reported by James Madison.* Athens, OH: Ohio University Press, 1966.

This volume contains the notes James Madison took at the Philadelphia Convention in 1787. Madison's notes are regarded as the most authoritative of those in attendance during that hot summer. By Madison's own legal will, these notes did not become available until after his death. Unfortunately, there is no index, so the reader needs to wade through the debates looking for the desired passages. This volume contains a preface by Madison and a fine introduction by Adrienne Koch.

Murphy, Paul L. *The Bill of Rights and American Legal History.* 20 vols. New York: Garland Publishing, 1990.

This set of volumes contains reproductions of over 300 articles that explore the history of civil liberties in the United States. The first three volumes treat the historical background of the Bill of Rights and the remaining volumes contain articles on each substantive topic in the Bill of Rights such as speech, press, religion, criminal procedure, and so on.

Prescott, Arthur Taylor. *Drafting the Federal Constitution.* New York: Greenwood Press, 1968.

The editor of this volume arranges Madison's notes by subject matter, making it easier to ascertain what was said at the Federal Convention in 1787. This volume contains both a thorough table of contents and index thereby permitting researchers to pinpoint their searches to particular subjects and delegates.

Rossiter, Clinton, ed. *The Federalist Papers: Alexander Hamilton, James Madison, and John Jay.* New York: New American Library, 1961.

Alexander Hamilton, James Madison, and John Jay authored under the name "Publius" eighty-five essays that advocated the adoption of the Constitution. Appearing in New York newspapers, these essays became widely known and had an impact on the ratification debates then occurring in the United States. These articles, the *Federalist Papers*, are sometimes cited by courts and others as evidence of the framers' intent. This collection of articles is available in several editions by different editors and publishers.

Storing, Herbert J., with the assistance of Murray Dry, eds. *The Complete Anti-Federalists.* 7 vols. Chicago: University of Chicago Press, 1981.

This seven-volume set presents what the so-called Antifederalists advocated. It includes the objections of the non-signers of the Constitution and essays written at the time that argued against the ratification of the Philadelphia Constitution. One may consult the index found in volume 7 for easy access to desired passages.

Legal Research Exercises

It would be wonderful if students could become accomplished legal researchers by simply reading this book. Unfortunately, this is not the case. Conducting legal research is a hands-on experience. The best way to learn how to use legal source materials is by researching a real problem. I have designed the exercises in this and the following chapter to acquaint students with many of the legal research materials found in this text. Upon completion of these short learning exercises, students can feel confident that they are capable of initiating a research effort. The correct answers appear at the end of this and the next chapter. Remember, however, that because publishers revise legal research materials to reflect changes in the law such materials are often modified over time. Consequently, the precise answers to these exercises may change over time.

Exercise 1—Court Reports

Read both chapter 1 of the text and the questions carefully before answering them.

1. According to the text, how many "official" as distinguished from "unofficial" reports of U.S. Supreme Court opinions are there?

2. The first ninety volumes of the *United States Reports (U.S.)* contain names of the respective court reporters. Identify the court reporter serving during 1828–1842.

3. A resident of New York gets involved in an Interstate Commerce Clause case that was first heard in a state court before 1940. In which *Regional Reporter* and series among the seven geographical regions is this court opinion found? How many states are in that region?

4. What are the parallel citations of the major hard-copy court reporters for the U.S. Supreme Court opinion in *Gibbons v. Ogden* (1824)?

5. Can the U.S. Supreme Court opinion in *Gibbons v. Ogden* be found on the following non-subscription Internet sites? (The actual addresses may change but try to locate the best current address to answer each question.)

a. http://www.lawschool.cornell.edu

b. http://www.findlaw.com

c. http://www.supremecourtus.gov

d. http://www. gpoaccess.gov

e. http://www.oyez.org/oyez/frontpage

6. In no more than 230 words, summarize the Supreme Court's holding in *National League of Cities v. Usery* (1976).

Exercise 2—Codes

Refer to the *United States Code* (*U.S.C.*).

1. In which title of the *Code* are provisions for commerce and trade found?

2. Which chapter of the *Code* contains provisions for consumer product safety?

3. Consult 15 U.S.C. section 77q. It contains the law on fraudulent interstate transactions under the general provision of "domestic securities"—the Securities Act of 1933. What is the exact date of this legislation and where in the *Statutes at Large* may the legislation be found in its original form?

4. Is Title 15, section 77q of the United States Code available through http://www4.law.cornell.edu/uscode? (The Legal Information Institute of Cornell University Law School is one additional way to locate this source.)

Answers for Legal Exercises

Exercise 1—Court Reports

1. 1 official

2. Richard Peters

3. North Eastern Reporter, 1st series; 5 states in the region

4. 22 U.S. (9 Wheat.) 1, 6 L. Ed. 23 (1824)

5a. Yes   5b. No   5c. No   5d. No   5e. Yes

6. The Court held that the imposition of a federal minimum-wage law on municipal employees represents an invasion of state power violating the Tenth Amendment of the U.S. Constitution.

Exercise 2—Codes

1. Title 15

2. Chapter 47

3. May 27, 1933, 48 Stat. 84

4. Yes

Endnotes

[1] J. Myron Jacobstein, Roy M. Mersky, and Donald J. Dunn, *Fundamentals of Legal Research*, 7th ed. (Mineola; NY: Foundation Press, 1998), p. 49.

[2] Jay Schuck, *Guide to West Group Legal Resources* (Eagan, MN: West Group, 1998), p. 7.

[3] Stephen R. Barnett, "From Anastasoff to Hart to West's Federal Appendix: The Ground Shifts Under No-Citation Rules," *Journal of Appellate Practice and Process* 4 (Spring 2002): 1–26.

[4] Ibid. Not all or even a majority of the opinions of federal district court judges are reported, but it is believed that opinions dealing with important matters find their way into print. See Robert A. Carp and C. K. Rowland, *Policymaking and Politics in the Federal District Courts* (Knoxville: University of Tennessee Press, 1983), p. 17.

[5] Jacobstein, Mersky, and Dunn, *Fundamentals of Legal Research*, pp. 768–769.

[6] For a more complete discussion of the matter of statutory interpretation see Albert P. Melone and Allan Karnes, *The American Legal System: Foundations, Processes, and Norms* (Los Angeles: Roxbury Publishing Co., 2003), pp. 132–140; William N. Eskridge, Jr., Philip Frickey, and Elizabeth Garrett, *Legislation and Statutory Interpretation* (New York: Foundation Press, 2000).

[7] H. B. Jacobini, Albert P. Melone, and Carl Kalvelage, *Research Essentials of Administrative Law* (Pacific Palisades, CA: Palisades Publishing, 1983), p. 1. For a thorough exposition, see Steven J. Cann, *Administrative Law*, 3rd ed. (Thousand Oaks, CA: Sage Publications, 2002).

[8] For greater specificity on the interpretivist/noninterpretivist debate and references to other sources, see Albert P. Melone and Allan Karnes, *The American Legal System,* pp. 140–152.

2

SECONDARY SOURCES AS RESEARCH AIDS

Introduction

Judges, justices, legislators, and executives including bureaucrats are the only legitimate source of law. In this sense, they represent the fountainhead of our legal tradition. In the first chapter, I introduced readers to primary sources for the law. There are also numerous secondary sources. These materials can help researchers to locate, describe, understand, and analyze what official lawmakers prescribe or proscribe. Editors and legal scholars of all sorts perform a vital function in helping busy attorneys, scholars, and ordinary laypersons to locate the law and to place it in context. The goal of this chapter is to acquaint readers with useful secondary sources, particularly as they apply to matters of constitutional law. These tools include compendia, guides and summaries, constitutional law treatises, encyclopedias, digests, cite-checkers, legal periodicals and indexes, newspaper sources, interest group resources, and law dictionaries. The bibliography at the end of this volume contains lists of numerous books on a variety of topics that researchers may consult when investigating particular substantive topics, interpretations of events, and historical trends.

Compendia, Guides, and Summaries

Bartholomew, Paul C. and Joseph F. Menez. *Summaries of Leading Cases on the Constitution*. 13th ed. Totowa, NJ: Littlefield Adams Quality Paperbacks, 1997.

This paperback contains summaries of almost 500 Supreme Court decisions. For each case it briefly states the facts, the legal issues, and the Court's decision and reasoning.

Biskupic, Joan and Elder Witt. *Guide to the U.S. Supreme Court*. 3d ed. Washington, DC: Congressional Quarterly, 1997.

This guide is an outstanding two-volume reference work on all aspects of the Supreme Court. It includes sections on the Court's history, the Court and federalism, the Court and presidential power, the Court and judicial power, the Court and the states, the Court and civil liberties and civil rights, political pressures on the Court, the internal operations of the Court, and the major decisions of the Court.

Cooke, Edward F. *A Detailed Analysis of the Constitution*. 7th ed. Blue Ridge Summit, PA: Rowman & Littlefield, 2002.

The author concisely explains each phrase in the Constitution. This volume also contains essays on making the American Constitution, its principles, and how to understand the constitutional system of government.

Congressional Research Service, Library of Congress. *The Constitution of the United States of America: Analysis and Interpretation*. Washington, DC: U.S. Government Printing Office, 1992 and latest supplement.

This large volume, first published in 1913, offers a lengthy, authoritative, narrative exposition of the Constitution, clause by clause. It includes listings of proposed constitutional amendments pending before the states, proposed amendments not ratified by the states, acts of Congress held unconstitutional in whole or in part by the Supreme Court, state constitutional and statutory provisions and municipal ordinances held unconstitutional on their face as administered, ordinances held unconstitutional, and Supreme Court decisions overruled by subsequent decisions. Annual pocket supplements are inserted at the back of the volume. This massive book is available in the reference section of most college libraries and online at http://www.access.gpo.gov/congress/senate/constitution/index.html.

Epstein, Lee, Jeffrey A. Segal, Harold J. Spaeth, and Thomas G. Walker. *The Supreme Court Compendium: Data, Decisions & Developments*. 3d ed. Washington, DC: Congressional Quarterly, 2002

This volume provides considerable data on voting behavior of Supreme Court justices, especially since 1953. It also contains biographical information on each justice and a variety of hard data, often in tables and figures, that elucidate Supreme Court behavior such as voting behavior and its consequences for U.S. political life. It contains tables of the ideological scores of justices beginning with the Vinson era (1946–1952) to the present Rehnquist Court (1986–) and interagreement scores among the justices in broadly defined issue areas.

Hall, Kermit L. *The Oxford Guide to United States Supreme Court Decisions*. New York: Oxford University Press, 2001.

This reference work contains summaries of over 400 significant decisions of the U.S. Supreme Court. It also contains essays of major issues facing the high court and biographies of every justice. This 448-page book also contains entries of prominent judges, nominees rejected by the Senate, and the role of U.S. presidents and their impact on the Court.

Hall, Kermit L., ed. *The Oxford Companion to the Supreme Court of the United States.* New York: Oxford University Press, 1992.

This volume contains in condensed form many interesting facts about the Supreme Court. Among its many features are summaries of its most important opinions, information about the justices, historical periods, subject-specific essays, and a host of trivia. Many serious students of the Court employ this volume as a ready desk reference.

Jost, Kenneth. *The Supreme Court Year Book.* Washington, DC: Congressional Quarterly, 2001.

This annual reference book beginning in the early 1990s summarizes every opinion written during the last completed Court term. This is a handy guide to what the Supreme Court has decided. Look for annual volumes as they are released by the publisher. Many libraries have standing orders for the latest volume.

Jost, Kenneth. *The Supreme Court A to Z.* Washington, DC: Congressional Quarterly, 2003.

This 600-page volume contains entries arranged in alphabetical order providing short definitions and extended essays on significant Supreme Court opinions, the justices of the Supreme Court, and a number of constitutional principles and concepts. This volume contains a useful bibliography and research tools and tips for pursuing interesting questions.

Maddex, Robert L. *The U.S. Constitution A to Z.* Washington, DC: Congressional Quarterly, 2002.

This 660-page volume is a comprehensive guide to the U.S. Constitution. It is useful to get a quick overview of constitutional law subjects listed in alphabetical order. Among its features are a table of important cases and annotations on constitutional provisions and historical documents.

Mitchell, Ralph, ed. *CQ's Guide to the U.S. Constitution.* 2d ed. Washington, DC: Congressional Quarterly, 1995.

This brief work provides a detailed index to the provisions found in the Constitution. It also contains the texts of the Constitution and the Declaration of Independence and a glossary of terms.

Peltason, J. W. and Sue Davis. *Understanding the Constitution.* 16th ed. Fort Worth: Wadsworth, 2004.

This book offers a thorough analysis of each provision of the Constitution and of related Supreme Court opinions as near to the publication date as practical. The authors examine how Supreme Court decisions as well as lower court decisions affect the interpretation of the Constitution. Look for new editions with the passing of time. Generations of college students are familiar with this text. It is an easy reference to what the Constitution means today.

United States Code Annotated (U.S.C.A): U.S. Constitution. St. Paul, MN: West, 1987/1999.

Along with an annotated version of the *U.S. Code,* West publishes an accompanying ten-volume set on the U.S. Constitution. It treats each article, section, and clause. First, the editors present the exact wording of each constitutional provision. They then present Westlaw Electronic Research suggestions and cross-references to other constitutional provisions and library references to pertinent law review articles, texts, and treatises. Notes of court decisions that interpret specific provisions may be used as a quick method for ascertaining the interpretation of each provision of the Constitution. Pocket supplements and paperback volumes update the hardbound set. This same information is available online through Westlaw Campus and Westlaw.

United States Code Service (U.S.C.S.): U.S. Constitution. Charlottesville, VA: LEXIS Law Publishing, 1986/1999.

The *U.S.C.S.* is a commercial product containing the various titles of the *U.S. Code.* The editors of this huge set also make available a five-volume accompanying set devoted exclusively to analysis of the Constitution, section by section and clause by clause. This set contains many of the same research aids as in the code. Under the Nineteenth Amendment, for instance, one finds the exact wording of the constitutional provision, cross references, a research guide, annotated references to court cases, and statutory law. In addition, there are interpretative notes and references to germane law review articles. It is very similar to the *U.S.C.A.* product discussed above. One may find this same information through the online subscription service Lexis-Nexis Academic. Go first to the *Federal Code* heading and find *Constitution* listed under the source list. Then type in the keyword that you are studying (for example, Contracts Clause) and find the same pertinent information one finds in the print volume set.

Treatises

Abraham, Henry J. and Barbara A. Perry. *Freedom and the Court: Civil Rights and Liberties in the United States.* 7th ed. New York: Oxford University Press, 1998.

This book offers an analysis of the conflict between individual rights and community welfare. Specific features include a historical discussion of the process of incorporation of the Bill of Rights by way of the Fourteenth Amendment; a discussion of religion, speech, due process, and political and racial equality; and an overview of the political development of civil liberties and rights in the United States. For those interested in locating other sources, the authors include pertinent bibliographic notes.

Baker, Thomas E. *Constitutional Analysis in a Nutshell.* 2d ed. Eagan, MN: West, 2003.

This book summarizes the main features of modern constitutional law. It serves as a good reference for beginning students to map the twists and turns of the subject.

Barron, Jerome A. and C. Thomas Dienes. *Constitutional Law in a Nutshell.* 5th ed. Eagan, MN: West, 2003.

A softcover book that is part of the West Nutshell series, this 632-page book traces the development of American constitutional law. The most recent edition is particularly useful because it treats the contemporary issue of congressional commerce power, the enforcement clause of the Fourteenth Amendment, pornography and the electronic age, and church/state issues.

Barron, Jerome A. and C. Thomas Dienes. *First Amendment Law in a Nutshell.* 2d ed. Eagan, MN: West, 2000.

The First Amendment is a complicated subject. The authors of this 531-page book create intellectual order from the apparent chaos of the subject matter. They provide background and methodology for understanding the general topic and explain specific topics including, for example, advocacy of illegal conduct, obscenity, commercial speech, expressive conduct, and the religion clauses.

Berg, Thomas C. *Berg's The State and Religion in a Nutshell.* Eagan, MN: West, 1998.

This handy paperback book relates the attention the Supreme Court has given to constitutional issues involving religion in the past two decades. It deals mostly with the Establishment and Free Exercise Clauses, but the author also provides a history of church/state relations.

Biskupic, Joan and Elder Witt. *The Supreme Court and Individual Rights.* 3d ed. Washington, DC: Congressional Quarterly, 1997.

This book offers a substantive treatment of the Court's role in protecting individual liberties and rights. Topics include: speech, religion, political participation, due process, and racial, alienage, sexual, and income discrimination. In addition, the authors provide excellent narratives with citations to relevant cases. Look for future editions.

Biskupic, Joan and Elder Witt. *The Supreme Court and the Powers of the American Government.* Washington, DC: Congressional Quarterly, 1997.

This book is a companion volume to *The Supreme Court and Individual Rights* by the same authors. It discusses the Court and its relationship to judicial power, Congress, the president, and the states. Both volumes are very readable and contain clear descriptions of cases, placing them in historical perspective. Look for future editions.

Cann, Steven J. *Administrative Law.* 3d ed. Thousand Oaks, CA: Sage Publications, 2001.

In the modern world, there is a close connection between constitutional law and administrative law and both are intimately connected to politics. In this volume the author discusses politics, democracy, bureaucracy, the administrative process, and substantive issues in administrative law.

Curry, James A., Richard B. Riley, and Richard M. Battistoni. *Constitutional Government: The American Experience.* 5th ed. Dubuque, IA: Kendall/Hunt Publishing Co., 2003.

This book offers a readable exposition on almost every aspect of the American constitutional system. Part I covers the history and the theory of constitutional government. Part II presents an in-depth discussion of the structure and processes of American constitutional government. Part III provides analyses of the Bill of Rights, civil liberties, and civil rights. Throughout the book, the authors summarize U.S. Supreme Court decisions and interpretations of the Constitution.

LaFave, Wayne R. *Search and Seizure: A Treatise on the Fourth Amendment.* 3d ed. St. Paul, MN: West, 1996.

This book offers in five volumes a thorough treatment of all aspects of the Fourth Amendment and the exclusionary rule. The book contains a useful table of cases and an annual pocket supplement to keep the volumes up to date. It is the best available source on search- and seizure-law.

Marks, Thomas C. and John F. Cooper. *State Constitutional Law in a Nutshell.* 2d ed. St. Paul, MN: West, 2003.

American federalism presupposes that state governments have governing rules of their own. Most students of American government know little about state constitutional law but in truth, the boundaries of political authority among the various institutions of state government and individuals are handled routinely by state courts interpreting state as well as federal constitutions. In recent decades, state supreme courts have received greater attention than in the past because some state courts are expanding constitutional rights while the U.S. Supreme Court has either retreated or failed to enlarge the scope of constitutional rights and liberties. This 365-page book is a good primer on the subject.

Rotunda, Ronald D. and John E. Nowak. *Treatise on Constitutional Law: Substance and Procedure.* 3d ed. St. Paul, MN: West, 1999.
　　　This five-volume set touches on all aspects of U.S. constitutional law. It contains an excellent table of contents, table of cases, and index for determining the law on a given topic. Each volume contains annual pocket supplements.

Vieira, Norman. *Vieira's Constitutional Civil Rights in a Nutshell.* 3d ed. Eagan, MN: West, 1998.
　　　This softcover text provides ready answers to how the courts deal with civil-rights issues of all sorts, especially equal-protection problems.

Legal Encyclopedias

　　　Legal encyclopedias are of three varieties: general, local, and specialized. For constitutional law students, general and specialized encyclopedias are most useful. Local law and most special-subject encyclopedias are of particular interest to legal practitioners. Local law encyclopedias cover the case and statutory law of specific state jurisdictions.[1] Unfortunately, less than a third of the fifty states have them. Special-subject encyclopedias contain comprehensive discussions of specific legal topics, for example, automobiles, private corporations, evidence, and constitutional law.

　　　The four general encyclopedias commonly held by law libraries are *West's Encyclopedia of American Law, Encyclopedia of the American Judicial System, American Jurisprudence 2d (Am. Jur. 2d),* and *Corpus Juris Secundum (C. J. S.).* Published in 1983, *The Guide to American Law* was created explicitly for laypersons. *West's Encyclopedia of American Law* superseded the *Guide* and remains available in many libraries. The *Encyclopedia of the American Judicial System* is intended for the well-read lay audience. The remaining general encyclopedias are designed and marketed for attorney use. *American Jurisprudence 2d* replaces *American Jurisprudence,* and *Corpus Juris Secundum* likewise supersedes the out-of-date *Corpus Juris.* All law-related encyclopedias are publications of private companies that employ subject experts who write on various topics; they are not official government documents.

　　　For the most part, encyclopedia articles on general or specific legal topics differ from legal treatises or articles appearing in legal periodicals in that there is no overt attempt to argue the merits of particular legal rules or principles. Unless otherwise indicated, the writers attempt to present clear, concise, and objective statements on the law of a particular topic or law-related matter. For laypersons, *West's Encyclopedia of American Law* is an excellent first source in the research process. Both *Am. Jur. 2d* and *C. J. S.* are also appropriate tools for beginning research into a specific legal question when the emphasis is on understanding legal rules. Besides an exposition on the law, the topical discussions cross-reference other legal research materials including cases, digests, statutory provisions, and annotations. Researchers should go from the encyclopedia exposition to more specific cited sources for a complete understanding of the subject matter.

West's Encyclopedia of American Law

This 12-volume set replaced the older *The Guide to American Law: Everyone's Legal Encyclopedia*, produced by West in 1998. *West's Encyclopedia of American Law* contains essays on a variety of law and law-related topics. Because it is designed for the non-specialist audience, it is ideal for undergraduate students. It contains over 4000 entries, many of which are not likely to be of direct interest to students of constitutional law. Yet, gleaning knowledge of important legal ideas and institutions may be helpful to laypersons by placing a constitutional law research topic in a broader context.

Volume 12 contains a dictionary of legal terms, a table of cases cited, a name index, and a subject index. A sample citation is *West's Encyclopedia of American Law*, s.v. "Symbolic Speech."

Encyclopedia of the American Judicial System

The *Encyclopedia of the American Judicial System*, published in 1987 by Charles Scribner's Sons, is a comprehensive, three-volume reference work on all aspects of the legal system. Students of constitutional law and judicial process will find this set particularly useful for beginning their research. Covered are broad generic topics such as legal history, substantive law, institutions and personnel, process and behavior, constitutional law and issues, and methodology. This set contains a comprehensive seventy-five-page index. A sample citation is H. Frank Way, "Religious Liberty," *Encyclopedia of the American Judicial System*, Robert J. Janosik, ed. (New York: Charles Scribner's Sons, 1987), p. 1214.

Encyclopedia of the American Constitution

The successor to the original 1986 four-volume set as supplemented in 1992, the *Encyclopedia of the American Constitution*, Second Edition, is a six-volume compilation of materials about the U.S. Constitution designed for use by laypersons. This edition was published in 2000 by Macmillan Reference USA. It contains over 2000 original signed articles by several hundred distinguished contributors. It is edited by Leonard W. Levy and Kenneth L. Karst.

The scope and organization of this specialized encyclopedia permit students to access information on the history of the Constitution, its concepts and terms, U.S. Supreme Court cases, biographical data on its authors, and public acts helpful for understanding the basic document. Researchers can find entries on the Constitutional Convention of 1787, the infamous *Dred Scott* case, Sandra Day O'Connor, and the Sherman Antitrust Act. This encyclopedia offers readers a variety of indexes to consult, including an index of subjects, an index of names, and an index of cases. A sample citation is Jack Greenberg, "Civil Rights," *Encyclopedia of the American Constitution*, 2d ed., Leonard W. Levy, and Kenneth L. Karst, eds. (New York: Macmillan Reference USA, 2000), 1: 387.

Encyclopedia of the Supreme Court

This one-volume reference manual with almost 500 terms contains discussions of important U.S. Supreme Court cases, judicial concepts, legal and constitutional issues, and portraits of the personalities central to an understanding of the nation's high court. Political scientist David Schultz is the editor. The volume is scheduled for publication by Facts on File in 2004.

Encyclopedia of the U.S. Supreme Court

Salem Press published in 2001 a three-volume set on the Supreme Court edited by Thomas T. Lewis and Richard L. Wilson. It contains biographies, historical topics, international perspectives, legislation and laws, organizations, procedural matters, issues addressed by the U.S. Supreme Court, and individual Court cases. Each of the essays, ranging in length from 50 to 2000 words, centers on the U.S. Supreme Court and each is written with the lay audience in mind. This set is an excellent starting point for research in constitutional law and for students of the Supreme Court.

Encyclopedia of Supreme Court Quotations

Edited by Christopher A. Anzalone and published in 2000 by M. E. Sharpe, this is a 13-chapter book containing 900 famous quotations of Supreme Court justices on many constitutional subjects. It also contains a table of cases with case summaries and a table of justices and decisions by justices. As stated in his preface, Anzalone chose these particular quotes for their "inherent beauty," "literary quality," and "profound philosophy."

American Jurisprudence 2d (Am. Jur. 2d)

American Jurisprudence 2d contains a discussion of both substantive and procedural aspects of American law arranged under more than 430 headings. This encyclopedia emphasizes federal statutory law and procedural rules, and although detailed references to state laws are few, the editors of *Am. Jur. 2d* make extensive references to the *Uniform State Laws*.

Volumes are arranged alphabetically by title. For researchers already familiar with a particular legal topic, access is easy. Abstracts and subject outlines precede the exposition of each legal topic. By reading the brief abstract and perusing the subject outline, the researcher can easily determine if he or she has turned to the appropriate discussion. This method, however, presupposes sophistication that laypersons sometimes lack. If necessary, one may refer to the *General Index* to locate the subject matter of interest. When appropriate, the publisher updates the index by issuing supplemental pamphlets or by completely replacing out-of-date volumes. For this reason, the example cited below may not be exactly consistent with what a researcher may find just a few months or years after the publication of this particular book. Yet, the illustration is indicative of the process researchers must use to locate discussions on topics of research interest.

Using the paperbound multivolume *General Index* (2003 edition) is simple. Assume that a student wants to research housing discrimination for a course in civil rights. Turning to the index item "Housing Discrimination (this index)" listed under the bold heading "Civil Rights" on page 180 in volume C–D of the *General Index*, the researcher knows that the topic of housing discrimination is contained under this heading and, turning to this index item, he or she will find the topic in the *General Index E–I*. If the researcher had focused immediately on the more specific subject of housing discrimination he or she would have turned to the *General Index*, volume F–I. On page 527 of this particular index is the entry "Housing Discrimination"; over four columns of subheading entries treating various aspects of housing discrimination follow. One also will find the subheading, "generally Civil Rights §§ 380–520." If the researcher begins the search with a broad or a specific subject category in mind and does not locate the topic immediately, he or she should use the available cross-referencing for easy access to substantive discussions of law.

Having located the correct subject entry in the *General Index*, the researcher then turns to the appropriate volume of *Am. Jur. 2d*. For the case of housing discrimination, we already know there is a general discussion under Civil Rights §§ 380–520. At times, *Am. Jur.* editors use abbreviations for their subject headings. For more difficult or uncommon abbreviations, one needs only to consult the table of abbreviations appearing at the front of each copy of the *General Index*. The symbol § refers to the section under Civil Rights where the discussion of the topic is found. Thus, volume 15 of *Am. Jur. 2d* contains materials ranging in alphabetical order from Charities to Civil Rights. Turning to §§ 380–520 under Civil Rights, one finds a discussion of housing discrimination beginning on page 543 and ending on page 615. From time to time, the editors at West make available a General Index Update. Consult this service for a complete search of one's research topic.

The legal exposition found in each encyclopedia entry contains extensive references to original source material such as statutes, executive orders, and case law. Secondary sources also are cited, including annotations to the *American Law Reports*. *American Jurisprudence 2d* is especially useful in obtaining a general overview of the law on a particular subject. Students should consult additional research materials often cited in this encyclopedia.

It is important to continue to emphasize that most publishers who market research tools for practicing attorneys update their publications. Each *Am. Jur. 2d* topic is written with current legal issues in mind. However, the legal environment continuously changes and so each volume is updated

annually by cumulative pocket supplements. Researchers should always
check these supplements for new materials. As the law changes, replacement
volumes are published. Consequently, *Am. Jur. 2d* is constantly undergoing
change, allowing researchers to be reasonably certain that they are aware of
recent developments in the law. Formerly published by Lawyers Cooperative
Publishing, *Am. Jur. 2d* is now a product of West. A sample citation is 15 Am.
Jur. 2d *Civil Rights* § 381 (2000). Those students with access to Westlaw Campus may search *Am. Jur. 2d* in electronic format.

Corpus Juris Secundum (C. J. S.)

Corpus Juris Secundum is a massive statement of U.S. case law. It has 101
numbered volumes in addition to lettered volumes (for example, 16B) added
to numbered volumes when the editors decide to expand treatments on given
topics. This encyclopedia features over 400 separate titles, many of which are
specifically labeled "constitutional law," and a multivolume *General Index*.

Included in *C. J. S.* are references to reported cases decided as long ago as
the mid-seventeenth century and extensive references to state as well as federal law. Each subject essay is made current with an annual pocket supplement found at the back of each bound volume. Whole volumes are
occasionally replaced with totally updated versions.

Written primarily for practicing attorneys, the publisher (West) has
devised time-saving methods for finding the law on any given subject. However, the use of these methods presupposes a general knowledge of law not
usually possessed by laypersons. Yet, any student can successfully use this
impressive encyclopedia by employing elementary techniques similar to
those described for *Am. Jur. 2d.*

First, consult the multivolume *General Index*, which lists all topics alphabetically. Beginning with the most general title, researchers can then proceed
to locate a more specific subtitle. The *General Index* is designed by the editors
to be used in close conjunction with the indexes to each *C. J. S.* subject volume. Therefore, before turning to the specific subject essay, it is advisable to
examine carefully the analysis that appears at the beginning of each subject
title. Consult the appropriate volume of the encyclopedia itself for a detailed
description of the discussion contained therein.

The analysis provides a brief description of a topic and an outline of its
related parts. By studying this aid, students can acquire an overview of the
subject matter and how the specific research topic fits into the general legal
framework. In addition to descriptive legal essays, each volume contains its
own index. Moreover, at the back of each volume is an index to words,
phrases, and legal maxims found there with dictionary-type definitions.

A simple example illustrates the research procedure. In a course on the
criminal justice system, the question arises whether prison officials may conduct strip searches of inmates. Because no one knows the answer to the question, the instructor asks one of the students to investigate and report his or
her findings to the class at its next meeting.

Turning to the *General Index M to Q* (2002 Edition), the student finds "Prisons and Prisoners" beginning on page 462 and ending on page 468. Since there are many subheadings, it is necessary to narrow the investigation further. On page 467 the researcher finds "Strip search permissible, Prisons § 58." One then turns from the *General Index* to the appropriate subject matter volume. Because "Prisons" falls alphabetically within volume 72—"Pledges–Process," one finds "Strip Search", with § 58 located on page 469. Back on page 467, directly under the title heading "Searches and Seizures," one finds a brief statement on the general rule of law with respect to lawful searches and seizures. A paragraph follows explaining applications of the rule with citations to a number of state and federal cases. In addition, the student should carefully check the *Cumulative Annual Pocket Part* for updated references and analyses. If the researcher also takes the time to consult the analysis under "Prisons," she will then be able to discuss prisoner privacy (Prisons § 57) within the general context of prisoner rights. Armed with this knowledge, she will truly impress her classmates and instructor with the breadth and quality of her knowledge and splendid contribution to the class. *C. J. S.* is accessible electronically at Westlaw but is unavailable through Westlaw Campus. The following is a sample citation: 72 C.J.S. *Prisons* § 58 (1987).

Digests

Court opinions are reported chronologically, but this creates a serious problem. How may we organize judicial opinions in a way that bears on particular facts and rules without reading all reported opinions from the beginning of the republic? Obviously, what researchers need is an indexing system that groups cases together by subject matter and/or legal rule. A digest is a research tool that does just that. Obviously, the ability to use a digest can ease the research process and lead to an up-to-date and thorough presentation.

A digest provides brief abstracts of the facts or holdings in a case. A digest, however, is not an encyclopedia because it does not present a full legal narrative with accompanying citations and references to authority. Because a digest acts as a subject index to reported cases, identifying only cases that deal with particular facts or legal problems, attorneys are able to read and analyze court opinions pertinent to the legal problem at hand.

Digests are available to fit a variety of needs. A national digest is necessary if a researcher wants to know all the reported cases in the United States on a given topic. If a researcher is interested in a particular part of the country, then regional digests are appropriate tools. Digests also exist for a number of state jurisdictions. Finally, there are digests that cover particular court systems.

Because all digests are useful research tools, it is necessary first to examine the digest system for all of American law and then focus on specialized court systems of interest to constitutional law scholars. The regional and state digests are segments of the national digest system, and researchers may use them in the same way.

American Digest System

The *American Digest System*, a massive work consisting of over 430 volumes, classifies by subject all reported cases appearing in the *National Reporter System*. The first set in this system, the *Century Digest*, covers the period from 1685 to 1896. For each succeeding ten-year period there are decennial digests from the *First Decennial* (1897–1906) to the *Eleventh Decennial* (1996–2000). The *General Digest*, a monthly bound supplement to the last *Decennial*, should be used if a complete enumeration of pertinent cases is desirable. In other words, until the publisher issues the *Twelfth Decennial* one can use the *General Digest* as an updating service beginning in 2001. The editors order all the abstracted cases according to West's Key Number System®.

West's Key Number System®

West's Key Number System® is a scheme for assigning cases or sections of cases to appropriate subject categories. This system first divides the law into seven main classes. Each class is then divided into 32 subheadings and each subclass is further divided into more than 400 digest topics. Finally, each topic is divided into subtopics to which a key number—not a word label—is assigned.[2] By first identifying the appropriate topic and key number, the researcher can locate all known reported cases on a specific legal topic during a particular time period. In fact, by going through each *Decennial* and *General Digest*, it is possible to identify all the reported cases known to the publisher on a given topic. Two indexes to the Key Number System® are best suited for layperson use: the *Table of Cases Index* and the *Descriptive-Word Index*.

Experience teaches that those without extensive legal training find using the *Table of Cases Index* the simplest and most time-effective method for locating case law on a given subject. For example, after reading the Supreme Court's decision in *Griswold v. Connecticut* (1965), the researcher may become interested in the right to privacy. Among other things, the researcher may want to identify all cases dealing with the constitutional protection of privacy. Each *Decennial* and *General Digest* contains an alphabetical listing of cases by plaintiff, for example, Griswold. Since *Griswold v. Connecticut* was decided in 1965, the correct reference is the *Table of Cases Index* for the *Seventh Decennial*. By looking up *Griswold v. Connecticut* the researcher can find its legal citation and the various topic and key numbers under which the case is digested. After deciding on the appropriate topic and key number, the researcher need only consult each *Decennial* and *General Digest* for a complete abstract of all reported cases under the selected topic and key number.

Although the *Descriptive-Word Index* sometimes provides a quicker method for locating topics and key numbers than the case-index approach, this approach requires more thought. There is a separate *Descriptive-Word Index* for each unit of the *Decennials* and *General Digest*. By thinking of a catchword, a researcher may consult this index to determine whether there is such an entry. For this example, "privacy" is an obvious catchword for cases involving the doctrine found in *Griswold v. Connecticut.* Selecting the right word usually proves more difficult, however. Because there are hundreds of word entries, the researcher can try additional catchwords until one finds the appropriate entry.

I must emphasize again that West has devised a variety of ways to find cases, but the editors at West created search methods for those who have had professional legal training, not laypersons. Those with little advanced legal training should use the tables of cases and the descriptive-word indexes. Although the Key Number System® may seem difficult to comprehend at first, working with the material builds confidence. Do not be intimidated by the undertaking. Hundreds of my students have successfully mastered the process. But it does take patience and perseverance.

Specialized Digests

As previously indicated, West also publishes several regional, state, and federal digests.[3] It is important to note that each of these more specialized digests is a segment of the *American Digest System.* Therefore, if the researcher has access to the parent *American Digest System,* there is no great need to consult the specialized digests. Sometimes, reflecting academic interests, college or university libraries will have one or more of the specialized digests and not the extensive *American Digest System.* Students of constitutional law will find the *Federal Practice Digest* and the *U.S. Supreme Court Digest* well suited for most research purposes.

Federal Practice Digest

There are four sets of digests produced by West that index only federal court opinions. All use the Key Number System®. Because this series includes all reported federal opinions of the ninety-four U.S. District Courts, the thirteen U.S. Courts of Appeals, and the U.S. Supreme Court, the Key Number System® is a valuable aid to those interested in ascertaining the known *corpus juris* of the federal judicial system. The special features of the *Federal Practice Digest* include entries indicating whether a case has been affirmed, reversed, or modified and references to secondary sources such as *Corpus Juris Secundum.*

Federal Practice Digest 3d indexes cases from 1975 to 1996 and should be used in conjunction with *Federal Practice Digest 4th,* which began publication in 1989. There is no distinct cut-off date for cases included in the *Federal Practice Digest 3d* and *Federal Practice Digest 4th.* If the researcher is interested only in locating cases from 1984 to the present, then the fourth set must be consulted.[4] *Federal Practice Digest 2d* indexes cases from 1961 to 1975. Researchers seeking to locate cases from 1939 to 1961 should consult *Modern Federal Practice Digest.* For all opinions before 1930, the *Federal Digest* is available. The series is made current by *Cumulative Pocket Parts* and by subsequent pamphlet supplements.

U.S. Supreme Court Digest

Typically, students conducting legal research in constitutional law focus their attention on the opinions of the highest court in the land. Consequently, they do not need to concern themselves with opinions of other federal courts. *U.S. Supreme Court Digest* indexes only decisions of the U.S. Supreme Court. Like other West publications, it uses the Key Number System® and duplicates the cases found in the *American Digest System* and the *Federal Practice Digest*. In addition, the editors at West bring it up to date with cumulative annual pocket supplements. Thus, if a research assignment calls for an examination of only Supreme Court opinions, using this set of over 30 volumes is the recommended digest tool.

Westlaw Campus and the Natural-Language Approach

A default search method for those students without legal training is available through the online subscription service Westlaw Campus. The natural-language method for finding cases allows researchers to search West's electronic database using plain English to retrieve pertinent court opinions in areas of interest, for example, the right to privacy. Using the *Quick Search* feature, one first selects the *Natural Language* or *Terms and Connectors* search method. Then, one simply types words that describe the sought cases in the *Search* for text box; for example, "Is a woman's right to privacy constitutionally protected?" Then select a date restriction if desired—let us say the last 10 years—and *All Federal Cases* as one's database. Finally, click *Go,* and within moments, the legal citations for the pertinent court opinions appear. I generally agree with many professional law librarians that the natural-language approach is not preferable to the digest system described above. Students are liable to include cases in their universe of study that are not as pertinent, and they will consequently spend considerable time and effort culling the list of cases. In addition, sometimes students will include discussion of court opinions in their research papers only because they are part of the list of opinions outputted by their computer terminals. This is a bad practice.

U.S. Supreme Court Reports Digest: Lawyers' Edition

U.S. Supreme Court Reports Digest: Lawyers' Edition is a publication of LEXIS Law Publishing, the same firm that issues *United States Supreme Court Reports: Lawyers' Edition* and *United States Code Service*. Because it is not a West product, it does not use the Key Number System®. Nevertheless, it is easy to use. *U.S. Supreme Court Reports Digest: Lawyers' Edition* contains both a table of cases and a word index.

The table of cases lists U.S. Supreme Court decisions under both plaintiff and defendant names as well as the popular names by which cases are sometimes known. Below the alphabetical listing for each case there is a full case citation, followed by the digest topic and section number(s). Instead of proceeding directly to the digest topic and number designation, it is advisable first to consult the scope-note and outline preceding each topic title. Scope-notes define the nature of each topic, enabling researchers to determine whether they have chosen the correct topic. The case of *Abrams v. United States,* for example, has four different digest topics: appeal and error, constitutional law, criminal law, and evidence. As is common for all digests, the editors abstract cases under many different topics. The researcher can choose the topic title of greatest interest by consulting the scope-notes and outlines before reading each digest entry. By doing so, effective researchers save time and considerable effort.

The word index to *U.S. Supreme Court Reports Digest: Lawyers' Edition* is used in the same way as West's *Descriptive-Word Index*. The researcher uses those catchwords which best describe the pertinent subject matter. As student researchers become more knowledgeable, they may find this method preferable to the table-of-cases approach. Yet, as indicated for the West product, for the relative novice the table-of-cases approach is more highly recommended. In addition to abstracts of each Supreme Court case, the editors have included references to *American Jurisprudence 2d,* the *American Law Reports* series, and annotations pertinent to the case.

Volume 17 of this set of forty-three contains several features particularly valuable to constitutional law students. First, each article, section, and clause of the Constitution appears with digest references. For example, listed under article I, section 8, clause 3 (the Commerce Clause) is the digest reference Commerce §§ 1–362. In this way, researchers may readily identify all Supreme Court opinions dealing with the Commerce Clause.

Serious students of the procedures of the U.S. Supreme Court will find volume 17 very informative. It contains the *Revised Rules of the Supreme Court of the United States* and answers such common questions as what constitutes a Court quorum and what rules govern the granting of the writ of certiorari. This *Rules* section also includes a research guide with references to the *U.S. Supreme Court Reports Digest: Lawyers' Edition* and other sources.

As with most legal research material, the editors of *U.S. Supreme Court Reports Digest: Lawyers' Edition* update this set with pocket supplements inserted at the back of each bound volume. As with all legal reference material, one should always consult the supplements.

Other Electronic Subject Search Techniques

I have referenced above the Westlaw Campus natural-language approach with respect to the West Digest system. However, there are other online services useful in accomplishing the same goal of finding related court opinions on the same or similar subjects.

LexisNexis Academic is one such service. First, click on *Legal Research* and scroll to and click *Area of Law by Topic.* On the new screen, type the desired term in the space next to the word *Keyword;* for example, privacy rights. This screen allows one to narrow the search with additional terms; for example, constitutional law. Click your choice for the various prelisted legal categories on the *Source List.* Researchers also have the option of how many years or months they want as their universe of cases—it ranges from six months to all available dates. Finally, click the *Search* button and a list of court opinions appears on the monitor. A problem with this method is that the computer program finds all cases with the word that is inputted, for example, "privacy", even though the particular court opinions may only be tangentially related to the topic of privacy. One way to cull the opinions is to use the *Find* feature on the browser. This allows researchers to locate the terms or phrases of particular interest. Obviously, this is an inefficient use of one's time.

Several prominent and well-known non-subscription online services group cases by subject matter or keyword. The Web site of the Legal Information Institute at Cornell University Law School allows users to search Supreme Court opinions by topic. Go to http://www.law.cornell.edu. Under *Law About*, click on *By Topic*. Each available topic is listed in alphabetical order. Unfortunately, as in our privacy example, one's particular topic of interest may not be listed. FedWorld/FLITE at http://www.fedworld.gov/supcourt/#FLITEinfo contains an easy-to-use self-explanatory keyword approach to finding U.S. Supreme Court opinions from 1937 to 1975 on topics of interest.

The Oyez project at Northwestern University allows student researchers to find cases by subject matter. Click on http://www.oyez.org/oyez/frontpage. Employ the *Advanced Search* option to find Supreme Court opinions on given subject topics or case names since 1955. It is important to emphasize that those electronic services that are not based on existing hard-copy digest systems are less useful, efficient, and reliable than the digest-based systems described above. In other words, researchers cannot be certain that they have located all the available court opinions on a given subject. If knowing all the cases on a given subject is not crucial to one's research project, then it is tolerable to proceed in this way.

Cite-Checking (Citators)

A citator is a research tool designed to determine the extent to which cases have been cited by subsequent court opinions or used in concurring or dissenting opinions. By using a citator, it is possible to quickly determine the status of a legal rule or precedent. This research process is commonly called cite-checking.

The attorney needs a citator for an obvious reason: to argue a case from a precedent that has long been overruled or modified would most certainly jeopardize the client's standing in the eyes of the court. Although professional consequences differ, researchers and teachers of constitutional law also need to know the standing of legal opinions. For example, if after reading Minersville School District v. Gobitis, 310 U.S. 586 (1940) a student concludes that compulsory flag salutes are constitutionally permissible, he or she would surely be wrong. In West Virginia State Board of Education v. Barnette, 319 U.S. 624 (1943), the Supreme Court overruled its 1940 decision. Using a citator would prevent this gross error.

Besides their use in checking for the precedential value of particular opinions, citators, like digests, help to locate opinions with similar subject matter, because the editors of citators list a case whenever an opinion writer cites it in support of one argument or another. The citator will pinpoint the exact page of those cases that cite the main case as precedent. Although we must qualify our enthusiasm, the basic premise of cite-checking is fundamentally sound. If a later court opinion cites the case under study, then the opinion writer must be discussing the same or similar legal or factual issue, or at least they believe the cases they are citing are pertinent to those legal or factual issues. Consequently, cite-checking leads researchers to judicial decisions involving factual or legal issues that may be pertinent to comprehending the subject that they are investigating. Hence, cite-checking is one way to ascertain the universe of pertinent cases for studying a specific subject. However, I advise caution when using legal citators for this purpose. Judges sometimes cite a case to make a point on a minor issue. Opinion writers do not always cite opinions particularly germane to their argument. Indeed, some cases they cite as authority may be highly debatable. Therefore, researchers should understand that the cited cases might be only tangentially related to the topic at hand. Thus a digest is more appropriate for finding cases of a similar nature.

Citators are available for several different jurisdictions and subjects. The Shepard's Citations series, the most widely known citator, is now part of LEXIS Law Publishing. Those citators most likely to be of use to constitutional law students include *Shepard's United States Citations: Cases*; *Shepard's United States Citations: Statutes*; *Shepard's United States Administrative Citations*; *Shepard's Acts and Cases by Popular Names, Federal and State;* and *Shepard's Code of Federal Regulations Citations*. Citators also are available for lower federal court cases, state cases, criminal justice cases, and law reviews. They are available in print, online, and on CD-ROM. For illustrative purposes, I will describe the citator for U.S. Supreme Court cases.

Shepard's United States Citations: Cases

Students commonly experience frustration when they examine one of the huge volumes in this set for the first time. The blur of tiny legal citations placed on very thin pages seems unwieldy, to say the least. A first reaction is to put the volume quietly back on the shelf and to forget the whole idea. But wait! Like most legal research material, the citator is easy to use. The process of using the Shepard's product has become so commonplace in American law that the noun Shepard has become a registered verb, to *Shepardize*®.

To check a cite, start with a legal citation to a court case and locate those cases that cite this central case in a significant fashion. Because a researcher may have a citation for only one reporting system, editors at Shepard's Citations have separate sections of each volume reserved for each of the three parallel citations; i.e., *United States Reports* (*U. S.*); the unofficial *Lawyers' Edition* (*L. Ed.*); or West's unofficial *Supreme Court Reporter* (*S. Ct.*). Beginning with a citation to a particular case (for example, 310 U.S. 586), locate the volume number of the citation (310) at the upper corner of each printed page of the citator—an easy task because case citations occur in numerical order. On the body of each page, printed in bold numerals, is the page number of each case, in our example 586. Immediately below this page number, one finds the case name and date: Minersville School District v. Gobitis 1940. Once the researcher finds the desired case by volume and page number, cite-checking may begin. See the sample page on page 49 of this chapter as you read the following description.

Because the editors have included a case citation whenever a judge cites another case, however vaguely or incorrectly, in his or her written opinion, often the number of citations is quite large. Obviously, reading each of these opinions would be an enormous and wasteful task. To circumvent this problem, Shepard's editors provide cues whenever a cited case is treated in a significant manner—for example, when a case is distinguished or overruled. These cues take the form of lower-case abbreviations appearing at the left edge of the cited or citing cases—these abbreviations indicate how the case is treated by the citing authority. A complete listing of abbreviations and definitions appears at the front of each volume. By running a finger down the left edge of the columns, the researcher may note the treatment cues. To determine the context of the case and the argument of the court in its decision, read the citing case in either the official or unofficial reports.

The compulsory-flag-salute cases provide an uncomplicated example to illustrate further the use of this citator. Here the research problem is to determine the rule of law about the flag-salute question. Armed with the *Gobitis* decision, the search begins. The official citation for *Minersville School District v. Gobitis* is 310 U.S. 586; 310 refers to volume 310 of the *U.S. Reports* in which *Gobitis* appears. Note that volume 1-4 of *Shepard's United States Citations* contains citations for Supreme Court cases reported in volumes 270–322 of *United States Reports*. Because the cases are in numerical order, turn directly to 310. On page 1224 of *Citations* we locate 310 U.S. 586 of this volume—see the sample page included on page 49.

Under 586, the researcher first sights the parallel citations, which include the *Lawyers' Edition* (84 LE 1375) and the *Supreme Court Reporter* (60 SC 1010). Immediately below these citations are several references describing the judicial history of the *Gobitis* case. At the left of these case citations are editor cues in the form of the lower-case *s*. To see what the various abbreviations signify, turn to the inside front cover of each Shepard's volume and locate the printed words "history and treatment abbreviations". There note that the lower-case *s* refers to "same case as case cited." The researcher knows at once that citations accompanied by lower-case *s* trace the history of the *Gobitis* controversy in the courts. Thus, the original federal district court opinion in *Gobitis* is at 21 FS 581, and the second opinion in that same court is at 24 FS 271. For the opinion of the U.S. Circuit Court of Appeals the researcher must consult 108 F. 2d 683. The Supreme Court's order for the grant of the petition for the writ of certiorari is referenced as 309 U.S. 645.

The next marginal notation sighted is a lower-case *d* followed by the citation 316 U.S. 598. The "history and treatment abbreviations" page indicates

Vol. 310 UNITED STATES REPORTS

126Wis2d333	(60SC1021)	719FS1432		j 343US268	
128Wis2d451	s 309US646	Cir. 8	P R	j 365US214	Cir. DC
168Wis2d480	s 311US570	113F2d701	73PRR383	j 366US62	120F2d735
335NW611	s 311US614	132F2d659	77PRR364	j 366US561	j 421F2d1103
377NW155	s 311US727	474F2d935	Tenn	392US246	206FS373
384NW360	s 107F2d70	165FS898	178Ten537	q 430US714	288FS443
484NW149	s 28FS131	194FS934	184Ten421	438US290	100TCt174
75CR1301	314US546	Cir. 9	29TnA539	450US153	Ariz
82CR938	319US318	d 35FS110	160SW415	457US882	58Az153
76Geo114	319US330	63FS396	198SW292	472US51	58Az449
77Geo2099	j 319US338	Cir. 10	199SW122	j 477US40	58Az454
57TxL563	320US352	36FS69	555SW400	j 478US213	90Az192
89YLJ1375	329US4	119FS862	Tex	j 490US824	118P2d101
	334US67	j 147FS645	152Tex447	Cir. 1	120P2d810
—563—	j 334US98	345FS88	162Tex289	117F2d664	120P2d812
	336US351	ECA	162Tex302	33FS846	367P2d232
Arkansas v	340US185	529F2d1026	146SW1086	Cir. 2	Ark
Tennessee	341US350	536F2d385	161SW1047	122F2d514	204Ark480
1940	343US392	536F2d1384	165SW503	j 122F2d524	163SW154
	Cir. 1	585F2d515	170SW570	c 172F2d409	Calif
(84LE1362)	202F2d704	f 598F2d603	186SW311	q 380F2d448	31C2d148
(60SC1026)	Cir. 2	2TCt1031	193SW834	638F2d414	5C3d616
s 296US545	128F2d224	Calif	215SW642	712F2d1542	264CA2d381
s 301US666	264F2d713	19C2d858	259SW177	q 307FS30	97CA3d638
s 308US511	319F2d27	164CA3d99	335SW432	325FS808	70CaR601
s 311US1	d 47FS947	210CaR337	346SW811	334FS594	96CaR624
s 312US664	160FS164	123P2d472	346SW821	387FS122	159CaR35
415US290	319FS732	Colo	380SW602	q 835FS146	187P2d775
430US605	400FS29	168Col165	387SW43	Cir. 3	487P2d1264
444US337	406FS365	176Col140	786SW677	130F2d656	Colo
Cir. 2	602FS1532	451P2d272	Wash	j 130F2d662	109Col235
956F2d388	674FS1106	490P2d278	10Wsh2d219	d 39FS32	112Col187
Cir. 5	Cir. 3	Me	116P2d521	310FS580	124P2d760
112F2d948	465F2d242	329A2d170	68Cor17	Cir. 4	147P2d825
e 220F2d355	641F2d116	Mass	73Cor50	47FS252	Fla
937F2d253	105FS618	328Mas683	85CR259	q 47FS253	570So2d335
Cir. 9	221FS846	106NE262	94HLR503	q 391FS447	Ill
811F2d1254	319FS413	Mich	88McL586	Cir. 5	101Il2d186
Cir. 10	372FS952	389Mch650	58MnL1071	124F2d70	461NE434
558FS744	Cir. 4	209NW221	13Æ536n	j 653F2d188	Kan
Ala	101FS653	Miss	37Æ435n	939F2d250	155Kan592
266Ala178	312FS716	190Mis253		103FS207	127P2d521
94So2d778	Cir. 5	199So304	—586—	q 142FS716	Ky
Calif	113F2d906	N Y		q 314FS294	291Ky441
14C3d276	118F2d847	296NY383	Minersville	Cir. 6	164SW974
123CaR57	e 124F2d468	296NY387	School District	114F2d914	Md
537P2d1306	e 128F2d336	270NYAD63	v Gobitis	178F2d41	217Md221
Mich	j 128F2d337	36NYAD266	1940	766F2d946	223Md58
347Mch184	e 130F2d14	73NE708		529FS37	262Md538
79NW621	130F2d19	73NE711	(84LE1375)	638FS579	262Md557
Miss	155F2d954	58NYS2d824	(60SC1010)	j 170F2d259	262Md558
240So2d140	229F2d199	320NYS2d284	s 309US645	44FS818	141A2d907
Mo	247F2d893	N C	s 108F2d683	e 49FS438	162A2d443
528SW161	253F2d381	222NC315	s 21FS581	295FS989	278A2d266
S D	255F2d778	275NC497	s 24FS271	296FS707	278A2d275
71SD65	322F2d600	22SE900	316US593	Cir. 7	278A2d277
21NW64	j 330F2d7	168SE384	d 316US598	c 426F2d458	Mass
	53FS178	Okla	j 316US623	e 43FS656	309Mas481
—573—	218FS620	199Okl173	319US587	q 82FS132	35NE804
	218FS621	203Okl41	319US625	Cir. 9	Miss
Railroad	353FS584	184P2d963	319US640	j 462F2d104	194Mis31
Commission	Cir. 6	220P2d285	o 319US642	819F2d880	194Mis71
of Texas	j 43FS1022	Ore	j 319US643	j 859F2d626	200Mis257
v Rowan &	56FS284	229Ore473	j 319US664	e 39FS30	11So2d671
Nichols Oil Co.	577FS524	365P2d1037	j 321US113	q 281FS516	11So2d688
1940	Cir. 7	Pa	321US665	Cir. 10	27So2d69
	178F2d908	11PaC612	j 340US308	177F2d599	478So2d1038
(84LE1368)	513F2d187	314A2d568	j 341US592		

1224

From *Shepard's United States Citations*, Case Edition, 1994, Vol. 1-4, page 1224. Reproduced by permission of Shepard's. Further reproduction of any kind is strictly prohibited.

that *d* signifies that the case at bar is different either in law or fact from the case cited; in this particular example, *Gobitis* is distinguishable from 316 U.S. 598. Thumbing down to the next entry the researcher finds a lower-case *j* adjacent to the citation, 316 U.S. 623. This means that on page 623 of volume 316 of the *U.S. Reports* a dissenting opinion cited *Gobitis*. Next, the researcher finds an entry for 319 U.S. 642 accompanied with the notation *o*. The lower-case *o* means that 310 U.S. 586 *(Gobitis)* is overruled by the Supreme Court at 319 U.S. 642: the case is West Virginia State Board of Education v. Barnette, 319 U.S. 624.[5] Following the *Barnette* entries are many citations to federal and state cases that cite *Gobitis* in some way.

Up to this point, it is apparent that Shepard's editors indicate *Barnette* has overruled *Gobitis*. To verify the editors' conclusion, and to determine the precise reasoning of the Court, turn to the actual opinion for reading and analysis. Yet, having done this, the researcher cannot report that *Barnette* is the contemporary rule of law. Once again, turn to the citator, repeating the research procedure, this time Shepardizing the *Barnette* case. In this same volume of *Shepard's United States Citations: Cases*, one can locate, beginning on page 1557, the citation for 319 U.S. 624, where there are numerous references to judicial opinions citing *Barnette*, but there are no editor notations indicating that *Barnette* has been overruled. Consulting the later supplements indicates the same. The researcher can be satisfied that *Barnette* is still the law of the land.

Shepard's Federal Statute Citations

Formerly named *Shepard's United States Citations: Statute and Court Rules*, *Shepard's Federal Statute Citations* includes citations to the *United States Code*, the *United States Code Annotated*, the *Federal Code Annotated*, the *United States Code Service*, the *United States Statutes at Large*, the *United States Treaties and other International Agreements*, and the *General Orders in Bankruptcy*. It also contains citations to the U.S. Constitution and the rules for several courts including the U.S. Supreme Court.

This multivolume set with supplements contains a variety of references, including citations to court decisions. If, for example, the researcher wants to know how the courts have construed the Eleventh Amendment, this citator provides a listing of cases citing the amendment. The same is true for the codes and other special features of this citator. For discussion and illustration, consult the preface and other explanatory remarks at the front of these volumes.

Electronic Citators

Cite-checking is also available electronically through LexisNexis and West. *Shepard's Citations* is integrated with other online tools including Lexis-Nexis and is available on CD-ROM. This helpful product is available on a subscription basis to law offices, law schools and law school libraries, and individual researchers. While the cost per search seems reasonable for attorneys who bill their clients accordingly, students conducting their own research may reasonably conclude that the print copies of Shepard's products available to them at libraries at no cost makes greater economic sense. The company maintains a Web site at http://www.lexis-nexis.com/shepards. As a competitor to Shepard's Citations, West is aggressively marketing *KeyCite*, a product that can be used online through Westlaw and Westlaw Campus. Online demonstrations are available through West at the Web address indicated below. As a practical matter, most college students are unable to bear the cost of either the LexisNexis or West cite-checking services. However, if their colleges or universities subscribe to LexisNexis Academic or Westlaw Campus it is possible for students to check cites electronically at no direct cost to themselves.

For those students that have access to LexisNexis Academic, the process of cite-checking is straightforward and easy to use. First, click *Legal Research* and scroll to *Shepard's for U.S. Supreme Court*. Following the simple instructions, type the citation of the opinion you want to cite-check (in our previous example, 310 U.S. 586). Then click the *Search* button option. Within moments, a complete listing of how this Supreme Court opinion has been subsequently treated appears on the screen. A convenient feature is a *Warning* signal that indicates negative treatment of the opinion—in our *Gobitis* example, that it has been overruled by the subsequent opinion in *Barnette*. The outputted display also provides researchers the number of times the studied case has been cited in subsequent opinions.

Westlaw Campus contains the same *KeyCite* program I mentioned earlier. Undergraduate and graduate students may be able to use this feature without cost to them if their college or university subscribes to the service. But students may also employ *KeyCite* for a price—as of May 2003, each retrieval cost $12.00 plus applicable taxes. The *KeyCite* system takes just a few minutes to learn. It uses colored symbols indicating the history of a case, statute, or administrative regulation to determine its present status as applicable law. *KeyCite* allows one to retrieve a list of all citing cases, to locate the most pertinent authority concerning the legal issue at hand, and more. It is possible to get an online demonstration of *KeyCite* by contacting West at http://west.thomson.com/store/product.asp?product%5Fid=westlaw+campus&catalog%5Fname=wgstore. As with most Web site addresses, it is important to recognize that in time addresses change or disappear altogether. Searching for the company Web site or keywords may be necessary in time. As time goes by, keying either http://www.west.thomson.com or http://www.west.thomson.com/Default.asp is probably the best approach.

Periodical Literature and Indexes

Law journal articles are useful for those researching a constitutional law topic. First, legal periodicals contain secondary source material for understanding what the law has been, what it is at any given historical moment, and what it might become. Second, law review articles reflect conflicting expert opinion about what the law should become. Third, law articles can teach students of the judicial process about the more subtle attempts to influence the bench and bar. Finally, law journals are publishing social science research at an increasing rate. Such articles assess the impact of court rulings on society, intra-court politics, and inter-institutional conflicts between and among the various branches and divisions of government.

Law journal articles are usually well-documented, meticulous discussions on a variety of legal or law-related topics. They often provide researchers with the history of the law and its more recent developments. A common error, however, is to treat these articles, no matter when or by whom they were written as authoritative, impartial statements on the law. Although law articles are substantial contributions to knowledge, often they are written from a distinct point of view; authors often attempt to shape the future direction of the law. The views expressed, therefore, are not necessarily those of the bench and bar. It is common for particularly controversial legal issues to have several competing perspectives. For a balanced outlook, make every effort to read as many law review articles on the subject as possible. As indicated earlier in this chapter, legal encyclopedias are usually an excellent source for impartial treatments of legal topics.

It is advisable for researchers to make a list of those articles that are pertinent to their subject matter. The various indexes to legal, public affairs, social science, and popular periodicals make such a task feasible.

Some legal periodicals are particularly useful for those conducting research on a constitutional law topic. The *Harvard Law Review* publishes an annual review of U.S. Supreme Court opinions. *Constitutional Commentary, Hastings Constitutional Law Quarterly, Constitutional Law Journal, Saint Louis University Public Law Review,* and two relatively new academic journals, *First Amendment Law Review* of the University of North Carolina Law School and the *University of Pennsylvania Journal of Constitutional Law,* focus on constitutional law topics. *Judicature,* the journal of the American Judicature Society, contains articles that bear on many judicial process topics. *Law and Society Review, Law & Policy Quarterly,* and the *Journal of Legal Studies* provide forums that bring together legal experts from related academic disciplines. Journals devoted to specialized legal subjects include *American Journal of Legal History,* the *Journal of Psychiatry and Law,* and the *Journal of Law and Economics.*

All law journals contain valuable material. Significant articles appear in the most famous as well as the most obscure journals, and to ignore them is perilous. For a first-rate research effort, always consult the various indexes. Consult chapter 5 of this volume for alternative styles for citing legal and other periodical literature.

Index to Legal Periodicals

A source of some confusion is the existence of three indexes with similar titles. Two of these are useful for identifying older materials.

An Index to Legal Periodical Literature consists of six volumes, the first of which specifies English-language legal articles and related materials published before January 1887. The remaining five volumes treat materials up to 1937. The editor, Leonard A. Jones, includes references to articles, papers, correspondence, annotated cases, and biographical notices in journals published in the United States, England, Ireland, and the English colonies. For research requiring vintage sources, this is an excellent tool. The *Index to Legal Periodicals*, published by the American Association of Law Libraries, is a second set of interest to those engaging in historical research. This eighteen-volume set covers the period 1910–1925.

Index to Legal Periodicals (renamed *Index to Legal Periodicals & Books* in 1997), published by H. W. Wilson, is the most accessible and widely known index at large. It contains entries beginning with the year 1926, and continues with periodic supplements to this day. It is the most complete index of legal periodicals published in the United States. It also contains entries for articles appearing in selected law journals of Canada, Great Britain, Ireland, Australia, and New Zealand. The *Index to Legal Periodicals* contains four main features: subject and author index, table of cases, table of statutes, and book review index.

Each cumulative volume and supplement contains a list of subject headings. By first determining the subject heading that best describes the research topic, students can save considerable effort. For example, if a researcher is interested in articles dealing with presidential impoundment of funds, he or she can find "impoundment" in the list of subject headings. By turning alphabetically to "impoundment" in the subject and author index, numerous relevant articles can be located.

Those interested in locating articles published before 1983 by author rather than subject matter may do so by a slightly more complicated process. For each volume of this index from 1926 to 1982, locate the last name of the author. Under the author's name is a listing of the subject headings under which his or her article(s) are classified. By turning to the appropriate subject heading(s), the author's name and article title are easily located. Depending on the scope of the research project, it is advisable to consult past and current volumes and to check all paperback supplementary indexes. Beginning in 1983, the subject and author listings are in alphabetical order with complete citations for each and therefore it is not necessary to follow the steps outlined above for index volumes before 1983.

Following the article listing under each subject heading, case notes or discussions of recent cases pertinent to the subject classification are found under the title "Cases." For example, in volume 17 (September 1973–August 1976) following the list of articles under the subject heading "freedom of press" there is a list of four different case notes dealing with the topic, which includes case names, followed by law journal names, volumes, pages, and dates of publication. These case notes, varying in length from a few to many pages, often are helpful in interpreting what a particular case might mean.

The "Table of Cases Commented Upon" lists articles that focus on particular judicial opinions. At the back of each volume and supplement, this table lists each case alphabetically by plaintiff, followed by law journal entries. This table is an excellent tool for researchers interested in finding what is written about specific cases, especially if issues surrounding the history or meaning of a statute are pertinent. For instance, the table yields no less than twelve law review articles for the statutory topic listed as the "Victim and Witness Protection Act of 1982."

The book review index of the *Index of Legal Periodicals* lists book reviews on legal subjects by name of author or title if the author's name is unknown.

The *Index to Legal Periodicals* is available in print and on CD-ROM. Wilson also publishes this index in electronic format on a subscription basis. It is called the *Index to Legal Periodicals & Books*, copyright 1999–present, and it contains periodical materials dating from 1981 to the present.

Current Law Index

The *Current Law Index (CLI)*, first appearing in 1980, is sponsored by the American Association of Law Libraries and references more than 875 law periodicals from the United States, Canada, the United Kingdom, Ireland, Australia, and New Zealand. This useful index, first a product of the Information Access Corporation and since 1999 the Gale Group, features a subject index, an author/title index, a table of cases, and a table of statutes. When statutes are discussed in an article, they are indexed by both their popular and official names. A listing of the titles of reviewed books appears in the author/title index. Each book is graded according to the reviewer's evaluation on a scale of A to F. As with other contemporary indexes, *CLI* is brought up to date with periodic supplements. At one time the *Current Law Index* had an easy-to-use companion microfilm service named *Legal Resource Index,* but in this high-tech age *LRI* is now accessible electronically through LexisNexis and Westlaw.

Legal Trac

Legal Trac, a legal periodical index, is a computer terminal system once offered by the Information Access Company but now owned by the Gale Group. Sitting at a keyboard with online instructions, researchers may access over 800 legal periodicals. Coverage begins with January 1980 and is updated every month. *Legal Trac* includes all the major law reviews, legal newspapers, specialty publications, bar association journals, and international law journals. The search process begins by entering a subject heading, author, case name, or statute name. Researchers should take their time in becoming acquainted with this powerful tool because if the wrong command is given it is possible to find only a few of the potential sources available for a given subject or author. In addition, the system has a *Power Trac* feature that allows for more advanced searches including dates, specific journals, or authors' names. By clicking the print function, users can have a bibliographical listing within seconds.

A growing number of law libraries and law firms are subscribing to *Legal Trac*. However, because *Legal Trac* contains entries beginning in 1980, it is of little use to researchers interested in obtaining earlier periodical sources.

Index to Foreign Legal Periodicals

The *Index to Foreign Legal Periodicals* is a tool for locating articles dealing with international law, comparative law, and the municipal law of non-common law countries. This index, published by the American Association of Law Libraries, contains article listings in over 500 legal journals published worldwide from 1960 to the present. Each year the editors analyze individually published collections of Festschriften, legal essays, mélanges, and congresses. It has an author index, subject index, geographical index, and book-review index. Growing interest in comparative legal topics makes this index invaluable. This index is available in hardbound volumes, on CD-ROM, and through the subscription Internet service *Ovid/SilverPlatter*.

Accessing Legal Periodicals in Electronic Format

Findlaw.com is a non-subscription site where researchers may access law reviews and journals. Findlaw has developed its own online legal library where they make available chapters from books and by-lined articles by legal practitioners. It also guides researchers to academic law reviews and journals and, when made available by the journal, one may print articles in PDF format. Unfortunately, however, not all academic journals make their publications available in electronic format and those that have taken this step have done so for only recent issues and years. These materials are located on the Web by keying *Findlaw: Academic Law Reviews and Journals* at http://stu.findlaw.com/journals.

LexisNexis Academic, the widely-held subscription service of colleges and universities, contains a universe of close to 700 law reviews. Click on *Law Reviews* and type the keyword of choice; there is a helpful feature to narrow the search with additional terms and dates (for example, establishment of religion, school prayer, last two years). Depending on the subject matter, citations for a large number of articles appear. From that list, researchers may click on articles of interest; they may then read and print the documents as they desire. However, like most databases, the articles are for recent years and do not extend backward beyond the 1990s.

Westlaw Campus is the other subscription service designed for undergraduate and graduate students that permits researchers to identify and to access law review articles. To search for legal periodicals, most students will want to employ the natural-language search method described in chapter 1 of this text. An added feature of considerable worth is that researchers may also identify encyclopedia articles on the same subject found in *Am. Jur. 2d* and *A. L. R.* Consequently, researchers may profit by first reading a relatively objective encyclopedia article on the subject and then may read and assess competing perspectives on the subject found in law journals.

PAIS International in Print

Many articles and books take a broad perspective on the law focusing in many cases on how it operates in a social, economic, and political context.

Such publications are often indexed in *PAIS International in Print,* formerly titled *Public Affairs Information Service Bulletin (PAIS).* It lists periodicals, books, pamphlets, and government documents useful for those conducting research on constitutional law topics. Most index entries include concise explanations of the item. Listings begin with 1915 and continue to the present. This index is available in print, on CD-ROM, and via the Web by direct database lease. Check with your library for availability.

Social Sciences Index

Social Sciences Index is among the best sources for developing an academic focus for a research paper. Students majoring in a social science discipline know this index well, and constitutional law students will find that it contains many items of interest. It contains references dating from 1916 forward. In a recent volume, over twenty subheadings are listed under the constitutional law subject heading. Before the mid-1960s, the name of this valuable tool was *International Index to Social Science and Humanities.* Today, there is a separate *Humanities Index,* and both indexes are available in print, on CD-ROM, and via online subscription. *Social Sciences Full Text* is part of this same service. It is available to subscribing libraries, making available to users the full text of articles from journals beginning in 1995. This same product has abstracts of articles to let readers know immediately if the piece is useful for their project. It also contains links to Web sites cited by articles, which are helpful in locating additional information on the subject of interest. In addition, beginning in 2003, H. W. Wilson made available to subscribing libraries the *Humanities & Social Sciences Index Retrospective: 1907–1984.* It indexes 600 periodicals and contains more than 1,100,000 articles and book reviews in electronic format.

U.S. Government Periodicals Index

Since 1994, the Congressional Information Service (CIS) has published the *U.S. Government Periodicals Index.* This service contains listings of articles appearing in government periodicals beginning in 1993. It is available in print, on magnetic tape, and through the LexisNexis subscription service. The LexisNexis service, not to be confused with LexisNexis Academic, has retrospective coverage beginning in 1988.

Readers' Guide to Periodical Literature

The *Readers' Guide to Periodical Literature* is the index of preference for citing popular articles such as those that appear in *Time, Newsweek, New Republic,* the *Nation,* or *National Review.* This index is particularly valuable when the research topic has widespread public interest. It contains items dating from 1901 to the present and features a single author and subject index. Many libraries make this index available on CD-ROM (updated monthly) and online, but it indexes periodicals back to only 1983. Also, a growing number of college and university libraries are subscribing to Wilson's *Readers' Guide*

Full Text, Mega Edition. Students may search for the full text of journal articles from 1994 to the present. Wilson has also produced the *Readers' Guide Retrospective: 1890–1982* in electronic format. It contains citations for more than 3,000,000 articles appearing in leading magazines, and through its Web site (WilsonWeb) researchers may have articles delivered to them.

Newspapers as Secondary Sources

Today, there are over 100 newspapers in the United States specializing in legal and business news. The *Chicago Daily Bulletin,* the *Los Angeles Daily Journal,* and the *New York Law Journal* are notable examples of large-circulation legal newspapers that provide daily information of particular importance for the practicing bar. Information about court calendars, changes in court rules, classified advertisements, and stories on members of the bench and bar are common features. These newspapers also print important court opinions of widespread interest. The *Legal Times* and the *National Law Journal* are weekly newspapers with a national circulation, and *The American Lawyer* is a monthly publication also with a national readership. A fair number of legal newspapers are accessible online through LexisNexis and Westlaw. See also the online subscription service http://www.law.com/index.shtml for the *Legal Times* and other notable legal newspapers. Findlaw.com provides a good non-subscription online service at http://news.findlaw.com. LexisNexis Academic has a huge offering of legal news articles from a wide variety of newspapers. Simply click on *Legal News* in the *Legal Research* section of this service. This function will lead you to articles that may go back ten years or reports as contemporary as just a few days old. These articles may be read on screen, printed, or saved on a disk or hard drive. Further, this service can access general news reports as well as specific legal news that may bear on particular research projects.

Because legal newspapers are sources of current information on court opinions, they are useful for staying current with court developments. However, from a social science perspective, these newspapers also can be used to understand the sociology and politics of the legal profession. Legal newspapers provide insight into what motivates lawyers, professional priorities, and information about the sociology and politics of bar stratification.

Many of the leading legal newspapers are indexed in the standard indexes to legal periodicals already discussed. Libraries typically keep back copies of newspapers for no more than a few weeks. However, thanks to microtext technologies, it is possible to access wanted stories through microfiche. The following is a sample citation for newspaper articles: Dan Mihalopoulos, "Trial Opens in Abortion Doctor Death," *Chicago Tribune,* 17 March 2003, p. 5.

The *New York Times* newspaper is among the best sources of information about developments in American law. It is clearly one of the best sources for news about the U.S. Supreme Court. Within academic circles, the *Times* is widely respected. The newspaper has made law-related articles, and all articles for that matter, accessible through *The New York Times Index*. News items are indexed for the periods from 1851 to 1906, and 1912 to the present. The *Times* may be accessed electronically at http://www.nytimes.com and through LexisNexis. As noted in chapter 1, the *Times* newspaper devotes a Web site specifically to the U.S. Supreme Court, but the address has changed over the years. I suggest that one seek articles online by locating the general Web site and then exercising the available options. By the way, the *New York Times* has made available a free online subscription service.

Radio and television are other sources of information about legal matters. Court TV, C-Span, the Public Broadcasting Service, and National Public Radio sometimes present live programs involving real court drama and public debates concerning legal issues. Often these organizations will present online transcripts or excerpts of significant legal opinions, debates, and events. Use your browser to locate the current address (URL) for each organization.

Electronic Book Review

The Law and Courts Section of the American Political Science Association maintains an electronic publication about books on law, courts, judges, the judicial process, criminal justice, law and society, jurisprudence, and related fields. *The Law and Politics Book Review* publishes reviews ranging between 800 and 2000 words and makes reviews available within six months of the editor's receipt of books submitted by publishers for review. Because this service began in the 1980s, it is of no use for books published earlier. One may subscribe to the service at no cost via the Internet. Alternatively, one may simply visit the Web site, where books are listed in alphabetical order by author. It is also possible to search by book title and by subject matter. For a reliable way to locate this Web site, one may first visit the home page for the Law and Courts Section of the American Political Science Association at that organization's main Web site: http://www.apsanet.org. Presently, *Law and Politics Book Review* is available at http://www.bsos.umd.edu/gvpt/lpbr. From time to time, however, the site will change when a new editor takes charge.

Legal Mobilization Sites

Interest groups in America have been responsible for the creation and maintenance of legal strategies designed to change the face of law. It is widely known, for example, that the National Association for the Advancement of Colored People (NAACP) was the prime instigator of lawsuits designed to eliminate the separate-but-equal rule devised by the Supreme Court in 1896. By mobilizing a variety of political and legal resources NAACP leaders and attorneys brought a number of test cases before the Supreme Court, and it overruled itself in 1954, holding that separate but equal facilities in public education are inherently unequal in violation of the Equal Protection Clause of the Fourteenth Amendment. Other interest groups have actively lobbied the courts to achieve their legal goals. These groups also have attempted to influence legislation at the state and national level and to create a favorable climate of opinion for the realization of their policy goals. Today, through a variety of legal mobilization strategies and tactics, numerous interest groups of all political persuasions are attempting to influence the law both here in the United States and abroad.[6] Many routinely publish their views and maintain Web sites with statements of their activities, analyses of issues, and databases pertaining to issue areas within their interests. Researchers may find these sources useful in developing their writing projects. However, everyone should realize that such Web sites are likely to obtain biased viewpoints and information. I have listed a small number of the many Web sites that sample the ideological landscape.

- American Civil Liberties Union at http://www.aclu.org
- Center for Constitutional Rights at http://www.ccr-ny.org/v2/home.asp
- NAACP Legal Defense Fund at http://www.naacpldf.org
- American Center for Law and Justice at http://www.aclj.org
- The Rutherford Institute at http://www.rutherford.org
- Landmark Legal Foundation at http://www.landmarklegal.org

Law Dictionaries

A common complaint leveled against the legal profession is that it has a language that only lawyers can understand. There is some truth to this charge, but law dictionaries are available to aid legal professionals and laypersons. Most law dictionaries define a word or phrase in its legal sense and give citations to court decisions or other references. In this sense, law dictionaries are elementary research tools. Although they tend to be expensive, a law dictionary can be a useful acquisition.

Four widely known and employed law dictionaries are: *Ballentine's Law Dictionary with Pronunciations*, 3d ed., Lawyers Co-operative Publishing Company, 1969; *Ballentine's Legal Dictionary and Thesaurus*, West, 1995; *Black's Law Dictionary*, 7th ed., West, 1999; and Bouvier, *Law Dictionary* (3rd revision), 8th ed., West, 1914 (reprinted in 1983 by William S. Hein). Two excellent, less technical, and relatively inexpensive dictionaries are: Oran's *Law Dictionary for Non-Lawyers*, 2d ed., West, 1991, and Garner's *Black's Law Dictionary (Pocket Edition)*, 2d ed., West, 2001. There are several online legal dictionaries. Two of the best are: *'Lectric Law Library* at http://www.lectlaw.com/ref.html and *Law.Com Dictionary* at http://www.law.com/index/shtml. *'Lectric Law*

Library maintains a Constitutional Law and Rights Topic Area at http://
www.lectlaw.com/tcon.htm. The University of Miami Law Library maintains a site listing legal dictionaries in English and other languages at http://
www. library.law.miami.edu/defguide.html. It may be easier to find this site
by searching first at http//www.library.law.miami.edu.

A two-volume dictionary focusing on constitutional law is *The Constitutional Law Dictionary* by Ralph C. Chandler, Richard A. Enslen, and Peter G.
Renstrom (Santa Barbara, CA: ABC-CLIO, 1987, 1988, 1991, 1995, 1998). It
contains hundreds of key cases, terms, and concepts. Volume 1 relates to individual rights and volume 2 deals with governmental powers. This set also features a glossary of terms and phrases. It contains many terms constitutional
law students are likely to encounter during their studies.

Finally, a growing number of undergraduate textbooks in constitutional
law and related subjects contain extensive glossaries of terms, as does this
text. It is a useful intellectual exercise for students to make themselves familiar with the glossary features of their textbooks early in their studies.

Legal Research Exercises

Especially true for secondary sources, researchers will discover that finding pertinent materials is often a matter of trial and error and hit and miss.
One must understand that going to a single or even a series of related sources
will not necessarily produce desired results. Instead, researchers must work
their way around the law library and the Internet, sometimes dusting off lit-
tle-used volumes or little-known electronic sources while often proceeding
down blind intellectual alleys. Do not become discouraged by the process.
Personal perseverance will pay off. The secondary source material discussed
in this chapter will present researchers with many challenges. Complete the
exercises below as a way to become acquainted with the task firsthand.

Exercise 1—Legal Encyclopedias

Use *Am. Jur. 2d* and your text to answer the following three questions.

1a. The constitutional phrase "to regulate commerce . . . among the several states" distinguishes between commerce that is wholly confined
within the boundaries of a state and does not affect other states and
commerce that affects more than one state. True or false?

1b. Where in *Am. Jur. 2d* is the correct answer found? Use the correct
citation format.

2. According to this text, is it preferable first to consult the "volume
index" or the "general index" to find the answer to the following
type of question: Is interstate commerce controlled by an act of Congress governing rights to parties to such transaction?

3a. The U.S. Supreme Court may decide what constitutes interstate commerce. True or false?

3b. In either case, give the correct legal citation for your answer.

Use *C. J. S.* to answer the next two questions.

4a. What is the legal definition(s) of interstate commerce as noted in *C. J. S.*, the legal encyclopedia?

4b. Where did you find the answer for 4a? Give the proper citation.

Exercise 2—Digests

You need to read the Digest section in the text *carefully* before starting this assignment.

1. Use the table of cases index of the appropriate decennial of the *American Digest System* to find the case Katzenbach v. McClung, 379 U.S. 294 (1964). Under what West key name and number is this case digested?

2. You are interested in locating constitutional law cases dealing with state power with respect to commerce. Use the *Descriptive-Word Index* of the *United States Supreme Court Digest* only. Under what West key name and section number is the topic digested?

3. You are interested in finding out whether the Supreme Court has ruled on the power of Congress to dictate to the states minimum-wage and working conditions of their employees. Cite the *U.S. Supreme Court Reports Digest: Lawyers' Edition* digest *name*(s) and *number*(s) where cases dealing with these issues are digested. Use the table of cases index to find *National League of Cities v. Usery*.

4. Identify at least three cases that address whether Congress may dictate to state and local governments the working and employment conditions of their employees. In 230 words or less, justify your selection of cases.

5. Using the Advanced Search feature available through Oyez, give the number of Supreme Court opinions rendered up until May 1, 2003, with respect to affirmative action. Write the names of each opinion.

Exercise 3—Citators

Refer both to your text and *Shepard's United States Citations: Cases.* Use bound volumes only to answer the following questions with reference to the case listed below. Cite as given in Shepard's.

1. For 426 U.S. 833:

   a. Give the parallel citation of the *United States Supreme Court Reports: Lawyers' Edition* for the same case.

   b. Give another citation to the same case in a lower court and/or the United States Supreme Court.

   c. Has this case been cited by the Illinois Supreme Court?

2. Repeat question 1 for 469 U.S. 528.

3. Has the U.S. Supreme Court decision in 426 U.S. 833 been *overruled* or *modified?* In either case, cite the case in which such a ruling was made.

Exercise 4—Legal Periodicals

For questions 1 and 2 state the *cumulative volume* and *page number* from the *Index to Legal Periodicals & Books.*

1. *Constitutional Law*—threats of mob violence as justification for restraint on exercise of right to travel in interstate commerce.

2. E. Celler, "Congress, Compacts, and Interstate Authority," *Law and Contemporary Problems* 26:682 (Autumn 1961).

3. Use the *Case Index* to the *Index to Legal Periodicals* to cite the volume(s), law review(s), page number(s), and date(s) in which the following case is discussed: U.S. v. Tobin, 195 F. Supp. 588.

4. Use volume 9 of the *Current Law Index.* How many law review articles on the subject of *Garcia v. San Antonio Metropolitan Transit Authority* are found there?

5. Using Findlaw.com, list the academic law reviews and journals treating constitutional law in which the full text of the articles appearing in each is available online.

Answers for Legal Exercises

Exercise 1—Legal Encyclopedias

1a. True

1b. 15 Am. Jur. 2d *Commerce* § 4 (2000).

2. General index

3a. True

3b. 15A Am. Jur. 2d *Commerce* § 7 (2000).

4a. "'Interstate commerce' means the free interchange of commodities between citizens of different states, without regard to state lines, or intercourse among the several states."

4b. 15 C.J.S. *Commerce* § 2 (2002).

Exercise 2—Digests

1. Commerce 3, 5, 7, 16, 40(1), 48, 60(3); Const. Law 47, 70(1); Courts 385(6); Decl Judgm 41, 44, 123, 254; Inj 85(1); States 4.16; Statut 40.

2. Commerce 3, 7, 10, 108, Const Law 283

3. Commerce 62, 63, 89, 96, 108; Const. Law 48, 513, 861.5; Jury 2; States 5, 16, 34, 37.

4. Answer depends on cases, but note that the *Usery* decision was effectively overruled in Garcia v. San Antonio Metropolitan Transit Authority, 469 U.S. 528 (1985).

5. Oyez found 12 Supreme Court opinions. The opinions are: *Richmond v. J.A. Croson Co.*, *Regents of the University of California v. Bakke*, *United Steelworkers of America v. Weber*, *Fillilove v. Klutznick*, *DeFunis v. Odegaard*, *Astroline Communications v. Shurberg Broadcasting*, *Local 28 v. EEOC*, *United States v. Paradise*, *Martin v. Wilks*, *Wygant v. Jackson Board of Education*, *Metro Broadcasting Inc. v. FCC*, and *Johnson v. Transportation Agency*.

Exercise 3—Citators

1a. 49 L. Ed. 2d 245

1b. 419 U.S. 1321, 406 F. S. 826

1c. No (Illinois Appellate Court, not the Supreme Court)

2a. 83 L. Ed. 2d 1016

2b. 838 F. 2d 1411, 557 FS 445

2c. No (Illinois Appellate Court, not the Supreme Court)

3. Yes, 469 U.S. 530

Exercise 4—Legal Periodicals

1. Vol. 13, page 146 or 423

2. Vol. 13, page 423

3. Columbia Law Rev. 62, p. 532 (March 1962); George Washington Law Rev. 30, p. 536 (March 1962); found in volume 13, p. 867.

4. Two entries

5. *First Amendment Law Review,* the *Journal of Constitutional Law,* the *East European Constitutional Review,* and the *Oregon Advocate.* (Note that while the *Hastings Constitutional Law Quarterly* is listed, the full text of its articles are not available online.)

Endnotes

[1] For a listing of extant state legal encyclopedias, see J. Myron Jacobstein, Roy M. Mersky, and Donald J. Dunn, *Fundamentals of Legal Research,* 7th ed. (Mineola, NY: Foundation Press, 1998), p. 385.

[2] Jay Shuck, *Guide to West Group Legal Resources: 1998–1999* (Eagan, MN: West, 1998), p. 15–23.

[3] The regional digests correspond to the regional reporter system. The regional digests are: *Atlantic Digest, North Western Digest, Pacific Digest, South Eastern Digest, South Western Digest, North Eastern Digest,* and *Southern Digest.* Some include additional series digests.

[4] Jacobstein, Mersky, and Dunn, *Fundamentals of Legal Research,* 7th ed., p. 107, n. 7.

[5] The observant reader will note that the page number citation for *Barnette* differs from the one presented earlier. The reason is that Shepard's editors provide the exact page within the *Barnette* opinion where *Gobitis* is directly overruled.

[6] For a fine treatment of this subject, see Charles R. Epp, *The Rights Revolution: Lawyers, Activists, and Supreme Courts in Comparative Perspective* (Chicago: University of Chicago Press, 1998).

3

WHY AND HOW TO BRIEF A CASE

Introduction

There is a major difference between *briefing a case* and *writing a legal brief*. When *briefing a case*, the task is to reduce the written opinion of a court to its most basic and essential elements. When *writing a legal brief*, the task is to assemble and present a legal argument to convince a court of the correctness of a client's conduct or an argument about a disputed point of law. Because briefing cases constitutes a first step in the learning process, instructors usually ask constitutional law students to brief cases; it is rare to assign a legal brief. Briefing court opinions is an essential skill in understanding legal thinking.

Full reports of court opinions are usually very long. Editors of instructional casebooks then reduce the full written opinions to those parts of cases they believe to be most pertinent to conveying an understanding of the important points of each case. Although casebook editors will occasionally summarize the facts of a case, they do not change the exact words of the opinion. Rather, they delete those words, sentences, paragraphs, or sections they regard as not particularly instructive.

Instructors will sometimes send students to the library to read and brief a case from the full reported opinion of the Court. Usually, however, instructors ask students to brief edited cases that appear in a course-required textbook. Consequently, textbook editors have already completed much of the required analysis. As a result, students need only to further reduce court opinions to their bare bones.

Many students find it difficult to believe that it is necessary to brief cases. Rather, they attempt to short-circuit the intellectual process by reading the assigned cases and writing marginal notes to help them recall pertinent points. This is a mistake! The dual act of intellectual analysis and writing is indeed necessary. There are five related reasons that justify taking what is admittedly much time to adequately brief cases.

First, the great number of complicated Court opinions discussed in a typical constitutional law course is impossible to recall from the memory of one or two readings. By writing down the essential elements of each case, students can firmly retain the pertinent information in their memory.

Second, student-composed briefs are an excellent study tool when preparing for examinations. Attempts to read, comprehend, and remember pertinent fact patterns and opinions the night before a scheduled examination almost inevitably meets with academic disaster. Read and brief cases as the course progresses. Then sit down before an examination to review the cases. It is at this cognitive juncture that students often begin to see the relationships necessary to discern the forest from the trees.

Third, by observing the intimate relationship between the facts and decisions of past and present cases, students gain an appreciation for the historical method of common law. In fact, most law school faculties believe that the case-method approach is the finest way to train lawyers—drilling students on the particulars of court opinions helps them to think like lawyers. Some legal educators contest this viewpoint because, as the argument goes, it tends to blind students to extralegal materials useful for understanding legal policymaking. Political scientists are alert to this problem. Yet, as faulty as the case-method approach may be, it is desirable to employ at least some of its aspects for two reasons. First, it is necessary to know what the courts have said. The courts make policy and it is important to know precisely what that policy might be. By reading written opinions, the primary and authoritative source material of judicial policymaking, students can avoid the confusion, misinformation, and improper interpretation often found in public debate about the meaning of court opinions. Second, political science students need to understand the workings of the legal mind. Serious students can best accomplish this goal by studying lawyers and judges in their own vernacular and on their own turf. No doubt, this intellectual process is narrow and confining. However, unlike the case for law students and working attorneys, a clear understanding of the legal opinion is not the end goal; for social scientists, it is the beginning of explanation. Therefore, political scientists must learn what the law is in order to explain scientifically why decisions are made the way they are, how cases reflect values in and outside of courts, and to consider the public policy consequences of adjudication. Remember that it is not the goal of political scientists and other social scientists to make constitutional lawyers out of undergraduates. Rather, the pedagogical task is to enable students to understand when, how, and why the law influences the allocation of authority within the political system.

Fourth, briefing cases provides students and teachers with a common point of departure for the discussion of meaningful problems. Using a common text in which people are in actual conflict allows a class to discuss not only what might appear to be mundane legal issues, but also the dramatic implications of those decisions for government and society. Because such issues touch on numerous aspects of the social sciences and the humanities, students can appreciate the interdisciplinary nature of the subject matter. In this lively environment, a synthesis of ideas is both possible and probable.

A final justification for briefing cases concerns the task itself. It sharpens the intellect and aids students in acquiring disciplined minds. Long after the cases are but dim recollections, the experience of rigorous reading and writing will endure. The careful and thoughtful process necessary for briefing cases should introduce an appreciation for critical thinking and prepare students to deal with future challenges. Training the mind to discern and carefully write analyses of actual problems in the political system remains a goal of practical value. In this sense, a rigorous constitutional law course is among the very best liberal arts courses offered on college campuses.

In the remaining sections of this chapter, I systematically treat the elements of a brief and provide a model brief to help students. However, students cannot learn how to brief a case by following a formula. The task is more art than science. When starting out, it is common for students to spend two or more hours briefing a single case. With experience, however, the task becomes less time-consuming and less difficult. In my experience, the average student takes up to six weeks of intense course work to become proficient at the art of briefing cases.

At first, students commonly exhibit stress and anxiety. They bring their briefs to class to find that the instructor and other students do not emphasize the same points. The reason for the apparent contradictions has little to do with questions of intelligence, however. Nonetheless, anxious individuals may request meetings with the instructor to review their briefs in detail. If you experience frustration, bear with it. Continue to brief cases and make changes in those briefs that seem dissimilar from what the instructor sanctions. Later, after you have expended genuine effort, you will come to understand the process and will feel confident with what you have done.

Elements of a Brief

There is no one right way to brief a case. Instructors often have their own individual recommendations. Differences aside, all well-done briefs carefully link together each major element of a court decision. Try to remember that briefs should be just that, brief! Given that along with the understanding that court opinions often contain key words and phrases without which important ideas may be lost, I suggest that brief writers make every effort to use their own words. Still, there are occasions when paraphrasing is not comparable to the justices' own verbal gems.

If working from a purchased textbook, feel free to mark it up. If using a reporter system found in a library, do not write on the printed pages. The reasons are obvious and need no further comment.

First, read each case quickly to comprehend the general nature of the case and the problems presented. Then read it again, this time with a pencil or pen in hand. Underline pertinent parts and make notations in the margins of each page. You then are ready to brief the case. Sit up in a hard chair and go to work. In the past, students used a pen and pad of paper to write their briefs. Today, however, using a personal computer with a spell checker and the ability to cut and paste makes the task less time-consuming than it once was. Below are elements of fundamental importance.

I. Name or Title of Case

The case name should appear at the top and center of the first page; e.g., Baker v. Carr.

II. Legal Citation

Place the legal citation below the case name. This provides the location in the various court reports where anyone will be able to locate the fully reported opinion. Usually, a single citation will suffice, for example, 369 U.S. 186 (1962). If available, the student may want to include parallel citations for the same case, 369 U.S. 186, 7 L. Ed. 2d 663, 82 S. Ct. 691 (1962). Exercising this option is a good idea because at some later point in time it may become necessary to read the fully reported opinion. Knowledge of the opinion's location in the reporter systems will ease the library search. In any event, knowing at least what court decided the case and the year it decided it is valuable information. It will help students to know where the case fits in time and where it is located within the structure of authority.

III. Statement of Facts

The facts include the pertinent circumstances of the dispute that gave rise to the lawsuit and the disposition of the case. Any legal dispute involves facts that may or may not be pertinent as far as the court is concerned. Indeed, circumstances surrounding events give rise to differing interpretations of what happened. However, for purposes of brief writing and for understanding the legal reasoning in each case, it is important to note only those facts treated by the opinion writer as relevant and those facts the writer specifically mentions to be irrelevant. Facts labeled as irrelevant by the court are important to note because the court deems them consequential in some sense. For instance, when a past case is distinguishable from the present case, irrelevant commonalties between the two cases may be as important as those elements considered pertinent. It is of no consequence to the brief writer whether the facts are true. Nor is it of particular concern that the brief writer thinks the opinion writer has identified the wrong facts. What is important is that the court treats the facts as pertinent.

While it is usual for the facts to appear at the beginning of the written opinion, at times it is necessary to search the court's entire opinion for the facts. This may include not only the court's majority opinion but also concurring and dissenting opinions. Consequently, the good brief writer must be able to dissect the full opinion, separating what is important from the body of the text from those words and lines that are not. Then the brief writer must reconstruct the opinion with only the most pertinent information attached. The last lines of the fact statement should include the decisions and actions of the lower courts, including how the case came before the Supreme Court, for example, writ of error, appeal, writ of certiorari.

Before the passage of the Judiciary Act of 1925, the Supreme Court had limited discretion in the cases it heard. The writ of error required the Court to hear cases coming to it upon proper application. In 1928, Congress passed legislation resulting in the demise of this method of appeal. Owing to the extraordinary lobbying efforts of Chief Justice William Howard Taft, which culminated in the passage of the 1925 statute, the Supreme Court today has considerable control over cases it wishes to hear. The Court grants the discretionary writ of certiorari when four of the nine justices agree that the full Court should hear a given case. The Supreme Court usually hears previously adjudicated cases in a state court of last resort or in a U.S. Court of Appeals by this method. It is important to note that most cases end at the lower levels of the judicial hierarchy without appeal to the Supreme Court.

Today it is fair to conclude that the U.S. Supreme Court is almost exclusively an all-certiorari tribunal. Before 1988, petitioners could bring a number of different types of cases from a variety of sources to the Court through an appeal method formally dubbed *Appeal* (ostensibly a form of appeal not within the discretion of the Supreme Court). Yet, even on *Appeal*, the Court found a way to reject jurisdiction. In such cases, the Supreme Court could simply find that the case or controversy does not present a "substantial federal question." With this important qualification, the U.S. Supreme Court must hear certain classes of cases coming from the U.S. District Courts, from the U.S. (Circuit) Courts of Appeals, and from the state courts of last resort. In 1988, however, Congress enacted Public Law 100-352, limiting the Court's mandatory jurisdiction to cases decided by three-judge federal district courts. This law spelled the virtual end of the Supreme Court's mandatory appellate jurisdiction.

A seldom-used appeal method is certification. In this instance, a lower court requests the Supreme Court to answer certain questions of law so that it may render a legally correct decision on a point of law in the case before it. This method is not within the control of the parties to the suit. Only the lower court may judge whether it needs clarification. Importantly, the Supreme Court may refuse the certificate. The Court might alternatively provide an answer that the lower court is obliged to apply, or the Supreme Court might decide the case itself without returning it to the lower court.

It is also useful for the brief writer to note if the Supreme Court is proceeding in its original jurisdiction consistent with article III, or if the case comes to the Court through extraordinary writs such as habeas corpus, writ of mandamus, or writ of prohibition. Lastly, it is a noteworthy fact whether petitioners pay the necessary court costs and attorney fees or the Court is hearing the case in *forma pauperis*, a method enabling indigents to sue without liability for costs.

IV. Statement of Issues

An issue is a statement of the legal or constitutional question the opinion writer deems necessary to answer to resolve the dispute. It is common for legal opinions to contain more than one issue. Sometimes the court must answer one issue affirmatively before it can or needs to answer following issues. Understand that editors of instructional casebooks often delete sections of a case they deem unimportant for understanding the topic under study. Students should be aware of this fact because cases in one context may stand for much more in another.

Often authors of judicial opinions place the statement of issues in one clearly identifiable place within the text—usually immediately following the recitation of the facts of the case. However, like facts, issues are sometimes scattered throughout the entire written opinion. This is another reason why it is wise to read the entire opinion and to write notes in the margins of your casebook before actually writing the brief.

Follow two rules when stating issues. First, issue statements should appear as yes-no questions. Second, phrase issues in a precise and specific way. A case always involves answering some specific legal or constitutional question. The U.S. Supreme Court does not deal with hypothetical or general issues. The statement of issues should reflect this fact. Avoid abstract conceptualizations of the problem. For example, it is not enough to write for *Baker v. Carr*: "May state legislatures fail to reapportion legislative districts consistent with population trends?" Note that the question does not raise a legal or constitutional issue; furthermore, the question is general—it deals with the general ability of state legislatures to discriminate against urban voters. This poorly conceived issue statement does not mention any constitutional provision or legal principle as particularly relevant. It does not address specific people with an actual controversy in law or in equity. Novice brief writers find this particular task difficult to master. It requires a careful focusing of mental energy and a development of intellectual habits necessary for understanding judicial opinions.

A proper statement of issues is important because it reflects an understanding of the facts, conditions, the legal decision, and, significantly, the reasoning of the court. Careful wording of issues, however, often produces long conditional interrogative sentences. When this occurs it is fair to conclude that although the sentence may not be elegant, the result is acceptable. Given the nature of the facts, statutes, or constitutional provisions, such sentences are often necessary because they admit no other ready alternative. In any event, always write issues so that you can clearly understand each as the need arises. At times, copying the issue(s) as stated by the court is the best format. However, once again, whenever practical put issues in your own words, making sure to keep those vital words or phrases of the opinion that are indispensable for understanding.

V. Decision and Action

For the decision, write a simple *yes* or *no* in response to each legal issue posed in the Statement of Issues above. No explanation or qualification is necessary at this point in the brief. The action is the court-ordered disposition of the case; for example, reversed, reversed and remanded, or affirmed. You can usually find this information by reading the last lines of the majority or plurality opinion of the court. Place both the court's decision and action on a single line.

VI. Reasoning of the Court

The reasons for the court's decision are the heart of the legal opinion. They contain the court's justification for its decision in the case. However, not everything written may be pertinent for purposes of the brief. Only that part of the opinion that is directly supportive of the decision is appropriate for inclusion in the brief. Be wary of statements and arguments not directly related to the issues and decision in the case. Legal professionals refer to such verbiage as *obiter dicta,* or simply *obiter*, *dicta*, or *dictum*. It is, so to speak, excess intellectual baggage—argumentation unnecessary for the court to come logically to its decision in the case.

It is necessary for the good brief writer to read the court's full opinion with a view toward separating those reasons that are central for the decision from those that are not. The key is the Statement of Issues. Only those arguments necessary for supporting the answers to the issues should be part of the brief. Ignore the remainder. This task requires careful attention to the expressions of the opinion writers. As previously discussed, when you read through opinions, it is advisable to make notations in the margins or underline those places in the text where the opinion writer offers essential justifications. While novice brief writers may have difficulty with this task, be assured it will become easier with experience.

On the first line of this section of the brief note the author of the court's opinion, for example, per Brennan. It is also wise to number the reasoning consistent with each issue statement. This permits quick eye movement between each issue, decision, and reasoning.

During the tenure of the first three chief justices—John Jay, John Rutledge, and Oliver Ellsworth—each member of the Supreme Court was entitled to write his own opinion in each case. This practice is known as *seriatim* opinion writing. Upon the accession of John Marshall as chief justice, the *seriatim* practice gave way to the institutional opinion. Since Marshall's day, typically the chief justice or a senior justice assigns to a single justice the task of writing the opinion of the Court. The chief justice makes that assignment only if in the voting majority. Otherwise, the senior-most justice in the majority makes the opinion-writing assignment. This leadership task is often delicate and complicated because it reflects conflicts and compromises within the Court.

VII. Concurring Opinion(s)

A concurring opinion agrees with the result of the majority or plurality opinion but disagrees with its reasons. Justices write concurring opinions when they believe it is necessary to indicate disagreement with the reasoning of the controlling bloc within the court. Indeed, at times an enlightened future court's majority adopts the reasoning found in today's concurring opinion as the preferred doctrine or rule in some later case. In addition, the frequency of concurring opinions is an indicator of the degree to which court members are united on a given issue. These opinions can point the way to how a court may alter its future course.

VIII. Dissenting Opinion(s)

A dissenting opinion expresses disagreement with the court's judgment in terms of both the decision and the reasoning supporting that decision. Note the justice(s) writing such opinions and the reasons for disagreement. Because dissenting justices sometimes disagree even among themselves, note each dissent separately.

IX. Voting Coalition

If the information is readily available, note the justices voting together. When studying particular courts or eras it often becomes plain that some justices often vote together. The dynamics of small-group interaction and ideological compatibility among certain members may aid in explaining judicial decision making. Sometimes a court changes its approach to a subject. It may be the result of a change in court personnel rather than an intellectual conversion resulting from studying case precedents. See chapter 4 for how to perform bloc analysis.

X. Summary of Legal Principle(s)

It is a useful learning exercise to summarize within a few lines the legal principles found in each case. This pulls the elements of the case together and is a valuable study aid when preparing for examinations. Also, note how the case at hand might differ from previously studied cases on the same topic.

XI. Free Space

Discussion of cases in class will reveal the flaws in individual briefs. Therefore, leave room at the end of the brief for classroom comments and further revisions. Some students prefer to use a separate notebook for such purposes.

Model Brief

I. Baker v. Carr

II. 369 U.S. 186, 82 S. Ct. 691, 7 L. Ed. 2d 663 (1962)

III. *Facts:* The Tennessee state legislature failed to reapportion its legislative districts in both houses for sixty years. This occurred despite the enactment of a 1901 statute governing the reapportionment process on a basis of qualified voters resident in each of the state's counties as determined by the population census. During this sixty-year period, the state's population became increasingly urban and yet urban voters found themselves underrepresented in the state legislature. Baker and other urban citizens sued in U.S. District Court under federal civil-rights statutes charging that the reapportionment scheme of the state legislature denied them the equal protection of the laws contrary to the Fourteenth Amendment. The plaintiffs sought a court declaration that the 1901 law was unconstitutional and asked the court for the alternative remedies of elections of state legislators at large or elections from districts based upon the 1950 census. The district court agreed with the plaintiffs' equal protection claims. However, the court found that it could not provide a remedy. The U.S. Supreme Court first heard arguments on appeal during the 1960 term.

IV. *Issues*:

   (1) Does the district court possess subject-matter jurisdiction in this case?

   (2) Do the litigants have standing to sue?

   (3) Is the malapportionment of state legislatures a justiciable controversy?

V. *Decision and Action*: (1) Yes, (2) Yes, (3) Yes. Reversed and remanded.

VI. *Reasoning*: Per Brennan.

   (1) There is a distinction between jurisdiction of the subject matter and the justiciability of the subject matter. If there is no jurisdiction, the cause of action does not arise under the Constitution, laws, or treaties of the United States. Nor may the case come under any of the categories found in article III, section 2, or is not a case or controversy within the meaning of that article and section. However, the matter of equal representation arises under the Equal Protection Clause of the Fourteenth Amendment and the U.S. District Court is authorized to hear such cases by congressional enactment (28 U.S.C. § 1343).

   (2) Voters who allege facts that disadvantage them as individuals have standing to sue. The 1901 statute injures the appellants because they are voters residing in underrepresented counties.

Voters have judicially enforceable rights against arbitrary impairment of the full enjoyment of that privilege.

(3) Simply because this suit seeks the protection of a political right does not render the case a political question and therefore nonjusticiable. The appellants' claim does not rest upon the Guaranty Clause of the Constitution, causes of action that the Supreme Court has declined to resolve. Rather, appellants' cause of action rests upon a denial of the Equal Protection Clause of the Fourteenth Amendment. The political-question doctrine applies to situations involving the separation of powers among the three coordinate branches of the federal government. The nonjusticiable-question doctrine is not applicable to the relationship between the federal judiciary and the states. The question to be decided in this case is not a conflict between coequal branches of government.

VII. *Concurring Opinion*: Per Douglas. There is no question that federal courts may restrain state agencies from violating citizen rights under the Equal Protection Clause of the Fourteenth Amendment. However, the test is whether the state has made "an invidious discrimination" as when it oppresses a race or nationality. The appellants should have an opportunity to prove that an "invidious discrimination" exists.

Concurring Opinion: Per Clark. It is not a good idea for the Supreme Court to intervene in such a delicate matter as legislative representation. However, the people in this instance have no other recourse open to them but to appeal to the courts for a remedy because the ordinary political channels are effectively closed to them.

Concurring Opinion: Per Stewart. The Court's opinion is limited to three points and nothing more: (1) The Court possesses subject-matter jurisdiction; (2) the case presents a justiciable cause of action; and (3) the appellants have standing to challenge the Tennessee apportionment statutes.

VIII. *Dissenting Opinion*: Per Frankfurter joined by Harlan. The Court reverses a uniformly decided set of cases on this subject. This case involves political questions and when the Court involves itself in such matters, it may suffer a loss of public confidence. Moreover, the Court does not provide any guidelines for the district court to enforce the claim. Finally, this case is not a simple one of blatant discrimination. Rather, Tennessee simply uses a method of geographical representation that the plaintiffs do not prefer.

Dissenting Opinion: Per Harlan joined by Frankfurter. The complaint should be dismissed for "failure to state a claim upon which relief can be granted." There is no equal protection requirement that legislative institutions must provide an equal voice for each voter. Lastly, if it is to remain a respected institution, the Supreme Court should exercise judicial self-restraint.

IX. *Voting Coalitions*: 6 to 2. For the majority, Brennan, Warren, Douglas, Black, Clark, Stewart. Dissenting, Frankfurter and Harlan. Not participating, Whittaker.

X. *Summary*: The question of the malapportionment of state legislatures is one in which the federal courts have subject-matter jurisdiction. It presents a justiciable cause of action. Citizens alleging deprivation of equal protection of the laws have standing to sue.

XI. *Free Space*: (Leave approximately one-third of a page for comments.)

4

QUANTITATIVE APPLICATIONS

Introduction

To discover the formal justifications for judicial decisions, it is vitally important to read and analyze the opinions and written thoughts of judges and justices. Yet, any intelligent person will learn after reading many cases over several years that behavior patterns separate some sets of judges and justices from others. Most members of the U.S. Supreme Court, for example, have a tendency to vote with certain other justices who together usually support or oppose the rights of criminal defendants. We can make the same statement for the existence of combinations of justices who uphold or oppose the claims and actions of the government. The same is true for other areas of litigation, including, for example, abortion rights, First Amendment rights, and states' rights. Indeed, it is common for observers to classify the choices of justices as liberal, conservative, or a variety of other labeling possibilities.

Some scholars and judges sincerely believe that judges only find the law, they do not make it. Judges, according to this view, simply identify preexisting legal rules and apply them objectively to the legal controversy at hand. If this were the case, however, then there would be very little disagreement among legal professionals about case outcomes. Obviously, judicial decision making is more complicated than the proponents of the judicial myth would have us believe. As social scientists, we must guard against confusing belief with behavior.

Once one concedes that judicial decision making involves more than the proponents of the mechanical view of jurisprudence assume, there remains nonetheless considerable disagreement. Some scholars argue that knowing the attitudes of the justices alone is a sufficient explanation for Supreme Court decision making. Others argue that the explanation is more complex. They suggest that any such theory should include analyses of the social backgrounds of justices, the role perceptions of individual justices, and the small-group dynamics of the Supreme Court including the strategic behavior of its members. Many outside factors also bear upon the judicial process, including the influence of interest groups, test cases, amicus curiae briefs, law clerks, congressional relations, public opinion, and so on.

We need not settle the debate here. However, it is important to recognize patterns of behavior and the need for researchers to present such tendencies in an objective, efficient, comprehensive, and reliable manner. Over the decades, social scientists have developed relatively simple quantitative approaches to achieve this goal. This chapter is devoted to describing three separate but related ways of summarizing the voting relationships among judges and justices on collegial courts. Although there are additional and more complicated methods, the three elementary methods described below include labeling "liberal" and "conservative" votes, unidimensional scaling of judicial opinions, and bloc analysis.

Labeling and Counting Judicial Votes

If justices vote in a case before them to support the claim of the criminal defendant, how might we label this decision? When the Rehnquist Court renders decisions against the congressional exercise of the commerce power and in favor of state power is that a liberal or a conservative opinion? Is a vote permitting civil suits against a sitting president a liberal or a conservative one? The correct answer is: It all depends on how one defines the words *liberal* and *conservative*. There is no reason in principle why a vote for or against any of these positions must be labeled one way or another. Yet, over the years, scholars have abided by certain imperfect conventions that reflect our collective understanding of American politics and ideology. Thus, in general, a liberal supports the underdog when the government is a party to a suit. A liberal believes in protecting civil liberties such as freedom of speech, press, and religion when the government seeks to curtail them. Matters become more complicated when considering choices between the goal of equality and the celebration of individual liberties; affirmative-action programs present such a challenge. A liberal generally supports the goals of equality even though they may compromise personal liberty in the process. With respect to government regulation of the economy, liberals generally are in favor of the exercise of governmental power while conservatives oppose government coming down on the side of business. In conflicts between labor and business, liberals generally favor organized labor over the interests of employers, particularly large corporations.

Clearly, it is important for researchers to stipulate the meaning of ideological labels. We call these stipulative definitions *decision rules*. One must keep the decision rules firmly in mind, applying them consistently from one judicial opinion to the next and one justice to the other. Those researchers who fail in this task find themselves with a mass of unreliable and unusable data.

Because we want to summarize the number of liberal and conservative votes in an efficient manner, it is convenient to simplify these terms by assigning plus (+) and minus (–) symbols to each vote. Thus, a liberal vote is usually, although not necessarily, given a plus sign (+). The symbol for a conservative vote is a minus (–) sign.

Calculating justices' attitudes is a simple matter of computing an arithmetic average. Sum the pluses (+), divide by the total number of cases in the issue category, and multiply by 100. Alternatively, sum the minuses (–), divide by the total number of cases in the issue category, and multiply by 100. Researchers may make the same calculation for all of the decisions in a single Court term or a number of Court terms divided by the total number of cases for each issue category.

Calculating attitude scores is easy enough for one or perhaps two Court terms. However, when researchers seek to ascertain trends over the years I advise them to consult the existing database known as the *United States Supreme Court Judicial Database*. Compiled under the direction of Harold J. Spaeth and other political scientists by virtue of grants from the National Science Foundation, the original data set contains a variety of information, including the votes on all the decisions of the U.S. Supreme Court from 1953 to 1993. The editors of this data set update the database annually, reflecting the opinions rendered by the Court each term. This huge data set may be examined and downloaded through a number of Internet sites including the Inter-University Consortium for Political and Social Research of the University of Michigan at Ann Arbor (ICPSR) at http://www. icpsr.umich.edu, the National Archive of Criminal Justice Data (NACJD) at http://www.icpsr.umich.edu:8080/NACJD-STUDY/09422.XML, and the Program for Law & Politics at Michigan State University at www.ssc.msu.edu. It may be possible to access this powerful database at other sites. The extensive codebook (available as a PDF file) describes the variables for each judicial opinion, including how the justices voted in each case, their interagreement, and the ideological direction of their votes. The data sets are available for data processing on the widely employed computer statistical packages SPSS and SAS.

A growing number of scholarly tomes are making the results of their computer analysis of the Spaeth data set available to readers. For example, see *The Supreme Court Compendium,* discussed earlier in this volume. It reports the aggregate voting records of all justices since the Warren Court.[1]

Scaling Cases

Though as a researcher you now know how to label and count the votes of justices, an important question remains: How do you know you have identified an attitude? Answering this question requires understanding what is meant by an attitude.

Quoting the social psychologist Milton Rokeach, political scientist Harold Spaeth defines an attitude as "a relatively enduring set of interrelated beliefs that describe, evaluate, and advocate action with respect to some object or situation."[2] Spaeth indicates that this definition possesses two important dimensions. First, attitudes are relatively stable. We can safely presume that judges and justices have acquired worldviews through their lifetimes with specific likes and dislikes that are not applied randomly. This is not to suggest that their attitudes never change, nor does this mean that judges are not amenable to a good argument that may change their attitudes. Nonetheless, unlike many adolescents, the attitudes of mature judges and justices are less likely to experience change with social fads and capricious mass behaviors and tastes. Specific attitudes, however, are not at the forefront of one's thoughts. Attitudes must be activated either by objects in our social environment or by social or political situations that we encounter. In the case of judicial decision making, the *object* is the litigant(s) at the bar of justice and the *situation* is their behavior that resulted in the litigation.

Given these definitions, if a researcher claims that justices possess certain attitudes, e.g., liberal and conservative, it is necessary for them to demonstrate a consistent voting pattern wherein these attitudes are manifest. Moreover, if researchers claim that justices share attitudes reflected in their bench votes for and against litigants, then their collective behavior should display patterns revealing an underlying attitude dimension. In other words, if a sufficient number of justices respond consistently in a given set of cases then it may be concluded that the cases scale, and, therefore, there is an underlying set of attitudes. Notice that this methodology infers attitudes from behavior. It would be better to first establish attitudes independent of judicial voting and then determine if there is a correlation between attitudes and votes.[3] However, this is not a practical approach because most judges and justices are not amenable to completing attitude questionnaires. Nonetheless, the judicial attitude approach, however faulty, possesses considerable predictive power. If nothing else, it is an excellent method for discerning and reporting patterns of behavior. In two stages, I describe a total of 13 steps in creating judicial scales. The first stage comprising five steps is preliminary. The second stage, steps 6–13, details the actual construction of a judicial scale.

Preliminary Stage

Step 1. Pick a substantive legal topic. The best advice is to choose a narrow topic. Most students are required to complete research projects within the span of a single quarter or semester. One is most likely to complete the project successfully if the topic is limited to a specific substantive legal topic. Also, the broader the legal topic the greater the chances that multiple attitudes will affect decision making and consequently the cases may not scale. However, it is possible to identify ideological cleavages that are manifest in broad subject categories. For example, researchers studying the Illinois Supreme Court located twenty-nine nonunanimous civil cases and seventeen nonunanimous criminal cases involving very diverse fact patterns from 1991 to 1993. The partisan-ballot-elected justices of that seven-member court display a remarkably consistent ideological voting pattern. Further, this ideological pattern is highly correlated with the party affiliation of the justices. Democrats are more "liberal" than their "conservative" Republican colleagues.[4]

Step 2.   After deciding on a substantive legal topic, researchers must locate cases on the topic. Before proceeding, readers should re-read the Digests and Cite-Checking sections of chapter 2. Researchers should know how to digest cases and how to use a citator. But because some researchers do not have access to a law library equipped with the full array of legal digests, they may opt to use instead Internet sites that arrange Supreme Court cases by subject matter. Chapter 2 describes particularly how to find categories of judicial opinions through LexisNexis Academic, Westlaw Campus, the Legal Information Institute at Cornell University Law School, FedWorld, and Oyez. One may also access a broad array of Supreme Court opinions through the *United States Supreme Court Judicial Database.* As useful as these cyberspace sites may seem, I think if the research problem treats a specific legal controversy, e.g., obscenity, death penalty, interstate travel, or juvenile justice, then a digest is the best available tool. In particular, if the research subject matter involves the U.S. Supreme Court I advise researchers to use *U.S. Supreme Court Digest* or the *U.S. Supreme Court Reports Digest: Lawyers' Edition.* Also, use a legal cite-checker such as *Shepard's United States Citations: Cases* or *Key-Cite.* With a legal citation for a case in hand, one may then find all citations for that particular case in subsequent cases. Although using legal cite-checkers often will yield good results, it is best not to rely solely on a cite-checker for this phase of the research project. Using digests and citators in tandem is a near certain way to identify all relevant cases for the universe of one's study.

If possible, scale cases only for a natural court. A natural court is one whose membership remains constant—there is no turnover in the Court's personnel. Because the Court membership is consistent, the same justices are reacting to the same stimuli at the same time. Though it is possible to construct scales with more than nine justices, working with more or fewer justices presents considerable problems that researchers may want to avoid. In such cases, the best course is to construct two or more scales of two or more natural courts. I provide some answers to this matter below when discussing the missing values problem.

Step 3.   The third preliminary step in constructing judicial scales is to read the opinions in each case to ascertain the votes of each participating justice. This requires using a court reporter or other source containing a court's written opinions. Before proceeding further, if you are not familiar with court reports, read the section in chapter 1 about Supreme Court opinions. It is a good practice to brief each opinion (per chapter 3), noting especially the vote of each justice—whether the justices joined the majority, concurred, or dissented. Also, note the vote of the court in each case (e.g., 5–4, 6–3, 8–1). Dissenting and concurring opinions include the names of those justices joining each opinion; however, the court reporters do not always list clearly in the body of the opinion the names of those justices joining the majority opinion. In such instances, it is necessary to infer the identity of those who are voting with the majority opinion writer. Each volume of the court reporter (e.g., *U.S.*) has a list of the names of the justices on the Court for that particular term. By logical deduction, the researcher can figure out all the justices who joined with the majority opinion. Sometimes, however, a justice may not participate in the opinion of the Court. In such rare instances, court reporters routinely provide that information in the text of the opinion.

Step 4. Make a list of how each justice voted in each case by indicating a plus sign (+) for a liberal vote and a minus sign (–) for a conservative vote. A concurring vote may be either a plus or minus depending on the substantive result of the case. Recall from chapter 3 that a concurring vote is one that agrees with the result of the majority or plurality opinion, so these opinions are treated the same way as winning votes. Also, specifically note the names of justices who did not participate in the opinion decision. I suggest the use of the symbol NP, meaning "not participating." Keep firmly in mind that the use of symbols does not consider the reasons for the opinion, only the result.

Step 5. The final preliminary step in creating judicial scales is to include a sufficient number of nonunanimous opinions. Unanimous opinions do not depict attitude differences. Consequently, as a general rule of thumb include only nonunanimous opinions in the analysis. One might justify the inclusion of one or perhaps two unanimous opinions when there are a large number of cases because the inclusion of these opinions may usefully serve as a baseline for ascertaining at what point agreement among the justices breaks down.

What is the optimum number of opinions for cumulative scaling? The greater the number of opinions, the more reliable the scale results. A good number is ten. In any event, do not attempt a scaling project with fewer than three nonunanimous opinions.

Constructing a Scale

The second stage of scaling cases entails the actual mechanics and construction of the scale. It is an eight-step process. Although it is an advisable practice, arranging the cases chronologically will not ordinarily result in a scale. Moreover, a chronological ordering of the votes alone will not provide a decision rule for rank ordering the justices from left to right. I use international-border cases involving searches of motor vehicles decided by the

Burger Court in the 1970s to illustrate scale construction. These cases provide a straightforward example, complete with problems student researchers are likely to encounter when constructing scalograms.

Step 6. I illustrate below the results of step 6—the scale production process in the form of an initial raw-data configuration. This matrix contains the votes of each justice for each case. The far right column contains the vote distribution for each case, and each row contains the vote distribution for each justice. I arranged the four cases along the rows in the order of how the cases were first located. Any random ordering, however, will suffice. As it so happens, the justices are ordered along the columns in order of rank and seniority on the Court. For both the row and column totals the first number represents liberal votes (+) and the second number symbolizes conservative votes (–).

Step 6: Initial Raw Data Configuration

Cases	Burger	Douglas	Brennan	White	Marshall	Stewart	Powell	Blackmun	Rehnquist	Case Votes
U.S. v. Martinez-Fuerte	–	(*)	+	–	+	–	–	–	–	(2–7)
Almeida-Sanchez v. U.S.	–	+	+	–	+	+	+	–	–	(5–4)
Bowen v. United States	–	+	+	–	+	+	–	–	–	(4–5)
United States v. Peltier	–	+	+	–	+	+	–	–	–	(4–5)
Justices' Votes	(0–4)	(3–1)	(4–0)	(0–4)	(4–0)	(3–1)	(1–3)	(0–4)	(0–4)	

Step 7. To achieve the proper rank order of the justices, follow the procedures as illustrated in the table below. Although there is no reason in principle why the researcher may not rank-order the justices based on their negative votes, place the justices from left to right in descending order by the total number of plus votes. I place Brennan and Marshall, both with 4–0 vote distributions, in the first and second columns. Douglas creates a special problem because he did not participate in all four cases. For reasons that I will explain later, I treat the missing vote as an inconsistency, and thus in this instance the vote is treated as a conservative vote. Douglas, therefore, occupies the third rank with a 3–1 vote distribution. Stewart is tied with Douglas, and Powell occupies the fifth rank at 1–3. Each of the remaining justices is rank-ordered in the same manner with White, Burger, Blackmun, and Rehnquist occupying the last four ranks.

Step 7: Proper Ordering of Justices

Brennan	Marshall	Douglas	Stewart	Powell	White	Burger	Blackmun	Rehnquist
(4–0)	(4–0)	(3–1)*	(3–1)	(1–3)	(0–4)	(0–4)	(0–4)	(4–0)

Step 8.   Step 8 comprises the proper rank ordering of the cases. The possible combinations of plus and minus votes in cases where all nine justices participate are as follows: 9–0, 8–1, 7–2, 6–3, 5–4, 4–5, 3–6, 2–7, 1–8, and 0–9. The case(s) with the most pluses appears in the first row (*Almeida-Sanchez v. U.S.*), those cases with the next highest number of pluses are placed in the second row, and so on. For cases exhibiting tie votes, the researcher may rank them chronologically, although this is an arbitrary decision.

Step 8: Proper Ordering of Cases

Almeida-Sanchez v. U.S.	(5-4)
Bowen v. U.S.	(4-5)
U.S. v. Peltier	(4-5)
U.S. v. Martinez-Fuerte	(2-7)

Step 9.   With the completion of steps 7 and 8, the researcher is in position to put the initial matrix together. I illustrate this mechanical process in the table below. If the researcher is fortunate, all the pluses (+) are in one region of the matrix, and all the minuses (–) are in the other. This is the case for the Burger Court motor-vehicle border-search cases. If this is not the case, the researcher needs to rearrange the matrix several times with the objective of minimizing *inconsistencies.*

Step 9: Putting the Initial Matrix Together

	Justices									
	Brennan	Marshall	Douglas	Stewart	Powell	Burger	Rehnquist	White	Blackmun	**Totals**
Cases										
Almeida-Sanchez v. U.S.	+	+	+	+	+	–	–	–	–	(5–4)
United States v. Peltier	+	+	+	+	–	–	–	–	–	(4–5)
Bowen v. United States	+	+	+	+	–	–	–	–	–	(4–5)
U.S. v. Martinez-Fuerte	+	+	*	–	–	–	–	–	–	(2–7)
Totals	(4–0)	(4–0)	(3–1)	(3–1)	(1–3)	(0–4)	(0–4)	(0–4)	(0–4)	

Step 10.   One cannot normally identify inconsistent votes until a stepline is drawn. An inconsistency is defined as the appearance of a plus or minus in the opposite region of the matrix where they are expected to be found. Thus, we treat a minus designation such as the case for Douglas in *U.S. v. Martinez-Fuerte* as an inconsistency because it appears in a place in the matrix where the other votes all are pluses. Drawing a *stepline* is the technique for dividing the pluses from the minuses and discerning whether inconsistencies are present in the matrix. This requires drawing a line from the upper right to the

lower left sector of the matrix, dichotomizing the votes between the pluses and the minuses and minimizing the number of inconsistent votes as the line progresses in the shape of steps or a stairway. See the final matrix on p. 86.

Step 11. For this step note the existence of any inconsistent votes—that is, whether there are any minus or plus votes where they do not belong by virtue of the stepline. One may accomplish this task by placing parentheses, circles, rectangles, or any other distinguishing notation marks in the inconsistent cells.

Step 12. Step 12 entails computing the coefficient of reproducibility (CR). To do this, count the number of inconsistent votes divided by the total number of responses (number of justices × the number of cases—in the international-border motor-vehicle-search cases, a total of 1 inconsistency divided by 9 justices times 4 cases ($9 \times 4 = 36$)). Applying the formula to our example yields a rounded CR figure of .97. The coefficient of reproducibility ranges from zero (0), meaning that the matrix bears no relationship to a perfect scale, to one (1), where there are no inconsistencies or errors, a perfect scale. The conventional benchmark for an acceptable approximation to a perfect scale is set at .90 or 90 percent reproducibility, although some researchers have set the cutoff figure as high as .95.

A score of .90 or higher suggests unidimensionality in the scale; in other words, the scale measures a single set of attitudes. The justices voted as they did in the border-search cases because of their individual attitudes toward the subject matter. Moreover, because the justices exhibit remarkable consistency in their pattern of agreement it may be inferred that they view the cases from the same or a very similar ideological framework. In brief, an underlying ideological or attitudinal dimension affects the way the justices respond to the stimuli of similar cases.

Step 13. Computation of scale scores for each justice is the thirteenth and final step in scale construction. As a practical tool, scale scores permit researchers to describe the relative position of each justice on the scale and to compare the relative positions of justices on two or more scales. We accomplish this latter function by collapsing the results, computing the average scale scores for justices in an effort to discern if the justices exhibit consistent ideological patterns of behavior over a number of different issue-specific scales.

The computation formula is: $SS = \dfrac{2P}{N} - 1$

P is the scale position of each judge. This represents the demarcation point at which the stepline partitioning the votes for each of the justices is drawn. Thus, in the motor-vehicle-search illustration, the scale position of Brennan and Marshall is 4; Douglas and Stewart is 3; Powell is 1; and Burger, Rehnquist, White, and Blackmun are all zero. N is the number of cases in the scale; in our illustration, 4. Scale score values range from +1.0 (all positive votes) to –1.0 (all negative votes). Thus, the scalogram analysis of the border-search cases during the Burger era indicates that Brennan and Marshall with perfect positive scale scores exhibit the most liberal attitudes relative to their colleagues, and the remaining justices exhibit different degrees of ideological commitment, including perfectly negative scale scores. On this basis, it is possible to array the justices on a liberal/conservative continuum as follows:

Justice	Scale Score	Ideology
Brennan	1.0	Liberal
Marshall	1.0	Liberal
Douglas	.5	Moderate Liberal
Stewart	.5	Moderate Liberal
Powell	−.5	Moderate Conservative
Burger	−1.0	Conservative
Rehnquist	−1.0	Conservative
White	−1.0	Conservative
Blackmun	−1.0	Conservative

Steps 10–13: Final Matrix

	Justices									
	Brennan	Marshall	Douglas	Stewart	Powell	Burger	Rehnquist	White	Blackmun	**Totals**
Cases										
Almeida-Sanchez v. U.S.	+	+	+	+	+	–	–	–	–	(5–4)
United States v. Peltier	+	+	+	+	–	–	–	–	–	(4–5)
Bowen v. United States	+	+	+	+	–	–	–	–	–	(4–5)
U.S. v. Martinez-Fuerte	+	+	*	–	–	–	–	–	–	(2–7)
Totals	(4–0)	(4–0)	(3–1)	(3–1)	(1–3)	(0–4)	(0–4)	(0–4)	(0–4)	
Scale Position	4	4	3	3	1	0	0	0	0	
Scale Score	1	1	0.5	0.5	-0.5	-1	-1	-1	-1	

Coefficient of Reproducibility = .97

(+ = vote in favor of protecting Fourth Amendment right (liberal))

(– = vote in favor of government intrusion (conservative))

* Justice Douglas did not participate in this decision.

Missing Values Problem

For a variety of good reasons, Supreme Court justices do not always participate in every decision of the Court. Justices may decline to participate because of temporary incapacitation due to illness. They may perceive a conflict of interest and therefore recuse themselves. At times, they may participate in all phases of a case but in the end decide not to vote on the merits of the case. Justices also have passed away during a Court term, leaving the

Court temporarily understaffed. Under these and other circumstances, we cannot infer justices' attitudes directly from the voting records found in the *U.S. Reports*. They represent missing values. The lack of participation by Justice Douglas in *U.S. v. Martinez-Fuerte* is one such instance. How should researchers treat these situations? First, signify nonparticipation. This is accomplished by leaving the particular missing cells empty, inserting (0) or (NP) or inserting an asterisk (*) as is done for Douglas. This seems easy enough. Yet, the insertion of symbols alone does not treat the more significant problem—how should researchers count missing values, if at all?

The most conservative procedure, the one adopted in our illustrative border-search cases, is to treat the missing value as an inconsistency. Unlike attorneys, social scientists endeavor to test the null hypothesis, not to prove a claim in order to win an argument. By treating missing values as inconsistencies, the researcher opts to reject the hypothesis that the decisions reflect an underlying set of attitudes. If they make the most conservative assumption in support of the null hypothesis, researchers may feel relatively confident when they confirm the alternative hypothesis, namely, that the cases do in fact scale with CR at or above .90.

A second approach is to make an educated guess about how each nonparticipating justice would have voted if he or she were willing and able to have participated. In many instances, this alternative is a reasonable choice. Given the liberal votes of Justice Douglas in three of the four cases and also knowing his general views on civil liberties it is reasonable to assume that if he had participated in the decision he would have voted for the civil liberty claim (+). If we make this assumption then the coefficient of reproducibility is a perfect 1.0. Obviously, if researchers exercise this option rather than the more methodologically conservative approach, CR results will be greater. Further, the point bears repeating that there will be a greater expectation that the null hypothesis will be rejected, allowing the researcher to conclude with reasonable confidence that there is indeed an underlying set of attitudes if the CR is nonetheless sufficiently high (.90 or above).

The same problem arises when researchers scale cases without a natural court. In such instances, the names of the justices arrayed across the columns exceed nine in number; consequently, there are empty cells, sometimes called missing values. The best option is to choose to study only natural courts. Sometimes a researcher may scale similar cases of two or more natural courts, first determining whether each set of cases scales and then comparing the scale scores of each justice between or among the studied natural courts. However, there are instances when it makes good sense to study "unnatural" courts. In such instances, employ the same options and thought processes as suggested for the usual occurrence of missing values.

Obviously, where there are more than nine justices there will be many more missing values than is ordinarily the situation. Therefore, if the conservative methodology is used, there is a greater likelihood that the coefficient of reproducibility will drop below the .90 threshold. Again, if the CR exceeds the .90 threshold, researchers can be confident in the conclusion that the cases do indeed scale.

When treating missing values as if the justices had actually voted in the specific cases, researchers should place the votes in parentheses—(+) or (–). Moreover, in the body of the text, researchers should inform their readers that they exercised such a choice and in the process should justify their decision to treat missing values as real votes. For example, Justice Douglas voted in a consistent liberal fashion in the three cases in which he participated and other cited studies confirm the proposition that he was a committed civil libertarian.

Bloc Analysis

Creating judicial scales contributes to our understanding of the ideological patterns among justices. Nevertheless, unidimensional scaling does not address whether jurists exhibit patterns of interagreement. It is a reasonable hypothesis that certain Supreme Court justices exhibit strong ties that manifest themselves in bloc voting. One might ask whether there are conservative, moderate, or liberal blocs of justices in certain issue areas or in more broadly conceived legal categories of interest. If so, researchers may precisely describe these interagreement patterns and predict outcomes in future cases. Thus, if a member of a five-person conservative bloc retires from the Supreme Court and an individual expected to exhibit liberal tendencies replaces that person, then the Court may change direction, at least with respect to issues around which the conservative bloc exists. Merely identifying voting blocs, however, does not provide the reason for justices' interagreement. Bloc analysis confirms only the existence of interagreement, nothing more. Justices may agree because of their mutual understanding of legal rules, their attitudes, strategic rational choice calculations, strong leadership, or bargaining. Consequently, researchers should view bloc analysis as an excellent descriptive technique, not as a scientific explanation of judicial decision making.

Researchers may use bloc analysis to study interagreement among decision makers for particular periods of time and issue areas. Scholars often construct voting blocs for one or more terms of the Supreme Court. This permits researchers to discern broad patterns of behavior, including, for example, whether newly appointed justices join blocs early in their tenures or whether they exhibit the so-called "freshman effect." This means that at the beginning of their Court tenures they fail to align themselves, taking time to investigate their political and interpersonal environment before joining a preexisting bloc. Bloc analysis also is useful for describing interagreement patterns when studying particular issue areas, such as cases involving border searches of motor vehicles. Again, these cases will serve as our illustrative example.

As is also the case for creating attitude scales, the most interesting questions worth studying involve the most contentious issues. Therefore, researchers most often opt to study nonunanimous opinions. Of course, as is true for unidimensional scaling, performing a bloc analysis on too few cases may create concerns about the reliability of one's findings. In the illustration presented below, there are only four cases. Yet the matter of reliability is inconsequential because these cases represent a complete enumeration for the Burger Court during the 1970s.

Constructing Blocs

There are four steps in constructing a bloc.

Step 1. The first is to calculate interagreement scores for all the justices. Count the number of times each pair of justices voted in the same case (both voted liberal, both voted conservative) and then divide this number by the total number of cases in which both justices participated. I illustrate the results of this simple arithmetic process in the table below. Notice, for example, that Brennan (Br) and Marshall (Mar) voted in the same way in all four of the border-search cases for an interagreement score of 100 (4 ÷ 4 = 1), in percentage terms 1 = 100%. Brennan (Br) and Douglas (Dg) participated together in three cases and in each instance they voted together (3 ÷ 3 = 100). In the case of Brennan (Br) and Powell (Pow) their interagreement score is .25 (1 ÷ 4 = 25). For this particular matrix, interagreement scores range from 0 to 100. Although the procedure recommended in this step results in duplicate interagreement scores for each pair of justices, be careful not to count the same pair of justices more than once when proceeding to the subsequent steps. An intellectually

Step 1: Initial Bloc Configuration

Br/Mar	Br/Dg	Br/Stew	Br/Pow	Br/Burg	Br/Reh	Br/Wh	Br/Bin
4/4=100	3/3=100	3/4=75	1/4=25	0/4=0	0/4=0	0/4=0	0/4=0
Mar/Br	Mar/Dg	Mar/Stew	Mar/Pow	Mar/Burg	Mar/Reh	Mar/Wh	Mar/Bin
4/4=100	3/3=100	3/4=75	1/4=25	0/4=0	0/4=0	0/4=0	0/4=0
Dg/Br	Dg/Mar	Dg/Stew	Dg/Pow	Dg/Burg	Dg/Reh	Dg/Wh	Dg/Bin
3/3=100	3/3=100	3/3=100	1/3=33	0/3=0	0/3=0	0/3=0	0/3=0
Stew/Br	Stew/Mar	Stew/Dg	Stew/Pow	Stew/Burg	Stew/Reh	Stew/Wh	Stew/Bin
3/4=75	3/4=75	3/3=100	2/4=50	1/4=25	1/4=25	1/4=25	1/4=25
Pow/Br	Pow/Mar	Pow/Dg	Pow/Stew	Pow/Burg	Pow/Reh	Pow/Wh	Pow/Bin
1/4=25	1/4=25	1/3=33	2/4=50	3/4=75	3/4=75	3/4=75	3/4=75
Burg/Br	Burg/Mar	Burg/Dg	Burg/Stew	Burg/Pow	Burg/Reh	Burg/Wh	Burg/Bin
0/4=0	0/4=0	0/3=0	1/4=25	3/4=75	4/4=100	4/4=100	4/4=100
Reh/Br	Reh/Mar	Reh/Dg	Reh/Stew	Reh/Pow	Reh/Burg	Reh/Wh	Reh/Bin
0/4=0	0/4=0	0/3=0	1/4=25	3/4=75	4/4=100	4/4=100	4/4=100
Wh/Br	Wh/Mar	Wh/Dg	Wh/Stew	Wh/Pow	Wh/Burg	Wh/Reh	Wh/Bin
0/4=0	0/4=0	0/3=0	1/4=25	3/4=75	4/4=100	4/4=100	4/4=100
Bin/Br	Bin/Mar	Bin/Dg	Bin/Stew	Bin/Pow	Bin/Burg	Bin/Reh	Bin/Wh
0/4=0	0/4=0	0/3=0	1/4=25	3/4=75	4/4=100	4/4=100	4/4=100

more challenging problem arises when a particular justice has participated in a relatively low number of cases, perhaps less than half. In this eventuality, consider carefully whether that person should be included in the analysis.

Step 2.   From the list of pairs of justices created by step 1, construct a matrix that rank orders the pairs of justices from the highest to lowest interagreement scores. Starting in the upper left-hand corner of the page, place the first pair of justices with the highest score in the first two cells of the matrix. In our illustration four justices (Burger, Rehnquist, White, and Blackmun), all have perfect interagreement scores (100). Justice Powell exhibits the next highest interagreement (75), followed by Stewart (25), and then the remaining justices (Douglas, Marshall, and Brennan), all of whom disagree substantially with the first five justices placed in the matrix. All of the justices with their respective interagreement scores are entered into the data matrix. Notice in this particular example I placed the conservative voting justices in the upper left-hand corner and the liberal voting justices in the bottom right-hand corner of the matrix. I make this decision because the conservative justices clearly are the larger of what appear to be two voting blocs. There is no reason in principle, however, why a researcher might not reverse the locations of each bloc. At the end of step 2, the matrix of interagreement should look something like the illustration below.

Step 2: Arranging the Pairs

	Burg	Reh	Wh	Bin	Pow	Stew	Dg	Mar	Br
Burger	–	100	100	100	75	25	0	0	0
Rehnquist	100	–	100	100	75	25	0	0	0
White	100	100	–	100	75	25	0	0	0
Blackmun	100	100	100	–	75	25	0	0	0
Powell	75	75	75	75	–	50	33	25	25
Stewart	25	25	25	25	50	–	100	75	75
Douglas	0	0	0	0	33	100	–	100	100
Marshall	0	0	0	0	25	75	100	–	100
Brennan	0	0	0	0	25	75	100	100	–

Step 3.   The third step is to determine what blocs, if any, actually exist, as well as the relative strength of these blocs. You can perform this operation in one of two ways, but today many scholars prefer the second method.

The first method is to compute and report the *index of interagreement*. It is the arithmetic average of the interagreement scores of the pairs included in the matrix per my example for the conservative bloc illustrated below: ((100 + 100 + 100 + 75 + 100 + 100 + 100 + 75 + 100 + 100 + 100 + 75 + 100 + 100 + 100 + 75 + 75 + 75 + 75 + 75) ÷ 20 = 90). But what pairs should the researcher include in the computed average? By studying the numbers in the matrix, the researcher searches out by trial and error the combinations of pairs of justices that exhibit the greatest number of justices with the highest levels of interagreement. Thus, in the illustration five justices clearly represent a conservative bloc; the index of interagreement for Burger, Rehnquist, White, Blackmun, and Powell is 90. The liberal-bloc index of interagreement for Brennan, Marshall, Douglas, and Stewart is slightly higher at 92. Yet, how high is high enough to conclude that a bloc exists? One option is based on the experience and practice of scholars in the field. Scholars regard an index of interagreement of 70 percent or higher as high, a moderate score as 60–69, and a low score as 59 or below. However, because this labeling approach is rather intuitive, a second method for proclaiming the existence of blocs is now widely regarded as preferable by many scholars. I describe it in step 4.

Step 3: Final Bloc Matrix

	Burg	Reh	Wh	Bin	Pow	Stew	Dg	Mar	Br
Burger	–	100	100	100	75	25	0	0	0
Rehnquist	100	–	100	100	75	25	0	0	0
White	100	100	–	100	75	25	0	0	0
Blackmun	100	100	100	–	75	25	0	0	0
Powell	75	75	75	75	–	59	33	25	25
Stewart	25	25	25	25	50	–	100	75	75
Douglas	0	0	0	0	33	100	–	100	100
Marshall	0	0	0	0	25	75	100	–	100
Brennan	0	0	0	0	25	75	100	100	–

Conservative bloc: Burger, Rehnquist, White, Blackmun, Powell = 90
Liberal bloc: Brennan, Marshall, Douglas, Stewart = 92
Court Mean = 46.75
Sprague Criterion = 73.34

Step 4. The final step is to compute the *Sprague Criterion*. Scholars often use this option to determine whether exceptionally high levels of interagreement exist based on all the available information found in the data matrix. First, compute the Court mean. You can accomplish this by summing all the scores of every pair of justices in the matrix and then dividing by the total number of pairs of justices in the matrix. For the border-search cases, the numbers are 1683 ÷ 36 = 46.75. Thus, based on the Court mean one may conclude that the average interagreement score for the entire Court is 47 percent. Off hand, it appears that the differences between the Court mean and the indexes of interagreement are substantial (47 compared to 90 and 92). Yet, Sprague's criterion sets the benchmark higher than a mere court average. Subtract the Court mean from 100 (100 – 46.75 = 53.25). Divide the resulting number by 2 (53.25 ÷ 2 = 26.63). Add the new number (26.63) to the Court mean (46.75) to produce the Sprague criterion (26.63 + 46.75 = 73.34). You may regard any pair of justices exceeding the criterion as a bloc.[5]

Cases and Data Analysis

The use of the elementary techniques described in this chapter need not preclude the careful reading of case law. In my view, if properly employed, data-analysis techniques inform researchers more fully about those issues dividing court members. Identifying particularly divisive cases may help researchers to focus on fact patterns that are likely to produce nonunanimous opinions. Carefully reading those particular opinions may point the way to how litigants and court blocs may proceed in the future. In some instances, researchers may anticipate a change in one or two votes by carefully reading the opinions of conflicted justices. Indeed, it is widely understood that interest groups that lobby courts carefully scrutinize opinions, looking for likely openings as they employ short- and long-range strategies to get their way with the judiciary.

Consequently, good student research papers often employ both traditional legal research tools and quantitative techniques. Both approaches are mutually reinforcing and one need not view them as antithetical. Most professors, however, have their own opinions on this subject and are usually keen to share them with their students.

Endnotes

[1] See, for example, Lee Epstein, Jeffrey A. Segal, Harold J. Spaeth, and Thomas G. Walker, *The Supreme Court Compendium: Data, Decisions & Developments*, 3d ed. (Washington, DC: Congressional Quarterly Press, 2003); Thomas R. Hensley, Christopher E. Smith, and Joyce A. Baugh, *The Changing Supreme Court: Constitutional Rights and Liberties* (St. Paul: West, 1997); Kenneth Lee Grambihler, "A Longitudinal Analysis of the Freshman Effect Hypothesis of United States Supreme Court Justices (1953–1988 Terms)," Ph.D. dissertation, Southern Illinois University Carbondale, 1993; Bradley J. Best, *Law Clerks, Support Personnel, and the Decline of Consensual Norms on the United States Supreme Court, 1935–1995* (New York: LFB Scholarly Publishing, 2002).

[2] Harold J. Spaeth, *Supreme Court Policy Making: Explanation and Prediction* (San Francisco: W. H. Freeman, 1979), pp. 119–120.

[3] Proponents of the attitude model argue that because there is a high correlation between the votes of the justices and how newspaper editors characterized their ideologies when they were nominated to the Court, the votes of justices are sound indicators of liberal and conservative attitudes. See Jeffrey A. Segal and Albert D. Cover, "Ideological Values and the Votes of U.S. Supreme Court Justices," 83 *American Political Science Review* (1989), p. 557–565.

[4] Rick A. Swanson and Albert P. Melone, "The Partisan Factor and Judicial Behavior in the Illinois Supreme Court," 19 *Southern Illinois University Law Journal* (Winter 1995): 303–332.

[5] John D. Sprague, *Voting Patterns of the United States Supreme Court: Cases in Federalism* (Indianapolis: Bobbs-Merrill, 1968), p. 54.

5

WRITING AND DOCUMENTING RESEARCH PAPERS

Introduction

Writing a paper on a law-related topic presents special problems of design and documentation. In addition to examining these difficulties, this chapter contains a practical discussion useful for other courses in the social sciences and humanities. In addition, some instructors in paralegal studies require the approved form for the citation of legal materials, and some instructors seek to acquaint their pre-law students with the citation format used in the legal profession. Therefore, I provide advice on how to cite papers following the general instructions of the *Chicago Manual of Style*, the in-text social-science notation style of the American Political Science Association, and the format for legal citations found in *The Bluebook: A Uniform System of Citation*, compiled by the law review editors at the Columbia, Harvard, Pennsylvania, and Yale university law schools.

One main goal of this chapter is to challenge students to think systematically about their research projects. Carefully considering what topic they choose to research saves students considerable time and effort. Moreover, formulating a research project by writing a research design helps students avoid mistakes along the research path. During the learning process, I hope that students will learn how to properly cite their sources, giving credit where credit is due.

Choosing a Topic

Course instructors usually determine the content and substance of student papers by setting requirements. If an academic unit offers many law-related courses, the instructor probably will narrow the range of topic choices. This range may reflect not only the specialized subject matter as defined by the curriculum, but the instructor's academic and policy interests as well. As a result, students should pay close attention to their instructors' expressions of expectations.

In courses on constitutional law and related subjects, instructors typically ask students to write a term paper that traces or analyzes the development of doctrine. Sometimes instructors ask students to research some aspect of judicial process and behavior, including the politics surrounding particular court decisions. Whatever the case, there is a wealth of material available for student papers; no student may legitimately claim that materials are nonexistent on a law-related topic.

For students without direct access to a law library the research task can pose difficulties. For students needing assistance, the interlibrary loan department of the college library is an appropriate place to start. They may photocopy materials at little or no expense. A visit to a law library some distance from campus may be worth the additional effort too. It is also advisable to explore the Internet for available material. However, do not rely solely on Web sites to complete the research task. I strongly recommend that students plan their research projects carefully. Because of the usual research problems just mentioned, never leave the paper to the last minute.

I advise students to choose narrow topics. While the initial impulse of an inexperienced researcher is to choose a broad topic, for example, "The Supreme Court and the Criminal Justice System," it is better to keep it narrow, for example, "The Rehnquist Court and the Fourth Amendment." Remember, when dealing with law-related topics, it is easy to write an excessively long and involved paper. If students conceive the topic as open-ended from the start, it will be difficult to contain it within reasonable bounds. A common pitfall for students is to become trapped in a project with no logical conclusion. A long and rambling paper usually raises more questions than it answers.

Before settling on a firm topic, conduct a preliminary investigation. Ask the following questions:

1. Am I interested in the topic?

2. Does the topic fulfill course requirements and instructor expectations?

3. Are the necessary library and other resource materials accessible to me?

4. What are my specific research questions?

Upon answering the first two questions affirmatively, it is necessary for the student to visit the library and access electronic resources for a careful appraisal of whether he or she may complete the task in a reasonable amount of time. Then the student-researcher should design the project carefully.

Do not needlessly expend time and energy compiling a bibliography without first narrowing your topic. A quick way to determine the scope and practicality of the research topic is to consult legal encyclopedias and indexes to periodical literature. Because of the nearly objective nature of most encyclopedia articles, a student can determine the scope and some key citations almost immediately. By consulting periodical literature indexes for recent years, it is possible to know what questions are of contemporary interest and need researching. Once satisfied with the ability to conduct the research, write out the specific research questions of interest. Armed with this knowledge, consult the instructor for advice—indicate the topic, specific research questions, and how you expect to conduct your research. The instructor might direct you to a better topic, a slightly different slant on the topic, or a superior way to conduct the research. Compile a complete bibliography only after narrowing the topic.

Designing the Research Project

Good researchers know what they want to study and they have a very good idea how to accomplish the task. There is no need to waste effort. To achieve this goal, writers should think of the research task as a two-fold process. First, write a research design. Second, execute the design in the form of a completed paper.

Research Design

What is a *research design*? It is a statement about how a researcher intends to answer a question or series of questions. It contains at least seven related parts that we may think of as separate, yet united, elements. Depending on the research problem, researchers are able to write satisfactory research designs in six to fifteen typewritten pages. Moreover, writers may easily incorporate their designs in the final paper submitted to the instructor for a grade. Place the *research design* at the beginning of the body of the paper, followed by a separate section that contains the *findings*, and a final section with *conclusions*. A good research design contains the following seven elements.

1. State the broad research interest.   Students of constitutional law might explain that they are interested in learning about how the U.S. Supreme Court interprets the Constitution over time. Alternatively, perhaps one's general interest is the investigation of decision-making patterns, if any, among members of the Court. This initial statement lays out the broad boundaries of the intellectual curiosity that drives the research effort. Yet, surely, these general statements of purpose are not specific enough. Researchers must narrow their subject further.

2. Recite a specific research problem. Researchers should indicate what subject in particular they have chosen to aid them in learning about their broad research interest. Thus, for example, discerning how the Supreme Court's interpretation of the Commerce Clause has changed since the decision in *Gibbons v. Ogden* (1824) to the present era is illustrative of how the Court interprets the Constitution over time. Alternatively, in the case of the general problem of learning about patterns of Supreme Court decision making, one might want to discern whether there is an underlying set of attitudes that differentiates justices about particular sets of policy issues; for example, justices' attitudes concerning the constitutional rights of the criminally accused.

3. Review the essential literature on the subject. Instructors may permit students to write a paper that does little more than reiterate what others have already discovered. Yet, if students make an additional effort by investigating what is also unknown about the subject, then they may claim that they have made an original contribution to our collective knowledge. First, however, the student researcher must discover what is already known about the subject.

Researchers may accomplish this goal by first reading the pertinent literature and then reporting on the state of existing knowledge. For example, the researcher interested in the Commerce Clause may report that the existing literature points to the conclusion that the Court's interpretation has changed considerably over time. Further, the writer may report that certain scholars indicate that the changing interpretation of the Commerce Clause is probably the result of competing views about the nature of American federalism. However, the existing scholarship does not provide a definitive explanation about the Rehnquist Court's handling of Commerce Clause litigation and how this Court fits the historical pattern; i.e., does it take a dual or a cooperative view of federalism? At this point in the research process, student researchers need not read and report every published study on the subject. Yet, students should be relatively certain that they have identified a researchable topic that is ripe for investigation. They will want to read the available works in detail as the research project progresses.

4. State specific hypotheses. A hypothesis is a declaratory statement purporting to test relationships among variables. It should state what the researcher expects to find in the real world. When stated, the hypothesis is an unproved proposition subject to testing. Posing hypotheses serves the important function of requiring researchers to focus their attention on discoverable relationships through empirical observation and analysis. In this way, researchers are forced to stick to the subject and not wander off into whatever nooks and crannies of constitutional law and politics the subject may take them. Consider the example of the Commerce Clause research project. The researcher may word the hypothesis as follows: "In cases dealing with the

Commerce Clause, the U.S. Supreme Court first interpreted congressional power broadly, then in the late nineteenth and early twentieth centuries the Court followed the doctrine of dual federalism opting for a narrow interpretation of congressional power. From the New Deal Court through most of the 1960s the Court adopted the cooperative view of federalism but in the 1990s the Court narrowed the commerce power once again." With respect to the attitudes of the justices of the Rehnquist Court one might devise the following hypothesis: "In cases dealing with the Fourth Amendment rights of criminal defendants, the Rehnquist Court displays a consistent voting pattern. Justices vote consistently either for or against the claims of criminal defendants, thereby displaying underlying attitudes that may be described as liberal or conservative." While researchers may word hypotheses in many different ways, it is important to remember that a hypothesis is a testable proposition, not a normative statement without real-world empirical referents.

 5. Specify the universe of the study. Given our hypothetical research project, will the researcher choose to study all Commerce Clause cases decided by the Supreme Court or only the leading opinions, and if the latter, how is a leading opinion defined? How do we know whether Court opinions exhibit a dual or a cooperative view of federalism? With respect to the research project attempting to uncover attitudes among Supreme Court justices, one needs to determine whether cases from certain years of the Rehnquist era will be the object of study. Alternatively, will the study include only those cases where the same nine members participate? It is also important to specify whether the universe of cases includes only nonunanimous opinions or all opinions in a given subject category, for example, Fourth Amendment or all criminal justice opinions. Too often students bite off more than they can chew. If the universe of the study is unspecified, then researchers may commit themselves to more time and energy than the assignment warrants. There is also a good chance that the poorly focused researcher will not complete the task or will submit an unacceptable paper to the instructor.

 6. Specify the variables to be studied with precision. Concepts are abstractions that permit humans to think about complex phenomena in efficient ways. However, abstractions are difficult to measure or test unless we reduce them to identifiable objects. In other words, concepts must be summarized in the form of variables subject to empirical verification. For instance, there is a need for the researcher studying the Commerce Clause to define the words *congressional commerce power, broad* versus *narrow interpretation,* and *dual* versus *cooperative federalism.* The researcher must specify these words and phrases with rigor, lest the researcher has an elusive definition of terms that permit any conclusion he or she may desire. With respect to the hypothetical judicial attitude study, researchers must pay careful attention to variable specification. What is the operational definition of criminal cases? Does it include cases involving the right to legal counsel, the right to a fair trial, the right to the confrontation of witnesses? Does the definition of a criminal case include white-collar tax cases? How do we define a judicial attitude? If a justice votes for the criminal defendant and against the government's claim, is that a liberal attitude, a conservative attitude, or something else? The final interpretation of the meaning of one's findings is dependent largely on the operational definition of each variable. Establish these decision rules when writing the research design, long before the research project is in the final stages of writing.

   7. Indicate how one plans to test each hypothesis. Think of this task as plotting a road map to travel from one physical place on a map to another—what interstate highways do I travel to get from to Los Angeles to San Francisco in the quickest and most economical fashion? I will want to know with precision how I get from my residence to the nearby freeway. I want to know when to switch from one highway to another. I will need a good estimate about how long it will take me to complete the journey. Will I need to stop for lunch? Where are the rest stops along the route so that I may walk my dog? To test the Commerce Clause hypothesis, for example, researchers may indicate that they will locate all of the Supreme Court opinions dealing with the Commerce Clause by consulting the *U.S. Supreme Court Reports Digest: Lawyers' Edition.* The digest topic is Commerce §§ 96–104. This will provide researchers with legal citations for all the cases for the years under study. Then the researcher will read each Court opinion in one of the Supreme Court reports, noting changes in the Court's interpretation of the Commerce Clause. To aid in the process of obtaining an objective professional evaluation of each case, researchers may indicate that they will consult *Shepard's United States Citations: Cases.* This source indicates when cases are overruled, distinguished, followed, and a host of other options. Researchers might also indicate that they intend to consult the U.S. Constitution volumes of one of the annotated versions of the *U.S. Code.* Perhaps they contemplate reading encyclopedia pieces as well as reading additional books and articles on the subject. For a specific way to test the judicial attitude hypothesis, see the complete discussion about scaling techniques found in chapter 4 of this text. Also, the first two chapters of this book contain information on locating and using primary and secondary sources. Often students forget what they thought they once learned. Therefore, it is a good idea to re-read these chapters before writing a research design to refresh one's memory and to avoid wasted effort.

   Appendix A contains a sample research design written by an undergraduate student in one of my constitutional law courses. The Supreme Court had granted the writ of certiorari to hear two cases from the University of Michigan concerning the constitutionality of that institution's affirmative action programs. I asked my students to first construct a research design that may prove useful in predicting how the Court might decide these highly controversial cases and then to execute their designs, resulting in a complete paper on the topic. It was well understood at the time that the Supreme Court would not in all likelihood render its decisions until after the term was completed. Note that the research design by Tyson Tanner was submitted to me on

March 12, 2003. The Supreme Court rendered its decisions on June 23, 2003. Also note the usefulness of the judicial attitude approach and bloc analysis in helping to explain in part the ultimate outcome of the closely divided Court in *Grutter v. Bollinger* (2003).

When conducting legal research, students should endeavor to explore all pertinent research materials. Because the nature of the research project will dictate where to begin, it is misleading to suggest that students should always begin in one place and end in another. Consult each of the following categories of research materials. Students who do this can be reasonably certain that they have adequately surveyed the topic. See the first two chapters of this volume for a description of the following research tools:

a. encyclopedias

b. books

c. articles

d. codes and statutory law

e. court opinions, case annotations

f. digests

g. cite checkers

h. case updating services and newspapers

i. briefs of counsel

j. interest-group Internet sites and publications

Writing a good research design is time well spent. If a design is without serious flaws, then the final research paper will be more than satisfactory. Your instructor may provide students with an opportunity to discuss their writing projects early in the course. You may ask your instructor to read and to criticize your design. During their graduate-school days, your instructors were specially trained by their professors for the task. Social scientists know that if a research design is poor then the resulting product is likely to possess little merit. After your research design is approved, then your journey to the end of the research task should proceed with few, if any, unanticipated roadblocks.

The Format for a Paper

Although requirements vary from instructor to instructor, law-related research papers often contain six elements: (1) A *title page* that should include the paper's title, student name, instructor name, course number and title, and date; (2) a *table of contents* that includes chapter or section headings; (3) a *table of cases*, listing in alphabetical order each case mentioned or cited in the paper, the legal citation for each case, and the multiple page numbers where each appears in the body of the text; (4) the *body of the text* that should include the introduction, the research design, the findings, and a conclusion; (5) a *bibliog-*

raphy that should be placed at the end of the paper; and (6) depending on course requirements, writers should place *notes* citing authority at the bottom of each page, at the back of each chapter, at the end of the paper just before the bibliography, or within the body of the text. Note that particular instructors may have their own expectations about the best citation format.

Always type and double-space papers. Use 8½″ × 11″ white bond paper of between sixteen and twenty pound weight. Set the margins at one inch on all sides and indent each paragraph one-half inch, and use a 12-point font in a conventional typeface such as Times New Roman or New Courier. Instructors are wise to student attempts to exaggerate their efforts by narrowing margins and increasing font sizes so that the paper appears to be longer than is actually the case. Do not demean your status by employing such low-brow tactics.

Writers should number each page. Use Arabic numbers beginning on the first page of the *body of the text* with the numbers placed at the upper right-hand corner of each page. Use lower case Roman numerals for the pages preceding the body of the text. Do not number the title page. When course instructors specify a particular page length they usually have in mind the length of the body of the text and not the other supportive pages such as the title page, table of contents, and so on. Do not right justify the margin of each page. You should firmly bind the pages together. A cover is optional.

Always be prepared to submit a second hard copy of your paper if the instructor misplaces the original. You should definitely back up your paper on a hard drive and a floppy disk. Increasingly, instructors are asking students to submit their papers as an electronic file. They use the comment feature on the browser in the case of Microsoft Word; on the Macintosh that same function appears on the Reviewing toolbar. This practice facilitates the criticism and grading process and reduces the need to cut down additional forests.

Special Writing Problems

Clear communication is the goal in all writing. However, a significant problem for writers of law-related papers is the phrasing of complex legal ideas and concepts. The first rule is to try to write in relatively short sentences. Whenever possible avoid writing long, complex sentences. Writers often can reduce such sentences to half their length by inserting periods following complete thoughts. You might regard any sentence that contains more than 25 words as a candidate for division. Further, in keeping with modern convention, try to avoid writing in the passive voice. Changing the verb tense in a sentence is not the way to change a sentence from passive to active voice. When the verb is active, it informs the reader that the subject of the sentence performs the action. When the verb form is passive, the reader learns that the subject of the sentence is acted upon.

Writers of law-related papers encounter the perplexing problem of what words to capitalize. There are some simple rules to internalize, but beyond these rules we enter the realm of ambiguity and uncertainty. When in doubt follow the modern practice; place words in lower case rather than upper case. Proper nouns are capitalized including the names of persons and their titles when they immediately precede a personal name (Justice Kennedy, Professor Pufong, Governor Schwarzenegger). But titles following a personal name or used in place of a personal name are usually placed in lower case (Earl Warren, chief justice of the Supreme Court). One oddity in legal writing is that when the writer refers to the United States Supreme Court the first letters of the words *supreme court* should be capitalized and if one simply uses the word *court* to refer to the U.S. Supreme Court the letter *c* should be capitalized. All other courts receive lower-case treatment.

When referring to a specific constitution, such as the U.S. Constitution, you should capitalize the word *constitution*. The problem is that as readers we see some writers referring to constitutional provisions in lower case and others in upper case. In the past, it was widely recommended to use lower case when referring to parts of the constitution (fifth amendment, due process clause, commerce clause). Today, however, U.S. Supreme Court opinion writers usually capitalize parts of the constitution (Fifth Amendment, Due Process Clause, Commerce Clause). Moreover, leading writing manuals including *The Bluebook: A Uniform System of Citation*, 17th edition,[1] as well as Microsoft's spell check feature, express a preference for the upper case. Consequently, to be consistent with modern usage, writers should capitalize parts of the U.S. Constitution. Finally, when referring to a particular term of the United States Supreme Court use the upper case, e.g., the 2004 Term.

Student researchers must schedule their time so that they are in the position to finish the research project during the course of the term. It is a good idea to ask peers to proofread papers and to write more than one draft. Today, this practice is eminently feasible with the editing functions of modern word-processing programs. Common mistakes that writers make when revising are clicking on the wrong word when substituting one word for another and failing to delete undesired words and phrases from the original draft. Always double-check your work to guard against making these common errors.

Documentation of Sources

There are usually a greater number of citations in constitutional law papers than for the average research project in the social sciences or humanities. Legal scholarship is particularly concerned with appropriate citation to authority.

What to Cite?

Ordinarily, cite ideas originating from another source. It is unnecessary to cite ideas, facts, and quotations of common knowledge, e.g., "The United States Constitution contains provisions for three branches of the national government." Particularly in the United States, academics regard the presentation of another's ideas or words as unacceptable conduct and deem it a punishable offense. Even if this failure is accidental, scholars regard it as plagiarism and constitute cause for a failing grade and more extreme penalties, including expulsion from college. Therefore, always document the source of your words or ideas if they are not your own or when these words or ideas are not widely known. This includes not only direct quotations but also paraphrasing the ideas of others.

Writers of law-related papers are obliged to note all court cases cited. These notes may appear in the middle or at the end of a sentence, for example, "The dispute, *Hawaii Housing Authority v. Midkiff* (1984)[86], arose out of a state-land reform statute. Writing for a unanimous Court Justice Sandra Day O'Connor, a Republican appointed by a Republican president, pointed out that the Contract Clause had never been used against the exercise of eminent domain power."

Writers may be tempted to quote extensively from judicial opinions. Though often useful, long quotations can be boring and consume too much space. Learn to use ellipses, three dots indicating omission of words within a sentence. Four dots, a period followed by three spaced dots (. . . .) indicate the omission of the last part of the sentence quoted, omission of the first part of the sentence, omission of a complete sentence, or more, including a paragraph or more. By employing ellipses writers may relate the essence of what is being quoted without requiring readers to plow through unnecessary verbiage, for example, "This conclusion was based upon an important stated assumption, that is, a state cannot be presumed to surrender its power to promote . . . the happiness and prosperity of the community by which it is established." Further, indent and single-space quotations of more than three lines in length. When using block quotations, it is unnecessary to use quotation marks unless one is quoting a word or phrase within the quote. In such instances, use single quotation marks. For example:

> Because these judicial institutions had not yet come into existence, the Socialist press dubbed them 'phantom courts.' Twenty-one of the 25 members of the SJC took part in the vote by secret ballot. But the elections were held after its ex officio chairman, Justice Minister Mladen Chervenyakov, had left the room and declared the meeting adjourned.

At times, it is desirable to alert readers to tangential facts or quotations. However, doing so distracts the reader's attention from the flow of ideas the writer is developing within the body of the text. In such an event, use reference notes, often called explanatory or discursive footnotes or endnotes. It is common, for example, to place a discussion of a minority court opinion in a footnote. Good writers appropriately make detailed methodological points in explanatory notes.

When referencing court opinions, writers often are confused as to when to underline or italicize case names. This is especially the case when referencing court opinions in the body of the text. I suggest the following practice. Do not underline or italicize a case name if it is followed by a legal citation, for example, Roth v. United States, 354 U.S. 476 (1957). If you are writing only the case name or the case name and date of the opinion, then italicize the case name including the abbreviation *v.* for the word versus, for example, *Roth v. United States* or *Roth v. United States* (1957). Do not underscore or italicize case names in footnotes and in bibliographies where legal citations are provided, for example, Roe v. Wade, 410 U.S. 113 (1973). Incidentally, from a typesetter's viewpoint, a word underlined by a writer signifies that she should set the word in italics. Because modern word-processing programs now contain the italic option, there is no longer a need to accept the limitation of the old typewriter technology.

Footnote or Endnote Format

Documentation style is one of the few things in academic life that can be justifiably arbitrary. There is no inherent reason to use one form rather than another, so long as the communication is clear and consistent. Writers of scholarly papers should cite works in the same form as in indexes, bibliographies, and library catalogs. In this way, a reader will be able to locate cited sources.

What follows are examples of the most frequently used documentation entries when writing a law-related paper in the social sciences. Most of the forms are based upon the various editions of *The Chicago Manual of Style*; Kate L. Turabian's *A Manual for Writers of Term Papers, Theses and Dissertations*; the American Psychological Association (APA) system of in-text citations in combination with the *Style Manual for Political Science,* revised edition (2001), and *The Bluebook: A Uniform System of Citation,* 17th ed. (Cambridge: Harvard Law Review Association, 2000). I also consulted two widely available excellent citation and writing guides: Diana Hacker, *A Pocket Style Manual,* 3d ed. (Boston: Bedford/St. Martin's, 2000), and Jane E. Aaron, *The Little, Brown Compact Handbook,* 3d ed. (New York: Longman, 1998). These latter two sources contain illustrations and explanations of the various documentation styles including the Modern Language Association (MLA) system of citation. I do not outline the MLA style system in this book because MLA is most often used in English and other humanities disciplines, not the social sciences or law.

The following examples of citation form conform to functional customs and conventions. For a book, provide the reader with the name of the author(s), a full title, the place of publication, the name of the publisher, the publication date, and the pages cited. For journal articles it is appropriate to indicate the name of the author, the title of the article, the name of the journal in which the article appears, the volume number, the date of publication, and the page(s) of the cited materials. The justification for providing documentation is that other researchers may need to access and read the cited material themselves. When others are able to read the source materials, they can evaluate how well the author accurately relates the true meaning of what the cited authority has written. Obviously, a writer may falsely report or have a mistaken view of what others have written. Good scholarship requires that others be able to retrace the steps of writers to guarantee the reliability and validity of what authors convey to readers. For those works that are not formally published but are nonetheless cited by writers, one should make every effort to make it possible for others to track down the source. Provide the author's name, the title of the unpublished material, the type of material (for example, a convention paper or an M.A. thesis), where a researcher may find the material, the date appearing on the material, and the page numbers when citing specific pages. It is preferable to reference legal articles in the same way as other academic articles when submitting a research paper in a social science or humanities course. However, sometimes instructors want students to be aware of how different legal citation style is from other academic disciplines, and they ask their students to use the legal style of citation. Instructors in paralegal studies courses often require that their students use a legal style of citation. This chapter contains examples of the legal format that writers may wish to employ. Pre-law students may wish to become familiar with the legal style of citation in anticipation of their vocational plans.

Students often ask their instructors whether to place documentation at the bottom of the page where they insert the citation or at the end of the paper. The usual answer is that they may place citations in either place. Once again, modern word-processing programs render either option practical. When professional scholars send manuscripts off to journals for possible acceptance and eventual publication, editors usually require that they use endnotes or in-text citations rather than footnotes. This journal convention is for the convenience of page designers. Though your instructors may not care, I think that because constitutional law term papers typically contain a large number of citations, student writers should place documentation at the foot (as in footnote) of the page. This makes it easier for the reader to evaluate the quality of your research effort.

Bibliography Form

A bibliography is a listing at the end of a research paper of all references a writer uses in preparation of his or her project. It includes all works cited in footnotes or endnotes as well as other works that the writer found useful in thinking about the topic. If one merely examines but does not use the work in a meaningful intellectual way, I do not recommend that it be included in the bibliography. However, some instructors demand that their students note all references found during the course of the research project.

A bibliography appears at the end of the research paper, is titled *Bibliography*, and typically is centered at the top of the page. List bibliographical entries in alphabetical order, last name first. When a person is the author of more than one work list the works chronologically with the earliest date first and the most recent scholarship listed last. If the list includes two or more works by the same author substitute a blank line (_____) instead of the author's or editor's name.

Bibliographies exist for the convenience of readers. Consequently, if a bibliography is long it is advisable to break it into categories of works, for example, books, articles, and government documents. Because law-related papers typically discuss many cases, writers should include a separate *table of cases*. Writers may place a table of cases either at the end of their papers or somewhere at the beginning of their papers, usually following the table of contents page. List the cases alphabetically together with their full legal citations, followed by the page number(s) in the text where mention is made of each case. If a paper references only a few court cases place them alphabetically in the bibliography. Cite only the first page in the court reporter where the judicial opinion begins.

A bibliographic entry is a transposition of a footnote or endnote entry. Although there are exceptions, change a footnote into a bibliographical entry by transposing the author's first and last names, removing parentheses from the facts of publication, omitting page references, and re-punctuating with periods instead of commas. One important exception is the inclusion of the first and last page numbers of an article appearing in periodical literature. Note the following examples:

Footnote or endnote: 5. Harry F. Stumpf, *American Judicial Politics,* 2d ed. (Upper Saddle River, NJ: Prentice Hall, 1998), pp. 369–370.

Bibliography: Stumpf, Harry F. *American Judicial Politics.* 2d ed. Upper Saddle River, NJ: Prentice Hall, 1998.

Footnote or endnote: 6. Neal C. Tate, "Personal Attribute Models of the Voting Behavior of U.S. Supreme Court Justices: Liberalism in Civil Liberties and Economic Decisions, 1946–1978," *American Political Science Review* 75 (June 1981): 359.

Bibliography: Tate, Neal C. "Personal Attribute Models of the Voting Behavior of U.S. Supreme Court Justices: Liberalism in Civil Liberties and Economic Decisions, 1946–1978." *American Political Science Review* 75 (June 1981): 355–367.

The examples found below are for footnote or endnote entries. I provide these examples with the understanding that students now know the general rules for transforming documentation citations into bibliographic entries. However, there are a few instances where the simple transformation rules do not apply. In such instances, I recommend through examples provided how the bibliographical entry should appear. Based on the seventeenth edition of *The Bluebook: A Uniform System of Citation,* I also provide examples of the dominant legal documentation style. Though this source is complete for writing legal documents and articles in professional journals, it is silent about the matter of bibliography format. That is, it is a suitable guide for footnotes or endnotes but is not useful for bibliographies. Using the now familiar language associated with computer word processing, my advice to those students who use the legal format for footnotes or endnotes is to adopt as a default the conventional bibliography format recommended for papers in the social sciences. Readers will also find below a section on how to document electronic sources, a matter that requires greater attention today that just a few years ago because of the growing presence of law-related materials on the World Wide Web and otherwise accessible information using personal computers.

Sample Citations

Footnoting or Endnoting Books

The following are examples of citations for many of the most common types of books. Below one will find examples for single-author books, books by more than one author, books in a series, books by an editor or translator, and many others. While this is not a complete list, writers will be able to find most of the examples they will require.

Book with One Author
1. Bradley J. Best, *Law Clerks, Support Personnel, and the Decline of Consensual Norms on the United States Supreme Court, 1935–1995* (New York: LFB Scholarly Publishing, 2002), p. 155

Book with One Author, Legal Format
1. BRADLEY J. BEST, LAW CLERKS, SUPPORT PERSONNEL, AND THE DECLINE OF CONSENSUAL NORMS ON THE UNITED STATES SUPREME COURT, 1935–1995 155 (2002).

Note especially the use of upper-case letters and the placement of the page number.

Book with Two Authors
2. Peter C. Hoffner and N. E. Hull, *Impeachment in America, 1635–1805* (New Haven: Yale University Press, 1985), pp. 50–65.

Book with Two Authors, Legal Format
2. PETER C. HOFFNER and N. E. HULL, IMPEACHMENT IN AMERICA, 1635–1805 50–65 (1985).

Book with Three Authors
3. Carl Kalvelage, Albert P. Melone, and Morley Segal, *Bridges to Knowledge in Political Science: A Handbook for Research* (Pacific Palisades, CA: Palisades Publishers, 1984), p. 138.

Book with Three Authors or More, Legal Format
3. CARL KALVELAGE et al., BRIDGES TO KNOWLEDGE IN POLITICAL SCIENCE: A HANDBOOK FOR RESEARCH 138 (1984).

Book with More than Three Authors
4. Donald Harris, et al., *Compensation and Support for Illness and Injury* (Oxford: Clarendon Press, 1984), p. 108.

Bibliography entry:
Harris, Donald, Mavis Maclean, Hazel Genn, Sally Lloyd-Bostock, Paul Feen, Peter Corfied, and Yvonne Brittan. *Compensation and Support for Illness and Injury.* Oxford: Clarendon Press, 1984.

Edition of a Book Other than the First
5. Laurence H. Tribe, *American Constitutional Law,* 2d ed. (Mineola, NY: Foundation Press, 1988), p. 1493.

Edition of a Book Other than the First, Legal Format
5. LAURENCE H. TRIBE, AMERICAN CONSTITUTIONAL LAW 1493 (2d ed. 1988).

Book in a Series
6. Lief H. Carter, *Contemporary Constitutional Law Making,* Pergamon Government and Politics Series (New York: Pergamon Press, 1985), p. 44.

Book in a Series, Legal Format
6. LIEF H. CARTER, CONTEMPORARY CONSTITUTIONAL LAW MAKING 44 (1985).

Book by Editor
7. Stuart S. Nagel, ed., *Handbook of Global Legal Policy* (New York: Marcel Dekker, 2000), p. 65.

Book by Editor/Translator, Legal Format
7. Stuart S. Nagel, ed. [trans.], HANDBOOK OF GLOBAL LEGAL POLICY 65 (2000).

If Nagel was the translator of the title then one should place the abbreviation for translator where the abbreviation for editor appears.

Book by Translator
8. Willi Paul Adams, *The First American Constitution: Republican Ideology and the Making of the State Constitutions in the Revolutionary Era,* trans. Rita Kimber and Robert Kimber (Chapel Hill: University of North Carolina Press, 1980), p. 164.

When both author and translator names appear on the title page, the translator's name should appear after the title. However, if the author's name is not on the title page, the translator's name should appear first, followed by the abbreviation *trans.*

Multivolume Book
9. Richard Loss, ed., *Corwin on the Constitution,* 2 vols. (Ithaca, NY: Cornell University Press, 1987), 2: 179–193.

Citation in One Book from Another Book
10. F. Frankfurter, *The Commerce Clause under Marshall, Taney and Waite,* pp. 80–82 as cited in David P. Currie, *The Constitution in the Supreme Court* (Chicago: University of Chicago Press, 1985), p. 449.

Bibliography entry:
Currie, David P. *The Constitution in the Supreme Court.* Chicago: University of Chicago Press, 1985.

Book Review

11. George Kannar, review of *Constitutional Choices* by Laurence Tribe, *The New Republic* (October 14, 1985), p. 33.

The first name cited is that of the reviewer of the book. The second name cited is the author of the book reviewed.

Book Review, Legal Format

11. David Sosa, *The Unintentional Fallacy,* 86 CAL. L. REV. 919 (1998) (reviewing ANTONIN SCALIA, A MATTER OF INTERPRETATION (1997)).

Book in a Series, One Author, Several Volumes, Each with a Different Title

12. Arthur M. Schlesinger, *The Age of Roosevelt,* 3 vols., *The Politics of Upheaval* (Boston: Houghton Mifflin, 1960), 3:215.

The first title is the name of the book series. The second title *(The Politics of Upheaval)* is the name of the specific cited volume.

Paperback Edition of a Book First Published in Hardcover

13. Bob Woodward and Scott Armstrong, *The Brethren: Inside the Supreme Court* (New York: Avon Books, paperback, 1979), pp. 85–92.

Introduction or Foreword of a Book by Another Author

14. Gilbert Y. Steiner, Foreword to *The Courts and Social Policy,* by Donald L. Horowitz (Washington, DC: Brookings Institution, 1977), p. i.

The first appearing name is the person writing the foreword or introduction to the book. It is his or her comments that are regarded as important and therefore are cited, not those of the author of the book.

Book with an Association as an Author

15. American Enterprise Institute for Public Policy Research, *Forming a Government under the Constitution* (Washington, DC: American Enterprise Institute for Public Policy Research, 1985), p. 35.

Author's Name Not on Title Page, but Known

16. (Alexander Hamilton), *Federalist,* No. 78 (New York: New American Library, 1961), p. 471.

Bibliography entry:
(Hamilton, Alexander; Madison, James; Jay, John). *The Federalist Papers.* New York: New American Library, 1961.

Ordinarily when citing generally to one of the *Federalist* papers it is acceptable to include the title of the work, the number, and the author in parentheses: *Federalist* No. 78 (Alexander Hamilton).

Article, Chapter, or Part of Another Book

17. John R. Coen, "On Worrying About the Constitution," in *The Humane Imagination,* edited by Charles L. Black, Jr. (Woodbridge: Ox Bow Press, 1986), p. 118.

Bibliography entry:
Black, Charles L., Jr., ed. *The Humane Imagination.* Woodbridge: Ox Bow Press, 1986.

Footnoting or Endnoting Journal and Magazine Articles

The following are examples of footnote or endnote citations for periodical literature. Readers will find examples for journal articles, magazines, and newspapers.

Academic Journal

18. Gregory A. Caldeira, "Public Opinion and the U.S. Supreme Court: FDR's Court-Packing Plan," *American Political Science Review* 81 (Dec. 1987): 1141.

Bibliography entry:

Caldeira, Gregory A. "Public Opinion and the U.S. Supreme Court: FDR's Court-Packing Plan." *American Political Science Review* 81 (Dec. 1987): 1139–1153.

See entry 19 for an example of the legal style for citing a law review article. However, I recommend for those writing a social science paper to cite all scholarly articles as suggested for entry 18.

Legal Periodical, Legal Format

19. Roger Handberg, *After the Fall: Justice Fortas' Judicial Values and Behavior After the Failure of His Nomination as Chief Justice,* 15 CAP. U. L. REV. 205 (1986).

Bibliography form:

Spell out the abbreviation for the law journal and employ the same usual rules for transforming a footnote or endnote into a bibliographical entry; see note 18.

Use this legal style only if requested by instructor. See entry 18 for the preferred style. Notice that the legal format style requires the abbreviation of law journal titles. For the list of abbreviations, see *The Bluebook: A Uniform System of Citation.* In the seventeenth edition, writers may locate the abbreviations in the contents under the heading "Abbreviations" (page xv).

Popular Magazine Article, No Author Given

20. "Supreme Court Ruling is Civil Rights Roadblock (Grove City Decision)", *Jet,* 7 April 1986, p. 10.

Popular Magazine Article, Author Given

21. Edwin Meese, "The Law of the Constitution," *National Review,* July 17, 1987, p. 30.

Popular Magazine Article, Author Given, Legal Format

21. Edwin Meese, "The Law of the Constitution," *National Review,* July 17, 1987 at 30.

Newspaper

22. Stephen Labotan, "Judges Mark 200 Years of Constitutional Law," *New York Times,* 19 July 1987, p. 88.

Some authorities suggest that because large-circulation newspapers have several editions with differing formats that writers drop the page numbers. I recommend, however, that page numbers always be included.

When the author byline is given, name the reporter at the beginning of the citation. For foreign newspapers that do not indicate the city in their titles, place the city name in parentheses, e.g., *Le Monde* (Paris).

Newspaper, Legal Format
22. Linda Greenhouse, *Election Case a Test and a Trauma for Justices*, N.Y. TIMES, February 20, 2001, at A18–19.

Footnoting Encyclopedias, Almanacs, and Other Works

Examples of footnote or endnote citations are given here for a variety of less commonly used sources. Examples included are for encyclopedias, almanacs, dissertations, and non-printed matter. Researchers should find that most contingencies have been addressed, or at least they should be able to fashion citations from the information given.

Signed Encyclopedia Article (not including legal encyclopedias)
23. Jeffrey Brandon Morris, "The Chase and Waite Courts and Era," *Encyclopedia of the American Judicial System*, Robert J. Janosik, ed. (New York: Charles Scribner's Sons, 1987), p. 95.

Bibliography entry:
Janosik, Robert J., ed. *Encyclopedia of the American Judicial System.* New York: Charles Scribner's Sons, 1987.

Unsigned Encyclopedia Article
24. *Encyclopedia Britannica*, 11th ed., s.v. "United States (of America)."

When citing popular encyclopedias or almanacs intended for the lay audience, writers normally omit the place of publication, publisher, date, and page numbers. Specify editions other than the first. When writers document the source more than a few times, they should reference page numbers when multiple pages are involved. The letters s.v. mean *sub verbo*, "under the word"; i.e., under the designated title.

Legal Encyclopedia
25. 70 Am. Jur. 2d *Sedition, Subversive Activities, and Treason* § 15 (1987).

Bibliography entry:
American Jurisprudence, 2d. s.v. *Sedition, Subversive Activities, and Treason* (1987).
25. 16 C.J.S. *Constitutional Laws* § 1256 (1985).

Bibliography entry:
Corpus Juris Secundum. s.v. *Constitutional Laws* (1985).

Legal Dictionary
26. *Black's Law Dictionary*, 95 6th ed. 1990, p. 95.

Almanac
27. *The World Almanac and Book of Facts 1985*, s. v. "Judiciary of the U. S."

Dissertation or Thesis
28. Marc Georges Pufong, "Trade Laws and the Class Dominance Thesis: The Role of the American Bar Association in National Trade Legislation and Policy" (Ph.D. dissertation, Southern Illinois University Carbondale, 1995), p. 414.
29. Jay T. Stokes, "The Issue of Judicial Recusals: An Investigation of Ideology, Impartiality, and the Recusal of Federal Judges" (M.A. thesis, Southern Illinois University Carbondale, 1997), p. 55.

Dissertation or Thesis, Legal Format

28. Allen Franklin Anderson, Jr., Plea Bargaining Rates in North Carolina: Some Determinants of Variability 41–42 (1984) (unpublished Ph.D. dissertation, Southern Illinois University Carbondale) (on file Morris Library, Southern Illinois University Carbondale).

Material from Manuscript Collections

30. Richard Richards, Administration of Justice and Courts, Richard Richards Papers, Library of University of California, Los Angeles, Los Angeles, California (1961), p. 4.

Material from Manuscript Collections, Legal Format

30. RICHARD RICHARDS, RICHARD RICHARDS PAPERS, ADMINISTRATION OF JUSTICE AND COURTS 4 (1961) Library of University of California, Los Angeles.

Radio or Television Program

31. NBC, NBC Nightly News, 9 March 1983, "President Reagan's Acceptance of Burford's Resignation," Chris Wallace, reporter.

Radio or Television Program, Legal Format

31. "President Reagan's Acceptance of Burford's Resignation" (NBC Nightly News Broadcast, Mar. 9, 1983).

Interview

32. Interview with Andrey Lukanov, member of Parliament, leader of the reform wing of the Bulgarian Communist Party, and former Prime Minister of Bulgaria, at the National Assembly Building, 1 Narodno Sabranie Square, Sofia, Bulgaria, October 14, 1993.

Interview, Legal Format

32. Interview with Andrey Lukanov, Bulgarian parliamentarian and former Prime Minister, at the parliament building, Sofia, Bulgaria (October 14, 1993).

Letter or Memorandum in Published Collection

33. Letter of Thomas Jefferson to Judge William Johnson, June 12, 1823, *The Writings of Thomas Jefferson,* Albert Ellery Bergh, ed., (Washington, DC: Thomas Jefferson Memorial Association, 1907), 15:447–48.

Bibliography entry:

Bergh, Albert Ellery, ed. *The Writings of Thomas Jefferson.* Washington, DC: Thomas Jefferson Memorial Association, 1907.

Nonprinted Report

34. Werner F. Grunbaum, "Selected Bibliography on Artificial Intelligence Applications and Expert Systems for Law," mimeographed (Law, Courts, and Judicial Process Section Newsletter, American Political Science Association, Spring, 1987), p. 12.

Booklet or Pamphlet

35. Alice O'Conner and Mary L. Henze, *"During Good Behavior": Judicial Independence and Accountability* (Washington, DC: The Jefferson Foundation, 1984), p. 5.

36. Illinois Office of Education, *Study Guide, Constitution of the State of Illinois and the United States* (Springfield, IL: State Board of Education, 1981), p. 21.

Italicize titles of booklets and pamphlets.

Booklet or Pamphlet, Legal Format

36. ILLINOIS OFFICE OF EDUCATION, STUDY GUIDE, CONSTITUTION
OF THE STATE OF ILLINOIS AND THE UNITED STATES 34 (1981).

Proceedings of a Meeting or Conference

37. The Bicentennial Conference of the United States Constitution, "Committee II—
Effectiveness of Governmental Operations," (Philadelphia, PA: April 5–8, 1986),
p. 123.

Paper Read or Speech Delivered at a Meeting

38. William Kitchin, "Russian Legal Reform: Judicial Aspirations and Political Realities" (Paper Delivered at the 1994 Interim Meeting of the Research Committee
on Comparative Judicial Studies, International Political Science Association)
Florence, Italy, August 2, 1994, p. 15.

Documenting Legal Sources

Examples of footnotes or endnotes for legal materials follow. In the past,
legal periodicals italicized case names in references but this is no longer the
case. Although the editors of *The Chicago Manual of Style,* 15th edition, recommend the use of italics for case names, I think this practice creates need-
less confusion. Therefore, italicize case names only when discussing cases in
the body of your text and when the case name is not followed by a full legal
citation. See also the discussion earlier in this chapter and in chapter 1 of
this volume.

U.S. Supreme Court (U.S.)

39. United States v. Lopez, 514 U.S. 549 (1995).

Bibliography entry:

United States v. Lopez. 514 U.S. 549 (1995).

Student writers all too often cite only the first page of an opinion and not
the particular page that a quotation or idea comes from. When referencing a
specific point found in a judge's opinion to a particular page, writers should
cite that specific page of the judicial opinion in the documentation. This rule
applies to all judicial opinions whatever the source; e.g., 446 U.S. 549 at 560
or 446 U.S. 549, 560.

In a bibliography or table of cases always list the first page on which the
judicial opinion appears in the court reporter. Do not cite a specific point
found in a judge's opinion on a particular page as one might do when footnot-
ing an opinion. This rule applies to all judicial opinions from whatever source.
Normally writers should list cases in a separate table of cases. However, when
the writer cites only a few cases it is appropriate to list them in alphabetical
order along with other references at the end of the paper in the bibliography.

U.S. Supreme Court (U.S.) **(reporter's name)**

40. Shelton v. Tiffin, 47 U.S. (6 How.) 163 (1848).

Federal Cases (F. Cas.)

41. Washington Mills v. Russell, 29 F. Cas. 336 (C.C.D. Mass. 1873) (No. 17,247).

Federal Reporter (F.), (F. 2d), (F. 3d)
42. Hong Kong Supermarket v. Kizer, 839 F. 2d 1078 (9th Cir. 1987).

Federal Appendix (Fed. Appx.)
43. U.S. v. Green, 53 Fed. Appx. 189 (4th Cir. 2003).

Federal Supplement (F. Supp.)
44. Pestrak v. Ohio Elections Commission, 670 F. Supp. 1368 (S.D. Ohio 1987).

Federal Rules Decisions (F.R.D.)
45. Hawthorne v. Gulf Shores, Inc., 115 F.R.D. 474 (1986).

American Law Reports (A.L.R.) **Annotation**
46. William B. Johnson, "Use of Plea Bargain or Grant of Immunity as Improper Vouching for Credibility of Witnesses in Federal Cases," 76 A.L.R. Fed. (1986), p. 409.

In bibliography entries include the first and last pages of the annotation and spell out the abbreviations.

American Law Reports (A.L.R.) **Annotation, Legal Format**
46. William B. Johnson, Annotation, *Use of Plea Bargain or Grant of Immunity as Improper Vouching for Credibility of Witness in Federal Cases*, 76 A.L.R. Fed. 409 (1986).

American Law Reports (A.L.R.) **Opinion**
47. Loose v. Offshore Navigation, 68 A.L.R. Fed. 318 (1984).

United States Law Week (U.S.L.W.)
48. Gulfstream Aerospace Corp. v. Mayacamas Corp., 56 U.S.L.W. 4243 (March 22, 1988).

State Cases
49. Adams v. Barrell, 132 A. 130 (Me. 1926).
50. Byrd v. Peterson, 66 Ariz. 253, 186 P. 2d 955 (1947).

When possible, cite both the official reporter and the West regional reporter. Include the state name when a state does not have its own reporter or if official reports are unavailable.

Briefs, Oral Arguments, Transcripts, and Records
51. Petitioner's Brief at 7. Mazer v. Stein, 347 U.S. 201 (1953), in 1953 FO No. 228, card 2, *Information Handling Service.*

Bibliography entry:
Petitioner's Brief. Mazer v. Stein, 347 U.S. 201 (1953), in 1953 FO No. 228, card 2, *Information Handling Service.*
52. Respondent's Brief at 594. Kissinger v. Halperin, 452 U.S. 713 (1981), in vol. 123, *Landmark Briefs and Arguments of the Supreme Court of the United States: Constitutional Law.*

Bibliography entry:
Respondent's Brief. Kissinger v. Halperin, 452 U.S. 713 (1981), in vol. 123, *Landmark Briefs and Arguments of the Supreme Court of the United States: Constitutional Law.*
53. Oral Argument by Harry D. Miller, Esq. on behalf of Appellants at 22. Pennell v. San Jose, 108 S. Ct. 849 (1988), on Fiche 28, *University Publications of America.*

Bibliography entry:
Oral Argument by Harry D. Miller, Esq. on behalf of Appellants. Pennell v. San Jose,
    108 S. Ct. 849 (1988), on Fiche 28, *University Publications of America.*
54. Transcript of Record at 23. Mazer v. Stein, 347 U.S. 201 (1953), in 1953 FO No.
    228, card 1, *Information Handling Service.*
Bibliography entry:
Transcript of Record. Mazer v. Stein, 347 U.S. 201 (1953), in 1953 FO No. 228, card
    1, *Information Handling Service.*

For briefs, oral arguments, transcripts, and records, first describe what is
being cited and end with a period. Follow the initial entry with the full legal citation to the case. As a courtesy to the reader, writers should provide the source
where the information is found. Cite petitions, complaints, and other court
records in the same way. The first words describe the nature of the document.

Briefs, Oral Arguments, Transcripts, and Records, Legal Format
51. Brief for Petitioner at 7. Mazer v. Stein, 347 U.S. 201 (1953) (No 228).

Federal Statute
55. *Department of Defense Authorization Act, 1985,* Publ. L. No. 98-525, 98 Stat. 2492
    (1984).

Cite statutes commonly referred to by their official or popular name. For
example: Comprehensive Employment and Training Act, 29 U.S.C. (1978) §
834 (Supp. IV 1980). It is permissible to substitute the word *section*, or its
abbreviation *sec.*, for the section symbol (§). Modern word-processing programs typically contain the symbol, so whenever possible, writers should use
the section character rather than the word *section* or its abbreviation. When
referring to more than one section of an act use two symbols as in §§ 834–837.

Federal Code
56. Fraud and Related Activity in Connection with Access Devices, U.S.C. § 1029 (2000).
57. Public Health Service Administration, 42 U.S.C.S. § 205 (LEXIS Law, 1994).
58. Departmental Regulations, 5 U.S.C.A. § 301 (West Group 2003 Supp. Pamph.).

U.S. Constitution
59. U.S. Const. art. II, § 3.

U.S. Constitution, Legal Format
59. U.S. CONST. art. II, § 3.

Federal Register (Fed. Reg.)
60. Visa Waver for Certain Cotton Terry Bar Mops, 50 Fed. Reg. 32,467 (1985).

Code of Federal Regulations (C.F.R.)
61. Standard for Nitrogen Oxides, 40 C.F.R. § 60.44a (1987).

Footnoting or Endnoting Government Documents
The form for government documents is unlike that adopted for books
and articles and often is a source of confusion. In general, references to government documents should include in the following order: (1) the country
(U.S.), (2) the branch of government (legislative, executive), (3) the sub-

branch or branches (House, Senate, Judiciary Committee), (4) the document title (italicized), (5) the name of the document series or sequence and the facts of publication (H. Rept. 342 to Accompany H.R. 6258, 95th Cong., 1st sess., 1977). For bibliographic entries follow the usual rules: substitute periods for commas, drop page references, and eliminate abbreviations with completely spelled words.

Legislative Bill

62. U.S. Congress, House, *Authorization for Childhood Immunization*, H.R. 5230, 99th Cong., 2d sess., 1986, p. 2.
63. U.S. Congress, Senate, *Violent Crime and Drug Enforcement Act of 1982*, S2572, 97th Cong., 2d sess., 1982, p. 7.

Legislative Bill, Legal Format

62. H.R. 5230, 99th Cong., 2d sess. 2 (1986).

Legislative Debate

64. U.S. Congress, Senate, Balanced Budget—Tax Limitation Constitutional Amendment, 97th Cong., 2d sess., 13 July 1982, *Congressional Record*, 128, no. 12, S15922.

Legislative Report

65. U.S. Congress, House, *The Changing Distribution of Industrial Profits: The Oil and Gas Industry Within the Fortune 500, 1978–1980.* H. Rept. 97-390, 97th Cong., 1st sess., 1981. p. 2.

Legislative Hearings

66. U.S. Congress, House, Committee on the Judiciary, *Immigration and Naturalization Act Amendments of 1986, Hearings before the Subcommittee on Immigration, Refugees, and International Law of the Committee on the Judiciary on H.R. 444*, 99th Cong., 2d sess., 1986, pp. 23–41.

Legislative Hearings, Legal Format

66. *Immigration and Naturalization Act Amendments of 1986, Hearings before the Subcommittee on Immigration*, 99th Cong., 2d sess., 23–41 (1986).

Executive Department

67. Executive Office of the President, Office of Management and Budget, *Budget of the United States Government, Fiscal Year 1987* (Washington, DC: U.S. Government Printing Office, 1987), p. 5/102–5/107.
68. General Accounting Office, *The Seizure of the Mayaguez: A Case Study of Crisis Management*, GAO ID-76-45 (May, 1976), pp. 114–128.

Government agencies often imprint documents with publication numbers and specify publication series. If such numbers are available, include them in citations. At times, author names are printed on documents and in such instances writers should cite the authors. However, libraries often do not catalog government documents by author name. Thus, do not neglect to include sponsoring agencies in citations.

Presidential Paper

69. U.S. President, "Veto of War Powers Resolution," *Weekly Compilation of Presidential Documents*, vol. 9, October 27, 1973, p. 1285.

Treaty

70. *U.S. Statutes at Large*, vol. 43, pt. 2 (December 1923–March 1925), "Naval Arms Limitation Treaty," February 26, 1922, ch. 1, art. 1, p. 1655.
71. U.S. Department of State, *United States Treaties and Other International Agreements*, vol. 27, pt. 2, "Soviet Socialist Republics, Union of—ABM Treaty," TIAS No. 8276, 3 July 1974.

Beginning in 1950, U.S. treaties are found in the publication *United States Treaties and Other International Agreements*. The United Nations also publishes a treaty series, formerly published by the League of Nations, that includes international agreements.

Treaty, Legal Format

70. Naval Arms Limitation Treaty, Feb. 26, 1922, 43 Stat Ch. 1, Art. 1, p. 1655.

International Organizations

72. United Nations, *Report of the Secretary-General Submitted under General Assembly Resolution 39/146 of 14 December 1984, Covering the Developments in the Middle East in All Aspects* (A/40/779), 1985, p. 2.

Kate Turabian has suggested that citations for international documents include authorizing body, topic or title, document or series number when available, and publication date.

State Document

73. Illinois, Secretary of State, *Handbook of Illinois Government*, April, 1999, p. 67.
74. Illinois Const. art. II, § 1.

Specify the date of the constitution if the constitution cited is not the one currently in force, for example, Illinois Const. (1848), art. I, § 2.

Local Document

75. Carbondale, Illinois, City Manager, "City of Carbondale, Illinois Annual Budget FY 1987–88," mimeographed (April 10, 1987), p. 16.

Often there is insufficient documentation for state and local materials. It may be necessary to improvise because many of these materials are often unknown to librarians and in many cases never find their way into public libraries. Citations for state and local government documents, however, should follow the same form as that used for U.S. government documents.

Documentation for Electronic Sources

Because today researchers often conduct their work using electronic sources including the Internet, writers are faced with the problem of how to properly document their research. Presently, there is no consensus on a uniform documentation format for electronic sources. *The Chicago Style of Manual*, the MLA, the APA, and the *Uniform System of Citation* each has a slightly differing approach. Other bodies and institutions have offered their own style sheets for documenting electronic sources. Bedford/St. Martin's provides an online site where writers may make themselves familiar with the various citation styles for online sources available today. As of mid-2003, that site is found at http://www.bedfordsmartins.com/online/cite7.html. But because sites change in time, you may be directed to another address or you may find it necessary to surf the Web for this information.

While the various style sheets are not consistent, writers should adhere to several basic rules when citing electronic sources. State the full facts of publication in the same way that one cites those facts for print sources. This means citations should include the author, the title of the work, the place of publication, the publisher, and the date of publication. Indicate that the source is available online at a specific URL address. And indicate the date that you accessed the source with the words *as of.* . . . I provide a number of examples below.

76. Gerhard Rempel, "Course Lecture Notes on Mercantilism, Western New England College," available online at http://www.mars.acnet.wnec.edu/~grempel/ courses/wc2/lectures/mechantilism.html, as of September 25, 2001.

Readers will find if they try to locate the source with the address given that they will be unable to do so. While the address was correct on September 25, 2001, as of July 27, 2003 this lecture is no longer available online. This example represents a major problem with using the Internet to write papers; it is not always possible to verify sources.

77. *Microsoft Encarta Online Encyclopedia 2001,* "Hudson's Bay Company," available at http://encarta.msn.com as of September 25, 2001.
78. U.S. Securities and Exchange Commission, *The Laws that Govern the Securities Industry,* available online at http://www.sec.gov.about/laws.html, as of November 27, 2001.

Case Law Citations to Electronic Sources

Alan L. Dworsky, the author of the *User's Guide to the Bluebook*,[2] offers excellent suggestions for citing case materials from LEXIS, Westlaw, and the Internet. Although his suggestions are made for formal legal writing, I urge readers to apply his general approach when citing court opinions and statutory law to LexisNexis Academic, Westlaw Campus, and the variety of Internet sources for case law and statutory law that I discuss in chapter 1 of this book. Dworsky names seven elements of a citation for electronic databases that I boil down to six. The recommended order of these elements for case law is as follows. (1) The name of the case (e.g., Board of Regents v. Southworth). (2) The case number that the court assigned to the case (e.g., No. 98-1189). (3) The date when the case was decided (e.g., 2000), not to be confused with the date a given dispute is argued before the court. (4) The name of the database (such as LexisNexis Academic or Westlaw Campus). (5) The number used by the database to identify the particular opinion (2196). (6) In parentheses give the abbreviated court name and full date of the opinion, e.g., (U.S. March 22, 2000). When we put the six parts of the citation together, the following is the result:

79. Board of Regents v. Southworth, No. 98-1189, 2000 LEXIS 2196 (U.S. March 22, 2000).

If the source for the court opinion is a non-subscription Internet service such as Findlaw.com, the Legal Information Institute of Cornell University Law School, or Oyez, then add *available at* . . . to the end of entry 79. The URL follows immediately and finally the date the researcher accessed the opinion.

80. Board of Regents v. Southworth, No. 98-1189, 529 U.S. 217 (U.S. March 22, 2000), available at http://www.oyez.org/oyez/resource/case/1372, as of June 13, 2003.

Statutory Law Citation to Electronic Sources

If print sources to statutory and codified law are unavailable, then the next best source is electronic. These sources may include, for example, Lexis-Nexis Academic, Westlaw Campus, the Legal Information Institute of Cornell University Law School, or the alternative sources one may locate on the World Wide Web for the *U.S. Code Gopher,* as well as other Web sites for state codes. Similar to the format recommended by Dworsky for case law, I urge writers to adopt one of two systems for documenting statutory law. The simplest and most straightforward method is to state the name of the act in question, followed by the title number and the name of the code, followed by the appropriate section number. Instead of placing only the year of the code in parentheses, also indicate the electronic source, for example, LexisNexis Academic (2002). See entry 81 for an example. The system adopted by Dworsky provides greater specificity than the simpler form just described because the writer documents the currency of the legislation in the citation itself, per entry 82.[3] The latter format is recommended for papers using the formal legal documentation system found in *The Bluebook: A Uniform System of Citation.*

81. Federal Tort Liability Act, 5 U.S.C.S § 8128 (LexisNexis Academic, 2003).
82. Federal Tort Liability Act, 5 U.S.C.S § 8128 (LexisNexis Academic through P.L. 108-30, May 29, 2003).

Later References to the Same Footnote or Endnote Source

A good research paper displays references to a wide variety of source material. However, it is common to reference a single source more than once. Shorten all second and later note references. Fortunately, the general rules for doing so have simplified over the years into the following three:

1. For references to the same work with no intervening notes simply use the Latin term *ibid.,* meaning "in the same place." Today, the word "ibid." is no longer italicized. Place the word in ordinary roman type.

2. For second references with no intervening note that are located on a different page of the same work, use ibid. and the page number, for example: Ibid., p. 101. Shortened versions are treated basically the same but use *Id.* or *supra* in place of *ibid.* Use *Id.* when employing the legal format. Notice that the word *Id.* is italicized when using the *Harvard Bluebook* format for legal citations.

3. For second references with intervening notes, indicate the author's last name, but not first name or initials unless another author of the

same name is cited. This information is followed by a shortened title of the work, and the specific page number that is being referenced. If one is employing the legal format use *supra* for intervening footnotes or endnotes.

Below are examples of second citations following first citations of a representative number of works.

Second References with Intervening Citations

Book, Single Volume
3. Lawrence Baum, *The Supreme Court* (Washington, DC: Congressional Quarterly Press, 1981), p. 42.
8. Baum, *The Supreme Court*, p. 101.

Book, Single Volume, Legal Format
8. BAUM, *supra* note 3, at 101.

Journal Article
4. James Murray, "The Role of Analogy in Legal Reasoning," *U.C.L.A. Law Review* 29 (1982): 833.
9. Murray, "Role of Analogy," p. 840.

Journal Article, Legal Format
9. Murray, *supra* note 4, at 840.

Government Document
11. U.S. Congress, Senate, Balanced Budget—Tax Limitation Constitutional Amendment, 97th Cong., 2d sess., 13 July 1982, *Congressional Record*, 128, no. 12, S15922.
15. U.S. Congress, Senate, Balanced Budget, S15922.

Government Document, Legal Format
15. U.S. Congress, *supra* note 11, at 129.

Judicial Opinion
2. Dames and Moore v. Reagan, 453 U.S. 654 (1981).
31. 453 U.S. at 655. *Or* 453 U.S. 654, 655.

Note that a second reference to a court opinion often references a different page number from the first citation. Writers may reference the actual page number alone. Alternatively, writers may indicate the original citation at the first page in the volume of the reporter in which the opinion appears followed by a comma and the actual page in the opinion from which a quote or idea is taken. A common error committed by students is failing to document the actual page in the court opinion from which they quote or paraphrase an idea. Writers always should provide precise page numbers so that readers may verify quotes or paraphrases.

In-Text Citation Form

Today, most political science and other social science journals have adopted systems of in-text citation based in large part on the documentation style first recommended by the American Psychological Association. Because social scientists publish many of their studies in these periodicals, they are familiar with the format and naturally encourage their students to employ the same documentation style. The in-text citation format allows readers to discern the source of a statement instantly and writers to edit and type a paper easily. It does present a disadvantage, however: the interruption of the flow of ideas and sentences caused by the intrusion of author names, publication dates, and pagination. Papers about constitutional law tend to exhibit more references than papers for other academic topics. As a result, I do not recommend the in-text format for law-related papers that document many court opinions. Cluttering the body of the text with parenthetical statements makes clear communication of complex ideas more difficult.

Writers using in-text citations do not use the conventionally numbered footnote or endnote. Instead, they employ parenthetical references that indicate the author's last name, the year of publication, and pagination, for example, "In general, seminal thinkers such as Weber (Gerth and Mills 1946, 85), Durkheim (1958, 7–8), and Tocqueville (1945, 275–276), admonish their readers to ponder the crucial or strategic position enjoyed by attorneys in the making of public policy."

The format for in-text references varies from journal to journal and from one discipline to another. In past editions of this book, I recommended a hybrid variety. However, because most papers in constitutional law written at the undergraduate and graduate level are in the discipline of political science, I now recommend with minor modifications the format adopted by the Committee on Publications of the American Political Science Association in *Style Manual for Political* Science.[4]

Guide to In-Text References

Place all but explanatory footnotes or endnotes (discursive comments) in the body of the text.

Parenthetical references should include author, year of publication, and pagination. It is unnecessary to cite page numbers if the documentation refers to the entire work. However, when working with constitutional law topics, pagination is usually required because references tend to be very specific.

Repeat earlier citation for second or later references. In other words, do not use the word *ibid.* or any other abbreviation when using in-text citations.

Notice that the parenthetical reference is part of the sentence and therefore is located within the punctuation of the sentence.

List all works cited in the text at the end of the paper under references. The list should include works found in the explanatory footnotes or endnotes and notes that may appear in tables and figures. Do not list as a reference any source that one might have consulted, but did not actually cite in the body of the paper.

Writers should reference explanatory comments in the same way as they do in the body of the text, but with footnote numbers placed in the body of the text. Writers may properly place comments on the page where the super-scripted numbers are located or together at the end of the manuscript immediately before the references. When using endnotes rather than footnotes, list each in numerical order under a heading "Notes." In general, editors of social science journals discourage but do not prohibit the use of discursive references. Indeed, such notes may be necessary to elucidate important points.

Author Surname Not in Body of Text

If as the writer you do not mention the author's name in the body of the text, then the author's surname should be the first item in the parentheses. The author's name is followed by the year of publication, followed by a comma and page number(s) if referencing specific pages.

He regards this "Populist-Progressive" position as historically untenable (Mendelson 1985, 264). (The word "He" in the sentence refers to Mendelson.)

Author Surname in Body of Text

If the author's name is mentioned in the body of the text, then the writer should provide readers with the year of publication listed first, followed by a comma, and then the page number.

Mendelson (1985, 264) regards this "Populist-Progressive" position as historically untenable.

More than One Author

Sometimes there is need to point to several sources supporting the same or similar points. Join single references with semicolons.

. . . public concern over crime and police protection have shown that these issues are tailor-made for politicians aspiring to office and ill-suited to incumbents . . . (Finckenauer, 1978; Buffum and Sagi, 1983; McPherson, 1983; and Guyot, 1983).

Reference to Same Author and Same Year

At times scholars publish more than one piece in the same year. Writers may distinguish among publications by inserting the letters *a, b, c,* and so on in both the manuscript body and on the references page at the end of the paper.

. . . (Nagel, 2000a, 6).
. . . (Nagel, 2000b, 38).
. . . (Nagel, 2000c, 154).

Judicial Opinion Cited in the Body of the Text

Writers citing court opinions and administrative-agency decisions should place them in the body of the text. Italicize the case name followed by the date in parentheses. When citing a particular page of a judicial opinion, place it after the date preceded by a comma. For second and later references, repeat the case name but delete the date.

... *United States Trust Co. v. New Jersey* (1977).
... *United States Trust Co. v. New Jersey* (1977, 13).
... *United States Trust Co. v. New Jersey*, 14.

Judicial Opinion Cited in the References

Writers citing court opinions in their papers must also include full documentation in the references appearing at the end of the paper. List each case alphabetically by case name, followed by the date of the decision, the volume of the reporter, the name of the reporter, and the first page where the opinion begins. If the citation is to a particular lower court then following the page number, writers should place the abbreviated name of the that court in parentheses.

Hill v. Colorado. 2000. 530 U.S. 703.
Republic of Philippines v. Marcos. 1987. 665 F. Supp. 793 (N.D. Cal.).
Armstead v. State. 1996. 673 A.2d 221 (Md. 1996).

Government Document

Writers should reference government documents parenthetically in the body of the text. The form is similar to other citations. List the country (U.S.), the branch of government (Congress), the sub-branch or branches (House or Senate), and the year of publication, followed by a comma and pagination.

... The commission submitted its report to President Nixon in 1971, who hailed the report as a "broad comprehensive framework in which to decide the issues involved in reform of the Federal Criminal Code" (U.S. Congress. Senate. 1971, 5).

Other Legal Material

Citation of other legal sources such as codes, encyclopedias, and annotations also should appear in the body of the text. Parenthetical references should include author, year of publication, and pagination. It is permissible to cite the title of the source itself when there is no author; instead of pagination, insert section numbers.

... (18 U.S.C. 2000, § 1028).

(This citation means Title 18 of the *United States Code* for the 2000 edition at section 1028.)

References at the End of the Paper

Because parenthetical citations are brief, it is necessary to provide readers with additional facts of publication so that they may actually locate the publications that the writer has cited. The in-text citation format requires writers to list all cited materials together at the end of the paper in alphabetical order by author. *References* differ from a *bibliography* in that they do not require under any circumstance the listing of all materials consulted in researching and writing. On the contrary, a reference includes only those materials actually cited in the body of the text. Include all author names in all works by multiple authors. The forms for books, articles, associations as author, and dissertations or theses differ. List judicial opinions alphabetically with full citation to volume, reporter series, first page where the opinion begins in the reporter, and year of the decision. When there are more than a few cases, place the list at the end of the paper under a separate title, "Cases Cited."

Sample Reference Page

Book

Barber, Sotirios. 1984. *On What the Constitution Means*. Baltimore: Johns Hopkins University Press.

Golding, Martin. 1983. *Legal Reasoning*. New York: Alfred A. Knopf.

McLaughlin, Andrew Cummingham. 1972a. *The Courts, the Constitution, and Parties: Studies in Constitutional History and Politics*. New York: Da Capo Press.

McLaughlin, Andrew Cummingham. 1972b. *The Foundations of American Constitutionalism*. Gloucester, MA: P. Smith.

Miller, Arthur Selwyn. 1982. *Towards Increased Judicial Activism: The Political Role of the Supreme Court*. Westport, CT: Greenwood Press.

Scheb, John M., and John M. Scheb, II. 1999. *Criminal Law and Procedure*. 3d ed. Belmont, CA: West/Wadsworth.

Articles

Dyer, James A. 1976. "Do Lawyers Vote Differently? A Study of Voting on No-Fault Insurance." *Journal of Politics* 38 (May):452–456.

Green, Justin J., John R. Schmidhauser, Larry L. Berg, and David Brady. 1973. "Lawyers in Congress: A New Look at Some Old Assumptions." *Western Political Quarterly* 26 (September): 440–452.

Associations

American Bar Association. 1985. *Report of American Bar Association*. Chicago: American Bar Association.

Theses or Dissertations

Prescott, James Frank. 1997. "A Comprehensive Analysis of United States Supreme Court Appropriations 1789–1994." Ph.D. diss. [alternatively, Master's thesis.] Southern Illinois University Carbondale.

Government Documents

U.S. Congress. Senate. Committee on the Judiciary. 1971. Reform of the Federal Criminal Laws. Hearings before the Subcommittee on Criminal Laws and Procedures, Part I. 92d Cong., 1st sess. 24 February. [Give the exact date of the hearing in place of the document number].

Judicial Opinions

Carson v. National Bank. 1974. 501 F. 2d 1082.

Ohio v. Wyandotte Chemicals Corp. 1971. 401 U.S. 493.

Endnotes

[1] (Cambridge, MA: The Harvard Law Review Association, 2000), p. 52.

[2] (Littleton, CO: Fred B. Rothman, 2000), pp. 15–16.

[3] Ibid., pp. 40–41.

[4] American Political Science Association, Committee on Publications, *Style Manual for Political Science*, revised edition (Washington, DC: American Political Science Association, 2001).

6

SUMMARIES OF LEADING SUPREME COURT DECISIONS

Introduction

This chapter contains summaries of 94 leading Supreme Court decisions. These cases are presented to acquaint students with the essential features of each decision. The summaries are only digests of the facts and decisions in each case—a two-paragraph summary cannot do justice to the richness found in most Supreme Court decisions. They are not substitutes for reading and studying each decision. Neither should these summaries be confused with a written brief of each case. Lower court holdings and actions typically are not included nor are discussions of dissenting opinions. Therefore, readers should view these summaries as nothing more than a study tool or a way to refresh one's memory.

There are several acceptable ways to use these summaries. Beginning students of constitutional law often encounter references to so-called landmark decisions. These references sometimes are made with the assumption that readers are already familiar with the case or that they will become acquainted at a later time, perhaps after several hundred pages of reading. The summaries, arranged in alphabetical order, provide a ready reference for the essential elements of each case. By turning to the cited decision, students may quickly obtain a working knowledge of the case. Second, as a quality control, these summaries may be used for comparison. Even after reading a case and completing an extensive written brief, students may be unsure of their understanding of the case. Certitude in such matters is difficult to obtain, even for the most seasoned scholar. Although it must be reemphasized that these summaries are not the equivalent of briefs, students may wish to refer to this chapter to determine whether their understanding of the case is roughly consistent. Third, both students and teachers need a quick reference when studying related topics and issues. For example, a course in political parties will often make reference to the case of Smith v. Allwright, 321 U.S. 649 (1944), which declared the Texas all-white primary system unconstitutional. The summary of this case can offer a quick reminder of its essentials. Lastly, the summaries may make a valuable contribution to an individual's private reference library for the years ahead.

Summaries

Abington Township v. Schempp
(*see*, School District of Abington Township v. Schempp)

Adarand Constructors, Inc. v. Pena
515 U.S. 200, 115 S. Ct. 2097, 132 L. Ed. 2d 158 (1995)

Adarand, a white-owned construction firm, submitted to a prime contractor the low bid on a subcontract for a federal highway project. Instead, a minority-controlled small business, Gonzales Construction, was awarded the contract. Federal law required a prime contractor be given a financial incentive to hire minority subcontractors; therefore, Gonzales was awarded this federal contract. A federal district court upheld the affirmative-action program, and a federal appeals court subsequently affirmed, concluding that previous Supreme Court precedents support the lower court decision.

Writing for a 6–3 majority, Justice Sandra Day O'Connor reversed the court of appeals. She applied the strict-scrutiny mode of constitutional interpretation employed in the state case of *Richmond, City of v. J.A. Croson Co.* (1989) to federal affirmative-action programs. Any preference based on racial or ethnic criteria must necessarily receive a most searching examination. The standard of review and the equal protection analysis applied under the Fourteenth Amendment to state cases is the same for Fifth Amendment cases involving the national government. The Supreme Court wrongly decided past cases requiring only intermediate scrutiny, and therefore overruled those cases.

Alden v. Maine
527 U.S. 709, 119 S. Ct. 2240, 114 L. Ed. 2d 636 (1999)

Probation officers in the employ of the state of Maine sought compensation due them for overtime work as required under the Federal Fair Labor Standards Act of 1938. A congressional act permits state employees to sue states in their own courts to recover under the law. However, a state trial court dismissed the action on the ground of sovereign immunity, and the Maine Supreme Judicial Court affirmed.

In a hotly contested 5–4 decision, the Court's majority, led by Anthony Kennedy, held that the Federal Fair Labor Standards Act authorizing private actions against states in their own courts without their consent violates Maine's sovereign immunity guaranteed under the Eleventh Amendment. Though the prohibition does not flow from a literal reading of the Eleventh Amendment, the Constitution's structure and its history argue for a view of federalism that does not violate the common law principle that a sovereign may not be sued without its consent.

Baker v. Carr
369 U.S. 186, 82 S. Ct. 691, 7 L. Ed. 2d 663 (1962)

The Tennessee General Assembly in 1901 enacted legislation apportioning its two chambers utilizing the federal census of 1900. It provided for subsequent reapportionment every ten years. Despite the fact that the state's population continually shifted from rural to urban centers, the legislature failed for more than sixty years to redistribute the legislative seats. In 1959, charging that as urban residents they were being denied the equal protection of the laws guaranteed by the Fourteenth Amendment, Baker and other qualified voters brought suit under federal civil-rights statutes.

Writing for the majority, Justice William Brennan first addressed the question of subject matter jurisdiction. Brennan made two points: (1) the appellants claim a denial of equal protection of the laws in violation of the Fourteenth Amendment and (2) since this claim was not deemed insubstantial and frivolous, the district court, by virtue of article III, section 2, as extended by Congress to the district courts by statutory enactment, does possess jurisdiction over the subject matter. As to the second important question, standing to sue, Brennan reasoned that because Baker and the others had a personal stake in the outcome of the controversy, effective voting power, they had satisfied the standing to sue requirement. Lastly, Brennan held that this ". . . challenge to an apportionment represents no nonjusticiable 'political question.'" The district court, argued Brennan, misinterpreted Colegrove v. Green, 328 U.S. 549, and other decisions of the Supreme Court in applying the political question doctrine to this case. The political question cases refer to the relationship between the judiciary and other coordinate branches of the national government, not to the federal judiciary's relationship to the state governments.

Barenblatt v. United States
360 U.S. 109, 79 S. Ct. 1081, 3 L. Ed. 2d 1115 (1959)

Lloyd Barenblatt, a former college instructor, refused to answer questions before a subcommittee of the House Committee on Un-American Activities. The subcommittee was investigating alleged communist infiltration in the field of education. Barenblatt claimed that compelling his testimony was neither authorized by Congress nor constitutionally permissible given the vagueness of Rule XI of the House of Representatives. Barenblatt also argued that he was not adequately apprised of the pertinence of the committee's questions to the subject matter under investigation. Lastly, he objected that the inquiry infringed on his First Amendment rights. Barenblatt was convicted in federal district court of contempt of Congress. After two appeals to the District of Columbia Court of Appeals, the U.S. Supreme Court decided the case.

With Justice John Harlan writing for a bare majority, Barenblatt's contempt conviction was upheld. Distinguishing the Court's decision in Watkins v. U.S., 354 U.S. 178 (1957), Harlan stated that the Court reversed the Watkins conviction "solely" on the ground that he had not been adequately apprised of the committee's subject matter or of the pertinency of the questions that he refused to answer. While Rule XI of the House is rather vague, the Court did not base its decision in *Watkins* on such a "broad and inflexible holding" as is claimed by Barenblatt. Moreover, given the fact that the House of Representatives has continued to support the life of the committee, it cannot be argued seriously that the investigation of communist activities and the use of the compulsory process was beyond that which the House had intended. Barenblatt's pertinency objection was not sustained because the subject matter of the inquiry was made plain by the subcommittee at the commencement of its proceedings, and given Barenblatt's own written memorandum there is little doubt that he was fully aware of the pertinency of the questions. Additionally, unlike Watkins, Barenblatt refused to answer queries concerning his own affiliation with the Communist Party. Harlan met the First Amendment argument with a balancing-of-interests approach. Ordinarily, argued Harlan, the activities of the Committee on Un-American Activities would be viewed as presenting a grave danger to First Amendment rights. But the Communist Party, stated Harlan, is not "an ordinary political party." The goal of the Communist Party is to overthrow the government of the United States by force and violence and since the self-preservation of society is of "ultimate value," the balance between the rights of society and the rights of individuals must be struck in favor of society.

Barron v. Baltimore
32 U.S. (7 Pet.) 243, 8 L. Ed. 672 (1833)

The city of Baltimore effectively destroyed John Barron's wharf. It redirected the course of several streams, which resulted in large deposits of sand surrounding the wharf. As a result, vessels could not approach Barron's wharf because of the shallow waters. A county court awarded Barron damages but an appellate court reversed the decision in favor of the city. Barron appealed to the U.S. Supreme Court arguing that Baltimore took his private property without just compensation violating the Fifth Amendment to the U.S. Constitution.

Writing for the Supreme Court, Chief Justice John Marshall held that the Fifth Amendment and the Bill of Rights in general are constraints on the national government, not state or local governments. The people of the United States established the general government for themselves, not for the governments of the individual states. The people intended for the Bill of Rights to operate against the possible abuses of the new central government, and not against the state governments.

Boerne, City of v. Flores
521 U.S. 507, 117 S. Ct. 2157, 138 L. Ed. 2d 624 (1997)

P. F. Flores, the Catholic Archbishop of San Antonio, applied for a building permit to expand the space available of the existing church at Boerne, Texas. City officials denied the permit because they felt the historic mission style of the church and its surroundings would be sacrificed. The church then brought suit under the Religious Freedom Restoration Act of 1993 (RFRA). It claimed that under the act the city is obliged to demonstrate a compelling state interest and not merely a rational basis for its action because freedom of religion is at issue. The Act was passed in an attempt to reverse a prior Supreme Court decision (*Employment Division of the Department of Human Resources of Oregon v. Smith* (1990)); the Supreme Court in that case employed the rational basis test instead of the commonly understood preferred freedoms approach of compelling state interest. A federal district court found in favor of the city holding RFRA unconstitutional. A federal appeals court, however, reversed the lower court.

Justice Anthony Kennedy, writing for the majority, held that the RFRA provision requiring a compelling state interest is an unconstitutional use of the Fourteenth Amendment's Enforcement Clause (section 5). Because Congress had attempted to decree the substance of the Fourteenth Amendment, it overstepped its authority under the amendment's enforcement provision. It is the task of the Supreme Court, not Congress, to say what the Constitution means.

Bolling v. Sharpe
347 U.S. 497, 74 S. Ct. 693, 98 L. Ed. 884 (1954)

This case arose when African-American children were denied admission to a public school in the District of Columbia solely because of their race. They alleged that such segregation deprived them of due process of law under the Fifth Amendment.

Delivered on the same day as Brown v. Board of Education of Topeka I, 347 U.S. 483 (1954), Chief Justice Earl Warren held for an unanimous Court that segregation in the District of Columbia public schools violated the Due Process Clause of the Fifth Amendment. Because the Fifth Amendment does not contain an Equal Protection Clause, the Court needed to ascertain whether the Due Process Clause, like equal protection, was also a bar to racial segregation. Warren argued that both the equal protection and due process concepts stem from the American ideal of fairness; these concepts are not mutually exclusive. Granting that the Court had not defined "liberty" in the Fifth or Fourteenth Amendments with any great precision, Warren reasoned that the term liberty is "not confined to mere freedom from bodily restraint." Rather, "Liberty under law extends to the full range of conduct which the individual is free to pursue, and it cannot be restricted except for a proper governmental objective." Warren then concluded that segregation of the District of Columbia public schools constituted an "arbitrary deprivation" of the liberty of African-American children in violation of the Due Process Clause.

Bowers v. Hardwick
478 U.S. 186, 106 S. Ct. 2841, 92 L. Ed. 140 (1986)

A Georgia statute makes it a felony for heterosexual or homosexual couples to engage in oral or anal sex. Hardwick violated this statute by performing prohibited acts with another male in the privacy of his bedroom. A Georgia district attorney decided not to take the matter to a grand jury, but Hardwick himself brought suit because he claimed that he was in imminent danger of arrest. He attacked the statute as unconstitutional because it applied to consensual sexual conduct. A federal district court dismissed the suit for failure of the plaintiff to state a claim. Later this judgment was overturned by a divided U.S. court of appeals that relied on the Ninth Amendment and the Due Process Clause of the Fourteenth Amendment to create a constitutionally protected zone of privacy. The appeals court remanded the case for trial on the issue of whether the state could satisfy the strict scrutiny test, i.e., could it demonstrate a compelling interest to support the law, and is the statute in question the most narrowly drawn means of advancing that interest. Bowers, the Georgia attorney general, appealed.

In a 6–3 opinion the Supreme Court held that a right to privacy does not extend to homosexuals. Opinion writer Justice Byron White found that one does not have a fundamental right to engage in homosexual sodomy. A right to engage in homosexual conduct does not exist in the concept of ordered liberty nor is it possible to make a case that the authors of the Bill of Rights had any such right in mind. A rational basis for the law exists and consequently the state has the right to proscribe homosexual conduct as immoral.

Boy Scouts of America v. Dale
530 U.S. 640, 120 S. Ct. 2446, 147 L. Ed. 2d 554 (2000)

James Dale, a Boy Scout and assistant scoutmaster, was removed from his scoutmaster position after he revealed that he was homosexual and a gay-rights advocate at Rutgers University. He filed suit under a New Jersey public-accommodations law alleging that the Boy Scouts violated the state law prohibiting discrimination in places of public accommodation based on sexual orientation. Dale lost in the state court of original jurisdiction but the appellate division of the state court found that the state's public accommodation law applied to the Boy Scouts. This court rejected the Scouts' claim that the organization had a First Amendment right of freedom of association to revoke Dale's membership in the organization. The New Jersey Supreme Court affirmed and the U.S. Supreme Court granted certiorari.

Chief Justice Rehnquist for a five-member majority held that because the Boy Scout leaders endeavor to inculcate their charges with a value system summarized in the pledges that Scouts make including an oath to be "morally straight" and "clean" and because the organization does not want to promote homosexual conduct as a legitimate form of behavior, the dismissal of Dale falls within the definition of expressive association protected by the First Amendment. While the right to expressive association is not absolute, the public accommodation provision of the New Jersey law that requires that the Scouts must not dismiss him from his position is unconstitutional. The intrusion into the internal affairs of the Boy Scouts by the state requiring it to accept members that it does not want violates the freedom of association guarantee found in the First Amendment of the U.S. Constitution.

Brown v. Board of Education of Topeka I
347 U.S. 483, 74 S. Ct. 686, 98 L. Ed. 873 (1954)

This case involved several consolidated cases concerning segregation in public schools. The African-American plaintiffs alleged that the denial of admission to public schools on a nonsegregated basis deprived them of the equal protection of the law guaranteed by the Fourteenth Amendment.

Writing for an unanimous Supreme Court, Chief Justice Earl Warren struck down segregated public schools. In all but one of the consolidated cases, the public schools were found by the lower courts to satisfy the separate but equal test first announced by the Supreme Court in Plessy v. Ferguson, 156 U.S. 537 (1896). Finding the evidence regarding the intention of the framers of the Fourteenth Amendment inconclusive, and concluding that consideration of only tangible factors in the separate but equal rule is inadequate, Warren framed the constitutional question. He wrote: "Does segregation of children in public schools solely on the basis of race, even though the physical facilities and other 'tangible' factors may be equal, deprive the children of the minority group of equal opportunities?" Noting that in previous cases (Sweatt v. Painter, 339 U.S. 629 (1950) and McLaurin v. Oklahoma State Regents, 339 U.S. 637 (1950)) the Supreme Court had considered the effects of intangible factors, Warren, citing social science studies, found that to separate black from white children in public schools "solely because of their race generates a feeling of inferiority as to their status in the community that may affect their hearts and minds in a way unlikely ever to be undone." Holding that segregation in public schools is a violation of the Equal Protection Clause of the Fourteenth Amendment, Warren concluded "in the field of public education the doctrine of 'separate but equal' has no place. Separate educational facilities are inherently unequal."

Brown v. Board of Education of Topeka II
349 U.S. 294, 75 S. Ct. 753. 99 L. Ed. 1083 (1955)

With its decisions in Brown v. Board of Education I, 347 U.S. 483 (1954) and Bolling v. Sharpe, 347 U.S. 497 (1954), the Supreme Court declared racial segregation in public education unconstitutional. Leaving open the question of the proper implementation of these decisions, the Court asked the U.S. attorney general and the attorneys general of all states requiring or permitting segregation to file briefs recommending proper relief.

Writing for the Court, Chief Justice Earl Warren noted that the primary responsibility for presenting solutions rests with local school authorities. The federal district courts were given the responsibility of overseeing the desegregation process because of their proximity to local conditions. The duty of the district courts was to consider whether the actions of authorities constitute "good faith implementation of the governing constitutional principles" found in *Brown I*. The Supreme Court ordered the district courts to be guided by equity principles of "practical flexibility in shaping its remedies and by a facility for adjusting the reconciling public and private needs." Once a "prompt and reasonable start toward full compliance" is made, the courts may permit additional time if they find it necessary for an effective implementation; the burden of proof, however, rests on the defendant school districts. The guiding principle for full implementation of desegregation plans is "all deliberate speed."

Buckley v. Valeo
424 U.S. 1, 96 S. Ct. 612, 46 L. Ed. 2d 659 (1976)

This case involves the constitutionality of the Federal Election Campaign Act of 1971. Characterized as the most far-reaching and comprehensive reform legislation involving the role of money in federal elections, the act limited financial contributions, regulated expenditures of money, and created a commission to oversee the regulations. Senator James Buckley and former Senator Eugene McCarthy brought suit against the Secretary of the U.S. Senate, Francis Valeo, and others challenging the various provisions of the act. Seeking declaratory and injunctive relief, the plaintiffs' action rested upon First and Fifth Amendment arguments and upon article II, section 2, clause 2 with respect to the appointment of the eight-member commission. After the Appeals Court for the District of Columbia upheld most of the act's provisions, the plaintiffs appealed to the U.S. Supreme Court.

In its lengthy per curiam opinion, the Court utilized a weighing process in determining whether the governmental interest in preventing corruption and the appearance of corruption justified the intrusion of the First Amendment rights of expression through political contributions and expenditures. The Court decided that the individual contribution limits, the disclosure and reporting provisions, and the public financing schemes are constitutional. However, the limitations on campaign expenditures, on independent expenditures by individuals and groups, and on expenditures by a candidate from his or her personal funds were found constitutionally defective. Since several of the eight members on the election commission were not appointed by the president, consistent with the Appointment Clause of the Constitution (art. II, sec. 2, cl. 2), the commission, as composed, was also found unconstitutional.

Bush v. Gore
531 U.S. 98, 121 S. Ct. 525, 148 L. Ed. (2000)

The 2000 presidential election came down to how the electoral votes from the state of Florida were to be counted. In several of its counties, votes cast were not counted because the voting machines were unable to detect the intent of voters with precision. The voters had failed to penetrate their paper ballots with the supplied metal stylus with sufficient force, resulting in dangling pieces of paper called "chads" or "hanging chads." With various deadlines looming when the votes had to be finally counted and certified, Vice President Albert Gore filed a motion in circuit court for Leon County, Florida to compel Secretary of State Kathleen Harris to accept amended returns from contested counties. The court denied the request. Nonetheless, the plaintiffs asked a state appeals court to review the matter, but this court certified the trial court's order to the Florida Supreme Court. The Florida high court then reversed the trial court. It cited ambiguities in the Florida Election Code and its understandings of the legislative intent of existing statutory law requiring that all the votes be counted. But the next day, the Bush election committee appealed the Florida high court decision to the U.S. Supreme Court. Within a few days, oral arguments were held and shortly thereafter the Court unanimously vacated the Florida Supreme Court decision with a request to the Florida Supreme Court to respond to the charge that it had violated the constitutional principle of separation of powers. In the meantime, a trial judge in Leon County, Florida was conducting a trial to ascertain whether Gore's request for a manual recount in four disputed counties should go forward. The judge ruled in favor of Bush and the decision was appealed to the Florida Supreme Court, which reversed the lower court ruling. On the following day, while the recount was beginning, the U.S. Supreme Court granted a request from the Bush campaign for a stay of the Florida high court order. Within a few days the U.S. Supreme Court heard oral arguments in the case.

In an unusual format, the Supreme Court in an unsigned five-person per curiam opinion ruled that the Florida Supreme Court's decision violated the Fourteenth Amendment's Equal Protection Clause. It found that the Florida high court failed to establish specific standards for counting votes to ensure its equal application throughout the state. The per curiam justices thought it possible a vote disqualified in one county because of some failure in voting machines reading chads may be machine-counted in another county without controversy. It was therefore necessary to conduct a statewide election recount under the direction of a single state judicial officer. But such a scheme was not practical because the deadline for selecting state electors to the Electoral College was too near and therefore there was no time to fashion any such remedy. The result was that none of the votes were recounted and George Bush became president of the United States.

Butchers' Benevolent Association v. Crescent City Livestock Landing and Slaughterhouse Co. (Slaughterhouse Cases)
83 U.S. (16 Wall.) 36, 21 L. Ed. 394 (1873)

Due to slaughterhouse activities, the city of New Orleans was ineffective in its efforts to deal with pollution of the Mississippi River. To remedy this problem, the state of Louisiana enacted a statute in 1869 granting an exclusive franchise to one large slaughterhouse. The Butchers' Benevolent Association brought suit to enjoin the monopoly from operating. It contended that the Louisiana law violated the Thirteenth Amendment anti-slavery provision and the Privileges and Immunities, Due Process, and Equal Protection clauses of the Fourteenth Amendment. The Louisiana Supreme Court ruled in favor of the monopoly. The Association appealed its case to the U.S. Supreme Court.

Rejecting the Thirteenth Amendment argument as applying to slavery historically understood, Justice Samuel Miller, writing for the majority, turned to an analysis of the meaning of the Fourteenth Amendment. Miller opted for a dual-citizenship interpretation, holding that the Privileges and Immunities Clause refers to a citizenship of the United States and a citizenship of a state—which are distinct. The sole purpose of this clause, wrote Miller, is ". . . to declare to the several states, that whatever those rights, as you grant or establish them to your own citizens, or as you limit or qualify, or impose restrictions on their exercise, the same, neither more nor less, shall be the measure of the rights of citizens of other states within your jurisdiction." Because the suit was brought by citizens of Louisiana and not citizens of other states, the Privileges and Immunities Clause could not justify a constitutional challenge. Refusing to recognize the notion of substantive due process, Miller expressed the majority of the Court's view that ". . . under no construction of that provision (due process) that we have ever seen, or any that we deem admissible can the restraint imposed by the state of Louisiana upon the exercise of their trade by the butchers of New Orleans be held to be a deprivation of property within the meaning of that provision." The equal protection claim was dismissed with the observation that it applies only to laws discriminating against Negroes.

Chandler v. Miller
519 U.S. 1051, 117 S. Ct. 1295, 137 L. Ed. 2d 513 (1997)

The Georgia state legislature enacted a law requiring candidates for state offices, the heads of various state bureaus, most judges, and state legislators to certify that they had submitted to and passed a urinalysis drug test prior to qualifying for nomination or election. Chandler, a Libertarian Party candidate, and others sued Governor Zell D. Miller claiming that the statute violated the Fourth and Fourteenth Amendments to the U.S. Constitution. A federal district court and the U.S. court of appeals upheld the statute.

In an 8–1 decision, Justice Ruth Bader Ginsburg concluded that there is nothing in the record to indicate a real danger to the public that would require the drug testing program. Ordinarily, for a search to pass constitutional scrutiny it must be based upon individualized suspicion of wrongdoing. Particularized exceptions to the rule are sometimes permissible based on special considerations. But this statute was not enacted in response to a fear that state officials are engaged in drug use. Rather, the law is a symbolic gesture, and does not address a real problem that might justify relaxing the basic constitutional rule.

Civil Rights Cases
109 U.S. 3, 3 S. Ct. 18, 27 L. Ed. 835 (1883)

The Civil Rights Act of 1875 prohibited any person from denying another the rights of access and enjoyment of accommodations, facilities, inns, public conveyances, theaters, and other places of amusement. In a number of consolidated cases, known here as the *Civil Rights Cases*, African Americans alleged that they were denied access to public facilities covered by the 1875 act solely because of their race.

Writing for the majority of the Supreme Court, Justice Joseph Bradley held that the Civil Rights Act of 1875 was not a valid application of the Fourteenth and Thirteenth Amendments and consequently was an infringement of the reserved powers of the states guaranteed by the Tenth Amendment. The Fourteenth Amendment applies to state, not individual, action since its opening lines refer to *state* abridgments of privileges and immunities, due process and equal protection. Bradley wrote, ". . . the legislation which Congress is authorized to adopt in this behalf is not general legislation upon the rights of the citizen, but corrective legislation; that is, such as may be necessary and proper for counteracting such laws as the states may adopt or enforce, . . ." Because the denial of rights to blacks by individuals cannot be regulated by Congress under the authority of the Fourteenth Amendment, such legislation violates the Tenth Amendment. Concluding that the Thirteenth Amendment refers to the abolition of slavery and that the refusal of accommodations to blacks "has nothing to do with slavery or involuntary servitude," Bradley found no constitutional authority for the Civil Rights Act.

Clinton v. Jones
520 U.S. 681, 116 S. Ct. 2545, 137 L. Ed. 945 (1997)

Paula Jones sued President Bill Clinton for the recovery of damages resulting from alleged sexual advances to her and subsequent punishments relating to her employment for the state of Arkansas while the president was governor of the state. The federal district court with jurisdiction in the case denied the president's motion to dismiss on presidential immunity grounds. It ordered that the discovery stage of the litigation go forward but stayed the actual trial until Clinton's term of office was completed. The judges of the Eighth Circuit Court of Appeals affirmed the dismissal denial but reversed the district court's order granting Clinton temporary immunity from trial.

Justice Stevens, writing for eight members of the Court, with Justice Breyer writing a concurring opinion, held that the president is not immune from suits for his unofficial conduct. Immunity is grounded in the function performed and not the identity of the actor who performs the function. The separation of powers doctrine does not require courts to stay all private legal actions against presidents until they leave office because of an assertion that such suits will make it difficult for chief executives to perform their official duties. Moreover, there is nothing in the record of the trial court that warrants the postponement of trial, permitting only the completion of discovery.

Clinton v. New York, City of
524 U.S. 417, 118 S. Ct. 1551, 141 L. Ed. 2d 393 (1998)

In 1996 Congress passed the Line Item Veto Act and President Clinton first employed the law to cancel a provision of the Balanced Budget Act of 1997 and two provisions of the Taxpayer Relief Act of 1997. In the first instance, the president struck a provision that waived the national government's right to recover taxes that New York had levied against Medicaid providers. In the second instance, the president struck a provision permitting owners of some food refineries to defer capital-gains taxes if they sold their stock to certain eligible farmers. The Line Item Veto Act contained a detailed set of conditions necessary for the president to exercise authority under the law including a method for Congress to disapprove of the president's decisions. However, a federal district court found that the two exercises of the president's power under the act violated the Constitution's Presentment Clause (article I, § 7, cl. 2).

Writing for the Court's majority, Justice Stevens found the Line Item Veto Act unconstitutional because it violates the Presentment Clause. The law authorizes the president to create a different law from the one voted on by either house of Congress and presented to the president for his signature. If there is to be a new procedure providing the president with discretion to delete from laws statutory provisions he thinks unwise after they are duly enacted, then it must be done through the amendment procedures set forth in article V of the Constitution.

Cooley v. Board of Wardens of the Port of Philadelphia
53 U.S. (12 How.) 299, 13 L. Ed. 996 (1852)

In 1803, the Pennsylvania legislature enacted a law requiring ships entering or leaving the port of Philadelphia to hire a local pilot for navigation purposes. Failure to comply would result in a fine of half the pilotage fee to be levied against the vessel. An act of Congress of 1789 provided that pilots shall continue to be regulated by state law until possible future congressional action might be taken. When Aaron Cooley violated the state law by failing to pay the fee on two of his vessels, the Board of Wardens filed suit to recover the fees. The Pennsylvania Supreme Court affirmed the lower court judgment rendered against Cooley. On a writ of error to the U.S. Supreme Court, Cooley maintained that the state statute was an unconstitutional tax on commerce.

Writing for the majority, Justice Benjamin Curtis first noted that pilots are an important part of navigation and it is well-established that navigation is part of commerce within the meaning of the Commerce Clause (art. I, sec. 8, cl. 3) of the Constitution. But the Commerce Clause does not per se deprive the states of all power to regulate pilots. Through its 1789 enactment, Congress manifested a clear intention not to regulate the subject matter, but rather to leave such regulation to the several states. Consequently, the Pennsylvania law was enacted by virtue of the power residing in the state to legislate and the law is not in conflict with congressional legislation.

Cruzan v. Director, Missouri Department of Health
497 U.S. 261, 110 S. Ct. 2841, 111 L. Ed. 2d 224 (1990)

As the result of an automobile accident, Nancy Cruzan lay in a vegetative state in a Missouri hospital. After it became clear that Nancy had no chance of regaining her mental faculties, her parents sought her removal from a life-support system to permit her to die. Hospital officials refused the request, but a Missouri court concluded that the parents' wishes should be honored because Nancy had expressed thoughts to a friend that she would not want to be kept alive under such circumstances. The Missouri Supreme Court, however, reversed the lower court finding because there was not clear and convincing evidence of Nancy Cruzan's wishes.

In a 6–3 opinion the Supreme Court, with Chief Justice William Rehnquist writing for the majority, held that although patients have a right to have life-support systems removed, and that this right is protected by the Constitution's Due Process Clause, the right is not absolute. Consequently, the state may determine the circumstances of life-support removal through the evidentiary protection of the clear and convincing rule. Moreover, the state need not accept the substituted judgment of close family members.

Dartmouth College v. Woodward
(*see*, Trustees of Dartmouth College v. Woodward)

Dennis v. United States
341 U.S. 494, 71 S. Ct. 857, 95 L. Ed. 1137 (1951)

In 1948, Eugene Dennis and ten other top leaders of the U.S. Communist Party were indicted under provisions of the 1940 Smith Act for organizing the Communist Party and for willfully and knowingly conspiring to teach or advocate the overthrow of the government of the United States by force or violence. After a lengthy trial, a U.S. district court found all defendants guilty. Convictions were upheld by the Circuit Court of Appeals.

On appeal to the U.S. Supreme Court, the Court affirmed the lower court decision limiting the scope of its review to First and Fifth Amendment questions. Writing for the majority, Chief Justice Vinson upheld the validity of the Smith Act both inherently and as applied to the First Amendment. Expanding the "clear and present danger" test, first established in Schenck v. U.S.,

249 U.S. 47 (1919), the Court concluded that Congress clearly possesses the authority to protect the government from violent overthrow, even though the danger is not imminent. Adopting the test set forth by U.S. Court Appeals Judge Learned Hand, the Supreme Court rejected the notion that it must consider success or probability of success as the criterion of clear and present danger. It stated: "In each case (courts) must ask whether the gravity of the 'evil,' discounted by its improbability, justifies such invasion of free speech as is necessary to avoid the danger." The Court also rejected the contention that the statute was too vague or indefinite so as to fail to present a clear standard of permissible behavior.

Dred Scott v. Sandford
60 U.S. (19 How.) 393, 15 L. Ed. 691 (1857)

Dred Scott, a black slave residing in the slave state of Missouri, was taken by his white master to the free state of Illinois. Later he was taken to the Louisiana Territory north of the line that forbade slavery by virtue of the 1821 act of Congress called the Missouri Compromise. In a test case, Scott brought suit in a Missouri court claiming that since he had once resided in a free state and in free territory he should be set free. Before the suit started, Scott was sold to Sandford, a New York citizen.

In a controversial 7–2 opinion, Chief Justice Roger Taney held that a slave is not included under the word "citizen" as understood in the Constitution. Further, because Scott is properly regarded as property, Congress could not pass a valid law depriving a slave owner of his property without due process of law. The Missouri Compromise is therefore void and the fact that Scott was taken from a "slave state" to a "free state" and free section of a federal territory does not alter the basic facts of property ownership.

Ex Parte McCardle
74 U.S. (7 Wall.) 506, 19 L. Ed. 264 (1869)

A federal military commission arrested and detained William McCardle, a Southern newspaper editor, for publishing articles alleged to be incendiary and libelous. McCardle, a civilian, argued that he was being illegally restrained and sought a writ of habeas corpus. A circuit court denied his petition, whereupon he appealed directly to the U.S. Supreme Court under an 1867 statute authorizing the Court to hear appeals in such cases. The Supreme Court granted review and heard the case. However, before a decision was delivered, Congress, over President Andrew Johnson's veto, repealed the statute. The resulting question before the Court was whether the Court still could exercise jurisdiction in the case.

Writing for the majority, Chief Justice Chase dismissed McCardle's appeal for want of jurisdiction. He found that appellate jurisdiction is subject to congressional regulation. Congress possesses constitutional authority to enlarge or diminish the Court's appellate jurisdiction.

Ex Parte Milligan
71 U.S. (4 Wall.) 2, 18 L. Ed. 281 (1866)

As a Civil War measure, President Lincoln suspended the habeas corpus privilege on September 24, 1862. Later, on March 3, 1863, Congress enacted a law in an attempt to modify the president's control of political prisoners. This act authorized, after the fact, suspension of habeas corpus but also required that the secretaries of state and war furnish to the federal courts lists of political prisoners. It provided that if a grand jury failed to indict the prisoners, they were to be released after taking an oath of allegiance. Milligan, a citizen of Indiana, where the administration of justice continued unimpaired in the civilian federal courts, was arrested, tried, found guilty of disloyalty and treason by a military commission, and sentenced to death. Objecting to the jurisdiction of the military commission, Milligan petitioned a U.S. circuit court for a writ of habeas corpus. The circuit court, unable to agree on a decision, certified unresolved queries to the Supreme Court for consideration.

With Justice David Davis writing for the Court, the military commission authorized by the president was found to be unlawful. A majority of five justices stated further that Congress, as well as the president, lacked the legal authority to create military commissions to try civilians in areas removed from the actual war zone and where the civilian courts remained open. A court established by Congress did not try Milligan. Only Congress, not the president, possesses the constitutional authority to establish courts. Milligan also was denied a trial by jury guaranteed by the Sixth Amendment. He was entitled to the habeas corpus writ. In a most emphatic pronouncement affirming the rule of law, Davis wrote, "The Constitution of the United States is a law for rulers and people, equally in war and in peace, and covers with the shield of its protection all classes of men, at all times, and under all circumstances. No doctrine, involving more pernicious consequences, was ever invented by the wit of man than that any of its provisions can be suspended during any of the great exigencies of government."

Fletcher v. Peck
10 U.S. (6 Cranch) 87, 3 L. Ed. 162 (1810)

In 1795, the legislature of the state of Georgia granted a large parcel of land to speculators resulting in part from bribery of several members. In 1796, the legislature declared the corrupt act of 1795 null and void. Peck took possession of the land in 1800, and in his deed that he signed over to Fletcher, he indicated that all of the past transactions involving the land were lawful. Fletcher sued Peck for breach of covenant because the original land grant was the result of an illegal agreement and, therefore, the land was not Peck's to sell. A circuit court entered judgment in favor of Peck and the case was appealed to the U.S Supreme Court on a writ of error.

Writing for the Court, Chief Justice John Marshall held that the land grant is a contract executed and because there is no constitutional difference between a contract that is executory and one that is executed, the legal agreement is one that is contemplated by article I, section 10 of the Constitution (the Contracts Clause). The Constitution does not make a distinction between a contract between individuals and one executed between a state and individuals. Therefore, the state of Georgia was restrained from passing the repealing legislation rendering the original grant null and void.

Furman v. Georgia
408 U.S. 238, 92 S. Ct. 2726, 33 L. Ed. 2d 346 (1972)

Furman and two other petitioners, each convicted in a state court and sentenced to death, sought review of the three state appellate court decisions affirming the imposition of the death penalty.

In the U.S. Supreme Court's per curiam decision (by the court as a whole), five of the nine justices agreed that the imposition of the death penalty *in these cases* constituted cruel and unusual punishment in violation of the Eighth and Fourteenth Amendments. In a concurring opinion, Justice Douglas argued that the death penalty has been applied selectively to minorities by judges and juries. But the death penalty itself may nevertheless remain unconstitutional if a mandatory death penalty were imposed. Also concurring, Justice Brennan concluded that the death penalty does not comport with principles of human dignity. The basis of Justice Stewart's concurring opinion was that the death penalty has been wantonly and freakishly imposed. Justice White emphasized that he did not hold that the death penalty is per se unconstitutional. Rather, because the legislatures delegated to juries and judges the responsibility for determining the circumstances where the death penalty should be imposed, there is an Eighth Amendment violation. Justice Marshall reasoned that the purposes served by capital punishment are not realized and that the death penalty is discriminatory against certain identifiable classes of people—there is evidence that innocent people have been wrongfully executed and the death penalty ". . . wreaks havoc with our entire criminal justice system." Four separate dissenting opinions, each joined by the other dissenters, invoked principles of judicial self-restraint. In Gregg v. Georgia, 428 U.S. 153 (1976), the Supreme Court upheld the constitutionality of the death penalty.

Garcia v. San Antonio Metropolitan Transit Authority
469 U.S. 528, 105 S. Ct. 1005, 83 L. Ed. 2d 1016 (1985)

The Supreme Court held in *National League of Cities v. Usery* (1976) that the minimum-wage and maximum-hour provisions of the Federal Fair Labor Standards Act (FLSA) did not bind cities. The Court reasoned that this federal regulation impairs the integrity and ability of the states to function effectively in the federal system. Notwithstanding the Court's 1976 opinion, Garcia, an employee of the San Antonio Metropolitan Transit Authority, invoking FLSA, sued his employer for lack of payment for overtime work. However, the San Antonio Metropolitan Transit Authority relied on the Court's decision in *National League of Cities* as justification for nonpayment.

The secretary of labor ruled in favor of Garcia, but a federal district court citing *National League of Cities* ruled in favor of the transit authority. The secretary of labor and Garcia took direct appeals to the Supreme Court.

Writing for the Court's 5–4 majority, Justice Harry Blackmun overruled *National League of Cities v. Usery.* He pointed out that it has been difficult to apply the principle laid down in *National League of Cities* that the national government should not invade the "traditional government functions" of the states. The legal boundary between traditional and non-traditional governmental functions has proven unworkable and is inconsistent with established principles of federalism. When the Court attempted this type of distinction in the area of intergovernmental tax immunity, for example, the results were also unworkable. The regulation of state or municipal employee wages and working conditions is a valid exercise of the congressional commerce power. Therefore, it is not an invasion of the power of the state reserved by the Tenth Amendment.

Gibbons v. Ogden
22 U.S. (9 Wheat.) 1, 6 L. Ed. 23 (1824)

The New York legislature granted Robert Livingston and Robert Fulton an exclusive twenty-year franchise to operate steamboats on New York waters. Under provisions of the statute, anyone operating a steamboat in New York waters not licensed to Fulton or Livingston would be subject to forfeiting their vessel. Aaron Ogden, securing a license from the two franchise holders, operated his boats between New York and New Jersey. Gibbons, on the other hand, secured a coastal license from the federal government to operate between the same two points. Ogden, contending that the federal coastal license conflicted with New York laws, brought suit to enjoin Gibbons from continuing his business. The injunction was granted and a New York State appellate court affirmed.

The U.S. Supreme Court ruled the New York statute invalid since it conflicted with an act of Congress. Chief Justice John Marshall ruled that commerce is more than traffic; commerce, he wrote: ". . . is intercourse. It describes the commercial intercourse between nations, and parts of nations in all its branches, and is regulated by prescribing rules for carrying out that intercourse." Commerce, however, does not comprehend activity that is completely internal within a state. The congressional power to regulate commerce is complete; it is plenary. Because the license granted by New York conflicts with the federal license granted to Gibbons, and since the federal Constitution is supreme (the Supremacy Clause), the state license is a nullity.

Gideon v. Wainwright
372 U.S. 335, 83 S. Ct. 792, 9 L. Ed. 2d 799 (1963)

Clarence Gideon was convicted of a felony under Florida law for breaking and entering a pool hall with the intent to commit a crime. Appearing at trial, without a lawyer and without the money to obtain one, Gideon requested that the judge appoint counsel for him. Citing Florida law, the judge explained that he may appoint counsel only in capital cases. Gideon conducted his own defense and was convicted and sentenced to five years in prison. After the Florida Supreme Court denied Gideon's habeas corpus petition against Wainwright (director of state corrections), Gideon proceeded *in forma pauperis* to the U.S. Supreme Court. Granting certiorari, the Court appointed well-known Washington, DC, attorney Abe Fortas to represent Gideon.

Delivering the opinion for the Court, Justice Hugo Black directly overruled Betts v. Brady, 316 U.S. 455 (1942). In a similar situation to Gideon's, the Court found in *Betts* that the Sixth Amendment guarantee of counsel is not one of those fundamental and essential rights so necessary to a fair trial that it should be made obligatory upon the states by the Due Process Clause of the Fourteenth Amendment. Black argued that the *Betts* Court had deviated from established precedent, in Powell v. Alabama, 287 U.S. 45 (1932). He held that the right to counsel is a fundamental right required by the Due Process Clause of the Fourteenth Amendment.

Gitlow v. New York
268 U.S. 652, 45 S. Ct. 625, 69 L. Ed. 1138 (1925)

Benjamin Gitlow was a leader of the Left Wing Section of the Socialist Party. He was tried and convicted of the New York Criminal Anarchy Act of 1902 for distributing a document similar in character to the *Communist Manifesto*. This publication, "Left Wing Manifesto," contained writings calling for the overthrow of capitalism and the necessity of bringing about a socialist society through mass political strikes and industrial revolts. There was no evidence that the publication had any effect. After his conviction was affirmed by the New York Court of Appeals, Gitlow appealed on a writ of error to the U.S. Supreme Court.

Writing for the majority, Justice Edward Sanford rejected counsel's First Amendment arguments and affirmed Gitlow's conviction. Employing *obiter dicta*, the Court agreed that the First Amendment protections of speech and press are applicable to the states by way of the Due Process Clause of the Fourteenth Amendment, but importantly, the Court found no First Amendment infringement. The New York statute does not prohibit utterance or publication of abstract ideas. Rather, the statute prohibits language advocating, advising, or teaching the advisability of overthrowing the government by unlawful means. The language in the "Left Wing Manifesto," concluded the Court, is a direct incitement to action. Moreover, it is within the power of the state legislature to determine generally which utterances create a substantive evil that may be punished. In short, the clear and present danger rule first announced in Schenck v. U.S., 249 U.S. 47 (1919) is not applicable where the legislature had previously determined the danger arising from speech of a specified nature.

Gratz v. Bollinger
2003 U.S. LEXIS 4801, 539 U.S.____(2003)

Announced on the same day as the University of Michigan Law School opinion in *Grutter v. Bollinger*, this dispute involved the admissions policy of undergraduates at that same institution. Unlike the law school case, however, underrepresented minorities including African Americans, Hispanics, and Native Americans were automatically awarded 20 out of a total of 100 minimum points required to qualify for admission. Gratz, a white Michigan resident, applied for admission as a freshman and one other party to the suit applied as a transfer student; both, however, were denied admission despite being within the qualified range for admission. At the same time, virtually all the members of the underrepresented minority groups were admitted, although they possessed only minimum qualifications for admission. The petitioners filed a class-action suit seeking compensatory and punitive damages and declaratory and injunctive relief. The U.S. district court that adjudicated the matter found in part for each side and appeals were pending in the Court of Appeals for the Sixth Circuit when the U.S. Supreme Court granted certiorari in this and the University of Michigan Law School case.

Chief Justice Rehnquist, writing for a five-member majority (in addition, one justice wrote a separate concurring opinion), found that educational diversity is a compelling state interest that the University may legitimately pursue. However, under the Court's strict scrutiny test, the point system as applied in this case failed the second element of the test—that the remedy must be narrowly tailored to achieve the legitimate educational goal. The 20-point automatic assignment to the named minorities on the basis of race runs counter to Justice Powell's view enunciated in his opinion in *Regents of the University of California v. Bakke* (1978); he held if race is treated as a "plus" among other factors wherein the qualifications of each applicant are assessed in a holistic fashion, then there is no violation of the Equal Protection Clause of the Fourteenth Amendment. Consequently, the University of Michigan undergraduate admissions policy fails the strict scrutiny test.

Griswold v. Connecticut
381 U.S. 479, 85 S. Ct. 1678, 14 L. Ed. 2d 510 (1965)

A long-standing but unenforced Connecticut statute made the use of contraceptives a criminal offense. Estelle Griswold, the executive director of the Planned Parenthood League, and others were convicted for having violated the law as accessories. They provided information and instruction to married persons on the use of contraceptives. A state circuit court of appeals upheld the conviction and on appeal to the Supreme Court of Errors of Connecticut the judgment was once again affirmed.

The United States Supreme Court reversed the state court decisions. Justice William O. Douglas delivered the judgment of the majority, but only Justice Clark fully accepted Douglas's reasoning. Expressly avoiding the implications of substantive due process reasoning as exemplified by Lochner v. New York, 198 U.S. 45 (1905), Douglas argued that several Court decisions established "that specific guarantees in the Bill of Rights have *penumbras*, formed by emanations from those guarantees that help them give life and substance." Five different amendments, the penumbras of which create zones of privacy, are the basis for the constitutional interpretation. They are the First Amendment's protection of the right of association; the Third Amendment's prohibition of quartering of soldiers in any house in time of peace without the consent of the owner; the Fourth Amendment's unreasonable search and seizure provision; the Fifth Amendment's prohibition against self-incrimination; and the Ninth Amendment's provision that "the enumeration in the Constitution, of certain rights, shall not be construed to deny or disparage others retained by the people."

Grutter v. Bollinger
2003 U.S. LEXIS 4800, 539 U.S. ___ (2003)

Barbara Grutter, a Michigan resident with a 3.8 G.P.A. and a 161 LSAT score, filed suit when she was denied admission to the University of Michigan Law School. While she possessed higher scores than minority applicants, she was not admitted, but they were under a program designed to further the goals of affirmative action by enrolling a "critical mass" of students that would enhance racial and ethnic diversity at the law school. A U.S. District Court found the admissions program unlawful but the Court of Appeals reversed holding that diversity is a compelling state interest consistent with Justice Powell's landmark opinion in *Regents of the University of California v. Bakke* (1978). The U.S. Supreme Court granted the writ of certiorari along with the companion case treating the affirmative-action program for undergraduate students at the University of Michigan (see *Gratz v. Bollinger*).

Writing for a 5–4 majority, Justice Sandra Day O'Connor upheld the law school affirmative action program. She cited favorably Mr. Powell's *Bakke* opinion, reasoning that the law school plan treated race as a plus factor in evaluating the qualifications of each applicant in a holistic fashion. The Court held that the value of diversity may be properly regarded by the university as a compelling state interest because many of the nation's leaders are trained in law schools. Further, other institutions including business and the military utilize affirmative action programs to train leaders with diverse backgrounds, contributing to the overall legitimacy of the social, economic, and political system. The goal of enrolling a "critical mass" of minority students is constitutionally permissible as long as race is one among many factors in determining admissions, satisfying the narrow tailoring feature of the strict scrutiny test when adjudicating Fourteenth Amendment Equal Protection Clause claims.

Hammer v. Dagenhart
247 U.S. 251, 38 S. Ct. 529, 62 L. Ed. 1101 (1918)

In 1916, Congress passed the Federal Child Labor Act. This act prohibited the shipment in interstate commerce of goods produced by companies employing children under the age of fourteen; it restricted children between the ages of fourteen and sixteen from working more than eight hours a day, more than six days a week, or at night. Dagenhart, the father of two children employed in a

North Carolina cotton mill, brought suit on behalf of himself and his children against Hammer, a U.S. attorney, enjoining the enforcement of the act. Granting the injunction, the district court held the act unconstitutional.

On appeal to the U.S. Supreme Court, the district court judgment was affirmed and the federal statute was invalidated. Writing for the Court, Justice Day held that the local production of goods was a state concern and the federal attempt to regulate, even though intended for transportation in interstate commerce, was a violation of the powers reserved to the states under the Tenth Amendment.

Heart of Atlanta Motel v. United States
379 U.S. 241, 85 S. Ct. 348, 13 L. Ed. 2d 258 (1964)

The owners and operators of the Heart of Atlanta Motel sought a declaratory judgment that Title II of the Civil Rights Act is unconstitutional. The motel, located close to downtown Atlanta and readily accessible to interstate highways, solicited out-of-state customers and prior to the passage of the act refused lodging to African Americans because of their race. A three-judge federal court sustained the validity of the act and issued a permanent injunction against the motel operators.

Delivering the opinion for the Supreme Court, Justice Tom Clark first noted that the history of the 1964 Civil Rights Act indicates that Congress based the legislation on the Equal Protection Clause of the Fourteenth Amendment and the congressional commerce power. The Court, however, anchored its holding to the Commerce Clause (art. I, sec. 8, cl. 3) alone. Basing its finding on extensive testimony, Congress determined that discrimination in lodging for African Americans had a detrimental effect on commerce. Though Congress may have been legislating in the commerce field to deal with "moral wrongs," Clark concluded that the act is nonetheless constitutional. The "power of Congress to promote interstate commerce also includes the power to regulate the local incidents thereof, including local activities in both the State of origin and destination, which might have a substantial and harmful effect upon that commerce." How Congress may, as a matter of policy, eliminate the obstructions in interstate commerce is within the discretion of Congress, not the courts. The only restriction on congressional power is that the means chosen must be "reasonably adapted to the end permitted by the Constitution." Finding that the legislation was reasonably related to the constitutional objective, the Supreme Court upheld the validity of the act.

Home Building and Loan Association v. Blaisdell
290 U.S. 398, 54 S. Ct. 231, 78 L. Ed. 413 (1934)

In 1933, the Minnesota legislature passed the Minnesota Moratorium Law, which was designed to prevent foreclosure of mortgages during the Great Depression. The law provided for the temporary postponement of payments on mortgages of homeowners and farmers. Under a provision of this law, John Blaisdell and his wife sought an extension of the period of redemption so they could retain ownership of their home. A state district court granted the extension but on the condition that Blaisdell make certain monthly payments to cover taxes, insurance, and interest. The Minnesota Supreme Court affirmed the judgment upholding the statute. Home Building and Loan then appealed to the U.S. Supreme Court.

Writing for the majority, Chief Justice Charles Evans Hughes, responding to the constitutional claim that the moratorium law exceeded state power, found no transgression of the Contracts Clause (art. I, sec. 10). Noting that while emergency does not create power, emergency may furnish the occasion for the exercise of power, Hughes established five criteria for determining when a contract is not impaired: an emergency is present; the legislation must be addressed to a legitimate end—for the protection of the basic interests of society, not for the mere advantage of particular individuals or interests; the relief must be appropriate to the emergency and may be granted only on reasonable conditions; the integrity of the contract is not impaired; and the legislation must be temporary in operation.

Hurtado v. California
110 U.S. 516, 4 S. Ct. 111, 28 L. Ed. 232 (1884)

Adopted in 1879, the California State Constitution provided that criminal prosecutions, which previously required a grand jury indictment, could be initiated by an information prepared by the prosecuting attorney. An information is a common law device whereby the prosecutor submits charges to a trial court in the form of an affidavit supported by sworn statements. Charged with murder, Hurtado was prosecuted through the use of an information. He was found guilty, and sentenced to death. Hurtado appealed arguing that the Due Process Clause of the Fourteenth Amendment comprehends grand jury indictment as is found in the Fifth Amendment's limitation on the power of the federal government. The California Supreme Court affirmed the conviction.

The U.S. Supreme Court affirmed the state court judgment. In the decision delivered by Justice Stanley Matthews, the Court held that the Due Process Clause of the Fourteenth Amendment does not provide a defendant charged with a state offense the right to indictment by a grand jury. Due process of law refers to "those fundamental principles of liberty and justice which lie at the base of all our civil and political institutions. . . ." Since the indictment process is ". . . merely a preliminary proceeding, and can result in no final judgment," the Court ruled it a legal proceeding not within the scope of the Due Process Clause as found in the Fourteenth Amendment.

Immigration & Naturalization Service v. Chadha
462 U.S. 919, 103 S. Ct. 2764, 77 L. Ed. 2d 317 (1983)

Under a provision of the Immigration and Nationality Act either the House or Senate could reverse a decision of the attorney general to deport or refuse to deport a specific alien. The attorney general refused to deport Chadha and five other deportable aliens. This decision was transmitted to

Congress, where the House of Representatives voted its disapproval. Chadha then filed for review of the deportation order with a U.S. Court of Appeals, which found in his favor. The federal government then appealed to the U.S. Supreme Court.

Writing for the Court's majority, Chief Justice Warren Burger focused on the constitutional issue raised by the provision of the act authorizing one house of Congress to invalidate the decision of the executive branch pursuant to authority delegated by Congress to the attorney general. He found that the one-house veto violates the Constitution's Presentment Clause (art. I, sec. 7, cl. 3). Reading the Constitution strictly, the chief justice reasoned that the procedures in the act amount to an amendment of a law. Various provisions of article I of the Constitution require all laws and amendments thereto must be the product of the vote of the two houses of Congress and must be presented to the president for his signature.

Katz v. United States
389 U.S. 347, 88 S. Ct. 507, 19 L. Ed. 2d 576 (1967)

Charles Katz was convicted in U.S. district court under an eight-count indictment charging him with transmitting wagering and betting information from a telephone booth in Los Angeles to Miami and Boston. During the trial, the federal government was permitted to present as evidence a recording of Katz's conversation that the FBI had obtained through the use of an electronic listening and recording device attached to the top of a public telephone booth. Katz objected to the use of the recordings as inconsistent with the Fourth Amendment protection against illegal searches and seizures. A U.S. circuit court affirmed Katz's conviction.

Justice Potter Stewart, expressing the views of seven members of the U.S. Supreme Court, held that the use of electronic surveillance equipment without first securing a warrant constituted a violation of Katz's general right to privacy. Overruling the underpinnings of Olmstead v. U.S., 277 U.S. 438 (1928) and Goldman v. U.S., 316 U.S. 129 (1942), on which the FBI based its conduct, the Court noted that the trespass doctrine can no longer be regarded as controlling. It is of no constitutional significance that the electronic listening device failed to physically penetrate the wall of the telephone booth.

Katzenbach v. McClung
379 U.S. 294, 85 S. Ct. 377, 13 L. Ed. 2d 290 (1964)

This case was argued along with Heart of Atlanta Motel v. U.S., 397 U.S. 241 (1964). It concerned the refusal to serve African Americans by a restaurant in Birmingham, Alabama. Ollie's Barbecue sought injunctive relief against the United States from the enforcement of the 1964 Civil Rights Act. A three-judge district court issued the injunction.

Writing for the Supreme Court, Justice Tom Clark found that the restaurant purchased food in interstate commerce and based on a congressional finding, discrimination against black patrons had a substantial impact on interstate commerce. The district court had erred when it found "no connection between discrimination and the movement of interstate commerce." Citing numerous precedents, Clark emphasized that even though business activity may be local in nature, Congress may reach such activity if it exerts a substantial economic impact on interstate commerce. The only limitation on the commerce power is found in Marshall's decision in Gibbons v. Ogden, 22 U.S. (9 Wheat.) 1 (1824); the activities beyond congressional reach are "those which are completely within a particular State, which do not affect other States, and with which it is not necessary to interfere, for the purpose of executing some of the general powers of the government." Furthermore, Clark concluded that it is not necessary for a case-by-case determination of discrimination in restaurant service. As long as it has a rational basis for finding a regulatory scheme necessary for the protection of commerce, Congress, and not the courts, may make the determination of what constitutes a burden on commerce.

Korematsu v. United States
323 U.S. 214, 65 S. Ct. 193, 89 L. Ed. 194 (1944)

Shortly after America entered World War II, Congress enacted a law authorizing the president, by executive order, to create military areas from which residents might be restricted in order to maintain national security. Under growing concern that Japan might invade the Pacific Coast, the Western Defense Command divided the entire coast into two military areas and imposed certain restrictions on those living there. The restrictions ranged from curfews that applied to aliens and persons of Japanese descent to an eventual forced removal to relocation camps of all persons of Japanese descent. Korematsu, a United States citizen, refused to leave his home and was convicted in federal district court for violating the exclusion order. A circuit court of appeals affirmed his conviction, whereupon Korematsu appealed to the U.S. Supreme Court.

Delivering the opinion of the Court, Justice Black found that exclusion was justified by the presence of an unknown number of disloyal citizens of Japanese origin. Congress and the executive branch, through the exercise of the war powers, possessed the constitutional authority to exclude citizens from certain areas during time of war.

Lawrence v. Texas
2003 U.S. LEXIS 5013, 539 U.S.___(2003)

Houston, Texas, police officers entered a private residence and found Lawrence and another person of the same sex engaged in intimate sexual acts and charged them with a misdemeanor under Texas law. They pleaded nolo contendere after failing to convince the local criminal court that the statute in question violated the Equal Protection Clause of both the U.S. and Texas Constitutions. The petitioner then challenged the statute in the Court of Appeals for the Texas Fourteenth District invoking the U.S. Constitution's Equal Protection and Due Process Clauses. Relying on the U.S. Supreme

Court's 1986 opinion in *Bowers v. Hardwick*, the court held that the right to privacy found in the Due Process Clause of the Fourteenth Amendment does not afford homosexuals a right to engage in sodomy. The U.S. Supreme Court granted the writ of certiorari to review the matter.

Justice Anthony Kennedy, writing for a 6–3 Court, held that the petitioners' private conduct is protected by the liberty provision of the Due Process Clause of the Fourteenth Amendment. The right to privacy is a fundamental right that the Court established in previous opinions dealing with private sexual conduct, and extends beyond marital relationships. Kennedy explicitly stated that *Bowers v. Hardwick* was wrongly decided, and it was specifically overruled.

Lemon v. Kurtzman
403 U.S. 602, 91 S. Ct. 2105 (1971)

Pennsylvania provided financial support to nonpublic elementary and secondary schools to defray the cost of teachers' salaries, textbooks, and instructional materials in specified secular subjects. Rhode Island law provided for a direct payment supplement to teachers in nonelementary schools. Both states included church-related schools in the class of schools aided through these laws.

Writing for the Supreme Court, Chief Justice Burger held that the Pennsylvania and Rhode Island laws foster an excessive entanglement with religion in violation of the Establishment Clause of the First Amendment as applied to the states through the Due Process Clause of the Fourteenth Amendment. While the state may be able to control the content of textbooks, it is not in a position to monitor how teachers interject faith and morals into secular subjects. Moreover, the matter of spending taxpayers' money to support religious schools will inevitably involve partisan and other political activity. Burger announced a three-fold test for ascertaining when the Establishment Clause is violated: (1) Does the statute possess a secular legislative purpose? (2) Is the principal or primary effect of the statute either to advance or inhibit religion? (3) Does the statute foster an excessive government entanglement with religion?

Lochner v. New York
198 U.S. 45, 25 S. Ct. 539, 49 L. Ed. 937 (1905)

Joseph Lochner, a bakery owner, was convicted of violating an 1897 New York statute prohibiting bakeries from allowing employees to work more than ten hours per day or more than sixty hours per week. After two New York appellate courts affirmed Lochner's conviction, the case was appealed to the U.S. Supreme Court.

Writing for the majority, Justice Rufus Peckham held that while the state, through the exercise of its police powers, may prohibit individuals from making certain contracts, limitations on the hours a baker may work transcends the power of the state. Because it bears no reasonable relationship as a health law safeguarding the public health or the health of bakers, the legislation is in violation of the liberty provision of the Due Process Clause of the Fourteenth Amendment.

Lucas v. South Carolina Costal Council
505 U.S. 1003, 112 S. Ct. 2886, 120 L. Ed. 2d 798 (1992)

David Lucas purchased two oceanfront lots for almost one million dollars. Subsequently, the state imposed a zoning regulation prohibiting the construction of buildings on such property. South Carolina sought to preserve the beach and dunes as storm barriers. Lucas sued the state claiming the state action in question represented a taking of his property without just compensation. A state trial court agreed with Lucas. It found that the building restriction is a complete denial of his use of the property. The South Carolina Supreme Court, however, reversed the lower court.

Writing for a divided U.S. Supreme Court, Justice Antonin Scalia, relying on the trial court finding, held that the zoning regulation denied Lucas all economic use of his property. Consequently, the state violated the just compensation provision of the Constitution's Fifth Amendment as applied to the states by the Due Process Clause of the Fourteenth Amendment. Whenever an owner's property is diminished fully, there is a taking and just compensation is required.

Luther v. Borden
48 U.S. (7 How.) 1, 12 L. Ed. 581 (1849)

Despite the Revolutionary War, the state of Rhode Island continued to operate under its Colonial Charter of 1663. Some of the charter's provisions, particularly voting requirements, were a source of dissatisfaction among a group of citizens led by Thomas Dorr. Under Dorr's leadership, a new government was formed and a new constitution was adopted. The existing charter government appealed to President Tyler for federal troops to put down the so-called rebellion, but the president failed to dispatch troops. Dorr and his men were defeated by the state militia, and the rival government collapsed. In an attempt to round up insurgents, Borden and other state militiamen were sent to arrest Luther, a Dorr supporter. Arrested at his home, Luther sued Borden for illegal trespass claiming that the charter government had been supplanted by the more representative insurgent regime, a republican form of government guaranteed under article IV, section 4 of the U.S. Constitution. Therefore, Borden had no authority to arrest him and to trespass on his property.

After a diversity of citizenship proceedings in federal circuit court, the case came before the U.S. Supreme Court. Writing for the majority, Chief Justice Roger Taney held that under the Guaranty Clause (art. IV, sec. 4) Congress, not the courts, has the responsibility to determine whether a state government is republican or not. Moreover, Congress through statutory enactment had authorized the president and not the courts to aid in putting down domestic violence. The case is consequently a political question and hence not within the appropriate sphere of authority of the Supreme Court.

McCulloch v. Maryland
17 U.S. (4 Wheat.) 316, 4 L. Ed. 579 (1819)

In 1816, Congress established a national bank, one branch of which was located in Baltimore, Maryland. Two years later the Maryland legislature enacted a statute taxing banks and bank branches not chartered by the state legislature. McCulloch, the cashier of the Baltimore branch of the Bank of the United States, refused to pay the $15,000 annual fee or a two-percent tax on all notes issued by the bank. McCulloch was convicted in a Maryland county court and a state court of appeals affirmed his conviction.

Reaching the Supreme Court on a writ of error, the state courts were reversed. Chief Justice John Marshall first reasoned that the powers of the national government do not emanate from the states, but rather from the people. Although the powers of the national government are specifically enumerated, the "Necessary and Proper" Clause (art. I, sec. 8, cl. 18) authorizes Congress to establish a national bank under its great powers to lay and collect taxes, to borrow money, to regulate commerce, and so on. Because the power to tax is the power to destroy, the state may not tax a federal instrumentality. The state law is inconsistent with the federal law establishing the bank. The Supremacy Clause (art. VI, sec. 2) makes the Constitution, laws, and treaties of the United States supreme over state laws. Thus, the state tax is unconstitutional.

Mapp v. Ohio
367 U.S. 643, 81 S. Ct. 1684, 6 L. Ed. 2d 1081 (1961)

Acting on information that a bombing case suspect and illegal gambling equipment might be found in the home of Dollree Mapp, three Cleveland police officers arrived at Mapp's home requesting entrance. After being refused admission and without a search warrant, the officers broke into the premises, roughed up and handcuffed Mapp, and conducted a search of the entire premises. In the basement, the officers searched a trunk and found obscene materials. Ultimately the contents of the trunk were used to convict Mapp under an Ohio law for possession of obscene books, pictures, and photographs. The Ohio Supreme Court affirmed her conviction.

The United States Supreme Court reversed the lower court and overruled an earlier decision in Wolf v. Colorado, 338 U.S. 25 (1949). The Court in *Wolf* held ". . . that in a prosecution in a state court for a state crime the Fourteenth Amendment does not forbid the admission of evidence obtained by an unreasonable search and seizure." Establishing the exclusionary rule for state proceedings, Justice Tom Clark, writing for the majority in *Mapp v. Ohio*, held that the Due Process Clause of the Fourteenth Amendment incorporates the protections of the Fourth Amendment. Hence, evidence obtained in a search and seizure in violation of the Fourth Amendment is inadmissible in state, just as in federal, prosecutions.

Marbury v. Madison
5 U.S. (1 Cranch) 137, 2 L. Ed. 60 (1803)

In his last days as president, John Adams nominated William Marbury as Justice of the Peace for the District of Columbia. The Senate confirmed the nomination, but the commission appointing Marbury was never delivered by Secretary of State John Marshall. The next president, Thomas Jefferson, ordered Marshall's successor James Madison not to deliver the commission. Under the provisions of section 13 of the Judiciary Act of 1789, Marbury petitioned the U.S. Supreme Court to issue a writ of mandamus ordering the secretary of state to deliver the commission.

Writing for the Court, Chief Justice John Marshall concluded that Marbury had a legal right to the commission he demanded, and that where there is a legal right there must be a remedy. However, the remedy sought, a writ of mandamus, is not within the authority of the Court to grant. Marshall reasoned that section 13 of the Judiciary Act of 1789 violates the Constitution because by granting to the Court the authority to issue writs of mandamus in its original jurisdiction it adds to that jurisdiction; article III strictly limits the Supreme Court's original jurisdiction. Marshall based his conclusion on the following interrelated arguments. First, the Constitution established by the people a government of limited powers. Second, the Constitution is superior to legislative enactments. To hold otherwise would make a written constitution useless. Third, the Court cannot close its eyes to an unconstitutional act. He stated, "It is emphatically, the province and duty of the judicial department, to say what the law is." Fourth, judges take an oath to uphold the Constitution. It would be immoral for them to give effect to an unconstitutional act. Lastly, the phrasing of article VI, paragraph 2 mentions the Constitution first before it mentions laws, not the other way around. Therefore, the framers of the Constitution must have intended that the basic document be held superior to laws.

Miller v. California
413 U.S. 15, 93 S. Ct. 2607, 37 L. Ed. 2d 419 (1973)

Miller was found guilty by a jury of mailing unsolicited written materials to California residents advertising "adult books" and a film found to be in violation of that state's obscenity statute. The mailed materials also contained explicit pictures and drawings of men and women engaged in a variety of sexual acts. A state appellate court affirmed Miller's conviction.

Chief Justice Warren Burger in a 6–3 opinion seized the opportunity to restate what was viewed as a confusing jurisprudence on the subject of obscenity. He first reiterated the long stated judicial holding that obscenity is not protected by the First Amendment. He then indicated that the test in Memoirs v. Massachusetts, 383 U.S. 413 (1966), requiring that the materials in question are "utterly without redeeming social value" is no longer workable. The new rule requires that state statutes must specifically define what depictions of sexual conduct are forbidden. Further, "the state offense must be limited to works which, taken as a whole, appeal to the prurient interest in sex, which portray sexual conduct in a patently offensive way, and which taken as a whole, do not have serious literary, artistic, political, or scientific value." In making any such determination, juries should not be asked to apply abstract national standards because the country is too large and diverse to make such a determination feasible. Rather, juries should be guided by the standards of their community—in this case the jury should apply the contemporary standards of decency in the state of California.

Milliken v. Bradley
418 U.S. 717, 94 S. Ct. 3112, 41 L. Ed. 2d 1069 (1974)

A class-action suit brought by the local branch of the NAACP alleged that Detroit public schools were segregated on the basis of race and were in violation of the Equal Protection Clause of the Fourteenth Amendment. The federal district court ruled in favor of the NAACP and ordered desegregation plans for the Detroit school system, as well as for several suburban districts within the metropolitan area. On appeal, the United States Court of Appeals affirmed the district court decision holding that the state had committed *de jure* acts of segregation in the Detroit area and that the district court had the remedial power to order interdistrict desegregation. The U.S. Supreme Court reversed the Court of Appeals decision and remanded the case back to the district court for further consideration.

Writing for the majority, Chief Justice Burger held that the lower courts had based their decisions on an erroneous standard that was unsupported by evidence that acts of outlying districts affected the discrimination found in the Detroit schools. Unless district lines were deliberately drawn to produce segregation or segregation in one district caused discrimination on the basis of race in another, a federal court does not possess the authority to order busing of students between school districts to remedy *de jure* segregation that exists in only one of the districts.

Miranda v. Arizona
384 U.S. 436, 86 S. Ct. 1602, 16 L. Ed. 2d 694 (1966)

Together with a group of state and federal cases, a controversy came before the U.S. Supreme Court dealing with the admissibility of statements or confessions made by defendants during custodial interrogations. The Court considered the question of what procedures are necessary to assure that defendants' Fifth and Sixth Amendment rights are protected.

Delivering the majority opinion for the Court, Chief Justice Earl Warren emphasized that the holding is not an innovation in American jurisprudence, but rather an application of long recognized principles of criminal justice. The Court held that in the absence of a clear, intelligent waiver of the constitutional rights involved, a suspect ". . . must be warned prior to any questioning that he has a right to remain silent, that anything he says can be used against him in a court of law, that he has the right to the presence of an attorney, and that if he cannot afford an attorney one will be appointed for him prior to any questioning if he so desires." The Court also noted that if the suspect does not wish to be interrogated, the police must cease the interrogation. Simply because the suspect may have answered questions or volunteered statements does not in any way deprive the suspect of the right to refrain from answering any additional queries until such time as the suspect has had an opportunity to consult with legal counsel and thereafter consents to the questioning.

Missouri v. Holland
252 U.S. 416, 40 S. Ct. 382, 64 L. Ed. 641 (1920)

In 1916, the United States and Great Britain entered into a treaty to protect various species of birds that migrate between the United States and Canada. In 1918, pursuant to the treaty, Congress passed a law authorizing the secretary of agriculture to establish seasons for hunting and other rules concerning the birds named in the treaty. The state of Missouri filed suit in federal district court to enjoin Ray Holland, a game warden of the United States government, from enforcement of the act. Following the district court's dismissal of the suit, Missouri appealed to the U.S. Supreme Court. It contended that the subject matter of both the treaty and the statute were beyond the enumerated powers of the national government and constituted an invasion of the powers of the state in violation of the Tenth Amendment.

Speaking for a majority of the Court, Justice Oliver Wendell Holmes held that the Tenth Amendment does not limit the power of the United States to make treaties. The treaty powers of the federal government are broader than the enumerated powers of Congress. He further stated, "Acts of Congress are the supreme law of the land only when made in pursuance of the Constitution, while treaties are declared to be so when made under the authority of the United States." Treaty-making authority cannot be ascertained in the same way as the authorities dictating congressional legislative power. Instead, Holmes maintained that the treaty-making power must be viewed in light of America's experience as a developing nation. The federal government must act in the national interest to protect the birds and with them our forests and crops. Reliance upon the states is insufficient.

Munn v. Illinois
94 U.S. 113, 24 L. Ed. 77 (1877)

The Granger movement was a protest movement that swept across the Midwest region of the United States against the felt exploitation of farmers by railroads and other business enterprises. In 1871, the Illinois state legislature responded by enacting a law requiring the licensing of grain elevator operators and establishing maximum rates elevators could charge for grain storage. Ira Munn refused to comply with the statute, and the state filed suit. A county court ruled against Munn, and on appeal to the Illinois Supreme Court, the lower court judgment was affirmed. On appeal to the U.S. Supreme Court, the judgment was once again affirmed.

Writing for the majority, Chief Justice Morrison Waite rejected Munn's Due Process and Commerce Clause arguments. First addressing himself to the Fourteenth Amendment Due Process Clause argument, Waite cited a common law principle of property law of at least two hundred years vintage. He wrote, "Property does become clothed with a public interest when used in a manner to make it of public consequence, and affect the community at large. When, therefore, one devotes his property to a use in which the public has an interest, he, in effect, grants to the public an interest in that use, and must submit to be controlled by the public for the common good, to the extent of the interest he has thus created. He may withdraw his grant by discontinuing the use; but, so long as he maintains the use, he must submit to the control." Since the state has not deprived Munn of property but is only controlling it in the public interest, there is no violation of the Due Process Clause of the Fourteenth Amendment. Munn also argued that he is entitled to a reasonable compensation for use of his property. However, the Supreme Court held that this is a matter of legislative judgment and not the courts. If protection against abuse by the legislature is sought, the proper remedy is at the polls, not the courts. Responding to Munn's Interstate Commerce Clause argument, Waite noted that the state has an interest in regulating business exclusively within the limits of Illinois. Although the regulation of grain elevators may incidentally touch upon interstate commerce, the state may regulate in the absence of congressional regulation.

Murray v. Curlett
(*see*, School District of Abington Township v. Schempp)

National Labor Relations Board v. Jones & Laughlin Steel Corp.
301 U.S. 1, 57 S. Ct. 615, 81 L. Ed. 893 (1937)

The National Labor Relations Act (Wagner Act) was passed in 1935 to guarantee the right of collective bargaining, and the act authorized the National Labor Relations Board to prevent unfair labor relations affecting interstate commerce. The Board found the Jones & Laughlin Steel Corporation had violated provisions of the Wagner Act when it fired ten workers because of their activities on behalf of the union. The NLRB ordered the steel company to reinstate the employees. When Jones & Laughlin refused to comply, the NLRB petitioned a U.S. circuit court to enforce its order, but the court agreed with Jones & Laughlin that the Wagner Act is a regulation of labor relations and not commerce within the meaning of the Constitution's Commerce Clause.

Writing for a five to four majority, Chief Justice Hughes found that the matter of labor relations bears a close and substantial relationship to interstate commerce. Congress cannot be denied the power to protect commerce from burdens and obstructions due to the paralyzing consequences of industrial strife. The decision in this case spelled an end to the judicially created distinction between direct and indirect effects on interstate commerce and paved the way for extensive congressional legislation in labor-management relations.

National Treasury Employees Union v. Von Raab
489 U.S. 656, 109 S. Ct. 1384, 103 L. Ed. 2d 685 (1989)

The U.S. Customs Service instituted a program of mandatory drug screening of those employees seeking transfer to positions that directly involve the interdiction of illicit drugs, require the carrying of a firearm, or involve access to classified information. Officials of the Customs Service justified the program on the grounds that it had a special responsibility to ensure a drug-free workforce because it was charged with the task of "stemming the tide of illicit drugs entering into the United States." The agency did not justify the program based upon individual suspicion that particular employees were involved in drugs. A federal district court granted the union declaratory and injunctive relief, but the U.S. Court of Appeals for the Fifth Circuit vacated the judgment.

Anthony Kennedy, writing for the Supreme Court's majority, held that the urine tests are a reasonable search under the Constitution's Fourth Amendment, and the public interest in controlling drugs outweighs the employees' right to privacy. Because it is sometimes impractical, a warrant, probable cause, or individualized suspicion are not indispensable components of what is reasonable government conduct. The government has a compelling interest in requiring Customs Service employees to undergo the drug tests because it is the first line of defense in the national crisis caused by the smuggling of illicit narcotics.

New York Times Co. v. Sullivan
376 U.S. 254, 84 S. Ct. 710, 11 L. Ed. 2d 686 (1964)

A paid advertisement in the *New York Times* made certain claims pertaining to the alleged mistreatment of African-American students and Martin Luther King in Montgomery, Alabama. Though not named directly in this advertisement, Sullivan, an elected county commissioner, contended the word *police* utilized in the ad referred to him as the supervisor of the Montgomery Police Department. Because particulars in the advertisement were not true, Sullivan sued the *New York Times* under Alabama libel laws. A state court awarded Sullivan $500,000 in damages, and the Alabama Supreme Court affirmed the judgment.

Justice William Brennan announced the constitutional rule that reversed the Alabama courts. To promote expression and robust criticism of government officials and to deter self-censorship, the First and Fourteenth Amendments offer a conditional shield against libel laws. Public officials may not recover damages for defamation of character unless they can prove actual malice. Defined by the Court, actual malice consists of a false statement made ". . . with knowledge that it was false or with reckless disregard of whether it was false or not."

New York Times Co. v. United States
403 U.S. 713, 91 S. Ct. 2140, 29 L. Ed. 2d 822 (1971)

The United States government sought an injunction to restrain the *New York Times* from publishing the contents of a Pentagon top-secret study entitled

History of U.S. Decision-making Process on Vietnam Policy. The government sought similar injunctive relief in an action against the *Washington Post.* Each district court in which suits were brought denied injunctive relief. The United States Court of Appeals for the District Court of Columbia affirmed the ruling of the district court for the District of Columbia, but the U.S. Court of Appeals for the Second Circuit remanded the case to the district court for further proceedings.

The Supreme Court affirmed the judgment of the Court of Appeals for the District of Columbia and reversed the order of the U.S. Court of Appeals for the Second Circuit with directions to enter a judgment affirming the judgment of the district court. In a per curiam decision, the Court held that the government had not overcome the heavy presumption against prior restraint by demonstrating sufficient justification for halting the publications.

Nixon v. Fitzgerald
457 U.S. 731, 102 S. Ct. 2690, 73 L. Ed. 2d 349 (1982)

A. Ernest Fitzgerald, a civil servant and Pentagon management analyst, appeared before a congressional subcommittee where he testified to waste and mismanagement in the development of a new military transport aircraft. Dismissed from his position, Fitzgerald had reason to believe that the Nixon administration punished him for his whistle-blowing testimony. Fitzgerald named the president and several of his aides in a civil suit for monetary damages. After several administrative and judicial actions, the matter was carried before the U.S. Supreme Court for final adjudication.

The Court concluded that as a former president, Nixon was entitled to absolute immunity from damages predicated on his official acts. Because of his central role in the government, the president must be free from diversions of private lawsuits. While the president has "absolute immunity" from civil suits for acts within the "outer perimeter" of his official responsibility, his aides are entitled to only "qualified immunity." Thus, in *Harlow v. Fitzgerald* (1982), the Court held that officials performing discretionary functions generally are shielded from civil liability to the extent that their conduct does not violate established rights that a reasonable person would have known.

Palko v. Connecticut
302 U.S. 319, 58 S. Ct. 149, 82 L. Ed. 288 (1937)

Frank Palko was found guilty of second-degree murder and was given a life sentence. A Connecticut statute, however, permitted the state to appeal criminal cases. The Connecticut Supreme Court of Errors ordered a new trial. Palko was tried again, found guilty of murder in the first degree and sentenced to death. The Connecticut Supreme Court of Errors then affirmed the conviction. Contending that the Fourteenth Amendment's due process provision makes the Fifth Amendment's double jeopardy provision applicable to the states, Palko appealed to the U.S. Supreme Court.

In the decision delivered by Justice Benjamin Cardozo, the Court affirmed the state court decision. The Fourteenth Amendment did not serve to incorporate the prohibition against double jeopardy found in the Fifth Amendment to the states. Cardozo justified the ruling by creating a distinction between those provisions of the Bill of Rights that are central to "principles implicit in the concept of ordered liberty" and those that are not.

Planned Parenthood of Southeastern Pennsylvania v. Casey
505 U.S.833, 112 S. Ct. 2791, 120 L. Ed. 2d 674 (1992)

Pennsylvania enacted a statute restricting a woman's legal right to an abortion. One provision permits an abortion in the case of a medical emergency, defined as a pregnancy that may cause death or severe bodily harm to a woman. Another provision allows for an abortion only after informed consent is granted. This provision requires a 24-hour waiting period. A spousal notification provision requires that a woman sign a statement that she has notified her spouse she is about to undergo an abortion procedure. With a provision for a judicial bypass procedure, an unemancipated woman under the age of eighteen may not obtain an abortion unless one of her parents or guardians provides informed consent. Finally, the law contains a record-keeping provision requiring a married woman's reason for her failure to provide notice to her husband of the abortion.

In an unusual approach to opinion writing, the controlling opinion was penned by three justices: O'Connor, Kennedy, and Souter. They agreed to abandon the trimester approach found in *Roe v. Wade* in favor of an undue burden test. They defined an undue burden as one that places "a substantial obstacle in the path of a woman seeking an abortion of a nonviable fetus." Following this approach to constitutional interpretation, the Court held: the medical-emergency provision constitutional; the informed-consent provision requiring a 24-hour waiting period constitutional; the spousal-notification provision unconstitutional; the parent-or-guardian-consent provision constitutional; and the record-keeping provision unconstitutional.

Plessy v. Ferguson
163 U.S. 537, 16 S. Ct. 1138, 41 L. Ed. 256 (1896)

In 1890, the Louisiana legislature enacted a statute requiring railroads to provide equal but separate accommodations for white and black passengers. The act made it unlawful for a person of one race to occupy a seat in a passenger car designated for passengers of another race. Homer Plessy, seven-eighths Caucasian, refused to give up his seat to a white passenger. During the course of criminal proceedings, Plessy petitioned the Louisiana Supreme Court to enjoin the trial judge, John Ferguson, from continuing the trial against him. After the state supreme court ruled against him, Plessy brought his case to the U.S. Supreme Court.

Writing for the majority, Justice Henry Brown, holding the equal but separate law a reasonable exercise of state power, determined that the state statute did not offend provisions of either the Thirteenth or Fourteenth Amendments. Brown noted that the state segregation law had not placed much stress upon the Thirteenth Amendment. He reasoned that the Louisiana law merely implies a legal distinction between the races based on color and possessed no tendency to reestablish slavery—the true purpose of the Thirteenth Amendment. The Fourteenth Amendment, Brown argued, was intended to enforce "the absolute equality of the two races before the law, but, in the nature of things, it could not have been intended to abolish distinctions based upon color, or to enforce social, as distinguished from political, equality, or a commingling of the two races upon terms unsatisfactory to either." Brown emphasized that even in states where the rights of blacks have been most vigorously enforced, segregation in education and laws against intermarriage have been upheld. Given the customs and traditions of the people, argued Brown, the reasonableness of the statute is within the discretion of the state legislature. This state law did not seem less reasonable than the acts of Congress requiring separate schools for blacks in the District of Columbia. Anticipating the dissent by Justice John Harlan, Brown argued that the enforcement of segregation does not stamp the colored race with a badge of inferiority. "If it be so," Brown stated, "it is not by reason of anything found in the act, but solely because the colored race choose to put the construction upon it." Finally, Brown stated, "If one race be inferior to the other socially, the constitution of the United States cannot put them upon the same plane."

Pollock v. Farmers' Loan and Trust Co.
158 U.S. 601, 15 S. Ct. 912, 39 L. Ed. 1108 (1895)

In 1894, Congress enacted the Wilson Gorman Tariff Act, which established a proportional tax on income. Pollock, a shareholder in Farmers' Loan and Trust Co., sued to enjoin the company from paying the tax. A U.S. circuit court upheld the tax and Pollock appealed to the Supreme Court. Initially, the Supreme Court, with Justice Howell Jackson absent because of illness, declared the law invalid insofar as it applied to the income from real estate and state and municipal bonds. The Court split on the question of whether stocks, bonds, wages, salaries, and professional earnings were subject to taxation. Following Justice Jackson's recovery, however, the Court granted a rehearing.

Writing for the majority, Chief Justice Fuller held the act unconstitutional. Because it was deemed a direct tax and was not apportioned among the states, the tax scheme was viewed as inconsistent with article I, section 8, clause 1. While the Court did not directly invalidate the provisions taxing income derived from wages and professional earnings, under the partial unconstitutionality of statute rule, established in a previous case, the entire act was held invalid.

Powell v. Alabama
287 U.S. 45, 53 S. Ct. 55, 77 L. Ed. 158 (1932)

Powell and six other African-American defendants were charged with the capital offense of the rape of two white women. The record indicates that the blacks had been riding in a freight train with seven white boys and two white girls. A fight took place between the black and white boys, during the course of which all but one white was thrown off the train. A message was sent ahead and the blacks were arrested. The two girls reported that each black youth raped them. In a hostile community atmosphere, the defendants were indicted and arraigned. They were not asked whether they had counsel or wished to have counsel appointed or whether friends or relatives might assist them. It was not until the morning of the trial that counsel was appointed. Prior to that time, the trial judge appointed all members of the local bar for the limited purpose of arraigning the defendants. Upon conviction, the defendants appealed to the Alabama Supreme Court for review. The trial court judgment was affirmed and the case was appealed to the U.S. Supreme Court.

Writing for the majority, Justice Sutherland held that in light of the circumstances of the case, the defendants were denied the right to legal counsel guaranteed by the Due Process Clause of the Fourteenth Amendment. Together with its sequel, Norris v. Alabama, 294 U.S. 587 (1935), the cases are popularly known as the "Scottsboro cases."

Prize Cases
67 U.S. (2 Black) 635, 17 L. Ed. 459 (1863)

After the Civil War broke out, but before Congress had an opportunity to meet in special session to declare war, President Abraham Lincoln instituted a blockade of all the naval ports of the Confederate states. During the period between the commencement of the blockade and the subsequent ratification of the blockade by Congress, the President ordered the seizure of several ships and their cargoes as confiscated "prize" because of their attempt to run the Union blockade. The ship owners argued that the blockade was illegal because Lincoln's action was not made subsequent to a congressional declaration of war.

Writing for a 5–4 majority, Justice Grier asked whether a state of war existed at the time the blockade was instituted that would justify the president imposing military power. He first conceded that the Constitution confers the sole power on Congress to declare a national (civil) or foreign war. But an 1807 act of Congress authorized the president to call out U.S. military forces in cases of foreign invasion or domestic insurrection. The president has a duty to meet the challenge. The declaration of the blockade by the president is official and conclusive proof that a state of war existed that demanded his action. Moreover, because Congress passed an act in 1861 after the blockade approving the president's actions, it is clear that he acted pursuant to war as understood by the U.S. Constitution.

Regents of the University of California v. Bakke
438 U.S. 265, 98 S. Ct. 2733, 57 L. Ed. 2d 750 (1978)

The medical school of the University of California at Davis established two admissions programs. A regular admissions program filled eighty-four of the one hundred student positions. The remaining sixteen positions were set aside for minority applicants considered economically or educationally disadvantaged. These minority applicants were not required to meet the same scholastic requirements as those admitted under the regular admissions program. Allan Bakke, a white, was twice denied admission but possessed higher academic qualifications than the minority admission applicants. Bakke sued alleging that he was denied admission because of his race. A California trial court decided against Bakke, but the California Supreme Court reversed the lower court, ordering Bakke's admission to the medical school. The California Supreme Court based its decision on a finding of a denial of equal protection of the laws. The University of California appealed to the U.S. Supreme Court.

The U.S. Supreme Court found the Davis medical-school admissions program invalid under the Fourteenth Amendment. However, there was considerable disagreement among the members of the Court about the proper basis for its decision. Justice Lewis Powell, apparently representing a middle position, but writing for himself, announced the judgment of the Court. He found that since the special admissions program involved the utilization of an explicit racial classification, it disregards individual rights as guaranteed by the Fourteenth Amendment. Yet, protections afforded individuals are not absolute. Classifications that withstand the strict scrutiny test supersede individual rights. But there must be a demonstration that any classification based on race is "necessary to promote a substantial state interest." Because the Davis medical school failed to show, as claimed, that the preferential classification was likely to have a beneficial impact on better health-care delivery to minorities, Powell concluded that it did not meet the test. The California Supreme Court's equal protection holding was therefore affirmed. However, that part of the California decision that enjoined the Davis medical school from any consideration of the race of any applicant was reversed. Limiting the Court's judgment to the particular affirmative action program at Davis, Powell notes that other programs currently in use at other institutions are constitutionally permissible. He held that programs that consider race as one particular "plus," together with a number of other factors relevant to producing educational pluralism, may be weighed without offending the Fourteenth Amendment. As Powell put it, "The applicant who loses out on the last available seat to another candidate receiving a 'plus' on the basis of ethnic background will not have been foreclosed from all consideration for that seat simply because he was not the right color or had the wrong surname. It would mean only that his combined qualifications, which may have included similar nonobjective factors, did not outweigh those of the other applicant."

Reynolds v. Sims
377 U.S. 533, 84 S. Ct. 1362, 12 L. Ed. 2d 506 (1964)

This case and fourteen companion cases involved the malapportionment of state legislative districts. Challenging the validity of the legislative apportionment for the bicameral state legislature, Sims and other Alabama residents brought suit against Reynolds and other state and party officials.

Despite the requirement in the Alabama Constitution that the legislature be reapportioned on the basis of population every ten years, no new apportionment had taken place since 1901. Because the state's population growth had been uneven, Sims asserted that some citizens were victims of serious discrimination. Although the Alabama Supreme Court found that the legislature had failed to comply with the state constitution, it ruled that it could not intervene in legislative apportionment matters. A three-judge federal district court, however, found that the state apportionment violated the Equal Protection Clause of the Fourteenth Amendment. As a result, the Alabama legislature adopted two reapportionment plans, both of which were rejected by the district court. The court then ordered a temporary reapportionment, whereupon Reynolds appealed to the U.S. Supreme Court.

Writing for the majority, Chief Justice Earl Warren held that the Equal Protection Clause of the Fourteenth Amendment requires that seats in both houses of a bicameral state legislature must be apportioned according to population. Insisting that legislators represent people, not trees or acres, Warren argued that diluting the weight of votes because of place of residence is a form of discrimination as invidious as race or economic status. In addition, Warren countered the argument that in adopting a bicameral scheme the state had employed the same plans as the federal government by making several points. First, thirty-six original state constitutions provided for representation in both legislative chambers ". . . completely, or predominantly, on population." Second, the founding fathers did not intend to establish a model for the states when they established the bicameral system for the national government. Third, unlike the relationship between the federal and state governments, the counties, cities, and other political subdivisions of state government have never been regarded as sovereign entities; rather, they have been regarded as governmental instrumentalities designed to assist the state in carrying out vital governmental functions. Lastly, from a positive viewpoint, bicameralism is in the modern sense highly functional; it provides for mature and deliberate legislative proceedings. Focusing on the implementation of the one man, one vote principle, Warren stated that ". . . the Equal Protection Clause requires that a state make an honest and good faith effort to construct districts, in both houses of its legislature, as nearly of equal population as is practicable. We recognize that it is a practical impossibility to arrange legislative districts so that each one has an identical number of residents, or citizens, or voters. Mathematical exactness or precision is hardly a workable constitutional requirement."

Richmond, City of v. J.A. Croson Co.
488 U.S. 469, 109 S. Ct. 706, 102 L. Ed. 2d 854 (1989)

The city of Richmond, Virginia, enacted a minority business plan requiring prime contractors to subcontract at least 30 percent of the dollar amount of their contracts to minority business enterprises. Minority business was defined to include a business from anywhere in the country at least 50 percent of which is owned and controlled by black, Spanish-speaking, Oriental,

Indian, Eskimo, or Aleut citizens. This program was instituted after a public hearing where no evidence was provided indicating that the city or its prime contractors had discriminated on the basis of race. The only evidence submitted was statistical; the data indicated that while the city's population was 50 percent black, less than one percent of the contracts let by its prime contractors had been awarded to minority businesses in recent years.

The U.S. Supreme Court found the city's plan in violation of the Equal Protection Clause of the Fourteenth Amendment. Most members of the Court agreed with Justice Sandra Day O'Connor that the case must be judged from a strict scrutiny approach. That is, the burden of proof is upon the city to demonstrate that the plan to remedy past evils is justified by a "compelling government interest," and the plan is "narrowly tailored" to accomplish a remedial purpose. A generalized assertion of past discrimination in the community, as is the case here, is insufficient to demonstrate a compelling interest to justify a racial quota.

Roe v. Wade
410 U.S. 113, 93 S. Ct. 705, 35 L. Ed. 2d 147 (1973)

An unmarried pregnant woman wishing to terminate her pregnancy by abortion challenged Texas statutes prohibiting abortions except those procured by medical advice for the purpose of saving the life of the mother in U.S. District Court. The three-judge district court heard her case together with two others and held that the woman and a physician who had suffered past prosecutions and was presently facing additional charges had standing to sue. Moreover, the district court held that the criminal abortion statutes were void because they were unconstitutionally vague and overbroad. On appeal to the U.S. Supreme Court, the physician's complaint was dismissed, but the district court judgment with respect to the unmarried pregnant woman was affirmed.

In a decision delivered by Justice Harry Blackmun, the Supreme Court held that a woman's decision to terminate her pregnancy is within her constitutional right to privacy protected under the liberty provision of the Due Process Clause of the Fourteenth Amendment. The Court acknowledged that while the right to privacy is a fundamental right, such rights might be limited by a compelling state interest. However, a compelling state interest cannot be demonstrated in the first trimester of pregnancy. For the stage beginning with the end of the first trimester, the state, in promoting its interest in the health of the mother, may, if it chooses, regulate the abortion procedure in ways that are reasonably related to maternal health. In the last trimester, the state may regulate and even prohibit abortion except where it might be necessary for the preservation of the life or health of the mother.

Rosenberger v. Rector and Visitors of the University of Virginia
515 U.S. 819, 115 S. Ct. 2510, 132 L. Ed. 2d 700 (1995)

As is the case with most state institutions of higher education, the University of Virginia authorized the payment from student-body funds for costs associated with the publication of materials distributed by recognized student groups. However, the UV administration withheld payment of printing costs for a newspaper distributed by a Christian student group called "Wide Awake." Rosenberger, a student founder of this organization, brought suit against the institution claiming that the policy violates First Amendment principles. A federal district court and court of appeals found for the university.

Writing for a sharply divided 5–4 majority, Justice Kennedy concluded that the University action prohibiting payment for the Christian publication is viewpoint discrimination in violation of the freedom of speech provision of the First Amendment. The state may not discriminate on the basis of the substantive content of a message conveyed in a public forum. Once the university opens its facilities as a public forum it must treat all speakers equally. Further, the university does not violate the First Amendment's Establishment Clause when it grants access to its facilities on a religion-neutral basis to a wide spectrum of students. The physical process of printing and paying costs does not involve the university in religion any more than when it provides meeting rooms to religious and nonreligious groups alike.

Saenz v. Roe
525 U.S. 489, 119 S. Ct. 1518, 143 L. Ed. 2d 689 (1999)

In 1992, California enacted a statute that limited the maximum welfare benefits available to residents who have lived in the state for less than twelve months to the same amount they would have received in their former states of residence. Because California provided welfare benefits that were considerably greater than most other states, the state would save tax dollars utilizing such a plan. Also, in 1992 the U.S. Secretary for Health and Human Services issued a waiver to the state for its lack of conformity to the federal rules. In addition, an amendment to the Social Security Act by Congress in 1996 authorized the California scheme. Several newly arrived residents from other states filed suit. A federal district court issued a preliminary injunction against the California law and a U.S. Court of Appeals affirmed. The U.S. Supreme Court granted a petition from California for a writ of certiorari.

Justice Stevens, writing for a 7–2 Court, held that the Privileges and Immunities Clause of the Fourteenth Amendment prevents California from enacting a law that treats newly arrived residents differently from other citizens. When states attempt to limit the right of citizens to travel, the highest level of judicial scrutiny must be applied, not some intermediate standard of review or the least difficult hurdle, the rational basis test. The state could have found other reasonable ways of reducing its costs of funding welfare programs. Consequently, the state's legitimate interest in saving funds provides no justification for its decision to discriminate among otherwise eligible citizens. Moreover, it is well established that Congress may not authorize states to violate the various provisions of the Fourteenth Amendment.

Schechter Poultry Corp. v. United States
295 U.S. 495, 55 S. Ct. 837, 79 L. Ed. 1570 (1935)

In 1933, in an attempt to stimulate business and reduce unemployment during the Great Depression, the National Industrial Recovery Act (NIRA) was enacted. Among its provisions, the NIRA authorized the president to approve state and local codes establishing standards on wages, hours, trade practices, working conditions, and methods of competition. The Schechter brothers owned slaughterhouses in New York City that received live chickens from other states. They were convicted in a federal district court of violating the Live Poultry Code on counts including filling false sales and price reports and selling diseased poultry. The U.S. Court of Appeals for the Second Circuit affirmed in part the decision of the district court, and both Schechter and the government appealed to the U.S. Supreme Court.

Writing for the Court, Chief Justice Charles Evans Hughes addressed two issues: first, the question of the delegation of legislative power and second, the application of the provisions of the Live Poultry Code to intrastate commerce. Because the NIRA supplies no standards for any trade, industry, or activity, the president is given unfettered discretion in approving or prescribing codes. The NIRA is therefore an unconstitutional delegation of legislative power. Second, the slaughtering and local sales of poultry are transactions in intrastate and not interstate commerce. For Congress to regulate this activity there must be a direct and not an indirect effect on interstate commerce. Thus, the slaughterhouse and sales activity of the Schechter brothers is not within the power of Congress to regulate.

Schenck v. United States
249 U.S. 47, 39 S. Ct. 247, 63 L. Ed. 470 (1919)

Charles T. Schenck, the general secretary of the Socialist Party, and others were charged and indicted under the Espionage Act of 1917 for conspiring to obstruct the recruiting and enlistment service of the United States during the war with Germany. Schenck printed and distributed 15,000 leaflets that urged men to oppose the draft. After conviction in federal district court, Schenck appealed to the U.S. Supreme Court.

Writing for the Court, Justice Oliver Wendell Holmes rejected the claim that the First Amendment guarantees absolute free speech. In peace time, the circulation of the leaflet would be protected. But Holmes argued, ". . . the character of every act depends upon the circumstances in which it is done. . . . The most stringent protection of free speech would not protect a man in falsely shouting fire in a theatre and causing a panic." The test in every case is ". . . whether the words used are used in such circumstances and are of such a nature as to create a clear and present danger that they will bring about the substantive evils that Congress has a right to prevent." Admitting that Schenck and his associates did not bring about the end of conscription, Holmes held that success is not necessary to convict for conspiracy. If the intent and the tendency of the act are the same, ". . . there is no ground for saying that success alone warrants making the act a crime."

School District of Abington Township v. Schempp
Murray v. Curlett
374 U.S. 203, 83 S. Ct. 1560, 10 L. Ed. 2d 844 (1963)

In *School District of Abington Township v. Schempp* the Schempp family, members of the Unitarian church, brought suit to enjoin the enforcement of a Pennsylvania statute requiring Bible readings at the beginning of each school day. Student participation, however, was voluntary. The Schempp family contended that the law is a violation of the Establishment Clause of the First Amendment. A three-judge district court panel granted injunctive relief. In the companion case of *Murray v. Curlett*, the school board, relying on a Maryland statute, adopted an opening exercise of Bible readings similar to those in Abington. Murray and her son, a student in a Baltimore school, both of whom were professed atheists, brought suit to compel Curlett, the president of the Maryland Board of School Commissioners, to rescind the Bible-reading requirement. A Maryland state court ruled against Murray, and the Maryland Court of Appeals affirmed.

Both cases were appealed to the U.S. Supreme Court. The Schempp judgment was affirmed, and the Murray decision was reversed. Writing for the majority, Justice Tom C. Clark expressed the constitutional doctrine with respect to religion. The constitutional test for the Establishment Clause is ". . . what are the purpose and primary effect of the enactment." If it either advances or inhibits religion then the enactment is unconstitutional. Demonstrating a violation of the Free Exercise Clause of the First Amendment requires showing a coercive effect as it operates against individuals in the practice of religion. The Court found the Abington and Baltimore practices were religious in character, and that these exercises violate the Establishment Clause of the First Amendment.

Scott v. Sanford
(*see*, Dred Scott v. Sanford)

Shelley v. Kraemer
334 U.S. 1, 68 S. Ct. 836, 92 L. Ed. 1161 (1948)

A majority of the deeds in a St. Louis neighborhood contained restrictive covenant provisions that prohibited property owners from selling their land to Negroes or members of the Mongolian race. Unaware of the restrictive covenant, Shelley, a Negro, purchased property in this neighborhood. When the restrictive covenant provision was discovered, Shelley refused to reconsider the purchase. Kraemer, a neighborhood resident and also a homeowner with a covenant provision on his property, sued to prevent Shelley from taking possession of the property. The trial court, however, found that the restrictive provision was technically faulty. The Missouri Supreme Court reversed the trial court and found that the property restriction did not violate constitutional rights. Shelley then appealed to the U.S. Supreme Court.

Delivering the unanimous opinion of the Court, Chief Justice Fred Vinson struck down the restrictive covenant as inconsistent with the Equal Protection Clause of the Fourteenth Amendment. Maintaining the distinction between state and private action, a principle established in the Civil Rights Cases, 109 U.S. 3 (1883), Vinson noted that the Fourteenth Amendment does not prohibit discrimination by private parties but refers only to official state conduct. The restrictive covenant agreements were, in the first instance, actions of private individuals. However, when as here, the state judiciary is utilized for the enforcement of private contracts, the action of a private citizen is transformed into state action. The chief justice wrote that because the "enjoyment of property rights was among the basic objectives sought to be effectuated by the framers of the Fourteenth Amendment," state discrimination had occurred.

Slaughterhouse Cases
(*see,* Butchers' Benevolent Association v.
Crescent City Livestock Landing and Slaughterhouse Co.)

Smith v. Allwright
321 U.S. 649, 64 S. Ct. 757, 88 L. Ed. 987 (1944)

In 1927, the Texas legislature enacted a law granting political parties the right to establish their own qualifications for party membership. Pursuant to this law, at its 1932 state convention, the Texas Democratic Party adopted a resolution imparting membership in the Democratic Party and full entitlement to participate in party deliberations to "all white" citizens of the state. Because only Democratic Party members were permitted to vote in Democratic Party primary elections, African Americans were denied the opportunity to vote in such elections. Smith, an African American, brought suit against Allwright, an election judge, for refusing him the opportunity to vote in a primary election. After lower court deliberations, the U.S. Supreme Court granted certiorari to hear the case.

Delivering the opinion for the majority, Justice Stanley Reed held the Texas practice a violation of the right-to-vote guarantee of the Fifteenth Amendment. Overruling its decision in Grovey v. Townsend, 295 U.S. 45 (1935), the Supreme Court found that the primary elections are "conducted by the party under state statutory authority." Reed further concluded, "The privilege of membership in a party may be, as this Court said in *Grovey v. Townsend* . . . no concern of a state. But when, as here, that privilege is also the essential qualification for voting in a primary to select nominees for a general election, the state makes the action of the party the action of the state."

Stuart v. Laird
5 U.S. (I Cranch) 299, 2 L. Ed. 115 (1803)

John Laird won a judgment against Hugh Stuart in the Fourth Circuit Court of the United States. However, because Congress repealed an 1801 law creating that court with the passage of the Judicial Repeal Act of 1802, Laird applied for and obtained judgment against Stuart. Stuart argued that because the fourth circuit court had decided the case, no other court, to wit, the Fifth Circuit Court, could proceed in the final disposition of the case.

Writing for the Supreme Court, Justice Paterson upheld the constitutionality of the Judicial Repeal Act of 1802. The Court found that the removal of the suit brought by Stuart against Laird from the court of the fourth circuit to the court of the fifth circuit is within the authority of Congress. In addition, the Judicial Repeal Act of 1802 did not deprive judges of good-behavior tenure as guaranteed under article III, section 1. Interpreting the statute narrowly, Justice Paterson found that the law did not deprive Stuart of the right to have his case heard by judges serving during good behavior. The law merely transferred his case from a court deriving its authority from an 1801 law to one organized under the Judicial Repeal Act of 1802. Congress has the power to organize the lower federal courts as it wants. Congress had also compelled Supreme Court justices to sit as circuit judges, as John Marshall had done in this cause of action. To this objection Justice Paterson argued that it had become accepted practice for Supreme Court justices to serve as circuit judges without having distinct commissions to do so. This has been true beginning with the commencement of the federal judicial system.

Texas v. Johnson
491 U.S. 397, 109 S. Ct. 2533, 105 L. Ed. 2d 342 (1989)

As part of a political demonstration outside the 1984 Republican National Convention in Dallas, Gregory Johnson burned an American flag while protesters chanted slogans. Although some bystanders were offended by the act, there were no physical injuries nor was any person threatened with injury. Johnson was arrested and convicted of intentionally desecrating a venerated object, a misdemeanor offense under Texas law. An intermediate state court affirmed the conviction, but the Texas Court of Appeals held that the flag-burning incident was an expressive form of behavior protected by the Constitution's First Amendment. The state appealed the case to the U.S. Supreme Court.

In a 6–3 vote, William Brennan delivered the opinion for the Court. He found that flag burning was a form of expressive behavior protected by the First Amendment. Though it is permissible to limit speech where the government has a compelling interest in regulating the nonspeech element of conduct, there is no evidence in this case that there was a disturbance or fighting words. Moreover, while the state may have an interest in preserving national unity and the flag is a symbol of that unity, the underlying principle of the First Amendment is to prohibit government from suppressing offensive or disagreeable ideas.

Tinker v. Des Moines Independent Community School District
393 U.S. 503, 89 S. Ct. 733, 21 L. Ed. 2d 731 (1969)

As part of a plan to protest U.S. involvement in the Vietnam conflict, two students, John Tinker and his sister Mary Beth, wore black armbands to school. The school board had previously declared that such action would result in suspension, and when the students refused to remove the armbands they were suspended until they would comply. Represented by their parents, the Tinkers sued in federal district court for injunctive relief. The district court dismissed the complaint. The U.S. Court of Appeals divided evenly. The case was then appealed to the U.S. Supreme Court.

Writing for the majority, Justice Abe Fortas held that the suspensions violated the First and Fourteenth Amendments and reversed and remanded the case. He maintained that the wearing of armbands in the circumstances of this case was entirely divorced from actual or potential disruptive conduct. Fortas characterized the activity as closely akin to "pure speech." Nor was there any demonstration that engaging in the protest would materially and substantially interfere with the requirements of appropriate student discipline. The Court also noted that other students have worn such political symbols as campaign buttons, including the Iron Cross, without penalty. In a vigorous defense of student rights, Fortas wrote, "Students in school as well as out of school are 'persons' under our Constitution. They are possessed of fundamental rights that the State must respect, just as they themselves must respect their obligations to the State. In our system, students may not be regarded as closed-circuit recipients of only that which the State chooses to communicate. They may not be confined to the expression of those sentiments that are officially approved. In the absence of a specific showing of constitutionally valid reasons to regulate their speech, students are entitled to freedom of expression of their views."

Trustees of Dartmouth College v. Woodward
17 U.S. (4 Wheat.) 518, 4 L. Ed. 629 (1819)

Before the Revolutionary War began, Dartmouth College had been granted a charter from King George. The charter authorized the establishment of a Board of Trustees to govern the college and to appoint successors. In 1816, however, the New Hampshire legislature enacted three laws amending the original charter and providing for a new governing body for the college to be appointed by the governor. Refusing to recognize the validity of the legislation, the incumbent trustees brought suit against William Woodward, the secretary-treasurer of the new board, to recover the college property. Argued before the New Hampshire Supreme Court, the legislation was upheld and the incumbent trustees brought the case to the U.S. Supreme Court on a writ of error.

Writing for the Court, Chief Justice John Marshall held that the corporate charter, possessing all the characteristics of a contract, was in fact a contract properly understood in article I, section 10 of the Constitution. Because the charter was effectively nullified by the state legislature, the contract was impaired in violation of the constitutional provision.

United States v. Butler
297 U.S. 1, 56 S. Ct. 312, 80 L. Ed. 477 (1936)

Congress enacted the Agricultural Adjustment Act of 1933 (AAA) in an attempt to rescue farmers from the Great Depression. Under terms of the law, farmers who reduced their crop production would receive payments from the government. The revenue obtained for these crop reduction payments was raised by imposing a tax on the commodity processor who prepared farm products for market. The tax was to be equal to the differences between current average farm prices and the price during an earlier base period (1909–1914). Butler, the receiver for a cotton processor, refused to pay the tax. A U.S. district court ordered the tax paid, but the U.S. Circuit Court of Appeals for the First District reversed the order. The government appealed to the U.S. Supreme Court.

Writing for the majority, Justice Owen Roberts affirmed the circuit court decision and invalidated the Agricultural Adjustment Act. His reasoning turned on the interpretation of three constitutional provisions: taxation, general welfare, and the Tenth Amendment. He first found that the tax on the processor was not a tax but rather an indispensable part of the regulation of agriculture. Although this does not necessarily render the tax unconstitutional, it does mean that the act cannot be held valid under the congressional taxing power. After discussing the opposing views of Madison and Hamilton, Roberts concluded that Hamilton's broad view of the General Welfare Clause is the correct one. That is, Congress possesses the power to appropriate for the general welfare, independent of the other enumerated powers found in article I. Yet after accepting this broad view, Roberts concluded that the AAA is in violation of the reserved powers of the states protected by the Tenth Amendment. Finding that the act imposed economic coercion to accept benefits and submission to regulation, Congress had misused its power under the General Welfare Clause. "It is an established principle," Roberts stated, "that the attainment of a prohibited end may not be accomplished under the pretext of the exertion of powers which are granted."

United States v. Curtiss-Wright Export Corp.
299 U.S. 304, 57 S. Ct. 216, 81 L. Ed. 255 (1936)

In 1934, Congress enacted a resolution granting to the president the power to forbid the sale of arms and munitions by American corporations to the hostile states of Paraguay and Bolivia. This power provided for such exceptions or limitations as the president should determine. President Roosevelt then issued a proclamation ordering an embargo on the sale of arms to these countries and charged the secretary of state with its enforcement. Subsequently, the Curtiss-Wright Corporation was charged with violating the proclamation by conspiring to sell fifteen machine guns to Bolivia. Sustaining its demurrer, a federal district court agreed with Curtiss-Wright that the congressional resolution was an unconstitutional delegation of legislative power. The government appealed to the U.S. Supreme Court.

Writing for the majority, Justice George Sutherland reversed the lower court decision, stressing that the power of the federal government when dealing with external affairs is vastly different from those concerning internal affairs. As Sutherland wrote, "The broad statement that the federal government can exercise no powers except those specifically enumerated in the Constitution, and such implied powers as are necessary and proper to carry into effect the enumerated powers, is categorically true only in respect to our internal affairs." Because the national union and not the individual states possess external sovereignty, the federal government alone may exercise power in foreign affairs. Moreover, because of the delicate nature of international relations, the president is the plenary and exclusive authority. Consequently, it is within the broad discretionary authority of the president to determine whether the enforcement of the congressional resolution might have a beneficial effect.

United States v. Darby
312 U.S. 100, 61 S. Ct. 451, 85 L. Ed. 609 (1941)

The Fair Labor Standards Act of 1938 prohibited the interstate shipment of goods produced by employees who worked more than forty-four hours per week, without overtime pay, or who were paid less than the minimum wage. The act also required employers to keep records of employee hours and wages. Fred Darby, the operator of a lumber business in Georgia, was indicted under provisions of this legislation. A federal district court held that the act was an unconstitutional regulation of manufacturing thereby setting aside the indictment. The government appealed directly to the U.S. Supreme Court.

Writing for a unanimous Court, Justice Harlan Stone noted that while manufacturing alone is not itself interstate commerce, "The shipment of manufactured goods interstate is such commerce and the prohibition of such shipment by Congress is indubitably a regulation of commerce." Directly and emphatically overruling the Child Labor Case, Hammer v. Dagenhart, 247 U.S. 251 (1918), Stone held that the commerce power is complete and Congress may exclude any good from interstate commerce subject only to the specific limitations found in the Constitution. Rejecting the suggestion that the Court should strike down the legislation because the motive of Congress was to invade the power of the states through the regulation of labor conditions, Stone rejoined, "The motive and purpose of a regulation of interstate commerce are matters for the legislative judgment upon the exercise of which the courts are given no control." Turning to the objection that the wage and hour provisions deal only with intrastate commerce and therefore are not subject to congressional regulation, Stone adopted the rule in National Labor Relations Board v. Jones & Laughlin Steel Corp., 301 U.S. 1 (1937). Because Congress could "regulate intrastate activities where they have a substantial effect on interstate commerce," the federal regulation of employees is a valid exercise of the commerce power. Finally, the record-keeping provisions of the act, even for intrastate transactions, were deemed "an appropriate means to the legitimate end."

United States v. E. C. Knight Co.
156 U.S. 1, 15 S. Ct. 249, 39 L. Ed. 325 (1895)

By purchasing the shares of four Philadelphia refiners with shares of its own stock, the American Sugar Refining Company acquired a monopoly on the manufacture of refined sugar in the United States. The U.S. government brought suit against the company seeking the cancellation of the stock transfer, claiming a violation of the 1890 Sherman Antitrust Act. Finding no violation of the Sherman Act, lower federal courts found for American Sugar Refining Company. The United States Supreme Court affirmed the decree.

Writing for an 8–1 majority, Chief Justice Fuller held that the Sherman Act is not applicable to monopolies in manufacturing or production. The regulation of commerce belongs to Congress, but manufacturing has only an incidental or indirect relationship to commerce. Consequently, the applicability of the Sherman Act in this case is an intrusion into the reserve power of the states under the Tenth Amendment. This case is important because it failed to extend Chief Justice Marshall's definition of commerce in Gibbons v. Ogden, 22 U.S. (9 Wheat.) (1824), from the distribution to the production of goods. Moreover, the Court used similar reasoning to strike down congressional attempts to regulate child labor, mining, and agriculture.

United States v. Leon
468 U.S. 897, 104 S. Ct. 3405, 82 L. Ed. 2d 677 (1984)

Following an investigation of drug trafficking, a federal magistrate signed a warrant to search Leon's private residence and automobile. Based on information supplied by a confidential informant of a local California police department, the application for the warrant was reviewed by several deputy district attorneys. Although the enforcement officials believed the informant to be reliable, they were mistaken. A federal district court and court of appeals ruled that the evidence seized under the authority of the warrant was issued in good faith, but the exclusionary rule created pursuant to the Fourth Amendment required its suppression.

The Supreme Court held in a 6–3 opinion of Justice Byron White that there is a good-faith exception to the exclusionary rule. The question before the Court required weighing the costs and benefits of preventing the use of inherently trustworthy evidence obtained by a search warrant based upon defective information. White concluded that in this case there were substantial social costs exacted by the exclusionary rule for the vindication of Fourth Amendment rights. Excluding evidence resulting from an honest police mistake fails to serve the purpose of the exclusionary rule to deter police from knowingly engaging in unreasonable searches and seizures. If they are honestly unaware of making a mistake, then police cannot be deterred from future unconstitutional conduct.

United States v. Lopez
514 U.S. 549, 115 S. Ct. 1624, 131 L. Ed. 2d 626 (1995)

In 1990 Congress enacted the Gun-Free Zones Act. This law made it a federal crime for any person to knowingly possess a firearm within 1,000 feet of the grounds of a public, private, or parochial school. Lopez, a senior at a San Antonio, Texas high school, carried a loaded gun to school; he was arrested and convicted in federal district court under the 1990 law. A federal appellate court reversed the conviction, finding that the law exceeds congressional power.

Chief Justice William Rehnquist, writing for a 5–4 majority, held that while lawyers for the federal government made the argument that guns in school have a substantial impact on interstate commerce, this view of the Constitution's Commerce Clause is too expansive to be sustained. The regulation of guns in a school is not an economic activity. To find otherwise, Rehnquist argued, it would be possible for the national government to regulate every aspect of local schools, including curriculum.

United States v. Nixon
418 U.S. 683, 94 S. Ct. 3090, 41 L. Ed. 2d 1039 (1974)

After hearing charges concerning the infamous Watergate break-ins, a federal grand jury returned indictments against former Attorney General John Mitchell and others for conspiracy to defraud the government and obstruction of justice in a cover-up. The grand jury also named President Richard Nixon as an unindicted co-conspirator. The special prosecutor sought, and the district court issued, a subpoena *duces tecum* directing the president to produce tape recordings made in the White House. These recordings contained conversations of the president and his advisors which were claimed by the special prosecutor to be relevant to the prosecution of the criminal cases. The president did release a number of edited transcripts, but he refused to release others requested by the prosecutor and the district court. Arguing that the dispute was nonjusticiable, the president's legal counsel then moved to quash the subpoena. Following legal maneuvers, the Supreme Court granted certiorari and heard oral arguments during a special session.

With Justice Rehnquist not participating, a unanimous Court rejected the president's claim of executive privilege. Chief Justice Warren Burger conceded that the president and his close advisors have need for confidential communication, but he clearly rejected the argument that the doctrine of separation of powers precludes judicial review of the president's claim for executive privilege. Citing John Marshall in Marbury v. Madison, 5 U.S. (1 Cranch) 137 (1803), the Court reaffirmed that "it is 'emphatically the province and the duty' of this Court 'to say what the law is' with respect to the claim of privilege presented in this case." Turning to the president's argument of absolute privilege, Burger noted that "when the privilege is based upon a broad, undifferentiated claim of public interest in the confidentiality of such conversations, a confrontation with other values arises. Absent a claim of need to protect military, diplomatic or sensitive national security secrets, we find it difficult to accept the argument that even the very important interest in confidentiality of presidential communications is significantly diminished by production of such material for in camera inspection with all the protection that a district court will be obliged to provide." Weighing the generalized interest in confidentiality against the fair administration of criminal justice, Burger concludes that the "privilege must yield to the demonstrated, specific need for evidence in a pending criminal trial." The district court acted properly when it treated the subpoenaed material as presumptively privileged and when the special prosecutor overcame the presumption. Therefore, the order for an in camera inspection of the tapes was justified.

United States v. United States District Court for Eastern District of Michigan
407 U.S. 297, 92 S. Ct. 2125, 32 L. Ed. 2d 752 (1972)

During the course of pretrial proceedings in a case involving prosecution for conspiracy to destroy government property, the defense moved to compel the government to disclose certain wiretap information that the government had obtained. The purpose of the defense motion was to determine if the information "tainted" the government's evidence against the defendants. The government responded by filing a sealed exhibit containing the surveillance logs for the court's in camera inspection. It also produced an affidavit certifying that the attorney general approved the wiretaps and such surveillance was authorized under an interpretation of Title III of the Omnibus Crime Control and Safe Streets Act of 1968. The district court found the surveillance a violation of the Fourth Amendment and ordered full disclosure. The United States Court of Appeals for the Sixth Circuit denied the government's request for a writ of mandamus. The government then appealed to the U.S. Supreme Court.

A unanimous Court, with Justice Rehnquist not participating, upheld the lower courts. First dealing with the government's argument that Title III relieves the government from the duty of obtaining a prior judicial warrant, Justice Lewis Powell held that the language of Title III, § 2511 (3), as well as the legislative history of the statute, refutes such an interpretation. Powell then rejected the government's contention that internal security matters are too complex for judicial evaluation. He wrote, "If the threat is too subtle or complex for our senior law enforcement officers to convey its significance to a court, one may question whether there is probable cause for surveillance." The Court also emphasized that its decision involves only the domestic aspects of national security. It left open the issues involved with respect to activities of foreign powers or their agents.

U.S. Term Limits, Inc. v. Thornton
514 U.S. 779, 115 S. Ct. 1842, 131 L. Ed. 2d 881 (1995)

By May 1995, Arkansas and twenty-two other states had enacted laws imposing term limits on members of the U.S. House of Representatives and the U.S. Senate. Arkansas enacted by ballot initiative term limits on members of their own state legislature and members of the U.S. House of Representatives from Arkansas who had already completed three two-year terms, as well as a two-term limitation for U.S. senators. The law, however, permitted write-in election of individuals who exceed the term limitation requirements. The Arkansas courts found the federal term limits unconstitutional, and the U.S. Supreme Court granted the petition for a writ of certiorari.

Writing for a 5–4 majority, Justice Stevens held that article I, section 2, clause 2 of the Constitution prohibits the states from adding qualifications for members of Congress. Such a power is not within the original grant by the people to the states under the Tenth Amendment. Further, Stevens reasoned, even if the states possess some original power in the matter of qualifications, the constitutional framers intended the Constitution be the exclusive source of qualifications for members of Congress. The ballot write-in provision does nothing to alleviate the fundamental constitutional infirmity.

University of California v. Bakke
(*see*, Regents of the University of California v. Bakke)

Walz v. Tax Commission of the City of New York
397 U.S. 664, 90 S. Ct. 1409, 25 L. Ed. 697 (1970)

Walz, a real estate owner, brought suit against the New York City Tax Commission for granting tax exemptions on property utilized for religious worship. Walz contended that such exemptions constitute a violation of the First Amendment's provision prohibiting government establishment of religion.

The U.S. Supreme Court affirmed the decisions of the New York courts in favor of the city of New York. Writing for the majority, Chief Justice Warren Burger reasoned that the legislative purpose of the property tax exemption is neither the advancement nor the inhibition of religion. Rather, the state has determined that certain organizations, including not only religious, but also nonprofit hospitals, libraries, scientific, and other entities, are beneficial to the community. The state is not attempting to ". . . establish religion; it is simply sparing the exercise of religion from the burden of property taxation levied on private profit institutions." Burger then argued that while the granting of tax exemptions to churches does afford an indirect economic benefit, it also serves to limit church and state entanglements. Taxing church property would involve excessive and continuing official state entanglement with religion. There is less state entanglement with religion by granting a tax exemption than if the state taxed such entities.

West Coast Hotel v. Parrish
300 U.S. 379, 57 S. Ct. 578, 81 L. Ed. 703 (1937)

In 1913, the state of Washington enacted a statute to protect women and minors by establishing a minimum wage and conditions of labor. Elsie Parrish and her husband, employed by the West Coast Hotel Company, brought suit to recover the difference between the wages paid her by the hotel and the minimum wage established by the state. The trial court decided against Parrish, but the Washington State Supreme Court reversed that decision finding the statute constitutionally valid. Relying on the U.S. Supreme Court's decision in Adkins v. Children's Hospital, 261 U.S. 525 (1923), West Coast Hotel appealed to the Supreme Court.

Directly overruling its decision in *Adkins,* the Supreme Court, with Chief Justice Charles Evans Hughes writing for the majority, held that the minimum-wage law was not an infringement of the Due Process Clause of the Fourteenth Amendment. While *Adkins* did involve the Due Process Clause of the Fifth Amendment, the fundamental issue remained the meaning of freedom of contract. Hughes reasoned that the Constitution does not speak in terms of freedom of contract; rather it ". . . speaks of liberty and prohibits the deprivation of liberty without due process of law." The Constitution does not define liberty in absolute terms. Rather, limitations on liberty are subject to the ". . . restraints of due process, and regulation which is reasonable in relation to its subject and is adopted in the interests of the community. . . ." It is, therefore, within the discretionary authority of the legislature to determine which working conditions are best suited to promote the well-being of the community. The community in the public interest may correct the abuses of employers.

West Virginia State Board of Education v. Barnette
319 U.S. 624, 63 S. Ct. 1178, 87 L. Ed. 1628 (1943)

In Minersville School District v. Gobitis, 310 U.S. 586 (1940), the U.S. Supreme Court sustained the constitutionality of an order by a local board of education in Pennsylvania to compel students and teachers to salute the flag. Soon thereafter, the West Virginia legislature passed a law requiring all state schools to conduct classes in civics and history, as well as in the U.S. and West Virginia Constitutions. The West Virginia State Board of Education further prescribed that all students and teachers must salute the flag as part of regular daily school activities. Refusal to comply was punishable by student expulsion and parents were subject to both a fine and jail term. Walter Barnette and other Jehovah's Witnesses brought suit after their children were expelled from schools for refusing to salute the flag; they objected to the compulsory flag salute as repugnant to a religious commandment not to worship graven images. A federal district court granted Barnette's petition for injunctive relief. The board of education then appealed directly to the U.S. Supreme Court.

Directly overruling its near-unanimous decision just three years earlier in *Gobitis,* Justice Robert Jackson based the Court's majority opinion on the clear and present danger doctrine. The compulsion of students to declare a belief is made without ". . . any allegation that remaining passive during a flag salute ritual creates a clear and present danger that would justify an effort even to muffle expression," wrote Jackson. "To sustain the compulsory flag salute we are required to say that a Bill of Rights which guards the individual's right to speak his own mind, left it open to public authorities to compel him to utter what is not in his mind." Responding to the argument that applying the First Amendment protection to state school boards would convert the Supreme Court into the school board for the country, Jackson held that the Fourteenth Amendment protects the citizen against all the creatures of the state, including school boards.

Youngstown Sheet and Tube Co. v. Sawyer
343 U.S. 579, 72 S. Ct. 863, 96 L. Ed. 1153 (1952)

During the Korean "police action," a dispute arose between the nation's steel companies and their employees over the terms of a new collective bargaining agreement. After long and bitter negotiations failed, the United Steelworkers of America gave notice of a strike. The Federal Mediation and Conciliation Service then intervened but was unsuccessful in bringing about a settlement. President Truman then referred the dispute to the Federal Wage Stabilization Board, but this attempt also met with failure. Given the repeated failures at a negotiated settlement and the union's strike announcement, President Truman acted to avert a felt threat to the "police action" in the event of a curtailment of steel production. Just a few hours before the strike was to begin, President Truman issued an executive order directing Secretary of Commerce Charles Sawyer to seize the steel mills and to keep them running. In a special message to Congress, President Truman reported the seizure inviting legislative action if Congress deemed it advisable. Congress, however, failed to act. The steel companies immediately attacked the order as unconstitutional, and a district court judge granted a preliminary injunction. After a court of appeals stayed the injunction, the Supreme Court granted certiorari.

In a 6–3 decision, marked by five concurring opinions, Justice Hugo Black delivered the opinion of the Court holding the seizure unconstitutional. Avoiding any discussion of executive prerogative in times of national emergency, Black observed that there was no statute expressly authorizing the president's argument that his authority flowed from his powers as chief executive or from his responsibilities as commander-in-chief. Black wrote, "In the framework of our Constitution, the president's power to see that the laws are faithfully executed refutes the idea that he is to be a lawmaker. The Constitution limits his functions in the lawmaking process to the recommending of the laws he thinks wise and the vetoing of the laws he thinks bad."

Zelman v. Simmons-Harris
536 U.S. 639, 122 S. Ct. 2460, 153 L. Ed. 2d 604 (2002)

The state of Ohio placed the Cleveland public schools under direct state control because of what was widely regarded as a failed system. This 1995 action was subsequently followed by a school-voucher plan that provided up to $2,250 per year to send Cleveland children outside of their home school districts to attend private or public schools of their parents' choosing. Eighty-two percent of the private schools had a religious affiliation, but one of the adjacent public schools participated in the program. One result was that 96 percent of the students participating in the voucher program attended religious schools. In response to a group of Ohio taxpayers that sought the enjoinment of the scholarship program, a federal district court and the Court of Appeals for the Sixth Circuit found the scholarship program unconstitutional. The U.S. Supreme Court heard the case on a writ of certiorari.

Writing for a 5–4 majority, Chief Justice Rehnquist reversed the appellate court. He found that the voucher program was enacted for the valid secular legislative purpose of providing educational opportunities to inner-city youth. The program does not advance religious institutions directly, he argued, but rather it provided the opportunity for private parties to make independent choices about where to send their children to school. The Court's own precedents established that programs designed to provide a benefit to a wide body of citizens in a neutral fashion without particular reference to religion does not violate the Establishment Clause of the First Amendment.

APPENDIX A

SAMPLE RESEARCH DESIGN

How Judicial Attitudes/Strategies of the Rehnquist Court (1994–present) may Impact the Outcome of *Grutter v. Bollinger*

Tyson Tanner
Dr. Melone
POLS 433B: Constitutional Law
March 3, 2003

INTRODUCTION—
History and Support for Affirmative Action

The United States of America was created with the words, "We hold these truths to be self-evident, that all men are created equal, that they are endowed by their Creator with certain unalienable rights, that among these are life, liberty, and the pursuit of happiness."[1] However, one should not be so naive in believing this has always, or ever, been the case in this great nation of freedom and liberty. In fact, this ideal proposed by our founding fathers may be one that is impossible to attain. One of the things we do know, however, is that there have been times in this country where the unalienable rights of all have been withheld to some due to discrimination based on a variety of characteristics such as race, religion, sex, national origin, and so on.

179

One such classification type, classifications based upon race, has generated so much emotion and debate surrounding the topic that the country became embattled in a Civil War to try and settle the dispute. Ultimately, the Civil War concluded and the newly reunited Union passed what are known as the "Reconstruction Amendments" (the Thirteenth, Fourteenth, and Fifteenth Amendments).[2] Of these three constitutional amendments, the Fourteenth Amendment became the most valuable weapon in the fight against state-sponsored acts of discrimination due primarily to the Equal Protection Clause.[3] This clause proved to be the supporting plank for the Supreme Court to rely upon in overruling school segregation policies,[4] as well as various other "Jim Crow" laws. The Court, through the Equal Protection Clause, seemed to be evolving into a great protector of minority rights in a nation that was slowly beginning to desegregate in the 1950s.

With the passage of the Civil Rights Act of 1964, Congress passed the first piece of legislation seeking to protect minorities from racial discrimination in the workplace.[5] Affirmative action itself was first introduced in 1972 within anti-discriminatory legislation, passed under the Civil Rights Act, intending to address problems in higher education.[6] With this new program minority students were given additional consideration in the admissions processes of colleges and universities across the country. However, opponents of the affirmative action program began challenging the program in the courts on the basis that affirmative action violates the Equal Protection Clause of the Fourteenth Amendment.

In *Regents of the University of California v. Bakke*,[7] the Supreme Court was faced with deciding this very difficult matter. The Court, in its plurality opinion, held that quota systems allotting for the placement of only minority students, such as the plan in place at Davis, were in violation of the Equal Protection Clause. Justice Powell, writer of the plurality's opinion, also went on to reason that laws dealing with affirmative action must be subjected to strict scrutiny, which means the law must serve a compelling state interest and be narrowly tailored to have only the intended effect of the law. However, the Court nevertheless affirmed the use of affirmative action where the policies were not designed to serve as a quota for minority students. In effect, the *Bakke* case allows for race to be considered in the admissions processes because the program helps to ensure diversity within a university setting.

While the Court's decision in *Bakke* is still controlling precedent on the issue, the Court will once again decide the fate of an affirmative action policy and its accordance with the Equal Protection Clause based upon an appeal of the Sixth Circuit Court of Appeals decision in *Grutter v. Bollinger*.[8] The policy in question is that of the University of Michigan School of Law, which states in its admissions policy that the university seeks to admit a "critical mass" of under-represented minority students in order for students to obtain a more diverse student body. The goal of diversity in the university is achieved through the process of giving minority applicants more "points" in the calculation of who is admitted to the law school. Ultimately, the fate of affirmative action policies in universities across the country will be determined by the nine members of the Supreme Court.

RESEARCH TOPIC—
How will the Court decide *Grutter v. Bollinger*?

The ability of the Supreme Court to make decisions on extremely controversial legal issues gives the Court a great deal of power in shaping public policy. Despite the Court's great power in the policymaking process, most people would expect the Court's role to be somewhat limited by their conceptions of how the Court should operate. Ideally, the Court is supposed to shape public policy by determining the outcomes of cases based solely on the facts and law applicable to the case. However, the reality is that in many cases the Supreme Court justices will base their decisions at least somewhat on their own beliefs and values in an effort to seek to produce outcomes that are similar, if not identical, to their own policy preferences.

In my initial research I have found a great deal of support for this general position, but there are also major differences between the positions of the scholars themselves. Jeffrey Segal and Harold Spaeth argue that the Court makes its decisions based upon what they call the "attitudinal model," which encompasses the Court deciding disputes "in light of the facts vis-à-vis the ideological attitudes and values of the justices."[9] Lee Epstein and Jack Knight carry Segal and Spaeth's argument one step further in arguing that, in addition the justices' personal values, group interaction among members of the Court also plays a role in the determination of a case in what they call the strategic account of judicial decision making.[10] Lawrence Baum further expands on Segal and Spaeth's findings by adding the influences of the state of the law, group interaction, and the Court's environment to the justice's values in order to determine the outcome of cases.[11]

These realizations provide us with several questions that must be answered throughout the research process in order to allow for the best possible prediction of the way the justices will vote in *Grutter v. Bollinger*. First and foremost, what are the underlying values that each current justice holds in regard to giving benefits to minority classes in order to "level the playing field" with members of the majority group? Are these attitudes consistent with each justice over time? Also, how will the interaction among the members of the Court alter or enforce each justice's values, subsequently causing that particular justice to cast a vote in one direction or the other? These questions must first be listed as testable hypotheses in order to determine if these particular factors will be influential in the decision making process.

Hypotheses

1. In cases dealing with discrimination by race, color, or condition, the justices will exhibit consistent underlying values in their decision making.

2. In cases dealing with discrimination by race, color, or condition, certain groups of judges will continue to vote in a similar fashion, causing them to be consistent voting blocs.

3. The beliefs expressed by the justices in hypotheses one and two will determine the vote of each justice on the Court, and eventually the outcome in the case of *Grutter v. Bollinger.*

Now that the hypotheses of the research topic have been formulated, it is necessary to review the process of how these propositions will be tested.

Testing Procedures

In order to limit the research to cases that are both relevant in time and subject matter, there are a number of filters that must be employed to limit the universe of the study. Obviously the cases must be decisions in which the United States Supreme Court rendered a decision. Additionally, limiting the time frame of the cases to those that have been decided since 1995 allows for collection of data on the natural court only. This will enable the research to focus on the current members of the Court, as well as their past voting tendencies within this specific makeup of the Court. Fortunately, this has been one of the longer periods of the Court where there has not been any turnover in the makeup of the Court.

Another limitation placed upon this research project involves the selection of the cases to be analyzed. The cases were limited to those that were found within *American Digest System's Tenth Decennial Digest: Part 2, Volume 12*[12] and *Eleventh Decennial Digest: Part 1, Volume 13*[13] under the "key note" heading of constitutional law. At this point the cases were narrowed further under subheading *XI: Equal Protection of Laws,* and eventually to key number 214: Discrimination by reason of race, color, or condition. Since this key number was subdivided, all relevant cases falling between key numbers 214 and 223 have been included within the case set. The case set will include the following cases: 1) *Adarand Constructors, Inc. v. Pena,*[14] 2) *Bush v. Vera,*[15] 3) *Hunt v. Cromartie,*[16] 4) *Kimel v. Florida Board of Regents,*[17] 5) *Miller v. Johnson,*[18] 6) *Reno v. Bossier Parish School Board,*[19] 7) *Rice v. Cayetano,*[20] 8) *Shaw v. Hunt,*[21] 9) *United States v. Armstrong,*[22] 10) *United States v. Martinez-Salazar,*[23] and 11) *Whren v. United States.*[24] While it is advantageous in determining voting behaviors of individual justices to have a set of cases that are decided nonunanimously by the Court, there are three cases (*Hunt v. Cromartie, United States v. Martinez-Salazar,* and *Whren v. United States*) within the case set that were unanimously decided by the Supreme Court. These cases will be included in the case set because I feel that it is important to include these cases in the scaling process to show the voting tendencies of the Court as a whole. As one may also notice, these cases are not leading opinions on the subject matter to be studied, rather, they are simply the only eleven cases that fit the criteria.

Now that the universe of the research has been specified, it is time to discuss the particular testing procedure for each hypothesis made in regard to this study. In order to determine the first hypothesis, it is necessary to construct a scale to determine the particular attitude of each justice in relation to his/her peers on the Court. Since attitudes remain fairly stable over time, it is assumed that the justice's decisions over time will enable the researcher to determine each justice's true attitude on the topic. In order to construct the scale in an appropriate manner, it is useful to follow the scale construction instructions set forth by Melone.[25] First, one must read the opinions in each case and ascertain the votes of each participating justice. Next, assign a (+) to each justice who voted for the liberal position, a (−) for each justice who voted for the conservative position, and a (0) for each justice who did not participate in a given case. For our purposes the liberal position will be the position of the Court that would benefit the minority in the case. Then, the justices must be ordered from the most liberal (left) to the most conservative (right). Thus, the justice with the most (+) will be the furthest left on the scale. Once the justices are in the proper order, the cases must be arranged in a manner that has the case with the most liberal voting justices at the top of the scale, while cases garnering the most conservative votes will be placed at the bottom of the scale. The cases should be placed in order of rank from most liberal (top) to most conservative (bottom). If done correctly, a neat division of the pluses and minuses should appear on the matrix. By drawing a stepline, one is able to separate these two positions. Any vote that is on the opposite side of the stepline as its mates is regarded as an inconsistency.

There are also two additional mathematical formulas that are useful in the scaling process.[26] The first is the coefficient of reproducibility, which is found by taking the number of inconsistencies divided by the total number of pluses, minuses, and zeros. Generally a scale is reproducible at .90, meaning it is 90% reproducible. The second equation involves each justice's scale score. These are calculated by finding the total number of liberal votes per justice, multiplying this by two, then dividing by the number of cases, and finally subtracting one from the number. Scale scores range from 1.0 (liberal) to −1.0 (conservative). For our purposes a liberal scale score (a score between 1 and 0) will equate with a liberal vote in *Grutter v. Bollinger*, a conservative scale score (a score between 0 and −1) will equate with a conservative vote in the case, and an even 0 score will equate with a justice joining the majority group, whether it is liberal or conservative.

In order to test hypothesis number two, it is necessary to construct a bloc analysis grid. Once again, this project will follow the bloc construction methods as described by Melone.[27] The first step is to calculate the agreement scores for each pair of justices. Once this is done, a matrix must be created that ranks the order of the pairs from highest agreement rate in the upper-left of the matrix, to the lowest agreement rate in the lower-right of the matrix. For the purposes of this study, the Sprague Criterion will also be used to determine if there is actual bloc of justices voting together in a consistent manner. This is calculated by finding the Court mean of interagreement, subtracting this number from 100, dividing this answer by 2, and adding this number back with the original Court mean. Any level of interagreement that exceeds this number is sufficient enough to regard that pair as a bloc.

In order to test hypothesis number three, it is necessary to further examine the results from the tests of hypotheses one and two. As mentioned earlier, a liberal scale score (a score between 1 and 0) will equate with a liberal vote, a conservative scale score (a score between 0 and −1) will equate with a conservative vote, and an even 0 score will equate with a justice joining the majority group, whether it is liberal or conservative. The real test for this hypothesis will be revealed once the Court issues its decision in the case. Only then will the facts indicate just how accurate this method of predicting the outcome of the Court's cases has been.

Bibliography

American Digest System: Eleventh Decennial Digest: Part 1, Volume 13. West. 2002. pp. 329–371.

American Digest System: Tenth Decennial Digest: Part 2, Volume 12. West. 1997. pp. 621–625.

Baum, Lawrence. 2001. *The Supreme Court, 7th edition.* Washington, DC: CQ Press.

Epstein, Lee, and Knight, Jack. 1998. *The Choices Justices Make.* Washington, DC: CQ Press.

Finn, John E., and Kommers, Donald P. 1998. *American Constitutional Law: Essays, Cases, and Comparative Notes.* Belmont, CA: Wadsworth.

Melone, Albert P. 2000. *Researching Constitutional Law, 2nd ed.* Prospect Heights, IL: Waveland Press.

Segal, Jeffrey A., and Spaeth, Harold J. 1993. *The Supreme Court and the Attitudinal Model.* New York: Cambridge University Press.

Woodhouse, Shawn. "The Historical Development of Affirmative Action: An Aggregated Analysis." *Western Journal of Black Studies.* (Fall 2002, Volume 26, Issue 3): 155–159.

Table of Cases

Adarand Constructors, Inc. v. Pena, 515 U.S. 200 (1995)

Bush v. Vera, 517 U.S. 952 (1996)

Grutter v. Bollinger, 288 F. 3d 732 (2002)

Hunt v. Cromartie, 526 U.S. 541 (1999)

Kimel v. Florida Board of Regents, 528 U.S. 62 (2000)

Miller v. Johnson, 515 U.S. 900 (1995)

Regents of the University of California v. Bakke, 438 U.S. 265 (1978)

Reno v. Bossier Parish School Board, 520 U.S. 471 (1997)

Rice v. Cayetano, 528 U.S. 495 (2000)

Shaw v. Hunt, 517 U.S. 899 (1996)

United States v. Armstrong, 517 U.S. 456 (1996)

United States v. Martinez-Salazar, 528 U.S. 304 (2000)

Whren v. United States, 517 U.S. 806 (1996)

Endnotes

[1] United States Declaration of Independence (1776).

[2] John Finn and Donald Kommers, *American Constitutional Law* (Belmont, CA: Wadsworth, 1998), p. 730.

[3] Ibid, p 731.

[4] See Brown v. Board of Education I, 347 U.S. 483 (1954).

[5] Shawn Woodhouse, "The Historical Development of Affirmative Action: An Aggregated Analysis," *Western Journal of Black Studies* (Fall 2002, Volume 26, Issue 3): 155.

[6] L. A. Connor, "The impact of affirmative action on the employment practices in Pennsylvania's state system of higher education," as cited in Woodhouse, "The Historical Development of Affirmative Action," 155.

[7] Regents of the University of California v. Bakke, 438 U.S. 265 (1978).

[8] Grutter v. Bollinger, 288 F. 3d 732 (2002).

[9] Jeffrey A. Segal and Harold J. Spaeth, *The Supreme Court and the Attitudinal Model* (New York: Cambridge University Press, 1993), p. 65.

[10] Lee Epstein and Jack Knight, *The Choices Justices Make* (Washington, DC: CQ Press, 1998), pp. 10–11.

[11] Lawrence Baum, *The Supreme Court, 7th edition* (Washington, DC: CQ Press, 2001), pp. 137–178.

[12] *American Digest System: Tenth Decennial Digest: Part 2, Volume 12* (West, 1997), pp 621–625.

[13] *American Digest System: Eleventh Decennial Digest: Part 1, Volume 13* (West, 2002), pp 329–371.

[14] 515 U.S. 200 (1995)

[15] 517 U.S. 952 (1996)

[16] 526 U.S. 541 (1999)

[17] 528 U.S. 62 (2000)

[18] 515 U.S. 900 (1995)

[19] 520 U.S. 471 (1997)

[20] 528 U.S. 495 (2000)

[21] 517 U.S. 899 (1996)

[22] U517 U.S. 456 (1996)

[23] 528 U.S. 304 (2000)

[24] 517 U.S. 806 (1996)

[25] Albert P. Melone, *Researching Constitutional Law, 2nd ed.* (Prospect Heights, IL: Waveland Press, 2000), pp. 67–75.

[26] Ibid., pp. 72–73.

[27] Ibid., pp. 76–78.

APPENDIX B
THE UNITED STATES CONSTITUTION

We the people of the United States, in order to form a more perfect union, establish justice, insure domestic tranquility, provide for the common defense, promote the general welfare, and secure the blessings of liberty to ourselves and our posterity, do ordain and establish this Constitution for the United States of America.

Article I

Section 1. All legislative powers herein granted shall be vested in a Congress of the United States, which shall consist of a Senate and House of Representatives.

Section 2. The House of Representatives shall be composed of members chosen every second year by the people of the several states, and the electors in each state shall have the qualifications requisite for electors of the most numerous branch of the state legislature.

No person shall be a Representative who shall not have attained to the age of twenty five years, and been seven years a citizen of the United States, and who shall not, when elected, be an inhabitant of that state in which he shall be chosen.

Representatives and direct taxes shall be apportioned among the several states which may be included within this union, according to their respective numbers, which shall be determined by adding to the whole number of free persons, including those bound to service for a term of years, and excluding

187

Indians not taxed, three fifths of all other Persons. The actual Enumeration shall be made within three years after the first meeting of the Congress of the United States, and within every subsequent term of ten years, in such manner as they shall by law direct. The number of Representatives shall not exceed one for every thirty thousand, but each state shall have at least one Representative; and until such enumeration shall be made, the state of New Hampshire shall be entitled to chose three, Massachusetts eight, Rhode Island and Providence Plantations one, Connecticut five, New York six, New Jersey four, Pennsylvania eight, Delaware one, Maryland six, Virginia ten, North Carolina five, South Carolina five, and Georgia three.

When vacancies happen in the Representation from any state, the executive authority thereof shall issue writs of election to fill such vacancies.

The House of Representatives shall choose their speaker and other officers; and shall have the sole power of impeachment.

Section 3. The Senate of the United States shall be composed of two Senators from each state, chosen by the legislature thereof, for six years; and each Senator shall have one vote.

Immediately after they shall be assembled in consequence of the first election, they shall be divided as equally as may be into three classes. The seats of the Senators of the first class shall be vacated at the expiration of the second year, of the second class at the expiration of the fourth year, and the third class at the expiration of the sixth year, so that one third may be chosen every second year; and if vacancies happen by resignation, or otherwise, during the recess of the legislature of any state, the executive thereof may make temporary appointments until the next meeting of the legislature, which shall then fill such vacancies.

No person shall be a Senator who shall not have attained to the age of thirty years, and been nine years a citizen of the United States and who shall not, when elected, be an inhabitant of that state for which he shall be chosen.

The Vice President of the United States shall be President of the Senate, but shall have no vote, unless they be equally divided.

The Senate shall choose their other officers, and also a President pro tempore, in the absence of the Vice President, or when he shall exercise the office of President of the United States.

The Senate shall have the sole power to try all impeachments. When sitting for that purpose, they shall be on oath or affirmation. When the President of the United States is tried, the Chief Justice shall preside: And no person shall be convicted without the concurrence of two thirds of the members present.

Judgment in cases of impeachment shall not extend further than to removal from office, and disqualification to hold and enjoy any office of honor, trust or profit under the United States: but the party convicted shall nevertheless be liable and subject to indictment, trial, judgment and punishment, according to law.

Section 4. The times, places and manner of holding elections for Senators and Representatives, shall be prescribed in each state by the legislature thereof; but the Congress may at any time by law make or alter such regulations, except as to the places of choosing Senators.

The Congress shall assemble at least once in every year, and such meeting shall be on the first Monday in December, unless they shall by law appoint a different day.

Section 5. Each House shall be the judge of the elections, returns and qualifications of its own members, and a majority of each shall constitute a quorum to do business; but a smaller number may adjourn from day to day, and may be authorized to compel the attendance of absent members, in such manner, and under such penalties as each House may provide.

Each House may determine the rules of its proceedings, punish its members for disorderly behavior, and, with the concurrence of two thirds, expel a member.

Each House shall keep a journal of its proceedings, and from time to time publish the same, excepting such parts as may in their judgment require secrecy; and the yeas and nays of the members of either House on any question shall, at the desire of one fifth of those present, be entered on the journal.

Neither House, during the session of Congress, shall, without the consent of the other, adjourn for more than three days, nor to any other place than that in which the two Houses shall be sitting.

Section 6. The Senators and Representatives shall receive a compensation for their services, to be ascertained by law, and paid out of the treasury of the United States. They shall in all cases, except treason, felony and breach of the peace, be privileged from arrest during their attendance at the session of their respective Houses, and in going to and returning from the same; and for any speech or debate in either House, they shall not be questioned in any other place.

No Senator or Representative shall, during the time for which he was elected, be appointed to any civil office under the authority of the United States, which shall have been created, or the emoluments whereof shall have been increased during such time: and no person holding any office under the United States, shall be a member of either House during his continuance in office.

Section 7. All bills for raising revenue shall originate in the House of Representatives; but the Senate may propose or concur with amendments as on other Bills.

Every bill which shall have passed the House of Representatives and the Senate, shall, before it become a law, be presented to the President of the United States; if he approve he shall sign it, but if not he shall return it, with his objections to that House in which it shall have originated, who shall enter the objections at large on their journal, and proceed to reconsider it. If after such reconsideration two thirds of that House shall agree to pass the bill, it shall be sent, together with the objections, to the other House, by which it shall likewise be reconsidered, and if approved by two thirds of that House, it shall become a law. But in all such cases the votes of both Houses shall be determined by yeas and nays, and the names of the persons voting for and against the bill shall be entered on the journal of each House respectively. If any bill shall not be returned by the President within ten days (Sundays excepted) after it shall have been presented to him, the same shall be a law, in like manner as if he had signed it, unless the Congress by their adjournment prevent its return, in which case it shall not be a law.

Every order, resolution, or vote to which the concurrence of the Senate and House of Representatives may be necessary (except on a question of adjournment) shall be presented to the President of the United States; and before the same shall take effect, shall be approved by him, or being disapproved by him, shall be repassed by two thirds of the Senate and House of Representatives, according to the rules and limitations prescribed in the case of a bill.

Section 8. The Congress shall have power to lay and collect taxes, duties, imposts and excises, to pay the debts and provide for the common defense and general welfare of the United States; but all duties, imposts and excises shall be uniform throughout the United States;

To borrow money on the credit of the United States;

To regulate commerce with foreign nations, and among the several states, and with the Indian tribes;

To establish a uniform rule of naturalization, and uniform laws on the subject of bankruptcies throughout the United States;

To coin money, regulate the value thereof, and of foreign coin, and fix the standard of weights and measures;

To provide for the punishment of counterfeiting the securities and current coin of the United States;

To establish post offices and post roads;

To promote the progress of science and useful arts, by securing for limited times to authors and inventors the exclusive right to their respective writings and discoveries;

To constitute tribunals inferior to the Supreme Court;

To define and punish piracies and felonies committed on the high seas, and offenses against the law of nations;

To declare war, grant letters of marque and reprisal, and make rules concerning captures on land and water;

To raise and support armies, but no appropriation of money to that use shall be for a longer term than two years;

To provide and maintain a navy;

To make rules for the government and regulation of the land and naval forces;

To provide for calling forth the militia to execute the laws of the union, suppress insurrections and repel invasions;

To provide for organizing, arming, and disciplining, the militia, and for governing such part of them as may be employed in the service of the United States, reserving to the states respectively, the appointment of the officers, and the authority of training the militia according to the discipline prescribed by Congress;

To exercise exclusive legislation in all cases whatsoever, over such District (not exceeding ten miles square) as may, by cession of particular states, and the acceptance of Congress, become the seat of the government of the United States, and to exercise like authority over all places purchased by the consent of the legislature of the state in which the same shall be, for the erection of forts, magazines, arsenals, dockyards, and other needful buildings;—And

To make all laws which shall be necessary and proper for carrying into execution the foregoing powers, and all other powers vested by this Constitution in the government of the United States, or in any department or officer thereof.

Section 9. The migration or importation of such persons as any of the states now existing shall think proper to admit, shall not be prohibited by the Congress prior to the year one thousand eight hundred and eight, but a tax or duty may be imposed on such importation, not exceeding ten dollars for each person.

The privilege of the writ of habeas corpus shall not be suspended, unless when in cases of rebellion or invasion the public safety may require it.

No bill of attainder or ex post facto Law shall be passed.

No capitation, or other direct, tax shall be laid, unless in proportion to the census or enumeration herein before directed to be taken.

No tax or duty shall be laid on articles exported from any state.

No preference shall be given by any regulation of commerce or revenue to the ports of one state over those of another: nor shall vessels bound to, or from, one state, be obliged to enter, clear or pay duties in another.

No money shall be drawn from the treasury, but in consequence of appropriations made by law; and a regular statement and account of receipts and expenditures of all public money shall be published from time to time.

No title of nobility shall be granted by the United States: and no person holding any office of profit or trust under them, shall, without the consent of the Congress, accept of any present, emolument, office, or title, of any kind whatever, from any king, prince, or foreign state.

Section 10. No state shall enter into any treaty, alliance, or confederation; grant letters of marque and reprisal; coin money; emit bills of credit; make anything but gold and silver coin a tender in payment of debts; pass any bill of attainder, ex post facto law, or law impairing the obligation of contracts, or grant any title of nobility.

No state shall, without the consent of the Congress, lay any imposts or duties on imports or exports, except what may be absolutely necessary for executing its inspection laws: and the net produce of all duties and imposts, laid by any state on imports or exports, shall be for the use of the treasury of the United States; and all such laws shall be subject to the revision and control of the Congress.

No state shall, without the consent of Congress, lay any duty of tonnage, keep troops, or ships of war in time of peace, enter into any agreement or compact with another state, or with a foreign power, or engage in war, unless actually invaded, or in such imminent danger as will not admit of delay.

Article II

Section 1. The executive power shall be vested in a President of the United States of America. He shall hold his office during the term of four years, and, together with the Vice President, chosen for the same term, be elected, as follows:

Each state shall appoint, in such manner as the Legislature thereof may direct, a number of electors, equal to the whole number of Senators and Representatives to which the State may be entitled in the Congress: but no Senator or Representative, or person holding an office of trust or profit under the United States, shall be appointed an elector.

The electors shall meet in their respective states, and vote by ballot for two persons, of whom one at least shall not be an inhabitant of the same state with themselves. And they shall make a list of all the persons voted for, and of the number of votes for each; which list they shall sign and certify, and transmit sealed to the seat of the government of the United States, directed to the President of the Senate. The President of the Senate shall, in the presence of the Senate and House of Representatives, open all the certificates, and the votes shall then be counted. The person having the greatest number of votes shall be the President, if such number be a majority of the whole number of electors appointed; and if there be more than one who have such majority, and have an equal number of votes, then the House of Representatives shall immediately choose by ballot one of them for President; and if no person have a majority, then from the five highest on the list the said House shall in like manner choose the President. But in choosing the President, the votes shall be taken by States, the representation from each state having one vote; A quorum for this purpose shall consist of a member or members from two thirds of the states, and a majority of all the states shall be necessary to a choice. In every case, after the choice of the President, the person having the greatest number of votes of the electors shall be the Vice President. But if there should remain two or more who have equal votes, the Senate shall choose from them by ballot the Vice President.

The Congress may determine the time of choosing the electors, and the day on which they shall give their votes; which day shall be the same throughout the United States.

No person except a natural born citizen, or a citizen of the United States, at the time of the adoption of this Constitution, shall be eligible to the office of President; neither shall any person be eligible to that office who shall not have attained to the age of thirty five years, and been fourteen Years a resident within the United States.

In case of the removal of the President from office, or of his death, resignation, or inability to discharge the powers and duties of the said office, the same shall devolve on the Vice President, and the Congress may by law provide for the case of removal, death, resignation or inability, both of the President and Vice President, declaring what officer shall then act as President, and such officer shall act accordingly, until the disability be removed, or a President shall be elected.

The President shall, at stated times, receive for his services, a compensation, which shall neither be increased nor diminished during the period for which he shall have been elected, and he shall not receive within that period any other emolument from the United States, or any of them.

Before he enter on the execution of his office, he shall take the following oath or affirmation:—"I do solemnly swear (or affirm) that I will faithfully execute the office of President of the United States, and will to the best of my ability, preserve, protect and defend the Constitution of the United States."

Section 2. The President shall be commander in chief of the Army and Navy of the United States, and of the militia of the several states, when called into the actual service of the United States; he may require the opinion, in writing, of the principal officer in each of the executive departments, upon any subject relating to the duties of their respective offices, and he shall have power to grant reprieves and pardons for offenses against the United States, except in cases of impeachment.

He shall have power, by and with the advice and consent of the Senate, to make treaties, provided two thirds of the Senators present concur; and he shall nominate, and by and with the advice and consent of the Senate, shall appoint ambassadors, other public ministers and consuls, judges of the Supreme Court, and all other officers of the United States, whose appointments are not herein otherwise provided for, and which shall be established by law: but the Congress may by law vest the appointment of such inferior officers, as they think proper, in the President alone, in the courts of law, or in the heads of departments.

The President shall have power to fill up all vacancies that may happen during the recess of the Senate, by granting commissions which shall expire at the end of their next session.

Section 3. He shall from time to time give to the Congress information of the state of the union, and recommend to their consideration such measures as he shall judge necessary and expedient; he may, on extraordinary occasions, convene both Houses, or either of them, and in case of disagreement between them, with respect to the time of adjournment, he may adjourn them to such time as he shall think proper; he shall receive ambassadors and other public ministers; he shall take care that the laws be faithfully executed, and shall commission all the officers of the United States.

Section 4. The President, Vice President and all civil officers of the United States, shall be removed from office on impeachment for, and conviction of, treason, bribery, or other high crimes and misdemeanors.

Article III

Section 1. The judicial power of the United States, shall be vested in one Supreme Court, and in such inferior courts as the Congress may from time to time ordain and establish. The judges, both of the supreme and inferior courts, shall hold their offices during good behaviour, and shall, at stated times, receive for their services, a compensation, which shall not be diminished during their continuance in office.

Section 2. The judicial power shall extend to all cases, in law and equity, arising under this Constitution, the laws of the United States, and treaties made, or which shall be made, under their authority;—to all cases affecting ambassadors, other public ministers and consuls;—to all cases of admiralty and maritime jurisdiction;—to controversies to which the United States shall be a party;—to controversies between two or more states;—between a state and citizens of another state;— between citizens of different states;—between citizens of the same state claiming lands under grants of different states, and between a state, or the citizens thereof, and foreign states, citizens or subjects.

In all cases affecting ambassadors, other public ministers and consuls, and those in which a state shall be party, the Supreme Court shall have original jurisdiction. In all the other cases before mentioned, the Supreme Court shall have appellate jurisdiction, both as to law and fact, with such exceptions, and under such regulations as the Congress shall make.

The trial of all crimes, except in cases of impeachment, shall be by jury; and such trial shall be held in the state where the said crimes shall have been committed; but when not committed within any state, the trial shall be at such place or places as the Congress may by law have directed.

Section 3. Treason against the United States, shall consist only in levying war against them, or in adhering to their enemies, giving them aid and comfort. No person shall be convicted of treason unless on the testimony of two witnesses to the same overt act, or on confession in open court.

The Congress shall have power to declare the punishment of treason, but no attainder of treason shall work corruption of blood, or forfeiture except during the life of the person attainted.

Article IV

Section 1. Full faith and credit shall be given in each state to the public acts, records, and judicial proceedings of every other state. And the Congress may by general laws prescribe the manner in which such acts, records, and proceedings shall be proved, and the effect thereof.

Section 2. The citizens of each state shall be entitled to all privileges and immunities of citizens in the several states.

A person charged in any state with treason, felony, or other crime, who shall flee from justice, and be found in another state, shall on demand of the executive authority of the state from which he fled, be delivered up, to be removed to the state having jurisdiction of the crime.

No person held to service or labor in one state, under the laws thereof, escaping into another, shall, in consequence of any law or regulation therein, be discharged from such service or labor, but shall be delivered up on claim of the party to whom such service or labor may be due.

Section 3. New states may be admitted by the Congress into this union; but no new states shall be formed or erected within the jurisdiction of any other state; nor any state be formed by the junction of two or more states, or parts of states, without the consent of the legislatures of the states concerned as well as of the Congress.

The Congress shall have power to dispose of and make all needful rules and regulations respecting the territory or other property belonging to the United States; and nothing in this Constitution shall be so construed as to prejudice any claims of the United States, or of any particular state.

Section 4. The United States shall guarantee to every state in this union a republican form of government, and shall protect each of them against invasion; and on application of the legislature, or of the executive (when the legislature cannot be convened) against domestic violence.

Article V

The Congress, whenever two thirds of both houses shall deem it necessary, shall propose amendments to this Constitution, or, on the application of the legislatures of two thirds of the several states, shall call a convention for proposing amendments, which, in either case, shall be valid to all intents and purposes, as part of this Constitution, when ratified by the legislatures of three fourths of the several states, or by conventions in three fourths thereof, as the one or the other mode of ratification may be proposed by the Congress; provided that no amendment which may be made prior to the year one thousand eight hundred and eight shall in any manner affect the first and fourth clauses in the ninth section of the first article; and that no state, without its consent, shall be deprived of its equal suffrage in the Senate.

Article VI

All debts contracted and engagements entered into, before the adoption of this Constitution, shall be as valid against the United States under this Constitution, as under the Confederation.

This Constitution, and the laws of the United States which shall be made in pursuance thereof; and all treaties made, or which shall be made, under the authority of the United States, shall be the supreme law of the land; and the judges in every state shall be bound thereby, anything in the Constitution or laws of any State to the contrary notwithstanding.

The Senators and Representatives before mentioned, and the members of the several state legislatures, and all executive and judicial officers, both of the United States and of the several states, shall be bound by oath or affirmation, to support this Constitution; but no religious test shall ever be required as a qualification to any office or public trust under the United States.

Article VII

The ratification of the conventions of nine states, shall be sufficient for the establishment of this Constitution between the states so ratifying the same.

Done in convention by the unanimous consent of the states present the seventeenth day of September in the year of our Lord one thousand seven hundred and eighty-seven and of the independence of the United States of America the twelfth. In witness whereof We have hereunto subscribed our Names,

G. Washington-Presidt. and deputy from Virginia

New Hampshire: John Langdon, Nicholas Gilman

Massachusetts: Nathaniel Gorham, Rufus King
Connecticut: Wm. Saml. Johnson, Roger Sherman
New York: Alexander Hamilton
New Jersey: Wil. Livingston, David Brearly, Wm. Paterson, Jona. Dayton
Pennsylvania: B. Franklin, Thomas Mifflin, Robt. Morris, Geo. Clymer, Thos. FitzSimons, Jared Ingersoll, James Wilson, Gouv Morris
Delaware: Geo. Read, Gunning Bedford jun, John Dickinson, Richard Bassett, Jaco. Broom
Maryland: James McHenry, Dan of St Thos. Jenifer, Danl. Carroll
Virginia: John Blair, James Madison Jr.
North Carolina: Wm. Blount, Richd. Dobbs Spaight, Hu. Williamson
South Carolina: J. Rutledge, Charles Cotesworth Pinckney, Charles Pinckney, Pierce Butler
Georgia: William Few, Abr. Baldwin

Amendments to the Constitution

Articles in Addition to, and Amendment of, the Constitution of the United States of America, Proposed by Congress, and Ratified by the Several States, Pursuant to the Fifth Article of the Original Constitution.

Amendment I

Congress shall make no law respecting an establishment of religion, or prohibiting the free exercise thereof; or abridging the freedom of speech, or of the press; or the right of the people peaceably to assemble, and to petition the government for a redress of grievances.

Amendment II

A well regulated militia, being necessary to the security of a free state, the right of the people to keep and bear arms, shall not be infringed.

Amendment III

No soldier shall, in time of peace be quartered in any house, without the consent of the owner, nor in time of war, but in a manner to be prescribed by law.

Amendment IV

The right of the people to be secure in their persons, houses, papers, and effects, against unreasonable searches and seizures, shall not be violated, and no warrants shall issue, but upon probable cause, supported by oath or affirmation, and particularly describing the place to be searched, and the persons or things to be seized.

Amendment V

No person shall be held to answer for a capital, or otherwise infamous crime, unless on a presentment or indictment of a grand jury, except in cases arising in the land or naval forces, or in the militia, when in actual service in time of war or public danger; nor shall any person be subject for the same offense to be twice put in jeopardy of life or limb; nor shall be compelled in any criminal case to be a witness against himself, nor be deprived of life, liberty, or property, without due process of law; nor shall private property be taken for public use, without just compensation.

Amendment VI

In all criminal prosecutions, the accused shall enjoy the right to a speedy and public trial, by an impartial jury of the state and district wherein the crime shall have been committed, which district shall have been previously ascertained by law, and to be informed of the nature and cause of the accusation; to be confronted with the witnesses against him; to have compulsory process for obtaining witnesses in his favor, and to have the assistance of counsel for his defense.

Amendment VII

In suits at common law, where the value in controversy shall exceed twenty dollars, the right of trial by jury shall be preserved, and no fact tried by a jury, shall be otherwise reexamined in any court of the United States, than according to the rules of the common law.

Amendment VIII

Excessive bail shall not be required, nor excessive fines imposed, nor cruel and unusual punishments inflicted.

Amendment IX

The enumeration in the Constitution, of certain rights, shall not be construed to deny or disparage others retained by the people.

Amendment X

The powers not delegated to the United States by the Constitution, nor prohibited by it to the states, are reserved to the states respectively, or to the people.

Amendment XI
(1798)

The judicial power of the United States shall not be construed to extend to any suit in law or equity, commenced or prosecuted against one of the United States by citizens of another state, or by citizens or subjects of any foreign state.

Amendment XII
(1804)

The electors shall meet in their respective states and vote by ballot for President and Vice-President, one of whom, at least, shall not be an inhabitant of the same state with themselves; they shall name in their ballots the person voted for as President, and in distinct ballots the person voted for as Vice-President, and they shall make distinct lists of all persons voted for as President, and of all persons voted for as Vice-President, and of the number of votes for each, which lists they shall sign and certify, and transmit sealed to the seat of the government of the United States, directed to the President of the Senate;— The President of the Senate shall, in the presence of the Senate and House of Representatives, open all the certificates and the votes shall then be counted;— the person having the greatest number of votes for President, shall be the President, if such number be a majority of the whole number of electors appointed; and if no person have such majority, then from the persons having the highest numbers not exceeding three on the list of those voted for as President, the House of Representatives shall choose immediately, by ballot, the President. But in choosing the President, the votes shall be taken by states, the representation from each state having one vote; a quorum for this purpose shall consist of a member or members from two-thirds of the states, and a majority of all the states shall be necessary to a choice. And if the House of Representatives shall not choose a President whenever the right of choice shall devolve upon them, before the fourth day of March next following, then the Vice-President shall act as President, as in the case of the death or other constitutional disability of the President. The person having the greatest number of votes as Vice-President, shall be the Vice-President, if such number be a majority of the whole number of electors appointed, and if no person have a majority, then from the two highest numbers on the list, the Senate shall choose the Vice-President; a quorum for the purpose shall consist of two-thirds of the whole number of Senators, and a majority of the whole number shall be necessary to a choice. But no person constitutionally ineligible to the office of President shall be eligible to that of Vice-President of the United States.

Amendment XIII
(1865)

Section 1. Neither slavery nor involuntary servitude, except as a punishment for crime whereof the party shall have been duly convicted, shall exist within the United States, or any place subject to their jurisdiction.

Section 2. Congress shall have power to enforce this article by appropriate legislation.

Amendment XIV
(1868)

Section 1. All persons born or naturalized in the United States, and subject to the jurisdiction thereof, are citizens of the United States and of the state wherein they reside. No state shall make or enforce any law which shall abridge the privileges or immunities of citizens of the United States; nor shall any state deprive any person of life, liberty, or property, without due process of law; nor deny to any person within its jurisdiction the equal protection of the laws.

Section 2. Representatives shall be apportioned among the several states according to their respective numbers, counting the whole number of persons in each state, excluding Indians not taxed. But when the right to vote at any election for the choice of electors for President and Vice President of the United States, Representatives in Congress, the executive and judicial officers of a state, or the members of the legislature thereof, is denied to any of the male inhabitants of such state, being twenty-one years of age, and citizens of the United States, or in any way abridged, except for participation in rebellion, or other crime, the basis of representation therein shall be reduced in the proportion which the number of such male citizens shall bear to the whole number of male citizens twenty-one years of age in such state.

Section 3. No person shall be a Senator or Representative in Congress, or elector of President and Vice President, or hold any office, civil or military, under the United States, or under any state, who, having previously taken an oath, as a member of Congress, or as an officer of the United States, or as a member of any state legislature, or as an executive or judicial officer of any state, to support the Constitution of the United States, shall have engaged in insurrection or rebellion against the same, or given aid or comfort to the enemies thereof. But Congress may by a vote of two-thirds of each House, remove such disability.

Section 4. The validity of the public debt of the United States, authorized by law, including debts incurred for payment of pensions and bounties for services in suppressing insurrection or rebellion, shall not be questioned. But neither the United States nor any state shall assume or pay any debt or obligation incurred in aid of insurrection or rebellion against the United States, or any claim for the loss or emancipation of any slave; but all such debts, obligations and claims shall be held illegal and void.

Section 5. The Congress shall have power to enforce, by appropriate legislation, the provisions of this article.

Amendment XV
(1870)

Section 1. The right of citizens of the United States to vote shall not be denied or abridged by the United States or by any state on account of race, color, or previous condition of servitude.

Section 2. The Congress shall have power to enforce this article by appropriate legislation.

Amendment XVI
(1913)

The Congress shall have power to lay and collect taxes on incomes, from whatever source derived, without apportionment among the several states, and without regard to any census of enumeration.

Amendment XVII
(1913)

The Senate of the United States shall be composed of two Senators from each state, elected by the people thereof, for six years; and each Senator shall have one vote. The electors in each state shall have the qualifications requisite for electors of the most numerous branch of the state legislatures.

When vacancies happen in the representation of any state in the Senate, the executive authority of such state shall issue writs of election to fill such vacancies: Provided, that the legislature of any state may empower the executive thereof to make temporary appointments until the people fill the vacancies by election as the legislature may direct.

This amendment shall not be so construed as to affect the election or term of any Senator chosen before it becomes valid as part of the Constitution.

Amendment XVIII
(1919)

Section 1. After one year from the ratification of this article the manufacture, sale, or transportation of intoxicating liquors within, the importation thereof into, or the exportation thereof from the United States and all territory subject to the jurisdiction thereof for beverage purposes is hereby prohibited.

Section 2. The Congress and the several states shall have concurrent power to enforce this article by appropriate legislation.

Section 3. This article shall be inoperative unless it shall have been ratified as an amendment to the Constitution by the legislatures of the several states, as provided in the Constitution, within seven years from the date of the submission hereof to the states by the Congress.

Amendment XIX
(1920)

The right of citizens of the United States to vote shall not be denied or abridged by the United States or by any state on account of sex.

Congress shall have power to enforce this article by appropriate legislation.

Amendment XX
(1933)

Section 1. The terms of the President and Vice President shall end at noon on the 20th day of January, and the terms of Senators and Representatives at noon on the 3d day of January, of the years in which such terms would have ended if this article had not been ratified; and the terms of their successors shall then begin.

Section 2. The Congress shall assemble at least once in every year, and such meeting shall begin at noon on the 3d day of January, unless they shall by law appoint a different day.

Section 3. If, at the time fixed for the beginning of the term of the President, the President elect shall have died, the Vice President elect shall become President. If a President shall not have been chosen before the time fixed for the beginning of his term, or if the President elect shall have failed to qualify, then the Vice President elect shall act as President until a President shall have qualified; and the Congress may by law provide for the case wherein neither a President elect nor a Vice President elect shall have qualified, declaring who shall then act as President, or the manner in which one who is to act shall be selected, and such person shall act accordingly until a President or Vice President shall have qualified.

Section 4. The Congress may by law provide for the case of the death of any of the persons from whom the House of Representatives may choose a President whenever the right of choice shall have devolved upon them, and for the case of the death of any of the persons from whom the Senate may choose a Vice President whenever the right of choice shall have devolved upon them.

Section 5. Sections 1 and 2 shall take effect on the 15th day of October following the ratification of this article.

Section 6. This article shall be inoperative unless it shall have been ratified as an amendment to the Constitution by the legislatures of three-fourths of the several states within seven years from the date of its submission.

Amendment XXI
(1933)

Section 1. The eighteenth article of amendment to the Constitution of the United States is hereby repealed.

Section 2. The transportation or importation into any state, territory, or possession of the United States for delivery or use therein of intoxicating liquors, in violation of the laws thereof, is hereby prohibited.

Section 3. This article shall be inoperative unless it shall have been ratified as an amendment to the Constitution by conventions in the several states, as provided in the Constitution, within seven years from the date of the submission hereof to the states by the Congress.

Amendment XXII
(1951)

Section 1. No person shall be elected to the office of the President more than twice, and no person who has held the office of President, or acted as President, for more than two years of a term to which some other person was elected President shall be elected to the office of the President more than once. But this article shall not apply to any person holding the office of President when this article was proposed by the Congress, and shall not prevent any person who may be holding the office of President, or acting as President, during the term within which this article becomes operative from holding the office of President or acting as President during the remainder of such term.

Section 2. This article shall be inoperative unless it shall have been ratified as an amendment to the Constitution by the legislatures of three-fourths of the several states within seven years from the date of its submission to the states by the Congress.

Amendment XXIII
(1961)

Section 1. The District constituting the seat of government of the United States shall appoint in such manner as the Congress may direct:

A number of electors of President and Vice President equal to the whole number of Senators and Representatives in Congress to which the District would be entitled if it were a state, but in no event more than the least populous state; they shall be in addition to those appointed by the states, but they shall be considered, for the purposes of the election of President and Vice President, to be electors appointed by a state; and they shall meet in the District and perform such duties as provided by the twelfth article of amendment.

Section 2. The Congress shall have power to enforce this article by appropriate legislation.

Amendment XXIV
(1964)

Section 1. The right of citizens of the United States to vote in any primary or other election for President or Vice President, for electors for President or Vice President, or for Senator or Representative in Congress, shall not be denied or abridged by the United States or any state by reason of failure to pay any poll tax or other tax.

Section 2. The Congress shall have power to enforce this article by appropriate legislation.

Amendment XXV
(1967)

Section 1. In case of the removal of the President from office or of his death or resignation, the Vice President shall become President.

Section 2. Whenever there is a vacancy in the office of the Vice President, the President shall nominate a Vice President who shall take office upon confirmation by a majority vote of both Houses of Congress.

Section 3. Whenever the President transmits to the President pro tempore of the Senate and the Speaker of the House of Representatives his written declaration that he is unable to discharge the powers and duties of his office, and until he transmits to them a written declaration to the contrary, such powers and duties shall be discharged by the Vice President as Acting President.

Section 4. Whenever the Vice President and a majority of either the principal officers of the executive departments or of such other body as Congress may by law provide, transmit to the President pro tempore of the Senate and the Speaker of the House of Representatives their written declaration that the President is unable to discharge the powers and duties of his office, the Vice President shall immediately assume the powers and duties of the office as Acting President.

Thereafter, when the President transmits to the President pro tempore of the Senate and the Speaker of the House of Representatives his written declaration that no inability exists, he shall resume the powers and duties of his office unless the Vice President and a majority of either the principal officers of the executive department or of such other body as Congress may by law provide, transmit within four days to the President pro tempore of the Senate and the Speaker of the House of Representatives their written declaration that the President is unable to discharge the powers and duties of his office. Thereupon Congress shall decide the issue, assembling within forty-eight hours for that purpose if not in session. If the Congress, within twenty-one days after receipt of the latter written declaration, or, if Congress is not in session, within twenty-one days after Congress is required to assemble, determines by two-thirds vote of both Houses that the President is unable to discharge the powers and duties of his office, the Vice President shall continue to discharge the same as Acting President; otherwise, the President shall resume the powers and duties of his office.

Amendment XXVI
(1971)

Section 1. The right of citizens of the United States, who are 18 years of age or older, to vote, shall not be denied or abridged by the United States or any state on account of age.

Section 2. The Congress shall have the power to enforce this article by appropriate legislation.

Amendment XXVII
(1992)

No law varying the compensation for the services of the Senators and Representatives shall take effect until an election of Representatives shall have intervened.

GLOSSARY OF TERMS AND PHRASES

Abrogate. The repeal, annulment, or destruction of an order or rule of a lower power by the same or higher authority.

Absolutism. (1) A view of constitutional interpretation that holds that judges must apply the strict meaning of the words or clear intentions of the constitutional framers regardless of whether it results in upholding or striking down legislation. See also, **interpretivism.** (2) A term often applied to the view that certain forms of expression are completely protected from government prohibition by the First Amendment. A doctrine most closely associated with Justice Hugo Black.

Abstention doctrine. A judicially created policy that federal courts should not exercise jurisdiction in those instances where a federal constitutional question depends on an uncertain interpretation of state law.

Accusatorial system. The legal system that presumes a person is innocent until proven guilty. This outstanding feature of Anglo-American criminal justice places the burden of proof on the accuser. Cf., **inquisitorial system.**

Actual malice. A judicial test in freedom of press defamation cases holding that a civil suit for money damages will not be sustained unless there is a finding that the defamatory statement was made with knowledge of its falsity or in reckless disregard of the truth.

Ad hoc. For a special or unique purpose; temporary and not permanent.

Ad valorem. A Latin term meaning according to value. An *ad valorem* tax is a levy on the value of something rather than a fixed tax regardless of value. For example, an *ad valorem* tax on a diamond ring worth $100 might be $5 while the tax on a $10,000 ring might be $250. The tax varies according to the worth or value of the item rather than a fixed tax of, say, $75 for all diamond rings.

Adjective law. A generic term referring to the procedural rules under which courts or agencies conduct their affairs as compared to the substantive law.

Administrative law. The branch of public law dealing with the rules and regulations promulgated by government agencies.

Administrative Procedure Act. First enacted by Congress in 1946, this law requires each agency of the U.S. government to describe its organization and locations, and the methods whereby the public may acquire information about it, make suggestions and other requests, and obtain agency rules and regulations. The act requires that agencies inform the public about their rules and regulations and the manner in which they make decisions and observe basic rules of due process of law.

Admiralty law. The branch of the law concerned with maritime matters.

Advisory opinion. A judicial ruling in the absence of an actual case or controversy; a ruling in a hypothetical case without bona fide litigants. Such opinions result from questions posed by a legislative body or government official, the answers to which are used to guide them in the exercise of their responsibilities. Such opinions may be influential, but they are not binding.

Affirmative action. Government programs requiring authorities or those benefiting from government programs to seek persons of racial, ethnic, or gender minority groups as employees or for admission to schools. It is a form of preferential treatment that proponents regard as benign discrimination.

Agency. (1) A relationship in which one party acts on behalf of another; the latter authorizes the former. (2) A name given for an administrative body of government such as the Bureau of the Budget or the Federal Trade Commission.

Alien and Sedition Acts. Passed in 1798 by a Congress controlled by Federalists, the Alien Act lengthened the residency requirement for citizenship from five to fourteen years and gave the president authority to banish aliens. The Sedition Act declared a crime any libel against the president or any attempt to cause disaffection against the government. Both laws were aimed at the Jeffersonian Republican opposition in the country and particularly the Jeffersonian Republican press.

All deliberate speed. This concept is an equity tool in which a court orders others to comply with its command with dispatch and with adequate and careful consideration of the consequences of its action.

Amicus curiae. A Latin term meaning friend of the court. It normally refers to an outside interest not directly a party to the suit. Usually presents a brief that provides information and argument relevant to a court in its deliberation as to matters of law.

Analytical jurisprudence. A school of jurisprudence that attempts to systematize the law utilizing tools of logic. Outstanding proponents include Hans Kelsen, John Austin, and H. L. A. Hart.

Answer. Usually a written statement or pleading by the defendant responding to the plaintiff's charges.

Appeal. A generic term referring to the movement of court proceedings from an inferior to a superior court. Depending on the context, the term may refer to a technical method of moving a case to a superior court.

Appellant. The name for a party who takes his or her case from a lower court to a higher court to seek review of the lower court decision. Cf., **appellee**.

Appellate court. A judicial body possessing the authority to review and sustain or reverse the decisions of a lower court.

Appellee. The party in a suit against whom the appeal to a superior court is taken; the party with an interest in sustaining the lower court judgment. Cf., **appellant**.

Arbitration. A third-party hearing settlement of a dispute among contending parties. The decision of the arbitrator(s) may be binding on the participants.

Arguento. A Latin term meaning sustaining the assumption that a statement of fact is true, although it may be in fact true or false. It is a method of illustrating a line of reasoning found in judicial opinions.

Arraignment. The name for the phase in the criminal legal process when an accused person answers an indictment with a plea of guilty, not guilty, or *nolo contendere*.

Arrest warrant. Upon finding that an accused person should stand trial for the commission of a crime, a court of competent jurisdiction authorizes police officials to take a person into custody.

Articles of Confederation. Between 1781 and 1789, the states composing the United States were governed under this document. It provided for a loose union of states wherein the powers of the central government were severely limited and the states retained their sovereign power.

Associate justice. In some appellate courts, this is the title given to judges other than the chief justice.

Bad tendency doctrine. The now discredited judicial doctrine permitting limitations on freedom of speech if there is a tendency, no matter how remote, to advance a prohibited activity. Cf., **clear and present danger**.

Bail. A legal device that guarantees in the form of cash or a bond that released prisoners will appear at their trials. Bail may be forfeited if the released prisoner does not appear at trial.

Bailiff. The name for an officer of the court who is in charge of prisoners and who guards the jurors in a court. This person is generally charged with keeping the peace in court.

Balancing of interests. One approach to judicial decision making wherein the judge weighs the competing interests in the case to arrive at a judgment. In constitutional adjudication, it sometimes requires judges to balance basic rights such as society's interest in freedom of expression and society's interest in the right to privacy.

Bar. The community of attorneys permitted to practice law in a particular jurisdiction or court.

Bicameral. Usually refers to a legislative body with two "houses"; for example, a Senate and a House of Representatives; it means two chambers.

Bifurcated trial. A judicial procedure in capital criminal trials that separates the guilt from the punishment segment of jury deliberations.

Bill of attainder. A legislative act declaring a person guilty of a crime and passing sentence without the benefit of a trial. Such legislation is specifically forbidden by the U.S. Constitution.

Black letter law. The most basic principle of law accepted by the courts. For example, "obscenity is not protected speech." It is generally rejected by political scientists and others as not explanatory of the judicial process.

Blackstone. Sir William Blackstone was the influential eighteenth-century jurist and author of *Blackstone's Commentaries on the Common Law.*

Blue law. A legislative enactment forbidding all or certain business activity on the Sabbath, usually Sundays.

Bona fide. A Latin term for good faith. It refers to persons acting without trickery, deceit, fraud, or dishonesty.

Brandeis Brief. A written argument presented before an appellate court containing extralegal social science information relevant to the case. It is named after Louis Brandeis whose brief in Muller v. Oregon, 208 U.S. 412 (1908) consisted of two pages of formal legal argument and one hundred pages of economic and social data.

Brief. (1) The oral or written argument presented by counsel to a court. (2) Summaries of the pertinent elements of a court opinion written by a student as a study guide and aid.

Burden of proof. Although possessing several technical meanings, the phrase burden of proof generally refers to the duty of one of the parties to a suit to demonstrate that the weight of evidence or law is on his or her side. Sometimes the burden of proof will shift. In Anglo-American criminal justice the burden of proof is on the prosecution.

Calendar. A list of cases in the order they are to be heard during a court term. Sometimes a calendar is known as a court docket or trial list.

Capitation tax. A head tax or a tax on persons regardless of such matters as income, assets, status, or personal wealth.

Capital crime. An offense against the people for which the death penalty may be imposed.

Carolene Products, footnote four. Justice Stone in United States v. Carolene Products Co., 304 U.S. 144 (1938) laid down, in footnote four of his opinion, guiding principles for when and how the Supreme Court should treat issues involving fundamental constitutional rights. The summary label for these principles today is the preferred freedoms approach; courts apply strict scrutiny to government regulations that limit fundamental rights.

Case and controversy. The Article III requirement of the U.S. Constitution that legal dispute with *bona fide* adversaries involve live and real issues, not hypothetical or abstract issues, rights, or claims to be protected.

Case-by-case approach to incorporation. The argument preferred by Justice Felix Frankfurter that whether a provision of the Bill of Rights applies to the states is dependent upon the particular facts in a case. That is, there is no constitutional requirement that any provision of the Bill of Rights must apply beyond the instance case. If, for example, police conduct is "shocking to the conscience" then the Due Process Clause of the Fourteenth Amendment is applicable, but only for that particular case.

Case law. As opposed to laws that are enacted by legislative bodies, the case law is law handed down in written judicial opinions.

Case method. A rigorous and dominant approach to legal education stressing the reading and in-depth analysis of leading judicial opinions. The growth of the law is traced through the reading of the cases. Professors employ the Socratic questioning method in connection with the court opinions.

Casebook. A law textbook containing leading edited judicial opinions on a particular legal subject. Cases are usually arranged chronologically by subject matter.

Cause of action. A commonly used phrase in law that refers to the existence of sufficient facts and accepted legal concepts to warrant a lawsuit brought by a plaintiff.

Censorship. A term that refers to government impositions or restrictions on what persons may read, speak, publish, or on other forms of communication. In such cases, First Amendment issues are raised.

Certification. A method of appeal by which a lower court requests a higher court to answer certain questions of law so that the lower court may make a correct decision in light of the answer provided.

Certiorari, writ of. An order from a superior to an inferior court to send the entire record of a case to the superior court for review. It is a discretionary writ employed by the U.S. Supreme Court. See also, **rule of four.**

Chambers. The private office of a judge. Legal activity transacted there is often referred to as "in chambers."

Charter. A document emanating from government granting certain rights, liberties, or powers to an organization, colony, local government, corporation, or people; for example, a city charter, colonial charter, or corporation charter.

Chattel. An old English legal term, the word chattel usually refers to personal property excluding land.

Checks and balances. A principle of limited government that refers to the ability of each branch of the government (legislative, executive, and judicial) to deter if not to prevent one branch of the government from dominating the others. In its operation, checks and balances serve as countervailing sources of governmental power in a way that promotes the goals of limited government.

Chief justice. The person appointed by the president with the advice and consent of the Senate to head the U.S. Supreme Court.

Chilling effect doctrine. A judicially created doctrine referring to an action by the government that discourages persons from exercising their civil liberties. The U.S. Supreme Court has used this concept to describe and discredit government conduct, particularly in the area of First Amendment rights.

Civil action. A lawsuit typically brought by a private party for the redress of a noncriminal act. Usually the plaintiff seeks money damages for the wrongful conduct of the defendant; for example, suits in negligence, contract, or defamation.

Civil law. (1) The system of jurisprudence based on Roman law found in most Western European nation-states. It is distinct from the common law. (2) In common law countries, civil law refers to noncriminal legal matters.

Class action suit. A legal suit brought by one person on behalf of him- or herself and all others similarly situated. For example, John Doe, as representative of the class of all persons similarly situated, and for himself, Plaintiff, v. Paul Smith, in his capacity as Chief of Police of the City of XYZ, Defendant.

Clear and present danger test. Created by Justice Holmes in Schenck v. United States, 249 U.S. 47(1919), the clear and present danger test is an alternative to an absolutist interpretation of the First Amendment. It indicates that limitations on free speech are permissible if the words are used in "such circumstances and are of such a nature as to create a clear and present danger that they will bring about the substantive evil that Congress has a right to prevent." Cf., **bad tendency doctrine**.

Close and substantial rule. The rule propounded in National Labor Relations Board v. Jones and Laughlin Steel Corporation, 301 U.S. 1 (1937) upholding the Wagner Act that established the right of labor to collectively bargain as a valid regulation of interstate commerce. It holds that "although activities may be intrastate in character when separately considered, if they have such a close and substantial relation to interstate commerce that their control is essential or appropriate to protect that commerce from burdens and obstructions, Congress may not be denied the authority to exercise that control."

Collusiveness. See **feigned cases**.

Comity. The willingness to extend courtesy and respect to another nation-state or a unit of government within a state motivated by good will and a desire for good relations.

Commander in chief. Article II, section 2, clause 1, of the U.S. Constitution provides that the president has authority over the armed services of the U.S. government.

Commercial speech. This concept treats the circumstances in which advertisement is protected speech under the First Amendment of the Constitution.

Common law. The system of law created by the English courts and brought to America by the colonists. Judges are said to find the law in the customs and habits of the people. It is largely judge-made law as distinct from statutory law made by legislators. Its chief competitor is the Roman-founded civil law system of Western Europe.

Commutation of punishment. An action by an executive officer of government that reduces a criminal penalty to a lesser punishment. It differs from a pardon in that it does not require the consent of the convict.

Compelling state interest. An intellectual tool of constitutional interpretation that places the burden of proof on the state to prove that the deprivation of a fundamental right or discrimination of certain classes of people is necessary for the public good. Cf., **rational basis test**.

Complaint. (1) A formal document in a civil suit containing the initial pleading in a lawsuit that frames the issues. (2) A criminal complaint is one person's statement taken under oath that accuses another of a criminal act.

Concurrent jurisdiction. The authority possessed by two or more courts to hear cases on a given subject.

Concurrent power. The political authority to exercise independent power by more than one government on the same subject matter; for example, the police and taxing powers in a federal system.

Confederation. An association or league among sovereign entities in which a central government is given certain limited responsibilities not affecting the basic powers of member entities or states. Cf., **federation**.

Conflict of laws. The field of law dealing with the situation in which a judge must choose among the laws of more than one jurisdiction as to which should apply in a particular case.

Conspiracy. A concept in criminal law that refers to two or more persons acting together to accomplish a criminal objective or to pursue a noncriminal purpose in an unlawful or criminal manner.

Constitutional courts. A court named in a constitution or a court given certain functions and protections independent of the other political branches of government. For the U.S. government, a constitutional court is one authorized under Article III of the Constitution or designated by the Congress as an Article III court. Article III courts are protected as to jurisdiction, appointment, and tenure.

Constitutionalism. The principle of the rule of law under which the rulers abide by certain rules limiting their official conduct in return for the right to exercise authority.

Contempt. An act that in some way obstructs or denigrates the dignity of a court, a legislative body, or an administrative agency. Contempt is usually a punishable offense.

Cooperative federalism. A general approach to the American federal system that views the relationship between the national and state governments as a working partnership by which the mutual interests of both may be satisfied. Some take a more extreme view by stressing the "necessity" of national supremacy. Cf., **dual federalism**.

Corpus delicti. A Latin term referencing the body of the crime. The production of material evidence indicating that the specific charges have in fact been committed and that some individual or group is criminally responsible.

Corruption of blood. Article III, section 3 of the U.S. Constitution prohibits the old English practice of preventing the heirs of a person convicted of treason from inheriting property.

Count. Refers to the separate and independent claims or charges in a civil or criminal matter. A criminal indictment, for example, may contain many counts; if the prosecution should lose on one or more counts it will still have others on which to convict.

Court of last resort. A popular term referring to a court from which there is no appeal.

Crime. The word used to indicate a violation of government's penal laws. The offense is against society and not just a violation of another's individual rights.

Criminal syndicalism statutes. Laws initially passed by Congress and the states in the early part of the twentieth century making it a crime to advocate political change through revolution or other violent means.

Criminology. A field of social science concerned with the causes, prevention, and punishment of crime. This discipline is considered by many as a branch of sociology.

Critical legal studies. A movement that began in the 1970s that seeks reform of the law school curriculum. It views the law as an instrument in the hands of the powerful to dominant and to manipulate the powerless in society. It has several branches including the neo-Marxist critical theory, critical race theory, and feminist critical theory.

Culpable. This word refers to blameworthy or wrongful conduct. It usually applies in the law of torts but sometimes it is used in a criminal context.

Damages. Money awarded by a court to a plaintiff for the wrongful conduct of a defendant.

De facto. This Latin term refers to the existence of something in fact or reality as distinguished from *de jure*, by right. Segregation in housing due to custom but not the result of official government action is often termed *de facto* segregation.

De jure. A Latin term referring to lawful, rightful, or legitimate; opposite of *de facto*. Segregation in public education mandated by state law was known as *de jure* segregation.

De minimus non curat lex. A Latin term meaning that the law is not concerned with trivialities.

De novo. A Latin term meaning anew, once more, again. Usually applies to a case being retried on order of an appellate court. Some court systems permit *de novo* appeals.

Declaratory judgment. A judicial determination of the legal rights of the parties involved in an actual case or controversy, but where the court does not require the parties to abide by the judgment. It differs from an advisory opinion because there is an actual case or controversy.

Decree. A court order or sentence specifying the details of a legal settlement; for example, terms of alimony, child custody, or an agreement between a business enterprise and the government. A consent decree is an agreement among the parties to conduct their affairs in a certain way. It cannot be amended without the consent of both parties.

Defamation. A concept in the law of torts referencing the damage to another's reputation by a false statement. Sometimes persons are found guilty of criminal defamation. See **libel; slander.**

Defendant. In a court case, the person or entity against whom a civil or criminal charge is brought.

Delegation of legislative authority. The grant of power by a legislative body to an administrative or regulatory agency to promulgate rules and regulations that are enforceable as law.

Deliberation. The process of weighing reasons or evidence for or against a course of action. A term that usually applies to the work of a jury when determining guilt or innocence.

Demurrer. A legal procedure permitting counsel to object to the sufficiency of a legal cause of action contained in the pleadings of the other side. Even if the act complained of did in fact occur, the law as presented by the other side does not cover that situation. In the U.S. Federal courts this term is no longer used in favor of the phrase "motion to dismiss."

Dicta. See **obiter dicta.**

Direct commerce. A now discredited interpretation of the Commerce Clause of the U.S. Constitution that favors dual federalism. It defined the congressional power to regulate commerce as limited to transportation or movement of goods and services across state lines.

Diversity jurisdiction. Article III of the U.S. Constitution provides for the trial of disputes in federal courts involving persons residing in different states.

Docket. A formal document that lists cases to be heard by a court.

Double jeopardy. Refers to being tried twice for the same crime. It is prohibited by the Fifth Amendment of U.S. Constitution, and this prohibition is applicable to the states through the Due Process Clause of the Fourteenth Amendment.

Dual federalism. The general approach to the American federal system that views the relationship between the national and state governments as adversarial. This perspective is best represented by the position of states' rights advocates that view the powers of the central government as strictly limited by the enumerated provisions in the Constitution; all other powers are reserved to the states by way of the Tenth Amendment. Cf., **cooperative federalism**.

Eavesdropping. The act of overhearing a conversation of others.

Eminent domain. The right and ability of government to take private property for a public use.

Emoluments Clause. Article I, section 6 of the Constitution prohibits the appointment of any member of Congress to a position in government during his or her elected term if, during that term, Congress created the office or increased the pay or benefits arising from the office.

En banc. Sometimes appearing as *En Banke*, this term means all the judges of a court or all jury members sitting together to hear a case.

Enabling legislation. A law enacted by a legislature that brings into existence a government agency or program. It contains the powers, purposes, and limitations of such an agency or program.

Enumerated powers of government. This phrase refers to those powers specifically spelled out in the body of the Constitution that government may exercise. For example, the enumerated powers of Congress are specified in Article 1, section 8 of the Constitution.

Equity. The administration of justice based on principles of fairness rather than strictly applied rules found in the common law. Because the common law courts of England became too rigid in the exercise of their jurisdiction, equity courts were created; in the United States, courts of law and courts of equity have been largely merged.

Erie doctrine. In Erie R. Co. v. Tompkins, 304 U.S. 64 (1938), the Supreme Court held that except for matters covered by the U.S. Constitution or by congressional enactment, a federal court is bound by the statutes and case precedents of the state in which it sits. Therefore, there is no federal common law about state matters. This doctrine prevents conflicts between federal and state courts reaching different results on the same issues.

Error, writ of. A method of appeal by which an appellate court orders a lower court to send a case to a higher court for review of alleged mistakes (errors) made by the lower court. Matters of law and not of fact are reviewed. The U.S. Supreme Court no longer employs this appeal method.

Establishment Clause. The First Amendment provision that prohibits Congress from making any laws respecting the establishment of religion. The clause has been made applicable to the states through the Due Process Clause of the Fourteenth Amendment.

Ex parte. A judicial hearing when only one party is present, such as when the appellant is in prison.

Ex post facto law. A Latin term for a law after the fact. An *ex post facto* law attempts to make an act a crime that was not a crime when it was done. It is specifically prohibited by Article I, section 9 of the U.S. Constitution.

Ex rel. An abbreviation for *ex relatione*. It means on relation or information. A designation appearing in case titles indicating that the suit is instituted by a state but at the instigation or insistence of an individual; for example, *Missouri ex rel. Gaines v. S.W. Canada*. The state of Missouri is bringing the suit at the instigation of Lloyd Gaines against S.W. Canada.

Exclusionary rule. A judicially created policy of the U.S. Supreme Court that evidence illegally obtained in violation of constitutional principles is inadmissible in a court of law to convict a criminal defendant.

Exclusive jurisdiction. The sole authority vested in one court to hear a case on a given subject matter; for example, for the U.S. Supreme Court, suits between and among the states, foreign ambassadors, bankruptcy, and prosecutions of federal criminal law.

Exclusive power. The sole exercise of authority by one governmental body; for example, only the federal government possesses the authority to make war.

Executive agreement. Presidents may make international agreements under their constitutional authority as commander-in-chief and in their capacity as the nation's spokesperson in foreign affairs. These agreements do not require senatorial approval, as is the case for a treaty.

Executive orders. Directives from presidents to bureaucratic officials requiring the implementation of policy. The source of this authority stems from congressional authorization with the president as chief executive delineating the details of policy implementation.

Executive privilege. A claim not found explicitly in the Constitution that executive officials including the president have the constitutional right to refuse to appear and give testimony before Congress or the courts. A fundamental premise is that communication between the president and subordinates must be protected from inspection by officials of other branches of government because of the separation of powers principle.

Exhaustion of remedies. As a maxim of judicial self-restraint, the judiciary requires that any party seeking review of an administrative or lower court ruling must first use all other legal options for the resolution of the conflict before the appellate court will hear the matter.

Expatriation. Either a voluntary or an involuntary act resulting in the abandonment, repudiation, or renouncement of citizenship.

Extradition. The legal process by which one jurisdiction surrenders a fugitive to another.

Federal preemption doctrine. When Congress properly legislates in a field of public policy in which state governments had previously exercised authority, the federal law exercises exclusive authority unless otherwise stated in law, thereby rendering the state law inoperable.

Federal question doctrine. A judicially created guideline that federal courts should adjudicate only those cases that directly involve the U.S. Constitution, the laws of the U.S., or treaties of the U.S. The U.S. Supreme Court often has maintained that its jurisdiction is limited to federal questions; it is one method of exercising judicial self-restraint.

Federation. A structure of government dividing powers between the central and state governments; both the state and national governments operate directly on the people.

Feigned case. A lawsuit in which there is no real controversy between the parties. The parties pretend there is a controversy to accomplish some other goal such as a wager.

Felony. A crime designated by statute as serious. More serious than a misdemeanor, a felony may involve capital punishment or imprisonment for a long duration.

Fiduciary. A relationship in which one person acts in a position of trust for another. It sometimes involves management of money or property.

Fighting words doctrine. This doctrine is a limitation on the exercise of free speech because the utterance of such words conveys an emotional message intended to incite a rapid and unthinking violent response by listeners.

Free exercise of religion. A provision of the First Amendment that prohibits government from interfering with how persons worship or choose not to engage in religious practices. It applies to the state governments through the liberty provision of the Due Process Clause of the Fourteenth Amendment.

Fruit of the poisonous tree. A judicially created doctrine that prohibits the introduction at trial of evidence that is traceable to illegally obtained evidence in the first instance. The poisonous tree is the original illegal activity by the police, for instance, the unlawful search of one's property, and the fruit is secondary evidence obtained by the police, for instance, illegal control substances. This doctrine was first enunciated in Silverthorne Lumber Co. v. United States, 251 U.S. 385 (1920).

Full Faith and Credit Clause. Article IV, section 1 of the Constitution provides that the public acts, records, and proceedings of each state are to be honored by every other state; for example, a divorce granted in one state is upheld in every other state.

Fundamental rights. Although a matter of controversy, Justice Cardozo defined fundamental rights in Palko v. Connecticut, 302 U.S. 319 (1937) as those "so rooted in the traditions and collective conscience of our people as to be ranked as fundamental." These rights are found in the Bill of Rights, and those that justices may determine.

Gag order. A popular term that has taken on legal meaning that refers to a judge's order prohibiting parties from speaking publicly about a matter before the court. It is designed to protect the rights of the parties.

Gerrymandering. The drawing of legislative or other political district boundaries in such a manner as to give advantage to one political party or interest.

Good faith exception. The U.S. Supreme Court in United States v. Leon, 468 U.S. 897 (1984) held that the exclusionary rule does not prohibit the introduction of evidence resulting from honest police mistakes because to exclude such evidence cannot deter police from knowingly engaging in unreasonable searches and seizures.

Grand jury. A jury of inquiry designed to determine whether there is sufficient evidence to justify a criminal trial.

Grandfather clause. Usually refers to a discriminatory practice in the southern states that prohibited African Americans whose ancestors had not voted prior to the enactment of the Fifteenth Amendment from voting. Today, the term is commonly used to refer to a legal provision in a law or regulation that protects a person from losing a legal right resulting from a change in public policy.

Guarantee Clause. Under Article IV, section 4 of the Constitution, the federal government owes a duty to every state to guarantee a "republican form of government." The Supreme Court has consistently held that this clause is nonjusticiable.

Guaranty Clause. See **Guarantee Clause.**

Habeas corpus, writ of. A writ directing that a person held in custody be brought before the court to determine if he or she is being lawfully detained.

Harmless error. Though judicial errors take place during trials, not all of them rise to levels that are detrimental to the rights of the parties. These errors therefore do not require correction by an appellate court and the consequent reversal and or remand to a lower court for action that affects the outcome of a case.

Hate speech. Offensive expressions aimed at individuals or groups based on certain characteristics including race, color, gender, religion, or sexual orientation. Some institutions such as cities and colleges have enacted laws and regulations punishing such speech.

Hicklin test. The now discredited rule enunciated in the English case, *Regina v. Hicklin* (1868). It held that materials are obscene if their tendency was to ". . . deprave and corrupt those whose minds are open to such immoral influences, and into whose hands a publication of this sort may fall."

High crimes and misdemeanors. Article II, section 4 of the U.S. Constitution provides for the removal from office of the president, vice-president, and all civil officers by way of impeachment for committing offenses such as treason, bribery, and other unspecified crimes.

Historical jurisprudence. A school of legal thought that applies the method of historical criticism to the study of law. Historical jurists study the customs and historical development of a people and their law. In the United States, the employment of the case method is its greatest manifestation. The writings of Karl von Savigny, Sir Henry Maine, and Christopher Columbus Langdell are preeminent in this area.

Hung jury. A jury that cannot agree upon a verdict, and may result in a new trial.

Ignoramus. Latin for we are ignorant or we ignore it. A formal designation employed by a grand jury when it finds insufficient evidence to warrant an indictment.

Immunity. An exemption from performing a duty. The grant of immunity in a criminal prosecution exempts a person from prosecution on the condition that he or she provides desired information.

Impeachment. The Constitution provides a procedure for the removal from office of the president, vice-president, and other civil officers for committing high crimes and misdemeanors. The House of Representatives possesses the sole power to bring a bill of impeachment and the Senate has the authority to try persons named in the bill of impeachment. The trial in the Senate is presided over by the chief justice of the U.S. Supreme Court and a vote of two-thirds of the members of the Senate is necessary to convict.

Implied powers. Those powers not specifically delegated to the national government but that may be inferred because they are necessary and proper for carrying out the delegated powers.

In camera. A Latin term for a vaulted chamber. A device by which a judge hears a case or part of a case in his or her chambers with spectators excluded.

In forma pauperis. A Latin term meaning in the manner of a pauper. It is a device enabling indigents to sue without liability for costs. It is provided for by U.S. statutory law, permitting any citizen upon the execution of an oath to enter proceedings in any federal court. The most celebrated case reaching the U.S. Supreme Court in this manner is Gideon v. Wainwright, 372 U.S. 335 (1963).

In personam. A Latin term meaning toward a person or individual. It is a legal action taken against an individual and not against the whole world.

In re. A Latin term referring to the matter of. Employed when titling judicial proceedings where there are no adversary parties; for example, *In re: Jones.*

In rem. A legal action to enforce property rights against the whole world and not one brought to enforce a legal right against individuals (in personam).

Incorporation of the Bill of Rights. The U.S. Supreme Court has employed the liberty provision of the Due Process Clause of the Fourteenth Amendment to make most of the provisions of the U.S. Bill of Rights applicable to the states.

Indictment. A written accusation presented by a grand jury to a court charging one or more individuals with having committed a public offense.

Indirect commerce. A one-time view of constitutional interpretation holding that manufacturing, agricultural production, mining, and labor taking place within a state have only an indirect impact on interstate commerce and therefore are not subject to congressional regulation. Cf., **direct commerce.**

Information. A device replacing indictment by grand jury in which the prosecutor submits his or her charges supported by evidence and sworn testimony to a trial court. This procedure is employed in England and many U.S. state jurisdictions.

Inherent power. The authority of an institution or officeholder that springs from the nature of the office or governmental institution itself and does not depend upon explicit legislative or constitutional sanction.

Injunction. Stemming from its equity jurisdiction, it is a court order directing someone to do something or refrain from doing something.

Inquisitorial system. A criminal justice system that assumes implicitly the guilt of the defendant, as opposed to common law systems. Civil law systems are said to employ this procedure; however, this characterization is not entirely correct because the highly professional magistrates are said to take great care in reaching truth. Cf., **adversarial system.**

Intelligible principle, delegation. When Congress delegates rule-making power to administrative bodies, it must provide these agencies with guidelines that may be clearly understood and are not so vague as to permit excessive administrative discretion.

Interest balancing test. This refers to a process of constitutional interpretation whereby a court weighs the interest of the community in a certain value against the community's interest in a competing value. For example, the community interest in national security is balanced against the community's interest in protecting the rights of aliens who may be connected with acts of terrorism. Sometimes the term ad hoc interest balancing test is used to describe competing interests in the particular context of specific disputes.

Intergovernmental tax immunity. A Supreme Court doctrine that holds that because the power to tax is the power to destroy, one division of government may not tax another. Its origin is found in the Supreme Court's opinion in McCulloch v. Maryland, 17 U.S. (4 Wheat.) 316 (1819).

Intermediate scrutiny. A constitutional standard for ascertaining violations of equal protection of the law under the Fourteenth Amendment or through the Due Process Clause of the Fifth Amendment. The burden of proof is on the government to demonstrate that its classification in certain instances of race, illegitimacy, or alienage where children are barred from a public education, serves an important government objective and that the tool used to achieve that goal is substantially related to that objective. This level of scrutiny is sometimes called middle tier analysis. Cf., **strict scrutiny test, rational basis test.**

International law. The law governing relations among nation-states, and the rules that determine the jurisdiction of national courts in disputes among private parties. It is a body of general principles and rules accepted by the international community as binding.

Interpretivism. Contemporary conservatives on and off the Supreme Court argue that judges must focus on the words and substantive intentions of the framers of the Constitution when interpreting the basic document. When judges conduct themselves in such a fashion, conservative proponents claim judicial decisions are objective or principled and not a matter of subjective value and moral judgments. Cf., **noninterpretivism.**

Interstate compact. An agreement between two or more states that is ratified by the law of each state and approved by Congress.

Intrastate commerce. Business and related activities including manufacturing and transportation wholly within state boundaries that have no substantial impact on interstate commerce are regarded as intrastate commerce and not within the power of Congress to regulate.

Ipse dixit. A Latin term meaning, he himself said it. It is regarded as an arbitrary statement depending on the authority of the one who said it.

Ipso facto. A commonly used Latin term meaning, by the fact itself. The fact speaks for itself.

Judicial review. Refers to the power of a court to examine legislative enactments and acts of executive officials to determine their validity with respect to a written constitution; for example, Marbury v. Madison, 5 U.S. (1 Cranch) 137 (1803).

Judicial self-restraint. The position accepted by many that judges should refrain from substituting their values for those of political decision makers closer to the sentiments of the people. Operationally, the U.S. Supreme Court has devised various techniques of restraint when deferring to the judgments of other decision makers.

Jurisdiction. Refers to the power or authority of a court to adjudicate disputes. Jurisdiction may extend over the person, the subject matter, or both. Jurisdiction is established either through statutory enactment or constitutional provision.

Jurisprudence of original intention. A view of constitutional interpretation popularized by Attorney General Edwin Meese. It is the attempt to ascertain what the framers of the Constitution really meant when they wrote the Constitution and to remain true to those principles when interpreting the basic document. It is one form of **interpretivism.**

Jurisprudence. (1) The philosophy or science of law. (2) Sometimes refers to a body of law.

Jury. A group of persons charged by a law court with the duty to examine facts and determine the truth.

Jus sanguinis. A Latin term standing for right of blood. It refers to gaining citizenship by virtue of being born of parents who are citizens. Cf., **jus soli.**

Jus soli. A Latin term standing for the right of land. It refers to gaining citizenship by virtue of place or country in which a person is born. Cf., **jus sanguinis.**

Just compensation. The Fifth Amendment of the U.S. Constitution requires that when government takes property from private parties it must adequately compensate them for their loss. Through judicial construction, this constitutional protection is applied to both national and state governments.

Justiciable question. A matter that may be properly adjudicated by a judicial body as within its competence. It is said that a political question is a nonjusticiable one because it is not a legal matter that judges have competence to adjudicate.

Larceny. The legal name given to the theft of the personal property of another person for stealing.

Legal realist school of jurisprudence. The views of a heterodox group of scholars sharing a cynical attitude toward the law. They are concerned with the actual as opposed to an idealized notion of the operation of law. They apply the social scientific approach to the study of law as defined by such figures as Karl Llewellyn and Jerome Frank.

Legislative courts. Courts established by the legislature. For the U.S. government, legislative courts are not protected by Article III. Cf., **Constitutional Courts**.

Legislative intent. It refers to the motives of legislators when enacting a law. It usually involves a reading and interpreting by a court of the legislative history of a statute.

Legislative veto. A device invented in this century by Congress to gain control over the expansion of executive power. It is part of some legislation that allows the rejection of an administrative or executive action by either the House of Representatives or the Senate, singularly or together, without the consent of the president. This procedure was declared unconstitutional in Immigration and Naturalization Service v. Chadha, 462 U.S. 919 (1983).

Lemon test. The rule, announced in Lemon v. Krutzman, 403 U.S. 602 (1971) to determine whether a government law or action violates the Establishment Clause of the First Amendment, contains three parts: (1) Does the statute possess a secular legislative purpose; (2) Is the principal or primary effect of the statute either to advance or inhibit religion; and (3) Does the statute foster an excessive government entanglement with religion?

Liability. The concept referencing the responsibility for performing a legally enforceable duty or obligation resulting from the commission of a wrongful act.

Libel. The form of defamation that is a written expression of a falsehood about another resulting or tending to result in damage to reputation. The other form of defamation of character is called slander, or spoken defamation. Cf., **slander.**

Liberty of contract. Refers to the viewpoint that persons should be able to enter into contractual agreements with others without government inference. In the later part of the nineteenth and early part of the twentieth centuries, advocates of Laissez-Faire economics championed the cause of limited government by using the liberty of contract argument to invalidate legislation protecting the rights of labor and other weak groups in the political system.

Line item veto. A practice permitted in some states permitting the state's chief executive to veto various sections of a bill without voiding the entire law. The U.S. Supreme Court in Clinton v. New York, 524 U.S. 417 (1998) declared unconstitutional a congressional law containing this feature.

Literacy test. A past practice employed by many states, particularly in the South, that required as a precondition for voting the passing of a reading and or writing skills test.

Litigant. An active participant in a lawsuit; for example, in *Smith v. Jones* both Smith and Jones are litigants.

Magna Charta. Literally the "great charter," this document represents a series of concessions of King John in 1215 to the barons to respect their rights. It signifies the great principle of constitutionalism that no person, even a king, is above the law.

Malapportionment. Usually refers to the drawing of legislative district lines in a way that violates the constitutional principle of one person one vote. See Reynolds v. Sims, 377 U.S. 533 (1964).

Malpractice. Professional misconduct or the below-standard performance of professional skills. Usually applies to suits against physicians and lawyers.

Mandamus, writ of. A Latin term for we command, it is a court order commanding a public official or government agency to perform a certain act. It may apply to all branches of government.

Manslaughter. The crime of taking the life of another without malice.

Martial law. The displacement of civilian law and government by the military. Rules usually depend solely on the commands of the military ruler in charge and often tend to be arbitrary. Martial law often is imposed in time of war, insurrection, or coup d'état.

Maxim. A certain precept or axiom of law applied to all cases covered by its usage.

Mechanical jurisprudence. The widespread belief, held by many judges but discounted by most political scientists, that judges only discover the law, they do not make it.

Memorandum decision. A court ruling stating only what has been decided and what should be done but without the reasons for the decision.

Mens rea. A Latin term referring to the mind or guilt of the defendant. A chief function of juries in criminal trials is to ascertain the criminal intent *(mens rea)* of defendants.

Ministerial. The execution of orders without making policy choices. It is a situation wherein no exercise of judgment or discretion is required or justified.

Miranda warnings. The rule laid down by the U.S. Supreme Court in Miranda v. Arizona, 384 U.S. 436 (1966) requires that in the absence of clear, intelligent waivers of constitutional rights the police must warn suspects prior to any questioning that they have a right to remain silent, that anything they say can be used against them in courts of law, that they have a right to the presence of an attorney, and that if they cannot afford an attorney one will be appointed for them prior to any questioning if they so desire.

Miscellaneous docket. The listing of *in forma pauperis* cases to be heard by the U.S. Supreme Court.

Misdemeanor. A criminal offense designated by statute to be of a lesser nature than a felony. Penalties are relatively minor.

Moot. A discussion or argument of a hypothetical situation.

Moot question. A term used in a lawsuit when the situation changes so that the relief sought is no longer applicable. For example, if during the course of a lengthy lawsuit for admission to a professional school, the student petitioner in fact graduates from the school then the question of admission becomes moot.

Motion. A request by an attorney to the judge to take some action; for example, dismiss the case.

Natural law. A higher law transcending positive law; it comes from God, nature, the universe, or reason. It lacks the ability to enforce commands.

Natural law school of jurisprudence. A view of legal philosophy that posits the existence of universal principles of justice. It is concerned with what the law ought to be and thus is an ideal perspective for criticizing what the law is. Although ancient in origin, this school is enjoying renewed interest.

Natural rights. By virtue of being human, persons have rights derived from nature and nature's laws that government has no authority to denigrate. These include life, liberty, and property. The U.S. Constitution is said to have a higher law background rooted in the natural law and natural rights.

Necessary and Proper Clause. Contained in the last paragraph of Article I, section 8 of the Constitution, this clause authorizes the passage of laws that may be "necessary and proper" for carrying out enumerated powers. This clause is also called the "elastic clause." It is the constitutional provision used by Chief Justice John Marshall in McCulloch v. Maryland, 17 U.S. (4 Wheat.) 316 (1819) to establish the concept of implied powers.

New Jersey Plan. One of the two prominent plans debated at the Philadelphia Convention of 1787, Congress would remain a single-house institution with each state possessing an equal vote without regard to population. Congress would have lawmaking authority in the fields of taxation and commerce. The plan called for a national Supreme Court appointed by the executive and an executive council. This plan was supported by the smaller states. Cf., **Virginia Plan.**

New judicial federalism. The belief that state supreme courts should take the lead to expand civil rights and liberties in view of the fact that the U.S. Supreme Court has, beginning with the Burger Court (1969–1986), tended to slow the advancement of rights.

Nisi prius. A Latin term meaning if not, unless before. This term is usually employed when referring to a jury trial before a single judge as distinguished from an appellate court.

Nolo contendere. It is Latin, meaning no contest. Without directly admitting guilt, it is a plea in a criminal proceeding in which the defendant does not offer a defense. A sentence is then handed down with the assumption of guilt.

Noninterpretivism. The view of constitutional interpretation that openly acknowledges the imprecise nature of constitutional provisions and maintains that many important constitutional provisions of contemporary interest require that judges give meaning beyond the literal words or specific intentions of the constitutional framers. Cf., **interpretivism.**

Novus homo. A Latin term meaning a new man. It is applied in reference to a person pardoned of a crime.

Obiter dicta. A Latin term referring to that part of the reasoning of a judicial opinion that is not necessary or pertinent to the result reached by the court. It is extra and unnecessary verbiage included for a variety of reasons. It is often simply referred to as *dicta* or *obiter.*

Obscenity. Expressions of a sexual nature that are offensive to a sense of decency in society are not protected by the First Amendment of the Constitution. The now long-standing U.S. Supreme Court rule for ascertaining whether an expression is protected speech is found in Miller v. California, 413 U.S. 15 (1973).

Ordinance. A term usually referring to a local law.

Original jurisdiction. The power of a court to hear certain cases where legal proceedings begin. It is the power of a court to hear a case in the first instance. The U.S. Supreme Court possesses both original and appellate jurisdiction but is basically an appellate court.

Original package rule. The rule that prohibited state taxation of products as part of interstate commerce until the commerce came to rest in a state and the interstate materials were dispatched from its original package.

Overbroad statute. A legislative enactment controlling activities not limited to constitutionally protected subjects or activities. The statute goes beyond that which is necessary to achieve a permissible legislative goal.

Pardon. An act by an executive exempting a person guilty of a crime from punishment under the law.

Parens patriae. The legal doctrine that sanctions government as the general guardian of dependent children and otherwise legally incompetent persons. This concept is the basis for the government's prominent role in the juvenile justice system. The term means, "father of the country."

Per curiam opinion. An opinion by the whole court expressing the views of the justice collectively. Typically, these opinions are unsigned.

Petit jury. A trial jury. Cf., **grand jury.**

Petitioner. The party to a lawsuit who brings the case to a court by way of a petition is called the petitioner; for example, the petition for a writ of certiorari. The party the petition is brought against is called the respondent.

Plain meaning rule. When the language of a statute is clear and may be interpreted in only one way, a court employing this rule considers only the language and not other sources for assigning meaning.

Plain view search. The judicial doctrine that sanctions a warrantless police search and seizure of clearly visible objects and to use such evidence in a criminal proceeding.

Plaintiff. The name given a party to a conflict who brings a lawsuit against another (defendant).

Plea. The first pleading made by a criminal defendant. It is a formal response to a criminal charge; for example, guilty, not guilty, or *nolo contendere.*

Plea bargain. The result of negotiation and compromise between the prosecution and defense by which the prosecution agrees to reduce the charges or counts in return for the defendant's guilty plea. The defendant, in these cases, is said to "cop a plea."

Pleadings. The formal and technical written statements made by the litigants framing the issues brought before a court.

Plenary power. The complete or whole power granted a body, such as the congressional power to regulate interstate commerce.

Police power. The authority of government to make and to enforce laws to provide for the health, safety, and morals of the people. This term is used most often in relation to state power.

Political question doctrine. A principle of judicial self-restraint holding that certain issues are best left to the other coordinate branches of government; such issues are said to be nonjusticiable.

Poll tax. A fee attached to voting and is outlawed in federal elections by the passage of the Twenty-Fourth Amendment in 1964. In 1966, the Supreme Court found the poll tax unconstitutional in state elections as a violation of the Equal Protection Clause of the Fourteenth Amendment.

Pornography. The production of writings, pictures, photographs, films, or other graphic representations that are intended to arouse sexual desire.

Positive law. Man-made laws enacted by a ruler, judge, or a legislature of some kind. Cf., **natural law.**

Precedent. A previously decided judicial opinion that serves as a guide for the decision in a present case. The facts of the past and present cases must be deemed sufficiently similar to serve as a precedent.

Preemption. See **federal preemption doctrine.**

Preferred freedoms doctrine. While certain rights such as economic ones may be important, rights thought essential for democratic procedures in the political system such as speech, press, association, assembly, and other liberties should receive special protection by the judiciary.

Presentment. A device by which a grand jury acting on its own, without the consent or participation of a public prosecutor, formally accuses persons of criminal offenses. It differs from an indictment because the grand jury acts without the prosecutor.

Presentment clause. Article I, section 7, clause 2 of the Constitution provides that bills passed by the House of Representatives and the Senate, shall, before becoming law, be presented to the president for approval.

Prima facie. A Latin term for at first sight, on first view. *Prima facie* evidence is such evidence that, if not later contradicted or in some way explained, is sufficient to sustain one's claim. A *prima facie* case is one that has proceeded to the point where it will support the charge if not later contradicted.

Prior restraint. A limitation or prohibition against expression before actual publication is regarded as an attack on freedom of the press.

Private discrimination. See **state action doctrine.**

Private law. (1) An enacted statute dealing with one person or a group; for example, a law passed to compensate Mr. Smith for damage to his property because of U.S. Army exercises. (2) A generic term referring to the law governing conflicts among private parties; for example, contracts, property, torts, or divorce.

Pro bono. A Latin term meaning for good. In the law, it means performing legal services for free.

Probable cause. The existence of evidence that reasonable persons believe will be found in a particular location that justifies the issues of a search warrant. It may also refer to the right of police officers to conduct warrantless searches, or whether a particular person has committed or is about to commit a criminal offense.

Procedural law. The various and often complex rules governing the conduct of court cases. Cf., **substantive law.**

Prohibition, writ of. An order issued by an appellate court to an inferior court ordering it not to exercise jurisdiction in a specific controversy.

Property. Ownership is divided into two major parts. The first is real property, ownership in land, and the second part is personal property, ownership in movable objects or chattels.

Prurient interest. This term is a major element in obscenity cases that come before the U.S. Supreme Court. It refers to lustful ideas or desires or those images that are by nature lascivious or lewd.

Public law. (1) A statute enacted dealing with the society as a whole; for example, minimum wage laws, energy legislation, and reorganization of governmental agencies. In Congress, such laws are given a number, for example, "Public Law No. 35." (2) A generic term referring to law governing operations of government and the government's relationships with persons; for example, constitutional law, criminal law, administrative law.

Punitive damages. Sometimes called "exemplary damages," they are awarded for malicious or willful harm inflicted by the defendant in a civil case. Money damages awarded by a court over and beyond actual and compensatory damages for the harm suffered are intended to act as a warning and deterrent against future wrongful conduct.

Pure speech. This concept expressed most forcibly by Justice Hugo Black defines speech as limited to written and oral expression, and it entails all speech not just political speech. It is absolutely protected by the First Amendment. Conduct, including for example, picketing, demonstrating, or marching, is more than speech and may be regulated by government.

Quaere. A question or query involving a matter in doubt.

Quid pro quo. A term associated with the law of contracts. It refers to that given in return for something else, something for something. In contract law, it constitutes legal consideration.

Quorum. The number of members in an organization or body required to conduct business. Often a quorum is set at a majority of the entire membership.

Ratio Decidendi. A Latin term for the ground or reason for the decision. It is the very essence or central core of a judicial opinion, the principle of the case. To find the *ratio decidendi* the reader must establish which facts are treated by the judge as material and immaterial and his or her decision based on them.

Rational basis test. Courts use this tool of constitutional interpretation placing the burden of proof on the individual challenging a government deprivation of a nonfundamental right or discrimination of nonsuspect classes of people. The court discerns if the government action is reasonable. The Supreme Court has employed this test in cases involving indigency, age, mental retardation, and certain instances involving alienage, international travel, education, welfare, and housing. This level of analysis is sometimes referred to as, lower tier analysis. Cf., **strict scrutiny, intermediate scrutiny.**

Real property. Ownership of land and the immovable objects placed upon it.

Recess appointment. The constitutional provision of Article II, section 2, clause 3 that provides the president shall have the authority to fill all vacancies that may occur during the recess of the Senate. The presidential commission ends at the end of the Senate's next session.

Recusation. Because of possible prejudice, a judge is disqualified from hearing a case. Recusal may be requested through motion of litigants or it may be voluntary.

Remedy. The legal means through a court order to enforce a right or to redress or compensate for harm.

Res judicata. A Latin term meaning a thing decided. It is a fundamental principle in civil proceedings that once a conflict has been decided by the court the decision is conclusive and the parties may not bring the same case before the court again.

Res nova. A Latin term for a new thing or matter, it refers to a new legal question that has not been decided before.

Reserved powers of the states. The Tenth Amendment of the U.S. Constitution provides that those powers not granted to the central government remain vested in the states and to the people. Consequently, if the central government enacts a law that may not be fairly traced to an enumerated or implied power, then that law is an invasion of the reserved powers of the states.

Respondent. The word standing for the party to a lawsuit against whom a petition is brought and who answers in various legal causes of action.

Restitution. The act of restoring or making good on something, for example, to return or pay for a stolen item.

Restrictive covenant. It is a contractual agreement among real property owners that prohibits the rent or sale of their property to certain classes of people. In Shelley v. Kraemer, 334 U.S. 1 (1948), the U.S. Supreme Court held that the Equal Protection Clause of the Fourteenth Amendment inhibits the judicial enforcement by state courts of such covenants based on race or color.

Reversal. The action of an appellate court when it concludes that the court below should have decided the dispute for the other side.

Right. The legal ability to perform or refrain from the performance of actions or the ability to control objects in one's possession. It also entails the ability to control the actions of others. In a legal sense, a right is enforceable as law as distinguished from a moral right.

Ripeness. A judicial doctrine that indicates a case is ready for final adjudication only after all preliminary actions or motions have been exhausted. It is one of several devices the U.S. Supreme Court uses to exercise self-restraint.

Rule of four. To grant the petition for a writ of certiorari, four justices must vote to do so.

Scienter. A situation where a person acts with prior knowledge that the act performed was wrong.

Scintilla. The word means a particle, the least bit. It usually refers to the least particle of evidence in a case.

Sedition. The criminal act of inciting civil insurrection or attempting to overthrow the government by force or violence.

Selective incorporation. The judicial doctrine ultimately adopted by the U.S. Supreme Court that was employed to determine which rights found in the Bill of Rights are applicable to the states by way of the Due Process Clause of the Fourteenth Amendment.

Self-executing. A term referring to legislative enactments, judicial decisions, agreements, or documents requiring no further official action to be implemented.

Self-incrimination. Refers to instances when persons admit to facts that may serve to convict them of crimes. The Fifth Amendment prohibits compulsory self-crimination and is applicable to both the national government and to the states through the Due Process Clause of the Fourteenth Amendment.

Separate but equal rule. A now defunct judicial doctrine interpreting the Equal Protection Clause of the Fourteenth Amendment that permitted racial segregation as long as the public facilities were separate but equal. See Plessy v. Ferguson, 163 U.S. 537 (1896).

Separation of powers. A constitutional concept designed to avoid tyranny by a single institution of government; the idea that all branches of the government (legislative, executive, and judicial) are separate and co-equal institutions.

Sequester. To isolate. For example, when during a trial the jury is kept from having contacts with the outside world.

Seriatim. A Latin word meaning individually, one by one, in order, point by point. It is the practice of each judge writing and recording his or her own views of a case. *Seriatim* opinion writing is in contrast to a collective opinion of the court representing the views of the majority, minority, or the whole court. Before the accession of John Marshall to the U.S. Supreme Court, the *seriatim* practice was employed generally.

Severability doctrine. When evaluating statutes to determine whether any or all of the parts of each can survive constitutional scrutiny, courts endeavor to invalidate only those sections that fail the constitutional test. Those sections of a statute that do not withstand the test are cut away from the statute so that the remainder of the statute may remain operable law.

Shield law. This is legislation that protects certain individuals from their obligation to give testimony in a case. Media shield laws that relieve news reporters from revealing in court confidential news sources are one instance of such laws.

Show cause order. A command to a person to appear in court to explain why the court should not take a proposed course of action against him or her or accept a point of law made before it.

Slander. The oral expression of a falsehood about another resulting or tending to result in damage to reputation. It is one form of defamation of character, the other is libel. Cf., **libel.**

Social Darwinism. The view that the biological laws of the survival of the fittest should be applied to the social world of human beings. The "liberty of contract" jurisprudence of the turn of the twentieth century reflected the view that government intervention in the economy interferes with the natural processes of selection and competition thereby deterring progress in society.

Sociological jurisprudence. A school of jurisprudence that attempts to make the study of law a social science by substituting social psychological conceptions for legal notions such as the origins of law and the impact of law on human society. It is also prescriptive. Roscoe Pound is generally viewed as the intellectual father of this school.

Sole organ theory. The view expressed by Justice George Sutherland in his majority opinion in United States v. Curtiss-Wright Export Corp., 299 U.S. 304 (1936). He argued that the president of the United States is the plenary and exclusive authority in the field of international affairs.

Sovereign immunity. The common law principle that the sovereign (crown) could not be sued without its permission. The Eleventh Amendment has been interpreted to protect state governments from suits that are authorized by federal legislation. See, for example, Alden v. Maine, 527 U.S. 709 (1999).

Special master in equity. A person appointed by a court in its equity jurisdiction. Such persons have the responsibility to discern the facts in a case and to report its findings and recommendations to the court.

Speech and Debate Clause. Article I, section 6 of the Constitution makes the conduct of members of Congress, when in the course of their official duties, immune from civil or criminal liability.

Standing to sue. Sometimes referred to simply as standing, it is the necessity of a plaintiff to demonstrate that he or she has a personal and vital interest in the outcome of the legal case or controversy brought before the court.

Stare decisis. Latin for the decision to stand, abide by, or adhere to decided cases. A deeply rooted common law tradition that once a court has determined a legal principle for a given set of facts, all future cases with similar facts should be decided in the same way.

State action doctrine. The requirement that those complaining against discriminatory conduct must show that it is the result of state government action or in some way is sanctioned by state government and is not simply the result of the conduct of private parties.

States' Rights. The view that emphasizes the sovereign powers of the states in relation to the national government. Strictly speaking, those powers not granted to the central government are reserved to the states and to the people through the Tenth Amendment of the Constitution. States' Rights advocates tend to view the relationship between the state and national governments as antagonistic.

Statute of limitations. A legislative enactment prescribing a limited time period within which a lawsuit may be commenced for given conduct.

Statute. A law enacted by a legislative body.

Stay of execution. A legal order halting the carrying out of a judgment.

Stewardship theory. An approach to presidential power best enunciated by Theodore Roosevelt. He argued that unless specifically prohibited by the Constitution or laws of the United States, the president may exercise any and all powers he thinks are in the public interest. President William Howard Taft took the opposite view.

Stop and frisk rule. As an exception to the warrant requirement of the Fourth Amendment, police officers may stop and search a person if they reasonably suspect such a person is engaged in criminal conduct. This rule was laid down in Terry v. Ohio, 392 U.S. 1 (1968).

Stream of commerce. The constitutional doctrine enunciated by Chief Justice Taft in Stafford v. Wallace, 258 U.S. 495 (1922). It states that federal authority over goods that have temporarily come to rest within a state remain part of interstate commerce as long as it is part of a movement across state lines.

Strict construction. A literal or absolutist interpretation of constitutional provisions. Today, the word interpretivism is used instead of this term to mean essentially the same thing, although it is only one form of interpretivism. See **interpretivism.**

Strict scrutiny test. This approach to constitutional interpretation is applicable when government uses a suspect class such as race or certain aspects of alienage to classify persons or when it is alleged that government abridges a fundamental right. When either condition is present, the government has the burden to demonstrate a compelling interest or a clear and present danger. The legislation or otherwise official action must be tailored narrowly to advance the legitimate government interest so that it does not unduly burden the exercise of constitutional rights. This level of analysis is sometimes referred to as upper tier analysis. Cf., **intermediate scrutiny, rational basis test.**

Sua sponte. A Latin term meaning of one's own will. When appellate courts raise and resolve legal issues not argued by the parties they are said to be acting, *sua sponte.*

Subpoena duces tecum. An order directed toward a person by a court or other duly authorized body to appear before it with certain papers, documents, or other things.

Subpoena. An order by a court or other duly authorized body to appear and testify before it.

Substantial evidence rule. A standard of proof commonly used by judges when reviewing decisions of administrative agencies. It is evidence that a reasonable mind may accept as adequate to support a conclusion of fact.

Substantive due process. The judicial doctrine requiring that the content of legislation must be fair and reasonable. It is a widely discredited practice of courts to look at the basis of legislation to determine whether it comports with principles of fairness or nature. Jurists using this conception of due process are said to substitute their judgments of good public policy for those of legislators.

Substantive law. The basic law governing relationships; for example, criminal law, constitutional law, property law, family law, torts. Substantive law is contrasted to procedural law; for example, the law of evidence. Cf., **procedural law.**

Suffrage. Refers to the right to vote.

Summary proceeding. Any judicial business conducted before a court, which is disposed of in a quick and simplified manner, sometimes without a jury or indictment. In the case of the U.S. Supreme Court, it entails a judgment without the benefit of hearing oral arguments.

Supremacy Clause. Article VI, section 2 of the Constitution has been interpreted by the U.S. Supreme Court to mean that the Constitution and the laws and the treaties of the United States are supreme over state action to the contrary. Thus, for example, when there is a conflict between a state law and a U.S. law the U.S. law trumps the state law. See McCulloch v. Maryland, 17 U.S. (4 Wheat.) 316 (1819).

Suspect class. A concept in constitutional law referring to government classifications that reflect prejudice against discrete and insular minorities, such as racial groups. When a suspect class is identified, the Supreme Court has ruled that the constitutional standard used to adjudicate claims is the strict scrutiny test.

Symbolic speech. The communication of ideas or beliefs without the use of words. Wearing armbands and displaying flags are examples of symbolic speech protected by the First Amendment.

Takings Clause. As part of the Fifth Amendment to the U.S. Constitution, this clause forbids government from confiscating private property without just compensation. The clause applies to the state governments through the Due Process Clause of the Fourteenth Amendment.

Test case. A lawsuit brought to clarify, overturn, or establish a legal principle. Usually sponsored by an interest group, but nevertheless there must be a *bona fide* litigant.

Time, place, and manner regulations. The courts have held that while expression is protected by the First Amendment, the government may impose reasonable regulations as to when, where, and how speech takes place. For example, a university may validly prohibit the use of loud speakers near and around classrooms and instead provide a "free forum" area of public debate and discussion where regular classroom activities will not be disturbed.

Total incorporation. Refers to the view that the Due Process Clause of the Fourteenth Amendment is shorthand for the Bill of Rights. The entire Bill of Rights applies to the states. This view was favored by Mr. Justice Hugo Black.

Total incorporation plus. Refers to the view that the Due Process Clause of the Fourteenth Amendment not only is shorthand for the Bill of Rights but also affords constitutional protection for unnamed rights that may be fairly inferred from that document. This view was expressed by Justices Frank Murphy and Wiley Rutledge in their dissenting opinion in Adamson v. California, 332 U.S. 46 (1947).

Transcript of record. A printed copy (sometimes typed) of the proceedings of a court case. The transcript is used by an appellate court in reviewing the proceedings of the court below.

Treaty. A formal agreement between or among sovereign states, creating rights and obligations under international law. In the United States all treaties must be ratified by a two-thirds vote of the Senate.

Trial de novo. See **De novo**.

Ultra vires. A Latin term meaning outside or beyond authority or power. It indicates an action taken outside the legal authority of the person or body performing it.

Use immunity. A legislative investigation tool designed to gain information from persons who might otherwise incriminate themselves. In exchange for immunity against prosecution, it forbids prosecutors from using information gained in this way.

Vagueness doctrine. A criminal statute that does not give fair notice about what activity is proscribed and consequently fails to inform the population and interpreting authorities about what conduct is criminal.

Venue. The location within a jurisdiction where a legal dispute is tried by a court.

Verdict. Refers to a jury declaration of its judgment in a civil or criminal trial.

Virginia Plan. One of the two prominent plans debated at the 1787 Philadelphia Convention to revise the Articles of Confederation, this plan favored by the larger states would have granted greater authority to the central government with a provision permitting the central government to veto state statutes that might be deemed inconsistent with the laws of the entire nation. The plan called for a bicameral legislature with one house chosen by the voters in each state and the upper house members chosen by the lower house. The national executive and judiciary would be chosen by the legislature. Cf., **New Jersey Plan.**

Voir dire examination. The examination by legal counsel and the judge of potential jury members as to their competency to serve. *Voir dire* is French for "speaking the truth."

Waiver. The relinquishing or giving up of a legally enforceable right, privilege, or benefit voluntarily, with full knowledge; for example, when criminal defendants give up their right to remain silent by taking the witness stand on their own behalf.

War Powers Resolution. A 1973 enactment during the Vietnam War requiring the president to consult with Congress before the introduction of armed forces into hostilities, and it set time limits on the use of combat forces abroad.

Warrant. A legal instrument issued by a judicial magistrate to arrest someone or to search premises.

Writ of certiorari. See **certiorari, writ of.**

Writ of Error. See **error, writ of.**

Writ of mandamus. See **mandamus, writ of.**

Writ of prohibition. See **prohibition, writ of.**

Writ. An order in the form of a letter from a court commanding that something be done.

BIBLIOGRAPHY

The Judicial System

Abraham, Henry J. *The Judicial Process: An Introductory Analysis of the Courts of the United States, England, and France.* 7th ed. New York: Oxford University Press, 1998.

Abramson, Jeffrey. *We, The Jury: The Jury System and the Ideal of Democracy.* Cambridge: Harvard University Press, 2000.

Agresto, John. *The Supreme Court and Constitutional Democracy.* Ithaca, NY: Cornell University, 1986.

Antieau, Chester J. *Adjudicating Constitutional Issues.* Dobbs Ferry, NY: Oceana, 1985.

Ball, Howard. *Courts and Politics: The Federal Judicial System.* 2d ed. Englewood Cliffs, NJ: Prentice-Hall, 1987.

Banks, Christopher P., and John C. Green, eds. *Superintending Democracy: The Courts and the Political Process.* Akron, OH: University of Akron Press, 2001.

Barnum, David G. *The Supreme Court & American Democracy.* New York: St. Martin's Press, 1993.

Bartee, Alice F. *Cases Lost, Causes Won: The Supreme Court and the Judicial Process.* New York: St. Martin's Press, 1984.

Baum, Lawrence. *The Puzzle of Judicial Behavior.* Ann Arbor: University of Michigan Press, 1997.

———. *The Supreme Court.* 7th ed. Washington, DC: Congressional Quarterly, 2000.

Berger, Raoul. *Government by Judiciary: The Transformation of the Fourteenth Amendment.* Cambridge: Harvard University Press, 1977.

Best, Bradley. *Law Clerks, Support Personnel, and the Decline of Consensual Norms on The United States Supreme Court, 1935–1995.* New York: LFB Scholarly Publishing, 2002.

Biskupic, Joan, and Elder Witt. *Guide to the U.S. Supreme Court.* 3d ed. Washington, DC: Congressional Quarterly, 1997.

Brenner, Saul, and Harold J. Spaeth. *Stare Decisis: The Alteration of Precedent on the Supreme Court.* New York: Cambridge University Press, 1995.

Cannon, Mark, and David O'Brien, eds. *Views from the Bench: The Judiciary and Constitutional Politics.* Chatham, NJ: Chatham House, 1985.

Canon, Bradley C., and Charles A. Johnson. *Judicial Policies: Implementation & Impact.* 2d ed. Washington, DC: Congressional Quarterly, 1998.

Carp, Robert A., and C. Y. Rowland. *Policymaking and Politics in the Federal District Courts.* Knoxville: University of Tennessee Press, 1983.

Carp, Robert A., and Ronald Stidham. *The Federal Courts.* 4th ed. Washington, DC: Congressional Quarterly, 2001.

———. *Judicial Process in America.* 5th ed. Washington, DC: Congressional Quarterly, 2001.

Carter, Lief H. *Contemporary Constitutional Lawmaking: The Supreme Court and the Art of Politics.* Elmsford, NY: Pergamon Press, 1985.

Chinn, Nancy, and Larry Berkson. *Literature on Judicial Selection.* Chicago: American Judicature Society, 1980.

Choper, Jesse H. *Judicial Review and the National Political Process: A Functional Reconsideration of the Role of the Supreme Court.* Chicago: University of Chicago Press, 1983.

Coffin, Frank M. *On Appeal: Courts, Lawyering, and Judging.* New York: W. W. Norton, 1994.

Cohen, Jonathan Matthew. *Inside Appellate Courts: The Impact of Court Organization on Judicial Decision Making in the United States Courts of Appeals.* Ann Arbor: University of Michigan Press, 2002.

Congressional Quarterly. *Guide to the U.S. Supreme Court.* 3d ed. Washington, DC: Congressional Quarterly, 1997.

———. *The Supreme Court.* 7th ed. Washington, DC: Congressional Quarterly, 2000.

DuBois, Philip, ed. *An Analysis of Judicial Reform.* Lexington, MA: Lexington Books, 1982.

Ducat, Craig R. *Modes of Constitutional Interpretation.* St. Paul, MN: West, 1978.

Ely, John Hart. *Democracy and Distrust: A Theory of Judicial Review.* Cambridge: Harvard University Press, 1980.

Epstein, Lee. *Contemplating Courts.* Washington, DC: Congressional Quarterly, 1995.

———, and Jack Knight. *The Choices Justices Make.* Washington, DC: Congressional Quarterly, 1998.

———, Jeffery A. Segal, Harold J. Spaeth, and Thomas G. Walker. *The Supreme Court Compendium: Data, Decisions & Development.* 3d ed. Washington, DC: Congressional Quarterly, 2002.

Fish, Peter. *The Office of Chief Justice.* Charlottesville: University of Virginia Press, 1984.

Frank, Jerome. *Courts on Trial.* Princeton, NJ: Princeton University Press, 1949.

Friedrichs, David O. *Law in Our Lives.* Los Angeles: Roxbury, 2001.

Gabin, Sanford Byron. *Judicial Review and the Reasonable Doubt Test.* Port Washington, NY: Kennikat Press, 1980.

Glick, Henry Robert. *Courts, Politics, and Justice.* 3d ed. New York: McGraw-Hill, 1993.

Goldman, Sheldon. *Picking Federal Judges: Lower Court Selection from Roosevelt Through Reagan.* New Haven, CT: Yale University Press, 1997.

———, and Thomas P. Jahnige. *The Federal Courts as a Political System.* 3d ed. New York: Harper & Row, 1985.

———, and Charles M. Lamb, eds. *Judicial Conflict and Consensus: Behavioral Studies of American Appellate Courts.* Lexington: University Press of Kentucky, 1986.

———, and Austin Sarat. *American Court Systems: Readings in Judicial Process and Behavior.* 2d ed. New York: Longman, 1989.

Goulden, Joseph C. *The Benchwarmers: The Private World of the Powerful Federal Judges.* New York: Weybright and Talley, 1976.

Hall, Kermit L., ed. *The Judiciary in American Life.* New York: Garland, 1987.

———, ed. *The Oxford Companion to the Supreme Court of the United States.* New York: Oxford University Press, 1992.

Halpern, Stephen C., and Charles M. Lamb. *Supreme Court Activism and Restraint.* Lexington, MA: Lexington Books, 1983.

Harrington, Christine. *Shadow Justice: The Ideology and Institutionalization of Alternatives to Court.* Westport, CT: Greenwood Press, 1985.

Higgins, Thomas J. *Judicial Review Unmasked.* Norwell, MA: Christopher Publications House, 1981.

Horowitz, Donald L. *The Courts and Social Policy.* Washington, DC: Brookings Institution, 1977.

Howard, Woodford. *Courts of Appeal in the Federal Judicial System: A Study of the Second, Fifth, and District of Columbia Circuits.* Princeton, NJ: Princeton University Press, 1982.

Jackson, Robert H. *The Supreme Court in the American System of Government.* Cambridge: Harvard University Press, 1955.

Jacobsohn, Gary J. *The Supreme Court and the Decline of Constitutional Aspiration.* Totowa, NJ: Rowman & Littlefield, 1986.

Jost, Kenneth. *The Supreme Court A to Z.* Washington, DC: Congressional Quarterly, 2003.

Klein, David E. *Making Law in the United States Courts of Appeals.* New York: Cambridge University Press, 2002.

Lazarus, Edward. *Closed Chambers: The First Eyewitness Account of the Epic Struggles Inside the Supreme Court.* New York: Times Books, 1998.

Levin, A. Leo, and Russell R. Wheller. *The American Judiciary.* San Mateo, CA: Sage, 1982.

Mays, Larry G., and Peter R. Gregware, *Courts & Justice: A Reader.* 2d ed. Prospect Heights, IL: Waveland Press, 2000.

McCann, Michael W., and Gerald L. Houseman, eds. *Judging the Constitution: Critical Essays on Judicial Lawmaking.* Glenview, IL: Scott Foresman, 1989.

McDowell, Gary L. *Taking the Constitution Seriously: Essays on the Constitution and the Constitutional Law.* Dubuque, IA: Kendall/Hunt, 1981.

———. *Equity and the Constitution: The Supreme Court, Equitable Relief and Public Policy.* Chicago: University of Chicago Press, 1982.

McGuire, Kevin T. *Understanding the U.S. Supreme Court: Cases and Controversies.* New York: McGraw-Hill, 2002.

Melone, Albert P., and George Mace. *Judicial Review and American Democracy.* Ames: Iowa State University Press, 1988.

———, and Allan Karnes. *The American Legal System: Foundations, Processes, and Norms.* Los Angeles: Roxbury, 2003.

Mendelson, Wallace. *Supreme Court Statecraft: The Rule of Law and Men.* Ames: Iowa State University Press, 1985.

Miller, Arthur Selwyn. *Toward Judicial Activism: The Political Role of the Supreme Court.* Westport, CT: Greenwood Press, 1982.

———. *Politics, Democracy and the Supreme Court: Essays on the Frontier of Constitutional Theory.* Westport, CT: Greenwood Press, 1985.

Murphy, Walter F., C. Herman Pritchett, and Lee Epstein. *Courts, Judges, and Politics: An Introduction to the Judicial Process.* 5th ed. Boston: McGraw-Hill Higher Education, 2001.

Neely, Richard. *How Courts Govern America*. New Haven, CT: Yale University, 1981.
———. *Judicial Jeopardy: When Business Collides with the Courts*. New York: Addison-Wesley, 1986.
Neubauer, David W. *America's Courts and the Criminal Justice System*. 7th ed. Belmont, CA: Wadsworth, 2001.
Oakley, John Bilyeu, and Robert S. Thompson. *Law Clerks and the Judicial Process: Perceptions of the Qualities and Functions of Law Clerks in American Courts*. Berkeley: University of California Press, 1980.
O'Brien, David M. *Storm Center: The Supreme Court in American Politics*. 6th ed. New York: W. W. Norton, 2003.
Pacelle, Richard L., Jr. *The Role of the Supreme Court in American Politics: The Least Dangerous Branch?* Boulder, CO: Westview Press, 2002.
Porto, Brian L. *May it Please the Court: Judicial Processes and Politics in America*. New York: Longman, 2001.
Powers, Stephen P., and Stanley Rothman. *The Least Dangerous Branch? Consequences of Judicial Activism*. Westport, CT: Praeger, 2002.
Peltason, Jack W. *Federal Courts in the Political Process*. New York: Random House, 1965.
Perry, H. W. *Deciding to Decide: Agenda Setting in the United States Supreme Court*. Cambridge: Harvard University Press, 1991.
Perry, Michael J. *The Constitution, the Court, and Human Right: An Inquiry into the Legitimacy of Constitutional Policy-Making by the Judiciary*. New Haven, CT: Yale University Press, 1984.
Pinkele, Carl, and William Louthan, eds. *Discretion, Justice, and Democracy: A Public Policy Perspective*. Ames: Iowa State University Press, 1985.
Posner, Richard A. *The Federal Courts: Crisis and Reform*. Cambridge: Harvard University Press, 1985, 1996.
Provine, Doris Marie. *Case Selection in the United States Supreme Court*. Chicago: University of Chicago Press, 1980.
———. *Judging Credentials: Nonlawyer Judges and the Politics of Professionalism*. Chicago: University of Chicago Press, 1986.
Pugh, J. Donna, et al. *Judicial Rulemaking: A Compendium*. Lanham, MD: University Publications of America, 1985.
Radcliffe, James E. *The Case or Controversy Provision*. University Park: Pennsylvania State University Press, 1978.
Rehnquist, William. *The Supreme Court: How It Was, How It Is*. Spec. ed. New York: William Morrow, 1992.
Rohde, David W., and Harold J. Spaeth. *Supreme Court Decision Making*. San Francisco: Freeman, 1976.
Scheb, John M., and John M. Scheb II. *An Introduction to the American Legal System*. Albany, NY: Delmar, 2002.
Schmidhauser, John R. *Judges and Justices: The Federal Appellate Judiciary*. Boston: Little, Brown, 1979.
Segal, Jeffrey, and Harold J. Spaeth. *The Supreme Court and the Attitudinal Model*. New York: Cambridge University Press, 1993.
———. *The Supreme Court and the Attitudinal Model Revisited*. New York: Cambridge University Press, 2002.
Shetreet, Shimon, and Jules Deschenes. *Judicial Independence: The Contemporary Debate*. Norwell, MA: Kluwer, 1985.
Slotnick, Elliot E. *Judicial Politics: Readings from Judicature*. 2d ed. Chicago: American Judicature Society, 1999.

Smith, Christopher. *Courts, Politics, and the Judicial Process.* Chicago: Nelson-Hall, 1993.

Spaeth, Harold J. *Supreme Court Policy Making: Explanation and Prediction.* San Francisco: W. H. Freeman, 1979.

Spaeth, Harold J., and Jeffrey A. Segal. *Majority Rule or Minority Will: Adherence to Precedent on the U.S. Supreme Court.* New York: Cambridge University Press, 1999.

Stern, Robert L., and Dale T. Irvin. *Supreme Court Practice: For Practice in the Supreme Court of the United States.* 8th ed. Washington, DC: The Bureau of National Affairs, 2002.

Storme, M. *Effectiveness of Judicial Protection and the Constitutional Order.* Norwell, MA: Kluwer, 1983.

Stumpf, Harry P. *American Judicial Politics.* 2d ed. New York: Prentice-Hall, 1997.

Tribe, Laurence. *God Save This Honorable Court.* New York: Random House, 1986.

———. *Constitutional Choices.* Cambridge: Harvard University Press, 1985.

Ulmer, S. Sidney, ed. *Courts, Law, and Judicial Processes.* New York: The Free Press, 1981.

Wasby, Stephen L. *The Supreme Court in the Federal Judicial System.* 4th ed. Chicago: Nelson-Hall, 1993.

Wolfe, Christopher. *The Rise of Modern Judicial Review: From Constitutional Interpretation to Judge-Made Law.* Rev. ed. New York: Basic Books, 1994.

Woodward, Bob, and Scott Armstrong. *The Brethren: Inside the Supreme Court.* New York: Simon & Schuster, 1981.

Jurisprudence

Ackerman, Bruce A. *Social Justice in the Liberal State.* New Haven, CT: Yale University Press, 1980.

Altman, Andrew. *Critical Legal Studies: A Liberal Critique.* Princeton, NJ: Princeton University Press, 1990.

Austin, John. *Lectures on Jurisprudence.* 2 vols. New York: James Crockcraft, 1875.

———. *The Province of Jurisprudence Determined.* H. L. A. Hart, ed. London: Weidenfeld & Nicolson, 1954.

Baer, Judith A. *Our Lives before the Law: Constructing a Feminist Jurisprudence.* Princeton, NJ: Princeton University Press, 1999.

Bartlett, K., and R. Kennedy. *Feminist Legal Theory.* Boulder, CO: Westview, 1991.

Bartlett, Katharine T. *Gender and Law: Theory, Doctrine, Commentary.* New York: New York University Press, 1991.

Beirne, Piers, and Richard Quinney, eds. *Marxism and Law.* New York: John Wiley & Sons, 1982.

Beirne, Piers, and Robert Sharlet. *Pashukanis: Selected Writings on Marxism and Law.* London: Academic Press, 1980.

Bentham, Jeremy. [1776]. *A Fragment on Government.* W. Harrison, ed. Oxford: Basil Blackwell, 1960.

———. [1789]. *An Introduction to the Principles of Morals and Legislation.* J. H. Burns and H. L. A. Hart, eds. London: Athlone Press, 1970.

Bishin, William R., and Christopher D. Stone. *Law, Language, Ethics: An Introduction to Law and Legal Method.* Mineola, NY: The Foundation Press, 1972.

Bodenheimer, Edgar. *Jurisprudence: The Philosophy and Method of the Law.* Rev. ed. Cambridge: Harvard University Press, 1974.

Brkić, Jovan. *Norm and Order: An Investigation into Logic, Semantics, and the Theory of Law and Morals.* New York: Humanities Press, 1970.

————. *Legal Reasoning: Semantic and Logical Analysis.* New York: Peter Lang, 1985.

Bronaugh, Richard. *Readings in the Philosophy of Constitutional Law.* 4th ed. Dubuque, IA: Kendall/Hunt, 1992.

Cain, Maureen, and Alan Hunt. *Marx and Engels on Law.* New York: Academic Press, 1979.

Campbell, Tom, and Jeffrey Goldsworthy, eds. *Judicial Power, Democracy and Legal Positivism.* Brookfield, VT: Ashgate, 2000.

Campos, Paul F. *Jurismania: The Madness of American Law.* New York: Oxford University Press, 1998.

Cardozo, Benjamin. *The Nature of the Judicial Process.* New Haven, CT: Yale University Press, 1945.

Carter, Lief H., and Thomas F. Burke. *Reason in Law.* 6th ed. Upper Saddle River, NJ: Pearson Longman, 2002.

Carty, Anthony, ed. *Post-modern Law.* Edinburgh, UK: Edinburgh University Press, 1990.

Clinton, Robert. *God, Man and the Law.* Lawrence: University Press of Kansas, 1997.

Cohen, Marshall, ed. *Ronald Dworkin and Contemporary Jurisprudence.* Totowa, NJ: Rowman & Littlefield, 1984.

Cohen, Morris. *Reason and Law.* New York: The Free Press, 1950.

Cohen, Ronald L. *Justice: Views from the Social Sciences.* New York: Plenum, 1986.

Cotterrell, Roger. *The Politics of Jurisprudence: A Critical Introduction to Legal Philosophy.* Philadelphia: University of Pennsylvania Press, 1989.

Crotty, Kevin M. *Law's Interior: Legal and Literary Constructions of the Self.* Ithaca, NY: Cornell University Press, 2001.

D'Amato, Anthony. *Jurisprudence: A Descriptive and Normative Analysis of Law.* Boston: Martinus Nijhoff, 1984.

Delgado, Richard, ed. *Critical Race Theory: The Cutting Edge.* Philadelphia: Temple University Press, 1995.

d'Entreves, A. P. *Natural Law: An Introduction to Legal Philosophy.* 2d ed. London: Hutchinson, 1970, 1977.

Dickson, Julie. *Evaluation and Legal Theory.* Oxford: Hart, 2001.

Dorsen, Norman, and Prosser Gifford, eds. *Democracy and the Rule of Law.* Washington, DC: Congressional Quarterly, 2001.

Duxbury, Neil. *Patterns of American Jurisprudence.* Oxford: Oxford University Press, 1995.

Dworkin, Ronald. *Taking Rights Seriously.* Cambridge: Harvard University Press, 1977.

————. *A Matter of Principle.* Cambridge: Harvard University Press, 1985.

————. *Law's Empire.* Cambridge: Harvard University Press, 1986.

————. *Life's Dominion.* New York: Alfred A. Knopf, 1993.

————. *Freedom's Law.* Cambridge: Harvard University Press, 1996.

————. *Sovereign Virtue: The Theory and Practice of Equality.* Cambridge: Harvard University Press, 2000.

Edelman, Martin. *Democratic Theories and the Constitution.* Albany: State University of New York Press, 1984.

Farber, Daniel A., and Philip P. Frickey. *Law and Public Choice: A Critical Introduction.* Chicago: University of Chicago Press, 1991.

Feldman, Stephen M. *American Legal Thought from Premodernism to Postmodernism: An Intellectual Voyage.* New York: Oxford University Press, 2000.

Fine, Bob. *Democracy and the Rule of Law: Liberal Ideals and Marxist Critiques.* Wolfeboro, NH: Longwood, 1984.

Finnis, John. *Natural Law and Natural Rights.* Oxford: Clarendon Press, 1980

Firth, Brian W. *The Constitution of Consensus: Democracy as an Ethical Imperative.* New York: Peter Lang, 1987.

Fletcher, George P. *Basic Concepts of Legal Thoughts.* New York: Oxford University Press, 1996.

Frank, Jerome. *Law and the Modern Mind.* Garden City, NY: Anchor, 1930.

———. *Courts on Trial: Myth and Reality in American Justice.* Princeton, NJ: Princeton University Press, 1973.

Friedrich, Carl J. *The Philosophy of Law in Historical Perspective.* 2d ed. Chicago: University of Chicago Press, 1963.

Fuller, Lon L. *The Law in Quest of Itself.* Boston: Beacon Press, 1940.

———. *Legal Fictions.* Stanford, CA: Stanford University Press, 1967.

———. *Anatomy of the Law.* New York: New American Library, 1968.

———. *The Morality of Law.* Rev. ed. New Haven, CT: Yale University Press, 1973, 1977.

———. *The Principles of Social Order.* Durham, NC: Duke University Press, 1981.

Garth, Bryant, and Austin Sarat, eds. *Justice and Power in Sociolegal Studies.* Evanston, IL: Northwestern University Press, 1998.

George, Robert P. *The Autonomy of Law: Essays on Legal Positivism.* Oxford: Clarendon Press, 1996.

———. *In Defense of Natural Law.* New York: Oxford University Press, 1999.

Glennon, Robert J. *The Iconoclast as Reformer: Jerome Frank's Impact on American Law.* Ithaca, NY: Cornell University, 1985.

Golding, Martin P., ed. *The Nature of Law: Readings in Legal Philosophy.* New York: Random House, 1966.

———. *Philosophy of Law.* Englewood Cliffs, NJ: Prentice-Hall, 1975.

Goldstein, L. *Feminist Jurisprudence: The Difference Debate.* Lanham, MD: Rowman & Littlefield, 1992.

Grossman, George S., ed. *The Spirit of American Law.* Boulder, CO: Westview Press, 2000.

Habermas, Jürgen. *Between Facts and Norms: Contributions to a Discourse Theory of Law and Democracy.* Cambridge: The MIT Press, 1970.

Hall, Jerome. *Foundations of Jurisprudence.* Indianapolis: Bobbs-Merrill, 1973.

———. *Readings in Jurisprudence.* Indianapolis: Bobbs-Merrill, 1973.

Halpin, Andrew. *Reasoning with Law.* Oxford: Hart, 2001.

Hart, H. L. A. *The Concept of Law.* Oxford: Clarendon Press, 1961.

———. *Law, Liberty and Morality.* New York: Vintage, 1963.

Hernandez-Truyol, Berta Esperanza, ed. *Moral Imperialism: A Critical Anthology.* New York: New York University Press, 2002.

Hirst, Paul Q. *Law, Socialism and Democracy.* London: Allen & Unwin, 1986.

Holmes, Oliver Wendell, Jr. *The Common Law.* Boston: Little, Brown, 1881.

Honeyball, Simon, and James Walter. *Integrity, Community and Interpretation: A Critical Analysis of Ronald Dworkin's Theory of Law.* Brookfield, VT: Ashgate, 1998.

Hutchinson, Allan C., ed. *Critical Legal Studies.* Totowa, NJ: Rowman & Littlefield, 1989.

James, Susan, and Stephanie Palmer, eds. *Visible Women: Essays on Feminist Legal Theory.* Oxford, UK and Portland, OR: Hart, 2002.

Jowell, Jeffrey, and Jonathan Cooper, eds. *Understanding Human Rights Principles.* Oxford: Hart, 2000.

Kairys, David. *The Politics of Law: A Progressive Critique.* New York: Basic Books, 1998.

Kelly, J. M. *A Short History of Western Legal Theory.* Oxford: Clarendon Press, 1992.

Kelman, Mark. *A Guide to Critical Legal Studies.* Cambridge: Harvard University Press, 1987.

Kelsen, Hans. [1934]. *Pure Theory of Law.* Berkeley: University of California Press, 1967.

———. *The Communist Theory of Law.* London: Stevens & Sons, 1955.

Kerruish, Valerie. *Jurisprudence as Ideology.* London: Routledge, 1991.

Klafter, Craig Evan. *Reason over Precedents: Origins of American Legal Thought.* Westport, CT: Greenwood Press, 1993.

Levi, Edward. *An Introduction to Legal Reasoning.* Chicago: University of Chicago Press, 1950, 1974.

Litowitz, Douglas E. *Postmodern Philosophy and Law.* Lawrence: University Press of Kansas, 1997.

Llewellyn, Karl. *The Bramble Bush.* New York: Oceana, 1930, 1951, 1960.

———. *Jurisprudence: Realism in Theory and Practice.* Chicago: University of Chicago Press, 1962.

———. *The Common Law Tradition: Deciding Appeals.* Boston: Little, Brown, 1962.

Lukes, Steven, and Andrew Scull, eds. *Durkheim and the Law.* Oxford: Martin Robertson, 1983.

Mackinnon, Catharine A. *Feminism Unmodified: Discourses on Life and Law.* Cambridge: Harvard University Press, 1987.

———. *Toward a Feminist Theory of the State.* Cambridge: Harvard University Press, 1989.

———. *Only Words.* Cambridge: Harvard University Press, 1993.

Maine, Henry. *Ancient Law.* London: Oxford University Press, 1986.

Maveety, Nancy, ed. *The Pioneers of Judicial Behavior.* Ann Arbor: University of Michigan Press, 2003.

Mercuro, N., and S. G. Medema. *Economics and the Law: From Posner to Post-Modernism.* Princeton, NJ: Princeton University Press, 1997.

Minda, Gary. *Postmodern Legal Movements: Law and Jurisprudence at Century's End.* New York: New York University Press, 1995.

Morawetz, Thomas. *The Philosophy of Law: An Introduction.* New York: Macmillan, 1980.

Morris, Clarence, ed. *The Great Legal Philosophers: Selected Readings in Jurisprudence.* Philadelphia: University of Pennsylvania Press, 1971.

Morrison, Wayne. *Jurisprudence: From the Greeks to Post-Modernism.* London: Cavendish, 1997.

Murphy, G. Jeffrie, and L. Jules Coleman. *The Philosophy of Law: An Introduction to Jurisprudence.* Rev. ed. Totowa, NJ: Rowman & Littlefield, 1989, 1990.

Olsen, Frances E. *Feminist Legal Theory.* Vols. I and II. New York: Washington Square Press, 1995.

Parisi, Francesco, ed. *The Economics of Public Law: The Collected Economic Essays of Richard A. Posner.* Vol. 3. Northampton, MA: Edward Elgar, 2001.

Patterson, Dennis, ed. *A Companion to Philosophy of Law and Legal Theory.* Cambridge: Blackwell, 1996.

Patterson, Dennis. *Law and Truth.* New York: Oxford University Press, 1996.

Patterson, Edwin W. *Jurisprudence: Men and Ideas of the Law.* Brooklyn: The Foundation Press, 1953.

Posner, Richard A. *Law and Literature: A Misunderstood Relation.* Cambridge: Harvard University Press, 1988.

———. *The Problems of Jurisprudence.* Cambridge: Harvard University Press, 1990.

———. *Overcoming Law.* Cambridge: Harvard University Press, 1995.

———. *The Economic Analysis of Law.* 4th ed. Boston: Little, Brown, 1998.

———. *The Problematics of Moral and Legal Theory.* Cambridge: Harvard University Press, 1999.

———. *Frontiers of Legal Theory.* Cambridge: Harvard University Press, 2001.

———. *Law, Pragmatism, and Democracy.* Cambridge: Harvard University Press, 2003.

Pound, Roscoe. *An Introduction to the Philosophy of Law.* Rev. ed. New Haven, CT: Yale University Press, 1982.

Quinney, Richard. *Critique of Legal Order.* Boston: Little, Brown, 1974.

———. *Class, State and Crime.* 2d ed. New York: McKay, 1980.

Rawls, John. *A Theory of Justice.* Cambridge: Belknap Press of Harvard University Press, 1973, 1980, 1986.

Robson, Ruthann. *Sappho Goes to Law School: Fragments in Lesbian Legal Theory.* New York: Columbia University Press, 1998.

Rosenfeld, Michel, and Andrew Arato. *Habermas on Law and Democracy.* Berkeley: University of California Press, 1998.

Rubin, Leslie G. *Justice v. Law in Greek Political Thought.* Lanham, MD: Rowman & Littlefield, 1997.

Sarat, Austin, and Thomas R. Kearns, eds. *Legal Rights: Historical and Philosophical Perspectives.* Ann Arbor: University of Michigan Press, 1997.

Sarat, Austin, Lawrence Douglas, and Martha Merrill Umphrey, eds. *Lives in the Law. The Amherst Series in Law, Jurisprudence, and Social Thought.* Ann Arbor: University of Michigan Press, 2002.

Savigny, Friedrich Karl von. [1831]. *On the Vocation of our Age for Legislation and Jurisprudence.* Birmingham, AL: Legal Classics Library, 1986.

———. *Of the Vocation of Our Age for Legislation and Jurisprudence.* Translated by A. Hayward. London: Littlewood, 1900.

Schauer, Frederick. *Free Speech: A Philosophical Inquiry.* New York: Cambridge University Press, 1982.

Schlegel, John Henry. *American Legal Realism and Empirical Social Science.* Chapel Hill: University of North Carolina Press, 1995.

Schuck, Peter H. *The Limits of the Law: Essays on Democratic Governance.* Boulder, CO: Westview Press, 2000.

Sellers, M. N. S. *The Sacred Fire of Liberty: Republicanism, Liberalism, and the Law.* New York: New York University Press, 1998.

Shiell, Timothy C. *Legal Philosophy: Selected Readings.* Fort Worth, TX: Harcourt Brace, 1993.

Shklar, Judith N. *Legalism.* Cambridge: Harvard University Press, 1964.

Smith, Patricia, ed. *Feminist Jurisprudence.* New York: Oxford University Press, 1993.

Smith, Roger M. *Liberalism and American Constitutional Law.* Cambridge: Harvard University Press, 1990.

Stacy, Helen M. *Postmodernism and Law: Jurisprudence in a Fragmenting World.* Burlington, VT: Ashgate, 2001.

Twining, William, ed. *Legal Theory and Common Law.* Oxford: Basil Blackwell, 1986.

Unger, Roberto. *The Critical Legal Studies Movement.* Cambridge: Harvard University Press, 1987.

Williams, Robert A., Jr. *The American Indian in Western Legal Thought: The Discourses of Conquest.* New York: Oxford University Press, 1990.

Wintgens, Luc J., ed. *Legisprudence: A New Theoretical Approach to Legislation.* Oxford, UK, Portland, OR: Hart, November 2002.

Zelermyer, William. *The Process of Legal Reasoning.* Englewood Cliffs: Prentice-Hall, 1963.

Constitutional Law—General

Baker, Thomas E. *Constitutional Analysis in a Nutshell.* 2d ed. Eagan, MN: West Group, 2003.

Barron, Jerome A., and C. Thomas Dienes. *Constitutional Law in a Nutshell.* 5th ed. Eagan, MN: West Group, 2003.

Bartholomew, Paul C., and Joseph F. Menez. *Summaries of Leading Cases on the Constitution.* 13th ed. Totowa, NJ: Littlefield Adams, 1997.

Bobbitt, Philip. *Constitutional Fate: Theory of the Constitution.* New York: Oxford University, 1984.

Congressional Research Service, Library of Congress. *The Constitution of the United States of America: Analysis and Interpretation.* Washington, DC: U.S. Government Printing Office, 1992 and latest supplement.

Cooke, Edward F. *A Detailed Analysis of the Constitution.* 7th ed. Blue Ridge Summit, PA: Rowman & Littlefield, 2002.

Corwin, Edward S. *The Constitution and What It Means Today.* 14th ed. Revised by Harold W. Chase and Craig R. Ducat. Princeton, NJ: Princeton University Press, 1978.

Crews, Kenneth D. *Edward S. Corwin and the American Constitution: A Bibliographical Analysis.* Westport, CT: Greenwood Press, 1985.

Curry, James A., Richard B. Riley, and Richard M. Battistoni. *Constitutional Government: The American Experience.* 5th ed. St. Paul, MN: Kendall/Hunt, 2003.

Federalist Society. *The Great Debate: Interpreting Our Written Constitution.* Washington, DC: The Federalist Society, 1986.

Hall, Kermit L. *The Oxford Guide to United States Supreme Court Decisions.* New York: Oxford University Press, 2001.

———, ed. *The Oxford Companion to American Law.* New York: Oxford University Press, 2002.

Jost, Kenneth. *The Supreme Court Year Book.* Washington, DC: Congressional Quarterly, 2001.

Kurland, Philip B., and Ralph Lerner. *The Founders' Constitution.* 5 vols. Chicago: University of Chicago Press, 1987.

Maddex, Robert L. *The U.S. Constitution A to Z.* Washington, DC: Congressional Quarterly, 2002.

Marks, Thomas C., and John F. Cooper. *State Constitutional Law in a Nutshell.* 2d ed. St. Paul, MN: Thomson West, 2003.

Mitchell, Ralph, ed. *CQ's Guide to the U.S. Constitution.* 2d ed. Washington, DC: Congressional Quarterly, 1995.

Padover, Saul K. *The Living U.S. Constitution.* Second Revised Edition by Jacob W. Landynski. New York: New American Library, 1983.

Peltason, J. W., and Sue Davis. *Understanding the Constitution.* 15th ed. Fort Worth, TX: Harcourt Brace, 2000.

Rotunda, Ronald D., John E. Nowark, and J. Nelson Young. *Constitutional Law: Treatise on Substance and Procedure.* 3d ed. St. Paul, MN: West, 1999.

Shaman, Jeffrey M. *Constitutional Interpretation: Illusion and Reality.* Westport, CT: Greenwood Press, 2001.

Sheldon, Charles H. *Essentials of the American Constitution: The Supreme Court and the Fundamental Law.* Stephen L. Wasby, ed. Boulder, CO: Westview Press, 2002.

Stark, Jack. *Prohibited Government Acts: A Reference Guide to The United States Constitution.* Westport, CT: Greenwood, 2002.

Vile, John R. *A Companion to the United States Constitution and its Amendments,* 3d ed. Westport, CT: Praeger, 2001.

Constitutional History

Adams, Willi Paul. *The First American Constitutions: Republican Ideology and the Making of the State Constitutions in the Revolutionary Era.* Translated by Rita Kimberg and Robert Kimberg. Chapel Hill: University of North Carolina Press, 1980.

Allen, W. B., and Gordon Lloyd, eds. *The Essential Antifederalist.* Lanham, MD: University Press of America, 1985.

————, and Kevin A. Cloonan. *The Federalist Papers: A Commentary.* New York: Peter Lang, 2000.

Amlund, Curtis Arthur. *Federalism in the Southern Confederacy.* Washington, DC: Public Affairs Press, 1966.

Bailyn, Bernard, ed. *Debates on the Constitution.* 2 vols. New York: The Library of America, 1993.

Banner, Stuart. *The Death Penalty: An American History.* Cambridge: Harvard University Press, 2002.

Barber, Sotirios A., and Robert P. George, eds. *Constitutional Politics: Essays on Constitution Making, Maintenance, and Change.* Princeton, NJ: Princeton University Press, 2001.

Beard, Charles Austin. *The Federalist.* New York: F. Ungar, 1959.

————. *The Supreme Court and the Constitution.* Englewood Cliffs, NJ: Prentice-Hall, 1962.

————. *An Economic Interpretation of the United States.* New York: Free Press, 1986.

Belsky, Martin, ed. *The Rehnquist Court: A Retrospective.* New York: Oxford University Press, 2002.

Beth, Loren P. *The Development of the American Constitution, 1877–1917.* New York: Harper & Row, 1971.

Biasi, Vincent. *The Burger Court: The Counter-Revolution That Wasn't.* New Haven, CT: Yale University Press, 1986.

Bloomfield, Maxwell. *Peaceful Revolution: Constitutional Change and American Culture from Progressivism to the New Deal.* Cambridge: Harvard University Press, 2000.

Boles, Donald E. *Mr. Justice Rehnquist, Justice Activist: The Early Years.* Ames: Iowa State University Press, 1987.

Boorstin, Daniel J. *The Americans: The Colonial Experience.* New York: Random House, 1988.

Bowen, Catherine Drinker. *Miracle at Philadelphia: The Story of the Constitutional Convention May to September 1787.* Boston: Atlantic-Little Brown, 1986.

Boyd, Steven R. *The Politics of Opposition: Antifederalists and the Acceptance of the Constitution.* Millwood, NY: KTO Press, 1979.

Brisbin, Richard A., Jr. *A Strike like No other Strike: Law and Resistance during the Pittston Coal Strike of 1989–1990.* Baltimore: Johns Hopkins University Press, 2002.

Burgess, John William. *Recent Changes in American Constitutional Theory.* New York: Arno Press, 1972.

Burns, Edward McNall. *James Madison: Philosopher of the Constitution.* New York: Octagon Books, 1968.

Clinton, Robert L. *From Precedent to Myth: Marbury v. Madison and the History of Judicial Review in America.* Lawrence: University Press of Kansas, 1989.

Cogan, Neil H. *The Complete Bill of Rights: The Drafts, Debates, Sources & Origins.* New York: Oxford University Press, 1997.

———. *Contexts of the Constitution: A Documentary Collection on Principles of American Constitutional Law.* New York: Foundation Press, 1999.

Cohen, Sherrill, and Nadine Taub, eds., *Reproductive Laws for the 1990s.* Clifton, NJ: Humana Press, 1989.

Collier, Christopher, and James Lincoln Collier. *Decision in Philadelphia: The Constitutional Convention of 1787.* New York: Random House Ballantine Books, 1987.

Conant, Michael. *The Constitution and the Economy: Objective Theory and Critical Commentary.* Norman: University of Oklahoma Press, 1991.

Cope, Alfred Haines. *Franklin D. Roosevelt and the Supreme Court.* Lexington, MA: Heath, 1969.

Corwin, Edward S. *The Doctrine of Judicial Review.* Princeton, NJ: Princeton University Press, 1914.

Cox, Archibald. *The Warren Court.* Cambridge: Harvard University Press, 1968.

Cripps, Louise L. *Human Rights in a United States Colony.* Cambridge: Schenkman Books, 1982.

Crosskey, William W. *Politics and the Constitution in the History of the United States.* 3 vols. Chicago: University of Chicago Press, 1980.

Currie, David P. *The Constitution in the Supreme Court: The First Hundred Years.* Chicago: University of Chicago Press, 1985.

———. *The Constitution in Congress: The Federalist Period, 1789–1801.* Chicago: University of Chicago Press, 1997.

Dewey, Donald O. *Union and Liberty: A Documentary History of American Constitutionalism.* New York: McGraw-Hill, 1969.

———. *Marshall Versus Jefferson: The Political Background of Marbury v. Madison.* New York: Knopf, 1970.

Donovan, Frank Robert. *Mr. Madison's Constitution: The Story Behind the Constitutional Convention.* New York: Dodd, Mead, 1965.

Douglas, William O. *The Court Years, 1935–1975.* New York: Random House, 1980.

Dunning, William Archibald. *Essays on the Civil War and Reconstruction.* New York: Harper & Row, 1965.

Duram, James C. *Justice William O. Douglas.* Boston: K. G. Hall, 1981.

Earle, Edward Meade, ed. *The Federalist: A Commentary on the Constitution of the United States* (Alexander Hamilton, James Madison, and John Jay). New York: The Modern Library, 1941, 1964.

Elliot, Jonathan. *Elliot's Debates.* 5 vols. Philadelphia: J. B. Lippincott, 1936, 1937.

———. *The Debates in the Several State Conventions on the Adoption of the Federal Constitution as Recommended by the General Convention at Philadelphia in 1787.* 2d ed. New York: B. Franklin, 1970, 1974.

Ely, James W., Jr., ed. *Property Rights in American History.* 6 vols. New York: Garland, 1997.

Faber, Doris, and Harold Faber. *We the People: The Story of the United States Constitution Since 1787.* New York: Charles Scribner's Sons, 1987.

Farrand, Max. *The Framing of the Constitution of the United States.* New Haven, CT: Yale University Press, 1940, 1967.

———, ed. *The Records of the Federal Convention of 1787.* 4 vols. New Haven, CT: Yale University Press, 1937, 1966, 1986.

Finkelman, Paul, and Melvin I. Urofsky. *Landmark Decisions of The United States Supreme Court.* Washington, DC: Congressional Quarterly, 2002.

Fisher, Louis. *Nazi Saboteurs on Trial: A Military Tribunal and American Law.* Lawrence: University Press of Kansas, 2003.

Ford, Saul Leicester, ed. *The Federalist.* New York: H. Holt, 1898.

Frankfurter, Felix. *The Commerce Clause under Marshall, Taney, and Waite.* Chicago: Quadrangle Books, 1964.

Friedman, Leon, and Fred L. Israel, eds. *The Justices of the United States Supreme Court 1789–1978: Their Lives and Major Opinions.* Rev. ed. New York and London: Chelsea House, 1995.

Funston, Richard Y. *Constitutional Counterrevolution: The Warren and the Burger Courts: Judicial Policy Making in Modern America.* New York: Halsted Press, 1977.

Garranty, John A. *Quarrels That Have Shaped the Constitution.* Rev. ed. New York: Harper and Row, 1988.

Goldstein, Robert J. *Burning the Flag: The Great 1989–1990 American Flag Desecration.* Kent, OH: Kent State University Press, 1996.

Graham, Fred P. *The Due Process Revolution: The Warren Court's Impact on Criminal Law.* New York: Hayden Books, 1970.

Graham, George J., and Scarlett G. Graham, eds. *Founding Principles of American Government.* Chatham, NJ: Chatham House, 1984.

Green, Fletcher M. *Constitutional Development in the South Atlantic States.* New York: W. W. Norton, 1966.

Grier, Stephenson D., Jr., *The Supreme Court and the American Republic: An Annotated Bibliography.* New York: Garland, 1981.

Haines, Charles G. *The Role of the Supreme Court in American Government and Politics, 1789–1835.* Berkeley: University of California Press, 1957, 1960.

———, and Foster H. Sherwood. *The Role of the Supreme Court in American Government and Politics, 1835–1864.* Berkeley: University of California Press, 1957.

———, *The American Doctrine of Judicial Supremacy.* 2d ed. Berkeley: University of California Press, 1959.

Hall, Kermit L., ed. *A Comprehensive Bibliography of Constitutional and Legal History, 1896–1979.* White Plains, NY: Kraus International Publications, 1991.

———. *Liberties in American History.* New York: Garland, 1987.

Harmon, M. Judd, ed. *Essays on the Constitution of the United States.* Port Washington, NY: Kennikat Press, 1978.

Hentoff, Nat. *The First Freedom: The Tumultuous History of Free Speech in America.* New York: Delacorte Press, 1988.

Higginbotham, A. Leon, Jr. *In the Matter of Color: Race and the American Legal Process, The Colonial Period.* New York: Oxford University Press, 1978.

Hirsch, H. N. *The Enigma of Felix Frankfurter.* New York: Basic Books, 1981.

Hixson, Walter L. *Murder, Culture, and Injustice: Four Sensational Cases in American History.* Akron, OH: University of Akron Press, 2001.

Hockett, Homer Carey. *The Constitutional History of the United States.* New York: Macmillan, 1939.

Hoffer, Peter C., and N. E. Hull. *Impeachment in America, 1635–1805.* New Haven, CT: Yale University Press, 1985.

Horwitz, Morton J. *The Transformation of American Law, 1780–1860.* Cambridge: Harvard University Press, 1977.

Howard, A. *The Road from Runnymede: Magna Carta and Constitutionalism in America.* Charlottesville: University of Virginia Press, 1968.

Hurst, Willard. *The Growth of American Law, The Law Makers.* Boston: Little, Brown, 1950.

Hyman, Harold Melvin. *A More Perfect Union: The Impact of the Civil War and Reconstruction on the Constitution.* Boston: Houghton Mifflin, 1975.

Irons, Peter. *A People's History of the Supreme Court.* New York: Viking Press; Penguin Books, 2000.

Jaffa, Harry V. *Original Intent and the Framers of the Constitution.* Washington, DC: Regnery Gateway, 1994.

———. *American Conservatism and the American Founding.* Durham, NC: Carolina Academic Press, 1983.

Jellinek, George. *The Declaration of the Rights of Man and of Citizens: A Contribution to Modern Constitutional History.* Westport, CT: Hyperion Press, 1985.

Jenson, Carol E. *Agrarian Pioneer in Civil Liberties: The Nonpartisan League in Minnesota During World War I.* New York: Garland, 1987.

Kahn, Paul W. *The Reign of Law: Marbury v. Madison and the Construction of America.* New Haven, CT: Yale University Press, 1997.

Kaplan, Alice. *The Collaborator: The Trial and Execution of Robert Brasillach.* Chicago: University of Chicago Press, 2000.

Kelly, Alfred H., Winfield A. Harbison, and Herman Beiz. *The American Constitution: Its Origins and Development.* 7th ed. New York: W. W. Norton, 1991.

Kenyon, Cecelia M., ed. *The Antifederalists.* Boston: Northeastern University Press, 1985.

Ketcham, Ralph, ed. *The Antifederalist Papers and the Constitutional Convention Debates.* New York: New American Library, 1986.

Kurland, Philip. *Politics, the Constitution, and the Warren Court.* Chicago: University of Chicago Press, 1970.

———, and Ralph Lerner, eds. *The Founders' Constitution.* 5 vols. Chicago: University of Chicago Press, 1987.

Kutler, I. Stanley. *Judicial Power and Reconstruction Politics.* Chicago: University of Chicago Press, 1968.

Lash, Joseph P., ed. *From the Diaries of Felix Frankfurter.* New York: W. W. Norton, 1975.

Leonard, Gerald. *The Invention of Party Politics: Federalism, Popular Sovereignty, and Constitutional Development in Jacksonian Illinois.* Chapel Hill: University of North Carolina Press, 2002.

Levy, Leonard Williams. *Essays on the Making of the Constitution.* New York: Oxford University Press, 1976.

Lloyd, Gordon, and Margie Lloyd. *The Essential Bill of Rights: Original Arguments and Fundamental Documents.* Lanham, MD: University Press of America, 1998.

Lofgren, Charles. *The Plessy Case: A Legal-Historical Interpretation.* New York: Oxford University Press, 1987.

Madison, James. *Notes of Debates in the Federal Convention of 1787 Report by James Madison.* Athens: Ohio University, 1966.

Magee, James J. *Mr. Justice Black: Absolutist on the Court.* Charlottesville: University of Virginia Press, 1980.

Main, Jackson Turner. *The Antifederalists: Critics of the Constitution.* New York: W. W. Norton, 1974.

Manaster, Kenneth A. *Illinois Justice: The Scandal of 1969 and the Rise of John Paul Stevens.* Chicago: University of Chicago Press, 2001.

Manley, John F., and Kenneth Dolbeare, eds. *The Case Against the Constitution: From the Antifederalists to the Present.* Armonk, NY: M. E. Sharpe, 1987.

Marcosson, Samuel A. *Original Sin: Clarence Thomas and the Failure of the Constitutional Conservatives.* New York: New York University Press, 2002.

Marks, Frederick W. *Independence on Trial: Foreign Affairs and the Making of the Constitution.* Baton Rouge: Louisiana State University Press, 1986.

Mason, Alpheus Thomas. *The Supreme Court from Taft to Warren.* Rev. ed. Baton Rouge: Louisiana State University Press, 1968.

————. *The States Rights Debate: Antifederalism and the Constitution.* 2d ed. New York: Oxford University Press, 1972.

————. *Supreme Court from Taft to Burger.* 3d ed. Baton Rouge: Louisiana State University Press, 1979.

McAffee, Thomas B. *Inherent Rights, the Written Constitution, and Popular Sovereignty: The Founders' Understanding.* Westport, CT: Greenwood Press, 2000.

McCloskey, Robert G. *The American Supreme Court.* 2d ed. Chicago: University of Chicago Press, 1994.

————. *The Modern Supreme Court.* Martin Shapiro, ed. Cambridge: Harvard University Press, 1979.

McDonald, Forrest. *A Constitutional History of the United States.* New York: Watts Franklin, 1982.

————. *Novus Ordo Seclorum: The Intellectual Origins of the Constitution.* Lawrence: University Press of Kansas, 1985.

McLaughlin, Andrew Cunningham. *A Constitutional History of the United States.* New York: Appleton-Century-Crofts, 1989.

————. *The Confederation and the Constitution.* New York: Collier Books, 1971.

————. *The Courts, the Constitution, and Parties: Studies in Constitutional History and Politics.* New York: Da Capo Press, 1972.

————. *The Foundations of American Constitutionalism.* Gloucester, MA: P. Smith, 1972.

Mendelson, Wallace. *Capitalism, Democracy, and the Supreme Court.* New York: Appleton-Century-Crofts, 1960.

Miller, Arthur S. *The Supreme Court and American Capitalism.* New York: Free Press, 1968.

Millett, Stephen M. *A Selected Bibliography of American Constitutional History.* Santa Barbara, CA: Clio Books, 1975.

Mitchell, Broadus. *A Biography of the Constitution of the United States: Its Origin, Formation, Adoption, Interpretation.* 2d ed. New York: Oxford University Press, 1975.

Morris, Richard B. *Witnesses at the Creation: Hamilton, Madison, Jay, and the Constitution.* New York: New American Library, 1985.

Murphy, Bruce Allen. *The Brandeis/Frankfurter Connection: The Secret Political Activities of Two Supreme Court Justices.* New York: Oxford University Press, 1983.

————. *Wild Bill: The Legend and Life of William O. Douglas.* New York: Random House, 2003.

Murphy, Paul L. *The Constitution in Crisis Times, 1918–1969.* New York: Harper & Row, 1972.

————. *World War I and the Origin of Civil Liberties in the United States.* New York: W. W. Norton, 1979.

————. *The Bill of Rights and American Legal History.* 20 vols. New York: Garland, 1990.

Nedelsky, Jennifer. *Private Property and the Limits of American Constitutionalism: The Madisonian Framework and Its Legacy.* Chicago: University of Chicago Press, 1990.

Nelson, William E. *Marbury v. Madison: The Origins and Legacy of Judicial Review.* Lawrence: University Press of Kansas, 2000.

————. *The Legalist Reformation: Law, Politics, and Ideology in New York, 1920–1980.* Chapel Hill: University of North Carolina Press, 2001.

Newmyer, Kent R. *Supreme Court Justice Story: Statesman of the Old Republic.* Chapel Hill: University of North Carolina Press, 1985.

Nieman, Donald G. *To Set the Law in Motion: The Freedmen's Bureau and the Legal Rights of Blacks, 1865–1868.* Millwood, NY: KTO Press, 1979.

Orth, John V. *Due Process of Law: A Brief History.* Lawrence: University Press of Kansas, 2003.

Paludan, Phillip S. *A Covenant with Death: The Constitution, Law and Equality in the Civil War Era.* Urbana: University of Illinois Press, 1975.

Papke, David Ray. *The Pullman Case: The Clash of Law and Capital in Industrial America.* Lawrence: University Press of Kansas, 1999.

Parrish, Michael. *Felix Frankfurter and His Times: The Reform Years.* New York: Free Press, 1982.

Patterson, James T. *The New Deal and the States: Federalism in Transition.* Westport, CT: Greenwood Press, 1981.

Pfeffer, Leo. *This Honorable Court: A History of the Supreme Court of the United States.* Boston: Beacon Press, 1965.

Phillips, Michael J. *The Lochner Court, Myth and Reality: Substantive Due Process from the 1890s to the 1930s.* Westport, CT: Praeger, 2001.

Pohlman, H. L. *Justice Oliver Wendell Holmes and Utilitarian Jurisprudence.* Cambridge: Harvard University Press, 1984.

Pollack, Louis. *The Constitution and the Supreme Court: A Documentary History.* 2 vols. Cleveland, OH: World, 1968.

Pound, Richard W. *Stikeman Elliott: The First 50 Years.* Montreal and Kingston, Canada: McGill-Queen's University Press, 2002.

Powell, H. Jefferson. *A Community Built on Words: The Constitution in History and Politics.* Chicago: University of Chicago Press, 2002.

Prescott, Arthur Taylor. *Drafting the Federal Constitution.* New York: Greenwood Press, 1968.

Pritchett, C. Herman. *The Roosevelt Court: A Study of Judicial Votes and Values, 1937–1947.* New York: Macmillan, 1969.

———. *Civil Liberties and the Vinson Court.* Chicago: University of Chicago Press, 1966.

Purcell, Edward A., Jr. *Brandeis and the Progressive Constitution, Erie, the Judicial Power, and the Politics of the Federal Courts in Twentieth Century America.* New Haven, CT: Yale University Press, 2000.

Ramos, Efren Rivera. *The Legal Construction of Identity: The Judicial and Social Legacy of American Colonialism in Puerto Rico.* Washington, DC: American Psychological Association, 2001.

Robarge, David. *A Chief Justice's Progress: John Marshall from Revolutionary Virginia to the Supreme Court.* Westport, CT: Greenwood Press, 2000.

Rodell, Fred. *Nine Men: A Political History of the Supreme Court from 1790–1955.* New York: Random House, 1964.

———. *55 Men: The Story of the Constitution.* 1987 edition. Washington, DC: Liberty Lobby, 1987.

Rossiter, Clinton. *1787: The Grand Convention.* New York: Macmillan, 1968.

———, ed. *The Federalist Papers: Alexander Hamilton, James Madison, and John Jay.* New York: The New American Library, 1961.

Rutland, Robert A. *The Birth of the Bill of Rights, 1776–1791.* Classics. New York: Macmillan, 1991.

Samples, John, ed. *James Madison and the Future of Limited Government.* Washington, DC: Cato Institute, 2002.

Sarat, Austin, Lawrence Douglas, and Martha Merrill Umphrey, eds. *Lives in the Law.* The Amherst Series in Law, Jurisprudence, and Social Thought. Ann Arbor: University of Michigan Press, 2002.

Savage, David S. *Turning Right: The Making of the Rehnquist Supreme Court.* New York: John Wiley & Sons, 1992.

Schmidhauser, John R. *Constitutional Law in American Politics.* Monterey, CA: Brooks/ Cole, 1984.

Schwartz, Bernard. *From Confederation to Nation: The American Constitution, 1835–1877.* Baltimore: Johns Hopkins University Press, 1973.

———. *Super Chief: Earl Warren and His Court.* New York: New York University Press, 1983.

Schwartz, Herman, ed. *The Burger Years: Rights and Wrongs in the Supreme Court, 1969– 1986.* New York: Viking-Penguin, 1988.

Scott, Eben G. *Development of Constitutional Liberty in the English Colonies of America.* 3d ed. Littleton, CO: Fred B. Rothman, 1982.

Sheldon, Garrett Ward. *The Political Philosophy of James Madison.* Baltimore: The Johns Hopkins University Press, 2001.

Silverstein, Mark. *Constitutional Faiths: Felix Frankfurter, Hugo Black, and the Process of Judicial Decisionmaking.* Ithaca, NY: Cornell University Press, 1984.

Simon, James F. *In His Own Image: The Supreme Court in Richard Nixon's America.* New York: David McKay, 1973.

———. *Independent Journey: The Life of William O. Douglas.* New York: Harper and Row, 1980.

Smith, David G. *The Convention and the Constitution: The Political Ideas of the Founding Fathers.* New York: St. Martin's Press, 1965.

Solberg, Winston U., ed. *The Federal Convention and the Formation of the Union of the American States.* Indianapolis: Bobbs-Merrill, 1958.

St. Clair, James E., and Linda C. Gugin. *Chief Justice Fred M. Vinson of Kentucky: A Political Biography.* Lexington: University Press of Kentucky, 2002.

Steamer, Robert J. *The Supreme Court in Crisis: A History of Conflict.* Amherst: University of Massachusetts Press, 1971.

———. *Chief Justice: Leadership and the Supreme Court.* Columbia: University of South Carolina Press, 1986.

Storing, Herbert J., ed. *The Abridged Anti-Federalist.* Chicago: University of Chicago Press, 1985.

Storing, Herbert J., with the assistance of Murray Dry, eds. *The Complete Anti-Federalists.* 7 vols. Chicago: University of Chicago Press, 1981.

Strum, Philippa. *Louis Brandeis: Justice for the People.* Cambridge: Harvard University Press, 1984.

Sutherland, Arthur E. *Constitutionalism in America: Origin and Evolution of its Fundamental Ideas.* New York: Blaisdell, 1965.

Swisher, Carl Brent. *The Growth of Constitutional Power in the United States.* Chicago: University of Chicago Press, 1966.

———. *American Constitutional Development.* Reprint. Boston: Houghton Mifflin, 1978.

Thomas, Andrew Peyton. *Clarence Thomas: A Biography.* San Francisco: Encounter Books, 2001.

U.S. Congress. The Debates and Proceedings in the Congress of the United States. *A Second Federalist: Congress Creates a Government.* New York: Appleton-Century-Crofts, 1967.

U.S. Constitution Sesquicentennial Commission. *History of the Formation of the Union Under the Constitution with Liberty Documents and Report of the Commission.* New York: Greenwood Press, 1968.

U.S. Constitutional Convention, 1787. *Notes of Debates in the Federal Convention of 1787, reported by James Madison.* Athens: Ohio University Press, 1966.

VanBurkleo, Sandra F., Kermit L. Hall, and Robert J. Kaczorowski, eds. *Constitutionalism and American Culture: Writing the New Constitutional History.* Lawrence: University Press of Kansas, 2002.

Virginia Commission on Constitutional Government. *The Constitution of the United States of America, with a Summary of the Actions by the States in Ratification of the Provisions thereof.* 6th ed. Richmond: Virginia Commission on Constitutional Government, 1967.

Vose, Clement E. *Constitutional Change: Amendment Politics and Supreme Court Litigation Since 1900.* Lexington, MA: Lexington Books, 1972.

Warren, Charles. *The Supreme Court in United States History.* 2 vols. Boston: Little, Brown, 1947, 1987.

———. *The Making of the Constitution.* New York: Barnes & Noble, 1993.

———. *Congress, the Constitution and the Supreme Court.* New York: Johnson Reprint Corp., 1994.

Wasby, Stephen L. *Continuity and Change: From the Warren Court to the Burger Court.* Pacific Palisades, CA: Goodyear, 1976.

Westin, Alan F. *An Autobiography of the Supreme Court.* New York: Macmillan, 1963.

White, G. Edward. *The Constitution and the New Deal.* Cambridge: Harvard University Press, 2000.

Wiecek, William M. *Constitutional Development in a Modernizing Society.* Washington, DC: American Historical Association, 1985.

Wilson, James G. *The Imperial Republic: A Structural History of American Constitutionalism from the Colonial Era to the Beginning of the Twentieth Century.* Aldershot, Hampshire, UK: Ashgate, 2002.

Wood, S. B. *Constitutional Politics in the Progressive Era.* Chicago: University of Chicago Press, 1968.

Woodward, C. Vann. *The Strange Career of Jim Crow.* 3d ed. New York: Oxford University Press, 1974.

Wright, Benjamin Fletcher. *The Growth of American Constitutional Law.* Chicago: University of Chicago Press, 1967.

Yarbrough, Tinsley E. *The Rehnquist Court and the Constitution.* New York: Oxford University Press, 2000.

Federalism

Ackerman, B. A. *Private Property and the Constitution.* New Haven, CT: Yale University Press, 1977.

Baxter, Maurice G. *The Steamboat Monopoly: Gibbons v. Ogden, 1824.* New York: Knopf, 1972.

Benson, Paul R., Jr. *The Supreme Court and the Commerce Clause.* New York: Dunellen, 1970.

Biskupic, Joan, and Elder Witt. *The Supreme Court and the Powers of the American Government.* Washington, DC: Congressional Quarterly, 1997.

Cooley, Thomas M. *Constitutional Limitations*. New York: Da Capo Press, 1972.

Cortner, Richard C. *The Jones and Laughlin Case*. New York: Knopf, 1970.

Corwin, Edward Samuel. *The Commerce Power Versus States Rights*. Magnolia, MA: Peter Smith, 1962.

Davis, S. Rufus. *The Federal Principle*. Berkeley: University of California Press, 1978.

Durchslag, Melvyn R. *State Sovereign Immunity: A Reference Guide to the United States Constitution*. Westport, CT: Praeger, 2002.

Elazar, Daniel J. *American Federalism: A View From the States*. 2d ed. New York: Harper and Row, 1984.

———, ed. *Federalism & Political Integration*. Lanham, MA: University Press of America, 1985.

———. *Exploring Federalism*. Tuscaloosa: University of Alabama Press, 1987.

Engdahl, D. E. *Constitutional Power: Federal and State*. St. Paul, MN: West, 1974.

———. *Constitutional Federalism in a Nutshell*. St. Paul, MN: West, 1987.

Flack, Horace. *The Adoption of the Fourteenth Amendment*. Baltimore: Johns Hopkins University Press, 1965.

Flynn, John J. *Federalism and State Antitrust Regulation*. Ann Arbor: University of Michigan Law School, 1964.

Folgelson, R. M., and L. E. Susskind. *American Federalism*. New York: Arno Press, 1977.

Frankfurter, Felix. *The Commerce Clause Under Marshall, Taney and Waite*. Chicago: Quadrangle Books, 1964.

Freilich, Robert H., and Richard G. Carlisle. *Section 1983, Sword and Shield: Civil Rights Violation and the Liability of Urban, State, and Local Government*. Chicago: American Bar Association, 1983.

Galliher, John F., Larry W. Koch, David Patrick Keys, and Teresa J. Guess. *America without the Death Penalty: States Leading the Way*. Boston: Northeastern University Press, 2002.

Gelfand, M. David. *Federal Constitutional Law and American Local Government*. Charlottesville, VA: Michie, 1984.

Glendening, Parris N., and Mavis M. Reeves. *Pragmatic Federalism: An Intergovernmental View of American Government*. 2d ed. Pacific Palisades, CA: Palisades, 1984.

Grodzins, Morton. *The American System*. Chicago: Rand McNally, 1966.

———. *The American System: A New View of Government in the United States*. New Brunswick, NJ: Transaction Books, 1983.

Hall, Kermit L., ed. *Federalism: A Nation of States*. New York: Garland, 1987.

Hallman, Howard W. *Emergency Employment: A Study of Federalism*. Tuscaloosa: University of Alabama Press, 1977.

Hawkins, Robert B., Jr., ed. *American Federalism: A New Partnership for the Republic*. 2d ed. San Francisco: ICS Press, 1983.

Hay, Peter, and Donald D. Rotunda. *The United States Federal System: Legal Integration in the American Experience*. Dobbs Ferry, NY: Oceana, 1982.

Hening, Jeffrey R. *Public Policy and Federalism: Issues in State and Local Politics*. New York: St. Martin's Press, 1985.

Hodgkinson, Virginia A., ed. *Impact and Challenges of a Changing Federal Role*. San Francisco: Jossey-Bass, 1985.

Holland, Randy J. *The Delaware State Constitution: A Reference Guide*. Westport, CT: Greenwood, 2002.

Hoose, Bernard. *Proportionalism: The American Debate and Its European Roots*. Washington, DC: Georgetown University Press, 1987.

Howitt, Arnold M. *Managing Federalism: Studies in Intergovernmental Relations*. Washington, DC: Congressional Quarterly, 1984.

Kens, Paul. *Judicial Power and Reform Politics: The Anatomy of Lochner v. New York*. Lawrence: University Press of Kansas, 1990.

Kenyon, Cecelia M., ed. *The Antifederalists*. New York: Bobbs Merrill, 1964.

Kettl, Donald F. *The Regulation of American Federalism*. Baton Rouge: Louisiana State University Press, 1983.

———. *The Regulation of American Federalism*. Baltimore: Johns Hopkins University Press, 1987.

Killenbeck, Mark R., ed. *The Tenth Amendment and State Sovereignty*. Lanham, MD: Rowman & Littlefield, 2002.

King, Preston. *Federalism and Federation*. Baltimore: Johns Hopkins University Press, 1983.

Langer, Laura. *Judicial Review in State Supreme Courts: A Comparative Study*. Albany: State University of New York Press, 2001.

Leach, Richard. *American Federalism*. New York: Oxford University Press, 1972.

Lee, Mark R. *Antitrust Law and Local Government*. Westport, CT: Greenwood Press, 1985.

Leonard, Gerald. *The Invention of Party Politics: Federalism, Popular Sovereignty, and Constitutional Development in Jacksonian Illinois*. Chapel Hill: University of North Carolina Press, 2002.

Lewis, Frederick P. *The Dilemma in the Congressional Power to Enforce the Fourteenth Amendment*. Washington, DC: University Press of America, 1980.

Lipkin, Robert Justin. *Constitutional Revolutions: Pragmatism and the Role of Judicial Review in American Constitutionalism*. Durham, NC: Duke University Press, 2000.

Low, Peter W., and John C. Jeffries, Jr. *Federal Courts and the Law: Federal-State Relations*. 3d ed. Mineola, NY: Foundation Press, 1994.

Magrath, C. Peter. *Yazoo: The Case of Fletcher v. Peck*. New York: W. W. Norton, 1966.

Mason, Alpheus Thomas. *The States Rights Debate: Antifederalism and the Constitution*. New York: Oxford University Press, 1972.

McDonald, Forrest. *States' Rights and the Union: Imperium in Imperio, 1776–1876*. Lawrence: University Press of Kansas, 2000.

Melnick, Shep. *Regulation and the Courts: The Case of the Clean Air Act*. Washington, DC: Brookings Institution, 1983.

———. *Between The Lines: Interpreting Welfare Rights*. Washington, DC: Brookings Institution, 1994.

Nagel, Robert F. *The Implosion of American Federalism*. Oxford: Oxford University Press, 2001.

Noonan, John T., Jr. *Narrowing the Nation's Power: The Supreme Court Sides with the States*. Berkeley: University of California Press, 2002.

Oesterle, Dale A., and Richard B. Collins. *The Colorado State Constitution: A Reference Guide*. Westport, CT: Greenwood Press, 2002.

Ostrom, Vincent. *The Political Theory of a Compound Republic: Designing the American Experiment*. Lincoln: University of Nebraska Press, 1987.

Parness, Jeffrey A. *Civil Procedure for Federal and State Courts*. Cincinnati: Anderson, 2001.

Peterson, Paul E., et al. *When Federalism Works*. Washington, DC: Brookings Institution, 1986.

Pinello, Daniel R. *The Impact of Self-Selection Method on State-Supreme-Court Policy: Innovation, Reaction and Atrophy*. Westport, CT: Greenwood Press, 1995.

Porter, Marty Cornelia, and Allan G. Tarr, eds. *State Supreme Courts: Policymakers in the Federal System*. Westport, CT: Greenwood Press, 1982.

Press, Charles, and Kenneth Verburg. *State and Community Governments in the Federal System*. New York: Macmillan, 1983.

Reagan, Michael D., and John Sanzone. *The New Federalism*. 2d ed. New York: Oxford University Press, 1981.

Redish, Martin H. *The Constitution as Political Struggle*. New York: Oxford University Press, 1995.

Ridgeway, Marian E. *Interstate Compacts: A Question of Federalism*. Carbondale: Southern Illinois University Press, 1971.

Riker, William. *Federalism: Origin, Operation, Significance*. Boston: Little, Brown, 1964.

———. *The Development of American Federalism*. Norwell, MA: Kluwer, 1987.

Roettinger, Ruth L. *The Supreme Court and State Police Power*. Washington, DC: Public Affairs Press, 1957.

Schmidhauser, John R. *The Supreme Court as Final Arbiter in Federal/State Relations, 1789–1957*. Westport, CT: Greenwood Press, 1977.

Shepard's Citation, Inc. *Civil Actions Against State Government, Its Divisions, Agencies and Officers*. Colorado Springs, CO: Shepard's McGraw-Hill, 1984.

Smith, Michael. *Qualified Immunity from Liability for Violations of Federal Rights: A Modification*. Chapel Hill: University of North Carolina, Institute of Government, 1983.

Sprague, John D. *Voting Patterns of the United States Supreme Court: Cases in Federalism, 1889–1959*. Indianapolis: Bobbs-Merrill, 1968.

Stewart, William H. *Concepts of Federalism*. Lanham, MA: University Press of America, 1984.

Sunquist, James L. *Making Federalism Work*. Washington, DC: Brookings Institution, 1969.

Tarr, George Alan. *Judicial Impact and State Supreme Courts*. Lexington, MA: Lexington Books, 1977.

Wheare, K. C. *Federal Government*. 4th ed. New York: Oxford University Press, 1963.

Wildavsky, Aaron. *American Federalism in Perspective*. Boston: Little, Brown, 1967.

Wilkins, David E., and K. Tsianina Lomawaima. *Uneven Ground: American Indian Sovereignty and Federal Law*. Norman: University of Oklahoma Press, 2001.

Wright, Benjamin Fletcher. *The Contract Clause of the Constitution*. Cambridge: Harvard University Press, 1938.

Congress

American Bar Association Staff, and Henry B. Cox. *War, Foreign Affairs, and Constitutional Power, 1829–1901*. Cambridge: Ballinger, 1984.

Bamberger, Michael A. *Reckless Legislation: How Lawmakers Ignore the Constitution*. New Brunswick, NJ: Rutgers University Press, 2000.

Barber, S. A. *The Constitution and the Delegation of Congressional Power*. Chicago: University of Chicago Press, 1975.

Baxter, M. G. *Daniel Webster and the Supreme Court*. Amherst: University of Massachusetts Press, 1967.

Berger, Raoul. *Congress Versus the Supreme Court*. Cambridge: Harvard University Press, 1969.

Bernner, Philip. *The Limits and Possibilities of Congress*. New York: St. Martin's Press, 1983.

Breckenridge, A. C. *Congress Against the Court*. Lincoln: University of Nebraska Press, 1970.

Campbell, Colton C., and John F. Stack, Jr., eds. *Congress Confronts the Court: The Struggle for Legitimacy and Authority in Lawmaking*. Lanham, MD: Rowman & Littlefield, 2001.

———, eds. *Congress and the Politics of Emerging Rights*. Lanham, MD: Rowman & Littlefield, 2002.

Claude, Richard. *The Supreme Court and the Electoral Process*. Baltimore: Johns Hopkins University Press, 1970.

Congressional Quarterly. *Guide to the Congress of the United States: Origins, History, and Procedure*. Washington, DC: Congressional Quarterly, 1971.

———. *Impeachment and the United States Congress*. Washington, DC: Congressional Quarterly, 1974.

Cortner, Richard C. *The Jones and Laughlin Case*. New York: Knopf, 1970.

Craig, Barbara H. *Chadha: The Story of an Epic Constitutional Struggle*. New York: Oxford University Press, 1990.

———. *The Legislative Veto: Congressional Control of Regulation*. Boulder, CO: Westview Press, 1984.

Elliott, Ward E. Y. *The Rise of Guardian Democracy: The Supreme Court's Role in Voting Rights Disputes, 1845–1969*. Cambridge: Harvard University Press, 1974.

Ely, John Hart. *War and Responsibility: Congressional Lessons of Vietnam and Its Aftermath*. Cambridge: Harvard University Press, 1993.

Ethridge, Marcus E. *Legislative Participation in Implementation: Policy Through Politics*. New York: Praeger Press, 1985.

Field, O. P. *Effect of an Unconstitutional Statute*. New York: Da Capo Press, 1971.

Fisher, Louis. *President and Congress: Power and Policy*. New York: Free Press, 1973.

———. *The Constitution Between Friends: Congress, the President, and the Law*. New York: St. Martin's Press, 1978.

Gallagher, Hugh Gregory. *Advise and Obstruct: The Role of United States Senate in Foreign Policy Decisions*. New York: Delacarte Press, 1969.

Goldwin, Robert A., and Art Kaufman, eds. *Separation of Powers: Does It Still Work?* Washington, DC: American Enterprise Institute for Public Policy Research, 1986.

Goodman, Walter. *The Committee: The Extraordinary Career of the House Committee on Un-American Activities*. New York: Farrar, Straus and Giroux, 1972.

Hamilton, James. *The Power to Probe*. New York: Vintage Books, 1977.

Harrell, Karen F. *The Constitutional and Political Aspects of the Legislative Veto*. Monticello, IL: Vance Bibliographies, 1985.

Keynes, Edward, with Randall K. Miller. *The Court vs. Congress: Prayer, Busing, and Abortion*. Durham, NC: Duke University Press, 1989.

Lakeman, Enid. *Power to Elect: The Case for Proportional Representation*. New York: Holmes and Meier, 1982.

Lee, R. Alton. *A History of Regulatory Taxation*. Lexington: University Press of Kentucky, 1973.

Letwin, William. *Law and Economic Policy in America: The Evolution of the Sherman Antitrust Act*. Edinburgh, UK: Edinburgh University Press, 1967.

Lucie, Patricia A. *Freedom and Federalism, Congress and Courts, 1861–1866*. New York: Garland, 1987.

Mansfield, Harvey C., Sr. *Congress Against the President*. New York: Praeger, 1975.

McGeary, M. Nelson. *The Development of Congressional Investigating Power*. New York: Octagon Books, 1973.

Merry, Henry J. *The Constitutional System: The Group Character of the Elected Institutions*. New York: Praeger, 1986.

Morgan, Donald Grant. *Congress and the Constitution: A Study of Responsibility.* Cambridge: Belknap Press of Harvard University Press, 1966.

Murphy, Walter F. *Congress and the Court: A Case Study in the American Political Process.* Chicago: University of Chicago Press, 1964.

Polsby, Nelson W. *Congress and the Presidency.* Englewood Cliffs, NJ: Prentice-Hall, 1986.

Pritchett, C. Herman. *Congress Versus the Supreme Court.* Minneapolis: University of Minnesota Press, 1961.

Reams, Bernard D., Jr., and Charles H. Haworth. *Congress and the Courts: A Legislative History: 1985–1992.* Buffalo, NY: William S. Hein, 1994.

Roche, John P., and Leonard Levy. *The Congress.* New York: Harcourt, 1964.

Rothman, David J. *Politics and Power: The United States Senate, 1869–1901.* New York: Atheneum, 1969.

Rush, Kenneth, et al. *The President, the Congress, and Foreign Policy: A Joint Project of the Association of Former Members of Congress and the Atlantic Council of the United States.* Lanham, MA: University Press of America, 1986.

Schmidhauser, John R., and Larry L. Berg. *The Supreme Court and Congress: Conflict and Interaction, 1945–1968.* New York: Free Press, 1972.

Shuman, Howard E. *Politics and the Budget: The Struggle Between the President and the Congress.* 3d ed. Englewood Cliffs, NJ: Prentice-Hall, 1992.

Vieira, Edwin, Jr. *Pieces of Eight: Monetary Powers and Disabilities of the United States Constitution.* Greenwich, CT: Devin-Adair, 1983.

Warren, Charles. *Congress, the Constitution and the Supreme Court.* New York: Johnston Reprint Corp., 1994.

Weeks, K. M. *Adam Clayton Powell and the Supreme Court.* New York: Dunellen, 1971.

Whalen, Charles W., Jr. *The House & Foreign Policy: The Irony of Congressional Reform.* Chapel Hill: University of North Carolina Press, 1982.

Wilson, Woodrow. *Congressional Government.* Cleveland: Meridian Books, 1885, 1967.

Wormuth, Francis D., and Edwin B. Firmage. *Proposals for Line-Item Veto Authority: Legislative Analysis.* Washington, DC: American Enterprise Institute for Public Policy Research, 1984.

———. *To Chain the Dog of War: The War Power of Congress in History and Law.* 2d ed. Dallas, TX: Southern Methodist University Press, 1989.

The Presidency

Abraham, Henry J. *Justices, Presidents, and Senators: A History of the U.S. Supreme Court Appointments from Washington to Clinton.* Rev. ed. Lanham, MD: Rowman & Littlefield, 1999.

Adler, David G. *The Constitution and the Termination of Treaties.* New York: Garland, 1986.

———, and Michael A. Genovese, eds. *The Presidency and the Law: The Clinton Legacy.* Lawrence: University Press of Kansas, 2002.

American Civil Liberties Union. *Why President Richard Nixon Should Be Impeached.* Washington, DC: Public Affairs Press, 1973.

Amlund, Curtis Arthur. *New Perspectives on the Presidency.* New York: Philosophical Library, 1969.

Anderson, Donald F. *William Howard Taft: A Conservative's Conception of the Presidency.* Ithaca, NY: Cornell University Press, 1973.

Baker, Peter. *The Breach: Inside the Impeachment and Trial of William Jefferson Clinton.* New York: Scribner, 2000.

Barber, James D. *The Presidential Character.* 4th ed. Englewood Cliffs, NJ: Prentice-Hall, 1992.

Barger, Harold M. *The Impossible Presidency: Illusions and Realities of Executive Power.* Glenview, IL: Scott, Foresman, 1984.

Benedict, Michael Les. *The Impeachment and Trial of Andrew Johnson.* New York: W. W. Norton, 1973.

Berger, Raoul. *Executive Privilege: A Constitutional Myth.* Cambridge: Harvard University Press, 1975.

————. *Impeachment: The Constitutional Problems.* Cambridge: Harvard University Press, 1974.

Bessett, Joseph M., and Jeffery Tulis, eds. *The Presidency in the Constitutional Order.* Baton Rouge: Louisiana State University Press, 1981.

Bickel, Alexander M. *Reform and Continuity: The Electoral College, the Convention and the Party System.* New York: Harper and Row, 1971.

Blackman, John L., Jr. *Presidential Seizure and Labor Disputes.* Cambridge: Harvard University Press, 1967.

Brandy, Gene F., and Donald L. Helmich. *Executive Succession: Toward Excellence in Corporate Leadership.* Englewood Cliffs, NJ: Prentice-Hall, 1984.

Brant, Irving. *Impeachment: Trials and Errors.* New York: Knopf, 1972.

Breckenridge, Adam Carlyle. *The Executive Privilege: Presidential Control over Information.* Lincoln: University of Nebraska Press, 1974.

Burns, James M. *Presidential Government: The Crucible of Leadership.* Boston: Houghton-Mifflin, 1973.

Cann, Steven J. *Administrative Law.* 3d ed. Thousand Oaks, CA: Sage, 2001.

Chase, Harold W. *Federal Judges: The Appointing Process.* Minneapolis: University of Minnesota Press, 1972.

Cheney, Dick, et al. *War Powers and the Constitution.* Washington, DC: American Enterprise Institute for Public Policy Research, 1984.

Cooper, Phillip. *By Order of the President: The Use and Abuse of Executive Direct Action.* Lawrence: University Press of Kansas, 2002.

Corwin, Edward S. *The President: Office and Powers, 1787–1984.* 5th ed. New York: New York University Press, 1984.

Crabb, Cecil V. *Invitation to Struggle: Congress, the President, and Foreign Policy.* 4th ed. Washington, DC: Congressional Quarterly, 1992.

Cronin, Thomas E., ed. *The Presidential Advisory System.* New York: Harper & Row, 1969.

Crovitz, L. Gordon, and Jeremy A. Rabkin, eds. *The Fettered Presidency: Legal Constraints on the Executive Branch.* Washington, DC: American Enterprise Institute, 1989.

De Chambrum, Adolphe. *The Executive Power in the United States: A Study of Constitutional Law.* Holmes Beach, FL: William W. Gaunt and Sons, 1974.

Denton, Robert E., Jr., and D. F. Hahn. *Presidential Communication: Description and Analysis.* New York: Praeger, 1986.

Dershowitz, Alan M. *Supreme Injustice: How the High Court Hijacked Election 2000.* Oxford: Oxford University Press, 2001.

Dionne, E. J., and William Kristol, eds. *Bush v. Gore: The Court Case and the Commentary.* Washington, DC: Brookings Institution Press, 2001.

Donovan, Robert J. *Conflict and Crisis: The Presidency of Harry S. Truman, 1945–1948.* New York: W. W. Norton, 1977.

Edwards, George C. III. *Presidential Influence in Congress.* San Francisco: Freeman, 1980.

Fausold, Martin, and Alan Shank, eds. *The Constitution and the American Presidency.* Albany: State University of New York, 1991.

Feerick, John D. *From Failing Hands: The Story of Presidential Succession*. New York: Fordham University Press, 1965.

Fisher, Louis. *President and Congress: Power and Policy.* New York: Free Press, 1973.

———. *Presidential Spending Power.* Princeton, NJ: Princeton University Press, 1975.

———. *The Constitution Between Friends: Congress, The President, and The Law.* Rev. ed. New York: St. Martin's Press, 1985.

———. *Constitutional Conflicts Between Congress and the President.* 3d ed. Princeton, NJ: Princeton University Press, 1991.

Fowler, Michael R. *Thinking About Human Rights: Contending Approaches to Human Rights in U.S. Foreign Policy.* Lanham, MD: University Press of America, 1987.

Friedland, Robert A. *Struggle for Supremacy: Presidential War Power & Foreign Policy.* Ardsley-on-Hudson, NY: Transnational, 1987.

Funderburk, Charles. *Presidents and Politics: The Limits of Power.* Pacific Grove, CA: Brooks/Cole, 1982.

Genovese, Michael A. *The Supreme Court, the Constitution, and Presidential Power.* Washington, DC: University Press of America, 1980.

Gillman, Howard. *The Votes That Counted: How The Court Decided The 2000 Presidential Election.* Chicago: University of Chicago Press, 2001.

Glennon, Michael J. *Constitutional Diplomacy.* Princeton, NJ: Princeton University Press, 1990.

Goldman, Jerry, ed. *Bush v. Gore.* Urbana: University of Illinois Press, 2002.

Goldsmith, William M., ed. *Growth of Presidential Power: A Documentary History.* New York: Chelsea House, 1983.

Greene, Abner. *Understanding the 2000 Election: A Guide to the Legal Battles that Decided the Presidency.* New York: New York University Press, 2001.

Haight, David, and L. Johnston, eds. *The President: Roles and Powers.* Chicago: Rand McNally, 1969.

Hardin, Charles M. *Presidential Power and Accountability.* Chicago: University of Chicago Press, 1974.

Hart, James. *The Ordinance-Making Powers of the President of the United States.* 2d ed. New York: Da Capo Press, 1971.

Hart, John. *The Presidential Branch.* Elmsford, NY: Pergamon Press, 1987.

Henkin, Louis. *Foreign Affairs and the Constitution.* New York: Foundation Press, 1972.

Hirschfield, Robert S. *The Power of the Presidency.* 2d ed. Chicago: Aldine, 1973.

Jackson, Carlton. *Presidential Vetos, 1792–1945.* Athens: University of Georgia Press, 1967.

Javits, Jacob Koppell. *Who Makes War: The President Versus Congress.* New York: Morrow, 1973.

Johnson, Loch K. *The Making of International Agreements: Congress Confronts the Executive.* New York: New York University Press, 1984.

Johnstone, Robert M. *Jefferson and the Presidency: Leadership in the Young Republic.* Ithaca, NY: Cornell University Press, 1978.

Kallenbach, Joseph E. *The American Chief Executive.* New York: Harper and Row, 1966.

Kessler, Francis P. *The Dilemmas of Presidential Leadership: Of Caretakers and Kings.* Englewood Cliffs, NJ: Prentice-Hall, 1982.

Keynes, Edward. *Undeclared War: Twilight Zone of Constitutional Power.* University Park: Pennsylvania State University Press, 1991.

Koenig, Louis W. *The Chief Executive.* 5th ed. New York: Harcourt, Brace and World, 1986.

———, et al. *Congress, the Presidency, and the Taiwan Relation Act.* New York: Praeger, 1985.

Labovitz, John R. *Presidential Impeachment.* New Haven, CT: Yale University Press, 1978.

Latham, Earl. *Kennedy and Presidential Power.* Lexington, MA: Heath, 1972.

Lofgren, Charles. *Government from Reflection and Choice: Constitutional Essays on War, Foreign Relations and Federalism.* New York: Oxford University Press, 1986.

Longaker, Richard P. *The Presidency and Civil Liberties.* Ithaca, NY: Cornell University Press, 1962.

Longley, Lawrence D., and Alan G. Braun. *The Politics of Electoral College Reform.* 2d ed. New Haven, CT: Yale University Press, 1975.

Lowi, Theodore J. *The Personal President: Power Invested, Promise Unfulfilled.* Ithaca, NY: Cornell University Press, 1986.

Lynn, Naomi B., and Arthur F. McClure. *The Fulbright Premise: Senator J. William Fulbright's Views on Presidential Power.* Cranbury, NJ: Bucknell University Press, 1973.

Mackenzie, G. Galvin. *The Politics of Presidential Appointment.* New York: Free Press, 1980.

Meltsner, Arnold J., ed. *Politics and the Oval Office: Toward Presidential Governance.* San Francisco: ICS Press, 1981.

Merry, Henry J. *Constitutional Function of Presidential-Administrative Separation.* Washington, DC: University Press of America, 1978.

———. *Five-Branch Government: The Full Measure of Constitutional Checks and Balances.* Urbana: University of Illinois Press, 1980.

Miller, Arthur S. *Presidential Power in a Nutshell.* St. Paul, MN: West, 1977.

Milton, George Fort. *The Use of Presidential Power, 1789–1943.* New York: Octagon Books, 1965.

Moore, John N. *Law and the Indo-China War.* Princeton, NJ: Princeton University Press, 1972.

Nathan, Richard P. *The Plot That Failed: Nixon and the Administrative Presidency.* New York: John Wiley & Sons, 1975.

Navasky, Victor. *Kennedy Justice.* New York: Atheneum, 1977.

Neustadt, Richard E. *Presidential Power: The Politics of Leadership from FDR to Carter.* New York: John Wiley & Sons, 1986.

Orman, John M. *Presidential Secrecy and Deception: Beyond the Power to Persuade.* Westport, CT: Greenwood Press, 1980.

Posner, Richard A. *An Affair of State: The Investigation, Impeachment, and Trial of President Clinton.* Cambridge: Harvard University Press, 1999.

———. *Breaking the Deadlock: The 2000 Election, the Constitution, and the Courts.* Princeton, NJ: Princeton University Press, 2001.

Pusey, Merlo J. *The Way We Go to War.* Boston: Houghton-Mifflin, 1971.

Raven-Hansen, Peter. *First Use of Nuclear Weapons: Under the Constitution, Who Decides?* Westport, CT: Greenwood Press, 1987.

Reveley, W. Taylor. *War Powers of the President and Congress: Who Holds the Arrow and Olive Branch?* Charlottesville: University Press of Virginia, 1981.

Roche, John, and Leonard Levy. *The Presidency.* New York: Harcourt, Brace and World, 1964.

Rossiter, Clinton. *The Supreme Court and the Commander-in-Chief.* Ithaca, NY: Cornell University Press, 1976.

Rozell, Mark J. *Executive Privilege: Presidential Power, Secrecy, and Accountability.* 2d ed. Lawrence: University Press of Kansas, 2002.

Rush, Kenneth, et al. *The President, the Congress, and Foreign Policy: A Joint Project of the Association of Former Members of Congress and the Atlantic Council of the United States.* Lanham, MA: University Press of America, 1986.

Schlesinger, Arthur M., Jr. *The Imperial Presidency.* Boston: Houghton-Mifflin, 1988/89.

Scigliano, Robert. *The Supreme Court and the Presidency.* New York: The Free Press, 1971.

Shull, Steven A., ed. *The Two Presidencies: A Quarter Century Reassessment.* Chicago: Nelson-Hall, 1991.

Silva, Ruth C. *Presidential Succession.* Westport, CT: Greenwood, 1968.

Smith, John Malcolm. *Powers of the President During Crises.* New York: Da Capo Press, 1972.

Sunstein, Cass R., and Richard A. Epstein, eds. *The Vote: Bush, Gore and the Supreme Court.* Chicago: University of Chicago Press, 2001.

Tatalovich, Raymond, and Byron W. Daynes. *Presidential Power in the United States.* Pacific Grove, CA: Brooks/Cole, 1984.

Thompson, Dennis F. *Just Elections: Creating a Fair Electoral Process in the United States.* Chicago: University of Chicago Press, 2002.

Tugwell, Rexford G., and T. E. Cronin. *The Presidency Reappraised.* 2d ed. New York: Praeger, 1977.

Westin, Alan F. *The Anatomy of a Constitutional Law Case.* Reprinted ed. New York: Columbia University Press, 1990.

Young, Donald. *American Roulette: The History and Dilemma of the Vice Presidency.* New York: Holt, Rinehart and Winston, 1972/74.

Civil Rights and Liberties

Abernathy, Glenn. *The Right of Assembly and Association.* 2d ed. Columbia: South Carolina University Press, 1981.

Abraham, Henry J., and Barbara A. Perry. *Freedom & the Court: Civil Rights & Liberties in the United States.* 8th ed. Lawrence: University Press of Kansas, 2003.

Ahdar, Rex H., ed. *Law and Religion.* Burlington, VT: Ashgate, 2000.

Alderman, Ellen, and Caroline Kennedy. *The Right to Privacy.* New York: Alfred Knopf, 1995.

Amar, Akhil Reed. *The Constitution and Criminal Procedure: First Principles.* New Haven, CT: Yale University Press, 1997.

Anastapolo, George. *The Constitutionalist: Notes on the First Amendment.* Dallas: Southern Methodist University Press, 1971.

Anderson, Lloyd C. *Voices from a Southern Prison.* Athens: University of Georgia Press, 2000.

Anzalone, Christopher A., ed. *Supreme Court Cases On Gender And Sexual Equality, 1787–2001.* Armonk, NY: M E. Sharpe, 2002.

———, ed. *Supreme Court Cases on Political Representation, 1787–2001.* Armonk, NY: M. E. Sharpe, 2002.

Auerbach, Jerold S. *Justice Without Law?* New York: Oxford University Press, 1983.

Aufderheide, Patricia, ed., *Beyond PC: Towards a Politics of Understanding.* St. Paul, MN: Graywolf Press, 1992.

Baer, Judith A. *Equality Under the Constitution: Reclaiming the Fourteenth Amendment.* Ithaca, NY: Cornell University Press, 1983.

———. *Women in American Law: The Struggle toward Equality from the New Deal to the Present.* New York: Holmes & Meier, 1991.

Baez, Benjamin. *Affirmative Action, Hate Speech, and Tenure: Narratives about Race, Law and the Academy.* New York: Routledge Falmer, 2002.

Baker, Gordon E. *The Reapportionment Revolution.* New York: Random House, 1966.

Baker, Liva Miranda. *Crime, Law and Politics*. New York: Atheneum, 1983.

Balkin, Jack M., ed. *What "Brown v. Board of Education" Should Have Said: The Nation's Top Legal Experts Rewrite America's Landmark Civil Rights Decision*. New York: New York University Press, 2001.

Ball, Howard. *The Bakke Case: Race, Education and Affirmative Action*. Lawrence: University Press of Kansas, 2000.

Barron, Jerome A., and C. Thomas Dienes. *First Amendment Law in a Nutshell*. 2d. ed. Eagan, MN: West Group, 2000.

Barsh, Lawrence, and James Youngblood Henderson. *The Road: Indian Tribes and Political Liberty*. Berkeley: University of California Press, 1982.

Beardslee, William R. *The Way Out Must Lead In: Life Histories in the Civil Right Movement*. Rev. ed. Westport, CT: Hill, Lawrence, 1983.

Becker, Carl L. *Freedom and Responsibility in the American Way of Life*. New York: Knopf, 1949, 1955, 1960, 1965.

Bedau, Hugo Adam. *The Death Penalty in America: Current Controversies*. New York: Oxford University Press, 1998.

Bell, Derrick A., Jr. *Race, Racism and American Law*. 2d ed. Boston: Little, Brown, 1980.

———. *And We are Not Saved: The Elusive Quest for Racial Justice*. New York: Basic Books, 1987.

———. *Faces at the Bottom of the Well*. New York: Basic Books, 1992.

Benokraitis, Nijole V., and Joe R. Feagin. *Affirmative Action and Equal Opportunity: Action, Inaction, Reaction*. Boulder, CO: Westview Press, 1978.

Berg, Thomas C. *Berg's The State and Religion in a Nutshell*. Eagan, MN: West Group, 1998.

Berger, Raoul. *Death Penalties: The Supreme Court's Obstacle Course*. Cambridge: Harvard University Press, 1982.

Berlowitz, Marvin J., and Ronald S. Edari, eds. *Racism and the Denial of Human Rights: Beyond Ethnicity*. Minneapolis, MN: MEP, 1984.

Berns, Walter. *Freedom, Virtue, and the First Amendment*. Baton Rouge: Louisiana State University Press, 1965, 1969, 1970.

———. *Religion and the Constitution*. Washington, DC: American Enterprise Institute for Public Policy Research, 1984.

Bernstein, David E. *Only One Place of Redress: African Americans, Labor Regulations, and the Courts from Reconstruction to the New Deal*. Durham, NC: Duke University Press, 2001.

Berry, Mary Frances. *Military Necessity and Civil Rights Policy: Black Citizenship and the Constitution, 1861–1868*. Port Washington, NY: Kennikat Press, 1977.

Bigel, Alan I. *The Supreme Court on Emergency Powers, Foreign Affairs, and Protection of Civil Liberties*. Lanham, MD: University Press of America, 1986.

Biskupic, Joan, and Elder Witt, eds. *The Supreme Court and Individual Rights*. 3d ed. Washington, DC: Congressional Quarterly, 1997.

Black, Charles L., Jr. *The Humane Imagination*. Woodbridge, CT: Ox Bow Press, 1986.

Blanck, Peter David, ed. *Employment, Disability, and the Americans with Disabilities Act: Issues in Law, Public Policy, and Research*. Evanston, IL: Northwestern University Press, 2000.

Blaustein, Albert P., and Clarence C. Ferguson, Jr. *Desegregation and the Law*. 2d ed. New Brunswick, NJ: Rutgers University Press, 1962.

Boles, Janet K. *The Politics of the Equal Rights Amendment: Conflict and the Decision Process*. New York: Longman, 1979.

Bollinger, Lee C., and Geoffrey R. Stone, eds. *Eternally Vigilant: Free Speech in the Modern Era*. Chicago: University of Chicago Press, 2002.

Boozhie, E. X. *The Outlaw's Bible: How to Evade the System Using Constitutional Strategy.* Scottsdale, AZ: Circle-A, 1988.

Bosmajian, Haig A., ed. *The Freedom to Read.* New York: Neal-Schuman, 1987.

Bosworth, Matthew H. *Courts as Catalysts: State Supreme Courts and Public School Finance Equity.* Albany: State University of New York Press, 2001.

Bowles, Samuel, and Herbert Gintis. *Democracy and Capitalism: Property, Community, and the Contradiction of Modern Social Thought.* New York: Basic Books, 1987.

Brant, Irving. *The Bill of Rights: Its Origin and Meaning.* Indianapolis: Bobbs-Merrill, 1967.

Breckenridge, Adam Carlyle. *The Right to Privacy.* Lincoln: University of Nebraska Press, 1970.

Brenton, Myron. *The Privacy Invaders.* New York: Coward-McCann, 1964.

Brown, Everett Somerville. *Ratification of the Twenty-first Amendment to the Constitution of the United States: State Convention Records and Laws.* New York: Da Capo Press, 1970.

Bullock, Charles, and Charles M. Lamb. *Implementation of Civil Rights Policy.* Monterey, CA: Brooks/Cole, 1984.

Bumiller, Kristin. *The Civil Rights Society: The Social Construction of Victim.* Baltimore: Johns Hopkins University Press, 1988.

Bunker, Matthew D. *Critiquing Free Speech: First Amendment Theory and the Challenge of Interdisciplinarity.* Mahwah, NJ and London, UK: Lawrence Erlbaum Associates, 2001.

Burnett, Cathleen. *Justice Denied: Clemency Appeals in Death Penalty Cases.* Boston: Northeastern University Press, 2002.

Cahn, Edmond, ed. *The Great Rights.* New York: Macmillan, 1963.

Carlson, Andrew. *The Antiquated Right: An Argument for the Repeal of The Second Amendment.* New York: Peter Lang, 2002.

Carr, Robert K. *Federal Protection of Civil Fights: Quest for a Sword.* Ithaca, NY: Cornell University Press, 1947.

Carter, Lief. *An Introduction to Constitutional Interpretation: Cases in Law and Religion.* New York: Longman, 1991.

Carter, T. Barton, et al. *The First Amendment and the Fourth Estate.* 6th ed. Atlanta, GA: Foundation Press, 1994.

Chaffee, Zechariah, Jr. *Free Speech in the United States.* Cambridge: Harvard University Press, 1942.

———. *How Human Rights Got into the Constitution.* Boston: Boston University Press, 1952.

———. *Documents on Fundamental Human Rights.* 3 vols. Cambridge: Harvard University Press, 1963.

———. *The Blessings of Liberty.* Philadelphia: J. B. Lippincott, 1973.

Chandler, Ralph. *The Constitutional Law Dictionary: Individual Rights Supplement.* Santa Barbara, CA: ABC-CLIO, 1987, 1991, 1995, 1997.

Chase, Harold W. *Security and Liberty, the Problem of Native Communists, 1947–1955.* Garden City, NY: Doubleday, 1955.

Choper, Jesse H., Richard H. Fallon, Jr., Yale Kamisar, and Steven H. Shiffrin. *Constitutional Rights and Liberties: Cases-Comments-Questions.* St. Paul, MN: West Group, 2001.

Commager, Henry S. *Freedom, Loyalty, Dissent.* New York: Oxford University Press, 1954.

Conwey, Flo, and Jim Siegelman. *Holy Terror: The Fundamentalist War on America's Freedoms in Religion, Politics, and Our Private Lives.* New York: Dell, 1984.

Cook, Constance Ewing. *Nuclear Power and Legal Advocacy: The Environmentalists and the Courts.* Lexington, MA: Lexington Books, D. C. Heath, 1980.

Cook, Joseph G. *Constitutional Rights of the Accused.* 2d ed. New York: Lawyers Cooperative Publishing Co., 1985.

———, and John L. Sobieski. *Civil Rights Actions.* New York: Bender, Matthew, 1986.

Cook, Thomas I. *Democratic Rights Versus Communist Activity.* Garden City, NY: Doubleday, 1954.

Cookson, Catharine. *Regulating Religion: The Courts and the Free Exercise Clause.* New York: Oxford University Press, 2001.

Corbin, Carole L. *The Right to Vote.* New York: Watts, Franklin, 1985.

Cortner, Richard C. *Civil Rights and Public Accommodations: The Heart of Atlanta and McClung Cases.* Lawrence: University Press of Kansas, 2001.

———. *The Supreme Court and the Second Bill of Rights: The Fourteenth Amendment and the Nationalization of Civil Liberties.* Madison: University of Wisconsin Press, 1981.

Corwin, Edward S. *Liberty Against Government.* Baton Rouge: Louisiana State University Press, 1948.

Cossman, Brenda, and Judy Fudge, eds. *Privatization, Law, and the Challenge to Feminism.* Toronto: University of Toronto Press, 2002.

Coutin, Susan Bibler. *Legalizing Moves: Salvadoran Immigrants Struggle for U.S. Residency.* Ann Arbor: University of Michigan Press, 2000.

Cover, Robert. *Justice Accused: Antislavery.* New Haven, CT: Yale University Press, 1975.

Cowles, Willard Bunce. *Treaties and Constitutional Law: Property Interferences and Due Process of Law.* Westport, CT: Greenwood Press, 1975.

Crosby, Faye J., and Cheryl Vandeveer, eds. *Sex, Race, and Merit: Debating Affirmative Action in Education and Employment.* Ann Arbor: University of Michigan Press, 2000.

Curtis, Michael Kent. *Free Speech, "The People's Darling Privilege": Struggles for Freedom of Expression in American History.* Durham, NC: Duke University Press, 2000.

Dahl, Robert A. *Democracy, Liberty & Equality.* Philadelphia: Coronet Books, 1986.

Davidson, Chandler, and Bernard Grofman, eds. *Quiet Revolution in the South: The Impact of the Voting Rights Act 1965–1990.* Princeton, NJ: Princeton University Press, 1994.

DeGrazia, Edward. *Girls Lean Back Everywhere: The Law of Obscenity and the Assault on Genius.* New York: Random House, 1992.

———, and R. K. Newan. *Banned Films: Movies' Censors and the First Amendment.* New York: R. R. Bowker, 1982.

DeLaet, Debra L. *U.S. Immigration Policy in an Age of Rights.* Westport, CT: Praeger, 2000.

Dilliard, Irving, ed. *The Spirit of Liberty: Papers and Addresses of Learned Hand.* 3d ed. New York: Knopf, 1960.

Dimond, Paul R. *Beyond Busing: Inside the Challenge to Urban Segregation.* Ann Arbor: University of Michigan Press, 1985.

Dixon, Robert G. *Democratic Representation: Reapportionment in Law and Politics.* New York: Oxford University Press, 1968.

Donner, Frank J. *The Age of Surveillance: The Aims and Methods of America's Political Intelligence System.* New York: Knopf, 1980.

Donson, Fiona J. L. *Legal Intimidation: A Slap in the Face of Democracy.* London: Free Association Books, 2000.

Dorn, Edwin. *Rules and Racial Equality.* New Haven, CT: Yale University Press, 1979.

Dorsen, Norman, ed. *The Rights of Americans: What They Are—What They Should Be.* New York: Vintage Books, 1972.

———, ed. *Our Endangered Rights: The ACLU Reports on Civil Liberties Today.* New York: Pantheon Books, 1984.

———, and Stephen Gillers, eds. *None of Your Business: Government Secrecy in America.* New York: Penguin Books, 1975.

Douglas, William Orville. *Freedom of the Mind.* Garden City, NJ: Doubleday, 1962.

Downs, Donald Alexander. *The New Politics of Pornography.* Chicago: University of Chicago Press, 1989.

Dudziak, Mary L. *Cold War Civil Rights: Race and the Image of American Democracy.* Princeton, NJ: Princeton University Press, 2000.

Eagles, Charles W., ed. *The Civil Rights Movement in America.* Jackson: University Press at Mississippi, 1986.

Easton, Susan M. *The Problem of Pornography: Regulation and the Right to Free Speech.* New York: Routledge, 1994.

Edds, Margaret. *Free at Last.* Bethesda, MD: Adler & Adler, Publishers, 1987.

Ehrlander, Mary F. *Equal Educational Opportunity: Brown's Elusive Mandate.* New York: LFB Scholarly Publishing, 2002.

Eisenberg, Theodore. *Civil Rights Legislation.* 3d ed. Charlottesville, VA: Michie, 1991.

Elam, Stanley M., ed. *Public Schools and the First Amendment.* Bloomington, IN: Phi Delta Kappa Educational Foundation, 1983.

Elliff, John T. *The Reform of FBI Intelligence Operations.* Princeton, NJ: Princeton University Press, 1979.

Emerson, Thomas I. *The System of Freedom of Expression.* New York: Random House, 1970.

Engberg, Edward. *The Spy in the Corporate Structure and the Right to Privacy.* Cleveland: World, 1967.

Ennis, Bruce, and Loren Siegel. *The Rights of Mental Patients.* New York: Avon Books, 1978.

Epstein, Lee, and Joseph F. Kobylka. *The Supreme Court and Legal Change: Abortion and the Death Penalty.* Chapel Hill: University of North Carolina Press, 1992.

Epstein, Richard A. *Takings: Private Property and the Power of Eminent Domain.* Cambridge: Harvard University Press, 1985.

Eskridge, William N., Jr. *Equality Practice: Civil Unions and the Future of Gay Rights.* New York: Routledge, 2002.

Evans, Tony, ed. *Human Rights Fifty Years Ago: A Reappraisal.* Manchester, UK: Manchester University Press, 1998.

Fager, Charles. *Selma, Nineteen Sixty-Five: The March That Changed the South.* New York: Beacon Press, 1985.

Failer, Judith Lynn. *Who Qualifies for Rights? Homelessness, Mental Illness, and Civil Commitment.* Ithaca, NY: Cornell University Press, 2002.

Fairman, Charles, and Stanley Morrison. *The Fourteenth Amendment and the Bill of Rights: The Incorporation Theory.* New York: Da Capo Press, 1970.

Farley, Reynolds. *Black and White.* Cambridge: Harvard University Press, 1986.

Farmer, James. *Lay Bare the Heart: An Autobiography of the Civil Rights Movement.* New York: Arbor House, 1985.

Felkenes, George T. *Constitutional Law for Criminal Justice.* 2d ed. Englewood Cliffs, NJ: Prentice-Hall, 1988.

Fellman, David. *The Constitutional Right of Association.* Chicago: University of Chicago Press, 1963.

———. *The Defendant's Rights Today.* Madison: University of Wisconsin Press, 1976.

Finkelman, Paul. *The Law of Freedom and Bondage: A Casebook.* New York: Oceana, 1986.

———. *Religious Liberty in America: Political Safeguards.* Lawrence: University Press of Kansas, 2002.

Flack, Horace Edgar. *The Adoption of the Fourteenth Amendment.* Gloucester, MA: P. Smith, 1965.

Fliter, John A. *Prisoners' Rights: The Supreme Court and Evolving Standards of Decency.* Westport, CT: Greenwood Press, 2001.

Franklin, Bob, ed. *The Rights of Children*. Oxford: Blackwell, 1986.

Frederickson, George H., and Ralph Clark Chandler, eds. *Citizenship and Public Administration*. Washington, DC: American Society for Public Administration, 1984.

Freund, Paul. *Religion and the Public Schools*. Cambridge: Harvard University Press, 1965.

Friedland, Martin L. *Double Jeopardy*. Oxford: Clarendon Press, 1969.

Friedrich, Carl J. *Transcendent Justice: The Religious Dimensions of Constitutionalism*. Durham, NC: Duke University Press, 1964.

Friendly, Alfred. *Crime and Publicity: The Impact of News and the Administration of Justice*. Millwood, NY: Kraus, 1975.

Garcia, Alfredo. *The Fifth Amendment: A Comprehensive Approach*. Westport, CT: Greenwood Press, 2002.

Garrow, David J. *Liberty and Sexuality: The Right to Privacy and the Making of Roe v. Wade*. New York: Macmillan, 1994.

Garvey, Stephen P., ed. *Beyond Repair? America's Death Penalty*. Durham, NC: Duke University Press, 2003.

Gelin, Jacques B., and David W. Miller. *The Federal Law of Eminent Domain*. Charlottesville, VA: Michie, 1982.

Gellhorn, Walter. *Individual Freedom and Governmental Restraints*. Baton Rouge: Louisiana State University Press, 1968.

Giles, Robert, and Robert W. Snyder, eds. *Covering the Courts: Free Press, Fair Trials and Journalistic Performance*. New Brunswick, NJ: Transaction, 1999.

Gillette, William. *The Right to Vote: Politics and the Passage of the Fifteenth Amendment*. Baltimore: Johns Hopkins University Press, 1969.

Gilliom, John. *Overseers of the Poor: Surveillance, Resistance, and the Limits of Privacy*. Chicago: University of Chicago Press, 2001.

Gillman, Howard. *The Constitution Besieged: The Rise and Decline of Lochner Era Police Powers Jurisprudence*. Durham, NC: Duke University Press, 1990.

Glick, Henry R. *The Right to Die*. New York: Columbia University Press, 1992.

Godwin, Mike. *Cyber Rights: Defending Free Speech in the Digital Age*. New York: Random House, 1998.

Gold, E. Richard. *Body Parts: Property Rights and the Ownership of Human Biological Materials*. Washington, DC: Georgetown University Press, 1996.

Goldberg-Hiller, Jonathan. *The Limits to Union: Same-Sex Marriage and the Politics of Civil Rights*. Ann Arbor: University of Michigan Press, 2002.

Goldstein, Robert Justin. *Flag Burning and Free Speech: The Case of Texas v. Johnson*. Lawrence: University Press of Kansas, 2000.

Gora, Joel M. *The Rights of Reporters*. New York: Avon Books, 1974.

Gottlieb, Stephen E. *Morality Imposed: The Rehnquist Court and Liberty in America*. New York: New York University Press, 2000.

Green, Philip. *Retrieving Democracy: In Search of Civic Equality*. Totowa, NJ: Rowman & Littlefield, 1985.

Grimes, Alan P. *Democracy and the Amendments to the Constitution*. Lexington, MA: Lexington Books, 1978.

Griswold, Erwin N. *Search and Seizure: A Dilemma of the Supreme Court*. Lincoln: University of Nebraska Press, 1975.

Grofman, Bernard, et al. *Representation & Redistricting Issues*. Lexington, MA: Lexington Books, 1982.

———. *Political Gerrymandering and the Courts*. New York: Agathon Press, 1990.

Guinn, David E. *Faith on Trial: Communities of Faith, the First Amendment, and the Theory of Deep Diversity*. Lanham, MD: Lexington Books, 2002.

Guliuzza, Frank III. *Over the Wall: Protecting Religious Expression in the Public Square.* Albany: State University of New York Press, 2000.

Guthrie, William Cameron. *Lectures on the Fourteenth Article of Amendment to the Constitution of the United States.* New York: Da Capo Press, 1970.

Hachten, William A. *The Supreme Court on Freedom of the Press: Decisions and Dissents.* Ames: Iowa State University Press, 1968.

Halpern, Stephen, ed. *The Future of Our Liberties: Perspectives on the Bill of Rights.* Westport, CT: Greenwood Press, 1982.

Hamburger, Philip. *Separation of Church and State.* Cambridge: Harvard University Press, 2002.

Hand, Learned. *The Bill of Rights.* New York: Atheneum, 1964.

Handlin, Oscar, and Mary Handlin. *The Dimensions of Liberty.* Cambridge: Harvard University Press, 1961.

Hanson, Royce. *The Political Thicket: Reapportionment and Constitutional Democracy.* Englewood Cliffs, NJ: Prentice-Hall, 1966.

Hardy, David T. *Origins and Development of the Second Amendment.* Southport, CT: Blacksmith, 1986.

Harris, Robert J. *The Quest for Equality: The Constitution, Congress, and the Supreme Court.* Baton Rouge: Louisiana State University Press, 1960.

Hawkins, Gordon, and Franklin E. Zimring. *Pornography in a Free Society.* Cambridge: Cambridge University Press, 1988.

Hayden, Trudy. *Your Rights to Privacy: The Basic ACLU Guide for Your Rights to Privacy.* New York: Avon Books, 1980.

Heins, Marjorie. *Not in Front of the Children: "Indecency," Censorship, and the Innocence of Youth.* New York: Hill and Wang, 2001.

Heller, Francis Howard. *The Sixth Amendment to the Constitution of the United States: A Study in Constitutional Development.* New York: Greenwood Press, 1969.

Hemmer, Joseph J. *Free Speech.* Millbrae, CA: Scarecrow, 1979.

Hempleman, Kathleen A. *Teen Legal Rights.* Rev. ed. Westport, CT: Greenwood Press, 2000.

Hentoff, Nat. *The First Freedom: The Tumultuous History of Free Speech in America.* New York: Delacorte, 1988.

Heumann, Milton. *Plea Bargaining: The Experiences of Prosecutors, Judges, and Defense Attorneys.* Chicago: University of Chicago Press, 1981.

Higginbotham, Leon, Jr. *In the Matter of Color: Race and the American Legal Process: The Colonial Period.* New York: Oxford University Press, 1978.

———. *Shades of Freedom: Racial Politics and Presumptions of the American Legal Process.* New York: Oxford University Press, 1996.

Hill, S. Samuel, and Dennis E. Owen. *The New Religious-Political Right in America.* Nashville: Abingdon Press, 1982.

Hollingsworth, Peggie J., ed. *Unfettered Expression: Freedom in American Intellectual Life.* Ann Arbor: University of Michigan Press, 2000.

Holzer, Henry M. *Sweet Land of Liberty? The Supreme Court & Individual Rights.* Medfield, MA: Common Sense Alternatives, 1983.

Howe, Mark De Wolfe. *Garden and the Wilderness: Religion and Government in American Constitutional History.* Chicago: University of Chicago Press, 1967.

Hudson, Edward. *Freedom of Speech and Press in America.* Washington, DC: Public Affairs Press, 1963.

Huey, Gary L. *Rebel with a Cause: P. D. East, Southern Liberation and the Civil Rights Movement, 1953–71.* Wilmington, DE: Scholarly Research, 1985.

Hull, N. E. H., and Peter Charles Hoffer. *Roe v. Wade: The Abortion Rights Controversy in American History.* Lawrence: University Press of Kansas, 2001.

Humphrey, Hubert H., ed. *School Desegregation, Documents and Commentaries.* New York: Thomas Crowell, 1964.

Hyman, Harold M., and William M. Wiecek. *Equal Justice under Law: Constitutional Development 1835–1875.* New York: Harper & Row, 1982.

Institute of Early American History and Culture Service. *The Development of American Citizenship.* Chapel Hill: University of North Carolina Press, 1984.

Irons, Peter. *The Courage of Their Convictions: Sixteen Americans Who Fought Their Way to the Supreme Court.* New York: Penguin Books, 1990.

———. *May It Please the Court: The First Amendment.* New York: New Press, 1997.

Jackson, Michael W. *Matter of Justice.* New York: Methuen, 1986.

Jamieson, Beth Kiyoko. *Real Choices: Feminism, Freedom, and the Limits of the Law.* University Park: Pennsylvania State University Press, 2001.

Johnson, Frank M., and Tony A. Freyer, eds. *Defending Constitutional Rights.* Athens: University of Georgia Press, 2001.

Kaczorowski, Robert J. *The Nationalization of Civil Rights: Constitutional Theory and Practice in a Racist Society, 1866–1883.* New York: Garland, 1987.

Kalven, Harry. *The Negro and the First Amendment.* Columbus: Ohio State University Press, 1965.

Karnig, Albert K., and Susan Welch. *Black Representation and Urban Policy.* Chicago: University of Chicago Press, 1981.

Katsh, M. Ethan. *The Electronic Media and the Transformation of Law.* New York: Oxford University Press, 1989.

Kaufman-Osborn, Timothy V. *From Noose to Needle: Capital Punishment and the Late Liberal State.* Ann Arbor: University of Michigan Press, 2003.

Kauper, Paul G. *Religion and the Constitution.* Baton Rouge: Louisiana State University Press, 1964.

Kendrigan, Mary Lou. *Political Equality in a Democratic Society: Women in the United States.* Westport, CT: Greenwood Press, 1984.

Kennedy, Randall. *Race, Crime and the Law.* New York: Pantheon Books, 1997.

Kersch, Ken I. *Freedom of Speech: Rights and Liberties under the Law.* Santa Barbara, CA: ABC-CLIO, 2003.

Keynes, Edward. *Liberty, Property, and Privacy: Toward a Jurisprudence of Substantive Due Process.* University Park: Pennsylvania State University Press, 1996.

Keyssar, Alexander. *The Right to Vote: The Contested History of Democracy in the United States.* New York: Basic Books, 2001.

King, Mary. *Freedom Song: A Personal Story of the Nineteen Sixty's Civil Rights Movement.* New York: William Morrow, 1986.

Klein, Irving J., and Christopher J. Morse. *Constitutional Law for Criminal Justice Professionals.* Flushing, NY: Looseleaf, 2003.

Kobylka, Joseph F. *The Politics of Obscenity.* Westport, CT: Greenwood Press, 1991.

Konvitz, Milton R. *Fundamental Liberties of a Free People: Religion, Speech, Press, Assembly.* Ithaca, NY: Cornell University Press, 1957.

———. *A Century of Civil Rights.* New York: Columbia University Press, 1967.

———. *Religious Liberty and Conscience: A Constitutional Inquiry.* New York: Viking Press, 1968.

Kousser, J. Morgan. *Colorblind Justice: Minority Voting Rights and the Undoing of the Second Reconstruction.* Chapel Hill: University of North Carolina Press, 1999.

Kramnick, Isaac, and Lawrence Moore. *The Godless Constitution: The Case against Religious Correctness.* New York: W. W. Norton, 1996.

Kurland, Philip B. *Religion and the Law.* Chicago: Aldine, 1962.

Ladenson, Robert F. *A Philosophy of Free Expression and Its Constitutional Applications.* Totowa, NJ: Rowman & Littlefield, 1983.

LaFave, Wayne R. *Search and Seizure: A Treatise on the Fourth Amendment.* 2d ed. St. Paul, MN: West, 1996.

Landynski, Jacob W. *Searches and Seizures and the Supreme Court.* Baltimore: Johns Hopkins University Press, 1966.

Lasson, Nelson Bernard. *The History and Development of the Fourth Amendment to the United States Constitution.* New York: Da Capo Press, 1970.

Lasswell, Harold D. *National Security and Individual Freedom.* New York: McGraw-Hill, 1950.

Law, Sylvia. *The Rights of the Poor.* New York: Avon Books, 1974.

Lawrence, Frederick M. *Punishing Hate: Bias Crimes under American Law.* Cambridge: Harvard University Press, 2002.

Lebsock, Suzanne. *A Murder in Virginia: Southern Justice on Trial.* New York: W. W. Norton, 2003.

Lee, Francis G. *Neither Conservative nor Liberal: The Burger Court on Civil Rights & Civil Liberties.* Melbourne, FL: Robert E. Krieger Publishing, 1983.

Leo, Richard A., and George C. Thomas III., eds. *The Miranda Debate: Law, Justice, and Policing.* Boston: Northeastern University Press, 2000.

Levy, Leonard. *Legacy of Suppression, Freedom of Speech and Press in Early American History.* Cambridge: Harvard University Press, 1960.

———. *Jefferson and Civil Liberties: The Darker Side.* Cambridge: Harvard University Press, 1963.

———, ed. *Freedom of the Press from Zenger to Jefferson: Early American Libertarian Theories.* Indianapolis: Bobbs-Merrill, 1966.

———. *Origins of the Fifth Amendment: The Right Against Self Incrimination.* New York: Oxford University Press, 1968.

Lester, Richard A. *Reasoning About Discrimination: The Analysis of Professional and Executive Work in Federal Antibias Programs.* Princeton, NJ: Princeton University Press, 1980.

Levine, Alan H., Eve Carey, and Diane Divoky. *The Rights of Students.* Rev. ed. New York: Avon Books, 1977.

Levitan, Sar A., William B. Johnston, and Robert Taggart. *Minorities in the United States.* Washington, DC: Public Affairs Press, 1976.

Lewis, Anthony. *Gideon's Trumpet.* New York: Random House, 1960.

———. *Make No Law: The Sullivan Case and the First Amendment.* New York: Random House, 1991.

Lien, Arnold Johnson. *Concurring Opinion: The Privileges or Immunities Clause of the Fourteenth Amendment.* Westport, CT: Greenwood Press, 1975.

Loeb, Ben F. *Eminent Domain Procedure Under General Statutes.* Chapel Hill: University of North Carolina, Institute of Government, 1984.

Lofton, John. *The Press as Guardian of the First Amendment.* Columbia: University of South Carolina Press, 1980.

Longnecker, Stephen. *Selma's Peacemaker: Ralph Smeltzer & Civil Rights Mediation.* Philadelphia: Temple University Press, 1987.

Lowenthal, David. *No Liberty for License: The Forgotten Logic of the First Amendment.* Dallas: Spence Publishing, 1997.

Mackey, Thomas C. *Pornography on Trial.* Santa Barbara, CA: ABC-CLIO, 2002.

Maguire, Daniel C. *The New Subversives: Anti-Americanism of the Religious Right.* Freedom, CA: Crossroads Press, 1982.

Manwaring, David P. *Render unto Caesar: The Flag-Salute Controversy.* Chicago: University of Chicago Press, 1962.

Martin, John Frederick. *Civil Rights and the Crisis of Liberalism: The Democratic Party 1945–1976.* Boulder, CO: Westview Press, 1979.

Martin, Robert W. T. *The Founding of American Democratic Press Liberty, 1640–1800.* New York: New York University Press, 2001.

Masaoka, Mike, and Bill Hosokawa. *They Call Me Moses Masaoka.* New York: William Morrow, 1987.

Mashaw, Jerry L. *Due Process in the Administrative State.* New Haven, CT: Yale University Press, 1985.

Matthews, John Mabry. *Legislative and Judicial History of the Fifteenth Amendment.* New York: Da Capo Press, 1971.

McClosky, Herbert, and Alida Brill. *Dimensions of Tolerance: What Americans Believe about Civil Liberties.* New York: Russell Sage Foundation, 1983.

McKay, Robert. *Reapportionment: The Law and Politics of Equal Representation.* New York: Twentieth Century Fund, 1965.

McNeil, Genna R. *Groundwork: Charles Hamilton Houston & the Struggle for Civil Rights.* Philadelphia: University of Pennsylvania Press, 1983.

McWhirter, Darien, and Jon Bible. *Privacy as a Constitutional Right.* New York: Quorum Books, 1992.

Meiklejohn, Alexander. *Political Freedom: The Constitutional Powers of the People.* New York: Harper and Row, 1960.

———. *Free Speech in Relation to Self-Government.* Port Washington, NY: Kennikat Press, 1972.

Meltsner, M. *Cruel and Unusual: Supreme Court and Capital Punishment.* New York: William Morrow, 1973.

Mendelson, Wallace. *Discrimination, Based on the Report of the United States Commission on Civil Rights.* Englewood Cliffs, NJ: Prentice-Hall, 1962.

Meyer, Hermine Herta. *The History and Meaning of the Fourteenth Amendment: Judicial Erosion of the Constitution Through the Misuse of the Fourteenth Amendment.* New York: Vantage Press, 1977.

Mian, Badshah K. *American Habeas Corpus: Law, History, and Politics.* San Francisco: Cosmos of Humanists Press, 1984.

Miller, Leonard G. *Double Jeopardy and the Federal System.* Chicago: University of Chicago Press, 1968.

Miller, Robert D. *Involuntary Civil Commitment of the Mentally Ill in the Post-Reform Era.* Springfield, IL: Charles C. Thomas Publishers, 1987.

Miller, Robert T., and Ronald Flowers. *Toward Benevolent Neutrality: Church, State, and the Supreme Court.* 4th ed. Waco, TX: Baylor University Press, 1992.

Mills, Henry E. *A Treatise Upon the Law of Eminent Domain.* Littleton, CO: Fred B. Rothman, 1982.

Milner, Neal A. *The Court and Local Law Enforcement: The Impact of Miranda.* Beverly Hills: Sage, 1971.

Monsma, Stephen V., ed. *Church-State Relations in Crisis: Debating Neutrality.* Lanham, MD: Rowman & Littlefield, 2002.

Mooney, Christopher F. *Boundaries Dimly Perceived: Law, Religion, Education and the Common Good.* Notre Dame, IN: University of Notre Dame Press, 1990.

Morgan, Richard E. *The Supreme Court and Religion*. New York: Free Press, 1972.

———. *The Politics of Religious Conflict: Church and State in America*. Lanham, MD: University Press of America, 1980.

———. *Disabling America: The "Rights Industry" in Our Time*. New York: Basic Books, 1984.

Morris, Aldon D. *The Origins of the Civil Rights Movement: Black Communities Organizing for Change*. New York: Free Press, 1986.

Mosley, Albert G., and Nicholas Capaldi. *Affirmative Action: Social Justice or Unfair Preference?* Lanham, MD: Rowman & Littlefield, 1996.

Murphy, Paul L. *The Meaning of Freedom of Speech: First Amendment Freedoms from Wilson to FDR*. Westport, CT: Greenwood, 1973.

Murphy, Walter F. *Wiretapping on Trial: A Case Study in the Judicial Process*. New York: Random House, 1965.

Mykkeltvedt, Ronald Y. *The Nationalization of the Bill of Rights: Fourteenth Amendment Due Process and Procedural Rights*. New York: Associated Faculty Press, 1983.

Nelson, Harold L., ed. *Freedom of the Press from Hamilton to the Warren Court*. Indianapolis: Bobbs-Merrill, 1967.

Newfield, J. *Cruel and Unusual Justice*. New York: Holt, Rinehart and Winston, 1974.

Norrell, Robert J. *Reaping the Whirlwind: The Civil Rights Movement in Tuskegee*. New York: Random House, 1986. Rev. ed. Chapel Hill: University of North Carolina Press, 1998.

Novak, Michael. *Human Rights and the New Realism: Strategic Thinking in a New Age*. New York: Associated Faculty Press, 1986.

Nuter, Harold F. *American Servicemembers' Supreme Court*. Lanham, MD: University Press of America, 1981.

O'Brien, Dan. *Eminent Domain*. Iowa City: University of Iowa Press, 1990.

O'Brien, David M. *Privacy, Law, and Public Policy*. New York: Praeger, 1979.

O'Brien, John L. *National Security and Individual Freedom*. Cambridge: Harvard University Press, 1955.

O'Connor, Karen. *Women's Organizations' Use of the Courts*. Lexington, MA: Lexington Books, 1980.

O'Rourke, Timothy G. *The Impact of Reapportionment*. New Brunswick, NJ: Transaction Books, 1980.

Oberweis, Trish, and Michael Musheno. *Knowing Rights: State Actor's Stories of Power, Identity, and Morality*. Burlington, VT: Ashgate, 2001.

Orfield, Gary. *Must We Bus? Segregated Schools and National Policy*. Washington, DC: The Brookings Institution, 1978.

Palmer, John W. *Constitutional Rights of Prisoners*. 6th ed. Cincinnati: Anderson, 1996.

Paterson, Judith, et al. *Civil Rights Held Hostage: The United States Catholic Conference and the Civil Rights Restoration Act*. Washington, DC: Catholics for a Free Choice, 1987.

Patterson, James T. *Brown v. Board of Education: A Civil Rights Milestone and its Troubled Legacy*. New York: Oxford University Press, 2001.

Paul, Ellen F. *Property Rights and Eminent Domain*. New Brunswick, NJ: Transaction Books, 1987.

———, and Howard Dickman, eds. *Liberty, Property, and Government: Constitutional Interpretation Before the New Deal*. Albany: State University of New York Press, 1989.

Peltason, Jack W. *Fifty-Eight Lonely Men: Southern Federal Judges and School Desegregation*. New York: Harcourt, Brace and World, 1971.

Perry, Richard L. *Sources of Our Liberties*. Chicago: American Bar Foundation, 1964.

Peters, Shawn Francis. *Judging Jehovah's Witnesses: Religious Persecution and the Dawn of the Rights Revolution.* Lawrence: University Press of Kansas, 2000.

Pfeffer, Leo. *The Liberties of an American.* Boston: Beacon Press, 1956.

———. *Church and State in the United States.* New York: Harper & Row, 1964.

———. *Church, State, and Freedom.* Boston: Beacon Press, 1967.

Phillips, Michael J. *The Dilemmas of Individualism: Status, Liberty & American Constitutional Law.* Westport, CT: Greenwood Press, 1983.

Pipel, Harriet E. *Obscenity and the Constitution.* New York: R. R. Bowker, 1973.

Post, Robert C., K. Anthony Appiah, Judith Butler, Thomas C. Grey, and Reva B. Siegel. *Prejudicial Appearances: The Logic of Antidiscrimination Law.* Durham, NC: Duke University Press, 2001.

Pound, Roscoe. *The Development of Constitutional Guarantees of Liberty.* New Haven, CT: Yale University Press, 1967.

———. *The Fourth Estate and the Constitution.* Berkeley: University of California Press, 1991.

Prettyman, Barrett, Jr. *Death and the Supreme Court.* New York: Harcourt, Brace and World, 1961.

Price, Don K. *America's Unwritten Constitution: Science, Religion, and Political Responsibility.* Baton Rouge: Louisiana State University Press, 1985.

Pritchett, C. Herman. *Civil Liberties and the Vinson Court.* Chicago: University of Chicago Press, 1954.

———. *The Political Offender and the Warren Court.* Boston: Boston University Press, 1958.

———. *Constitutional Civil Liberties.* Englewood Cliffs, NJ: Prentice-Hall, 1984.

Provenzano, Johanna Z. *Guide to Title XII.* Wheaton, MD: National Clearinghouse for Bilingual Education, 1984.

Pyle, Christopher H. *Military Surveillance of Civilian Politics, 1967–1970.* New York: Garland, 1986.

———. *Extradition, Politics and Human Rights.* Philadelphia: Temple University Press, 2001.

Rankin, Robert S., and Winifred R. Dallmayr. *Freedom and Emergency Powers in the Cold War.* New York: Appleton-Century-Crofts, 1964.

Redish, Martin H. *Money Talks: Speech, Economic Power, and the Values of Democracy.* New York: New York University Press, 2001.

Reed, Douglas S. *On Equal Terms: The Constitutional Politics of Educational Opportunity.* Princeton, NJ: Princeton University Press, 2001.

Rhode, Deborah. *Justice and Gender.* Cambridge: Harvard University Press, 1989.

Richey, Charles R. *Manual on Employment Discrimination and Civil Rights Actions in the Federal Courts: Attorney's Edition.* New York: Kluwer, 1988.

Riles, Annelise. *The Network Inside Out.* Ann Arbor: University of Michigan Press, 2000.

Ringer, Benjamin B. *We the People and Others: Duality and America's Treatment of Its Racial Minorities.* New York: Methuen, 1986.

Rivkin, Robert S. *The Rights of Servicemen.* New York: Avon Books, 1972.

Roche, John T. *Courts and Rights, The American Judiciary in Action.* 2d ed. New York: Random House, 1966.

Romero, Francine Sanders. *Civil Rights Policymaking in the United States: An Institutional Perspective.* Westport, CT: Praeger, 2002.

Rosenblum, Nancy L., ed. *Obligations of Citizenship and Demands of Faith: Religious Accommodation in Pluralist Democracies.* Princeton, NJ: Princeton University Press, 2000.

Rosengart, Oliver. *The Rights of Suspects.* New York: Avon Books, 1974, 1983.

Ross, Susan C. *The Rights of Women.* 3d ed. New York: Avon Books, 1993.

Rudovsky, David. *The Rights of Prisoners.* New York: Avon Books, 1973.

Rush, Mark E., and Richard L. Engstrom. *Fair and Effective Representation?: Debating Electoral Reform and Minority Rights.* Lanham, MD: Rowman & Littlefield, 2001.

Rutland, Robert A. *The Birth of the Bill of Rights, 1776–1791.* Chapel Hill: University of North Carolina Press, 1966.

Sackman, Julius, and Russell Van Brunt. *Nichols on Eminent Domain.* New York: Matthew Bender, 1986.

Samet, Andrew J., ed. *Human Rights Law and the Reagan Administration: 1981–1983.* Washington, DC: International Law Institute, 1984.

Scheb, John M., and John M. Scheb II. *Criminal Law and Procedure.* 3d ed. Belmont, CA: West/Wadsworth, 1999.

Scheingold, Stuart A. *The Politics of Law and Order.* White Plains, NY: Longman, 1984.

———. *The Politics of Street Crime: Criminal Process and Cultural Obsession.* Philadelphia: Temple University Press, 1991.

Schlesinger, Steven R. *Exclusionary Injustice: The Problem of Illegally Obtained Evidence.* New York: Marcel Dekker, 1977.

Schreibman, Vigdor. *The Doctrines on Race, Economics and Sex.* McLean, VA: Americas Publications, 1988.

Schuck, Peter H. *Suing Government: Citizen Remedies for Official Wrongs.* New Haven, CT: Yale University Press, 1983.

Schuck, Peter H., and Rogers M. Smith. *Citizenship Without Consent: Illegal Aliens in the American Policy.* New Haven, CT: Yale University Press, 1985.

Schwartz, Bernard. *Statutory History of the United States: Civil Rights.* 2 vols. New York: Chelsea House, 1970.

———, ed. *The Fourteenth Amendment: Centennial Volume.* New York: New York University Press, 1970.

———. *Swann's Way: The School Busing Case and the Supreme Court.* Oxford: Oxford University Press, 1986.

———. *The Great Rights of Mankind: A History of the American Bill of Rights.* New York: Oxford University Press, 1992.

Scorer, Catherine, and Ann Sedley. *Amending the Equality Laws.* New York: State Mutual Book and Periodical Service, 1983.

Scotch, Richard K. *From Good Will to Civil Rights: Transforming Federal Disability Policy.* Philadelphia: Temple University Press, 1984.

Shapiro, Martin. *Freedom of Speech: The Supreme Court and Judicial Review.* Englewood Cliffs, NJ: Prentice-Hall, 1966.

———. *The Pentagon Papers and the Courts: A Study in Foreign Policymaking and Freedom of the Press.* San Francisco: Chandler, 1972.

Shiell, Timothy C. *Campus Hate Speech on Trial.* Lawrence: University Press of Kansas, 1998.

Shiffrin, Steven H. *The First Amendment, Democracy, and Romance.* Cambridge: Harvard University Press, 1990.

Shilts, Randy. *Conduct Unbecoming: Gays & Lesbians in the U.S. Military.* New York: St. Martin's Press, 1993.

Sigler, Jay A. *Double Jeopardy: The Development of a Legal and Social Policy.* Ithaca, NY: Cornell University Press, 1969.

Simon, James F. *The Antagonists: Hugo Black, Felix Frankfurter, and Civil Liberties in Modern America.* New York: Simon & Schuster, 1989.

Sindler, Allan P. *Bakke, Defunis, and Minority Admissions: The Quest for Equal Opportunity.* New York: Longman, 1978.

Skrentny, John David, ed. *Color Lines: Affirmative Action, Immigration, and Civil Rights Options for America.* Chicago: University of Chicago Press, 2001.

Slavin, Sarah, ed. *The Equal Rights Amendment: The Policy and Process of Ratification of the 27th Amendment to the U.S. Constitution.* New York: The Harworth Press, 1982.

Smith, Bradley A. *Unfree Speech: The Folly of Campaign Finance Reform.* Princeton, NJ: Princeton University Press, 2001.

Smith, Michael. *Qualified Immunity From Liability for Violations of Federal Rights: A Mollification.* Chapel Hill: University of North Carolina, Institute of Government, 1983.

Smith, Rodney K. *Public Prayer and the Constitution.* Wilmington, DE: Scholarly Resources, 1987.

Smithburn, J. Eric. *Case and Materials in Juvenile Law.* Cincinnati: Anderson, 2002.

Snepp, Frank. *Irreparable Harm: A Firsthand Account of How One Agent Took on the CIA in an Epic Battle over Free Speech.* Lawrence: University Press of Kansas, 2001.

Sornarajah, M., ed. *The Pursuit of Nationalized Property.* Norwell, MA: Kluwer, 1986.

Southwestern Legal Foundation. *Annual Institute on Planning and Zoning and Eminent Domain: Sixteenth Annual Institute.* New York: Matthew Bender, 1987.

Spitzer, Robert J. *The Right to Bear Arms: Rights and Liberties under the Law.* Santa Barbara, CA: ABC-CLIO, 2001.

Spurrier, Robert L., Jr. *Rights, Wrongs and Remedies: Section 1983 and Constitutional Rights Vindication.* New York: Associated Faculty Press, 1986.

Stefan, Susan. *Unequal Rights: Discrimination against People with Mental Disabilities and the Americans with Disabilities Act.* Washington, DC: American Psychological Association, 2001.

Stephens, Otis H. *The Supreme Court and Confessions of Guilt.* Nashville: University of Tennessee Press, 1973.

Stephens, Steven Scott. *The Uncertainty of Legal Rights.* New York: Routledge, 2001.

Stouffer, Samuel A. *Communism, Conformity, and Civil Liberties.* Garden City, NY: Doubleday, 1955.

Strum, Philippa. *Women in the Barracks: The VMI Case and Equal Rights.* Lawrence: University Press of Kansas, 2002.

Sullivan, Harold J. *Civil Rights and Liberties: Provocative Questions and Evolving Answers.* Upper Saddle River, NJ: Prentice-Hall, 2000.

Sunstein, Cass. *Democracy and the Problem of Free Speech.* New York: Free Press, 1993.

Taper, Bernard. *Gomillion v. Lightfoot, the Tuskegee Gerrymander Case.* New York: McGraw-Hill, 1962.

Taylor, Telford. *Two Studies in Constitutional Interpretations: Search, Seizure, and Surveillance, and Fair Trial and Free Press.* Columbus: Ohio State University Press, 1969.

Tedford, Thomas. *Freedom of Speech.* 2d ed. New York: Random House, 1993.

Ten Broek, Jacobus. *Equal Under Law (Anti-Slavery Origins of the Fourteenth Amendment).* New York: Collier Books, 1965.

Theoharis, Athan. *Spying on Americans: Political Surveillance from Hoover to the Huston Plan.* Philadelphia: Temple University Press, 1978.

Thomas, Robert J. *Citizenship, Gender, and Work: The Social Organization of Industrial Agriculture.* Berkeley: University of California Press, 1985.

Thompson, Dennis F. *Just Elections: Creating a Fair Electoral Process in the United States.* Chicago: University of Chicago Press, 2002.

Tribe, Laurence. *Abortion: The Clash of Absolutes.* New York: W. W. Norton, 1990.

Uviller, H. Richard, and William G. Merkel. *The Militia and the Right to Bear Arms, or, How the Second Amendment Fell Silent*. Durham, NC: Duke University Press, 2002.

Van Alstyne, William. *Interpretations of the First Amendment*. Durham, NC: Duke University Press, 1984.

Van Gerpen, Maurice. *Privileged Communication and the Press: The Citizen's Right to Know versus the Law's Right to Confidential News Source Evidence*. Westport, CT: Greenwood Press, 1979.

VanBurkleo, Sandra F. *"Belonging to the World": Women's Rights and Constitutional Culture*. New York: Oxford University Press, 2001.

Vance, Mary A. *Civil Rights in the U.S. Material Published 1980–1984*. Monticello, IL: Vance Bibliographies, 1985.

Vestal, Theodore M. *The Eisenhower Court and Civil Liberties*. Westport, CT: Praeger, 2002.

Vieira, Norman. *Vieira's Constitutional Civil Rights in a Nutshell*. 3d ed. Eagan, MN: West/Wadsworth, 1998.

Von Hirsch, Andrew. *Past or Future Crimes: Deservedness and Dangerousness in the Sentencing of Criminals*. Manchester, UK: Manchester University Press, 1987.

Vose, Clement E. *Caucasians Only: The Supreme Court, the NAACP, and the Restrictive Covenant Cases*. Berkeley: University of California Press, 1967.

Walentyrowicz, Len. *How to Stay in America Legally*. Bethesda, MD: National Press, 1988.

Walker, Sam. *Hate Speech: The History of an American Controversy*. Lincoln: University of Nebraska Press, 1987.

Walker, Samuel. *In Defense of American Liberties: A History of the ACLU*. New York: Oxford University Press, 1990.

———. *The Rights Revolution: Rights and Community in Modern America*. New York: Oxford University Press, 1998.

Walton, Hanes, Jr. *When the Marching Stopped: The Politics of Civil Rights Regulatory Agencies*. Albany: State University of New York Press, 1988.

Walzer, Lee. *Gay Rights on Trial: A Reference Handbook*. Santa Barbara, CA: ABC-CLIO, 2002.

Walzer, Michael. *Obligations: Essays on Disobedience, War, and Citizenship*. Cambridge: Harvard University Press, 1982.

Warren, Earl. *The Bill of Rights and the Military*. New York: University Law Center, 1962.

Warsoff, Louis A. *Equality and the Law*. Westport, CT: Greenwood, 1975.

Wasby, Stephen L., Anthony A. D'Amato, and Rosemary Metrailer. *Desegregation from Brown to Alexander: An Exploration of Supreme Court Strategies*. Carbondale: Southern Illinois University Press, 1977.

Weizer, Paul I. *Sexual Harassment: Cases, Case Studies, & Commentary*. New York: Peter Lang, 2002.

Welch, Michael. *Flag Burning: Moral Panic and the Criminalization of Protest*. New York: Walter de Gruyter, 2000.

———. *Detained: Immigration Laws and the Expanding I.N.S. Jail Complex*. Philadelphia: Temple University Press, 2002.

Welner, Kevin G. *Legal Rights, Local Wrongs: When Community Control Collides with Educational Equity*. Albany: State University of New York Press, 2001.

West, Cornell. *Race Matters*. Boston: Beacon Press, 1993.

Westin, Alan. *Privacy and Freedom*. New York: Atheneum, 1968.

Whalen, Charles, and Barbara Whalen. *The Longest Debate: A Legislative History of the 1964 Civil Rights Act*. Bethesda, MD: Seven Locks Press, 1985.

Whitney, Sharon. *The Equal Rights Amendments: The History and the Movements*. New York: Watts, Franklin, 1984.

Wiener, Solomon. *Questions and Answers on American Citizenship*. New York: Regents, 1982.

Williams, Jerre, et al. *Our Freedoms: Rights and Responsibilities*. Austin: University of Texas Press, 1985.

Williams, Juan. *Eyes on the Prize: America's Civil Rights Years, 1954–1965*. New York: Viking Penguin, 1987.

Williams, Patricia J. *The Alchemy of Race and Rights*. Cambridge: Harvard University Press, 1991.

Williamson, Joe. *A Rage for Order: Black-White Relations in the American South Since Emancipation*. New York: Oxford University Press, 1986.

Wills, Garry. *Under God: Religion in American Politics*. New York: Simon & Schuster, 1990.

Wise, David. *The American Police State*. New York: Random House, 1976.

Yalof, David A., and Kenneth Dautrich. *The First Amendment and the Media in the Court of Public Opinion*. New York: Cambridge University Press, 2002.

Yarbrough, Tinsley E. *Judge Frank Johnson and Human Rights in Alabama*. Tuscaloosa: University of Alabama, 1981.

———. *A Passion for Justice: J. Waties Waring and Civil Rights*. New York: Oxford University Press, 1987.

———. *Race and Redistricting: The Shaw-Cromartie Cases*. Lawrence: University Press of Kansas, 2002.

Zagel, James. *Confessions and Interrogations After Miranda: A Comprehensive Guideline of the Law*. Alexandria, VA: National District Attorneys Association, 1982.

Zalman, Marvin, and Larry J. Siegel. *Criminal Procedure*. 2d ed. Belmont, CA: West/ Wadsworth, 1997.

Zangrando, Robert L. *The NAACP Crusade Against Lynching, 1909–1950*. Philadelphia: Temple University Press, 1980.

Zelden, Charles L. *Voting Rights on Trial: A Handbook with Cases, Laws, and Documents*. Santa Barbara, CA: ABC-CLIO, 2002.

Zimring, Franklin E. *The Contradictions of American Capital Punishment*. New York: Oxford University Press, 2003.

Zinn, Howard. *SNCC: The New Abolitionists*. Westport, CT: Greenwood Press, 1985.

Comparative Constitutional Politics

Abel, Richard L., and Philip S. C. Lewis, eds. *Lawyers in Society: The Common Law World*. Berkeley: University of California Press, 1988.

———. *Lawyers in Society: The Civil Law World*. Berkeley: University of California Press, 1988.

Addo, Michael K., ed. *Freedom of Expression and the Criticism of Judges: A Comparative Study of European Legal Standards*. Burlington, VT: Ashgate, 2000.

Allott, A. N. *Judicial and Legal Systems in Africa*. London: Butterworths, 1970.

Anderson, Ellen. *Judging Bertha Wilson: Law as Large as Life*. Toronto: Osgoode Society for Canadian Legal History and University of Toronto Press, 2001.

Bagehot, Walter. Paul Smith, ed. *The English Constitution*. Cambridge, UK: Cambridge University Press, 2001.

Baker, H. E. *The Legal System of Israel*. Jerusalem: Israel Universities Press, 1968.

Beer, Lawrence W., and John M. Maki. *From Imperial Myth to Democracy: Japan's Two Constitutions, 1889–2002*. Boulder: University Press of Colorado, 2002.

Bell, Daniel A. *East Meets West: Human Rights and Democracy in East Asia*. Princeton, NJ: Princeton University Press, 2000.

Berman, Harold J. *Law and Revolution: The Formation of the Western Legal Tradition*. Cambridge: Harvard University Press, 1983.

Biebesheimer, Christina, and Francisco Meja, eds. *Justice beyond our Borders. Judicial Reforms for Latin America and the Caribbean*. Washington, DC: Inter-American Development Bank, 2000.

Blackshield, Tony, Michael Coper, and George Williams, eds. *The Oxford Companion to the High Court of Australia*. New York and Melbourne: Oxford University Press, 2001.

Blackstone, William. [1765–1769]. *Commentaries on the Laws of England*. Chicago: University of Chicago Press, 1979.

Blair, P. *Federalism and Judicial Review in West Germany*. Oxford: Clarendon Press, 1984.

Blankenburg, Erhard, and Freek Bruinsma. *Dutch Legal Culture*. 2d ed. New York: Kluwer, 1994.

Bodde, D., and C. Morris. *Law in Imperial China*. Philadelphia: University of Pennsylvania Press, 1973.

Brodie, Ian. *Friends of the Court: The Privileging of Interest Group Litigants in Canada*. Albany: State University of New York Press, 2002.

Bryce, James. *Studies in History and Jurisprudence*. London: Oxford University Press, 1901.

Burnett, Christina Duffy, and Burke Marshall, eds. *Foreign in a Domestic Sense: Puerto Rico, American Expansion, and the Constitution*. Durham, NC: Duke University Press, 2001.

Butler, W. *Soviet Law*. London: Butterworths, 1983.

Butler, W., ed. *Basic Documents on the Soviet Legal System*. New York: Oceana, 1983.

Calisse, C. *A History of Italian Law*. New York: Augustus M. Kelley, 1969.

Cappelletti, Mauro. *Judicial Review in the Contemporary World*. Indianapolis: Bobbs-Merrill, 1971.

———. *The Judicial Process in Comparative Perspective*. Oxford: Oxford University Press, 1989.

Cappelletti, Mauro, and W. Cohen. *Comparative Constitutional Law: Cases and Materials*. Indianapolis: Bobbs-Merrill, 1979.

———, eds. *The Modern Systems of Judicial Review: Comparative Constitutional Law*. Indianapolis: Bobbs-Merrill, 1979.

Cappelletti, Mauro, J. H. Merryman, and J. M. Perillo. *The Italian Legal System*. Palo Alto, CA: Stanford University Press, 1967.

Cappelletti, Mauro, and J. M. Perillo. *Civil Procedure in Italy*. The Hague: M. Nijhoff, 1965.

Central Office of Information for British Information Services. *The Legal Systems of Britain*. London: Her Majesty's Stationery Office, 1976.

Cheffins, R. R., and R. N. Tucker. *The Constitutional Process in Canada*. Toronto: McGraw-Hill, 1976.

Chesterman, Michael. *Freedom of Speech in Australian Law: A Delicate Plant*. Burlington, VT: Ashgate, 2000.

Christelow, Allen. *Muslim Law Courts and the French Colonial State in Algeria*. Princeton, NJ: Princeton University Press, 1985.

Claude, Richard, ed. *Comparative Human Rights*. Baltimore: Johns Hopkins University Press, 1976.

Cohen, J. A., R. Edwards, and F. C. Chen, eds. *Essays on China's Legal Tradition*. Princeton, NJ: Princeton University Press, 1980.

Cole, Daniel H. *Pollution and Property: Comparing Ownership Institutions for Environmental Protection*. New York: Cambridge University Press, 2002.

Conant, Lisa. *Justice Contained: Law and Politics in the European Union.* Ithaca, NY: Cornell University Press, 2002.

Cowen, Z., and L. Zines. *Federal Jurisdiction in Australia.* Melbourne: Oxford University Press, 1978.

Crabb, J. H. *The Constitution of Belgium and the Belgian Civil Code.* Littleton, CO: Fred B. Rothman, 1982.

Cruz, Julio Baquero. *Between Competition and Free Movement: The Economic Constitutional Law of the European Community.* Oxford: Hart, 2002.

Daniels, Ronald J., Patrick Macklem, and Kent Roach, eds. *The Security of Freedom: Essays on Canada's Anti-Terrorism Bill.* Toronto: University of Toronto Press, 2001.

Dashwood, Alan, and Angus Johnston, eds. *The Future of the Judicial System of the European Union.* Oxford: Hart, 2001.

David, R., and P. de Vries. *The French Legal System: An Introduction to Civil Law Systems.* New York: Oceana, 1958.

David, Rene, and J. E. C. Brierly. *Major Legal Systems in the World Today: An Introduction to the Comparative Study of the Law.* London: Stevens and Sons, 1978.

Deere, Carmen Diana, and Magdalena Leon. *Empowering Women: Land and Property Rights in Latin America.* Pittsburgh: University of Pittsburgh Press, 2001.

Dias, C. J., R. Luckhamn, D. O. Lynch, and J. C. N. Paul, eds. *Lawyers in the Third World: Comparative and Developmental Perspectives.* Uppsala, Sweden: Scandinavian Institute of African Studies, 1981.

Dicey, A. V. *Introduction to the Study of the Law and the Constitution.* 10th ed. London: Macmillan, 1961.

Dillon, Sara. *International Trade and Economic Law and the European Union.* Oxford: Hart, 2002.

Dinnage, James D., and John F. Murphy. *The Constitutional Law of the European Union.* Cincinnati: Anderson, 1996.

Doern, G. Bruce, and Markus Sharaput. *Canadian Intellectual Property: The Politics of Innovating Institutions and Interests.* Toronto: University of Toronto Press, 2000.

Duchacek, I. D. *Comparative Federalism: The Territorial Dimension of Politics.* Lanham, MA: University Press of America, 1987.

Dunne, Timothy, and Nicholas J. Wheeler, eds. *Human Rights in Global Politics.* New York: Cambridge University Press, 1999.

Dussich, John P. J., Paul C. Friday, Takayuki Okada, Akira Yamagami, and Richard D. Knudten. *Different Responses to Violence in Japan and America.* Monsey, NY: Criminal Justice Press, 2001.

Eberle, Edward J. *Dignity and Liberty: Constitutional Visions in Germany and the United States.* Westport, CT: Praeger Press, 2002.

Edelman, Martin. *Courts, Politics, and Culture in Israel.* Charlottesville: University of Virginia Press, 1994.

Ehlermann, Claus Dieter, and Isabela Antanasiu, eds. *European Competition Law Annual 2000: The Modernisation of EC Antitrust Policy.* Oxford: Hart, 2001.

Ehrmann, H. W. *Comparative Legal Cultures.* Englewood Cliffs, NJ: Prentice-Hall, 1976.

Elliot, Catherine. *French Criminal Law.* Cullompton, UK: Willan, 2001.

Ellmann, Stephen. *In a Time of Trouble: Law and Liberty in South Africa's State of Emergency.* Oxford: Clarendon Press, 1992.

Engelmann, A., S. Williston, and W. C. Holdsworth. *A History of Continental Civil Procedure.* New York: Augustus M. Kelly, 1969.

Eorsi, G. *Comparative Civil (Private) Law.* Budapest: Akademiai Kiado, 1979.

Epp, Charles R. *The Rights Revolution: Lawyers, Activists and Supreme Courts in Comparative Perspective.* Chicago: University of Chicago Press, 1998.

Evans, Tony, ed. *Human Rights Fifty Years Ago: A Reappraisal.* Manchester, UK: Manchester University Press, 1998.

Falk, Richard, Lester Edwin J. Ruiz, and R. B. J. Welker, eds. *Reframing the International: Law, Culture, Politics.* New York and London: Routledge, 2002.

Faure, Murray, and Jan-Erik Lane, eds. *South Africa: Designing New Political Institutions.* Newbury Park, CA: Sage, 1996.

Feldman, Eric. *The Ritual of Rights in Japan: Law, Society, and Health Policy.* New York: Cambridge University Press, 2000.

Fields, Charles B., and Richter H. Moore, Jr. *Comparative Criminal Justice.* Prospect Heights, IL: Waveland Press, 1996.

Franklin, Daniel P., and Michael J. Baun, eds. *Political Culture and Constitutionalism: A Comparative Approach.* Armonk, NY: M. E. Sharpe, 1995.

Gall, G. L. *The Canadian Legal System.* 2d ed. Toronto: Carswell Legal Publications, 1983.

Galligan, Brian. *Politics of the High Court: A Study of the Judicial Branch of Government in Australia.* St. Lucia, Australia: University of Queensland Press, 1987.

Gessner, Volkmar, ed. *Foreign Courts: Civil Litigation in Foreign Legal Cultures.* The Onati International Institute for the Sociology of Law. Aldershot, UK: Dartmouth, 1996.

Gibney, Mark, and Stanislaw Frankowsi, eds. *Judicial Protection of Human Rights: Myth or Reality.* Westport, CT: Praeger, 1999.

Glendon, M., W. M. Gordon, and C. Osawke. *Comparative Legal Traditions in a Nutshell.* St. Paul, MN: West, 1982.

Glennon, Michael J. *Limits of Law, Prerogatives of Power: Interventionism after Kosovo.* New York: Palgrave, 2001.

Goldstein, Judith, Miles Kahler, Robert O. Keohane, and Anne-Marie Slaughter, eds. *Legalization and World Politics.* Cambridge: The MIT Press, 2001.

Goldstein, Leslie Friedman. *Constituting Federal Sovereignty: The European Union in Comparative Context.* Baltimore: Johns Hopkins University Press, 2001.

Gower, Karla K. *Liberty and Authority in Free Expression Law: The United States and Canada.* New York: LFB Scholarly Publishing, 2002.

Greenberg, Douglas, Stanley N. Katz, Melanie Beth Oliviero, and Steven C. Wheatley, eds. *Constitutionalism and Democracy: Transitions in the Contemporary World.* New York: Oxford University Press, 1993.

Guild, Elspeth, and Carol Harlow, eds. *Implementing Amsterdam: Immigration and Asylum Rights in EC Law.* Oxford: Hart, 2001.

Halmai, Gabor, ed. *The Constitution Found?: The First Nine Years of the Hungarian Constitutional Review of Fundamental Human Rights.* Budapest: Indok—Human Rights and Information Documentation Center, 2000.

Hamilton, V. Lee, and Joseph Sanders. *Everyday Justice: Responsibility and the Individual in Japan and the United States.* New Haven, CT and London: Yale University Press, 1992.

Harris, Douglas C. *Fish, Law, and Colonialism: The Legal Capture of Salmon in British Columbia.* Toronto: University of Toronto Press, 2001.

Harvey, Colin J., ed. *Human Rights, Equality and Democratic Renewal in Northern Ireland.* Oxford: Hart, 2000.

Hesse, Joachim Hens, and Nevil Johnson, eds. *Constitutional Policy and Change in Europe.* New York: Oxford University Press, 1995.

Heuston, R. G. *Lives of the Lord Chancellors, 1885–1940.* Oxford: Clarendon Press, 1964.

Hiebert, Janet L. *Charter Conflicts: What is Parliament's Role?* Montreal and Kingston, Canada: McGill-Queen's University Press, 2002.

Humana, Charles. *World Human Rights Guide.* 3d ed. New York: Oxford University Press, 1992.

Hutchinson, T. W., et al., eds. *Africa and Law: Developing Legal Systems in African Commonwealth Nations.* Madison: University of Wisconsin Press, 1968.

Ioffe, O. S. *Soviet Law and Socialist Reality.* Dordrecht/Boston: Martinius Nijhoff, 1985.

Ioffe, O. S., and P. B. Maggs. *Soviet Law in Theory and Practice.* New York: Oceana, 1983.

Jackson, Donald W. *The United Kingdom Confronts the European Convention on Human Rights.* Gainesville: University Press of Florida, 1997.

Jackson, Vicki, and Mark V. Tushnet. *Comparative Constitutional Law.* New York: Foundation Press, 1999.

Jacob, Herbert, Erhard Blankenburg, Herbert M. Kritzer, Dorris Marie Provine, and Joseph Sanders. *Courts, Law, and Politics in Comparative Perspective.* New Haven, CT: Yale University Press, 1996.

Jamieson, Alison. *The Antimafia: Italy's Fight against Organized Crime.* New York: St. Martin's Press, 2000.

Jhappan, Radha, ed. *Women's Legal Strategies in Canada.* Toronto: University of Toronto Press, 2002.

Johnson, David T. *The Japanese Way of Justice: Prosecuting Crime in Japan.* New York: Oxford University Press, 2002.

Johnston, David, and Reinhard Zimmermann, eds. *Unjustified Enrichment: Key Issues in Comparative Perspective.* New York: Cambridge University Press, 2002.

Kassim, Husain. *Sarakhsi Hugo Grotius of the Muslims: The Doctrine of Juristic Preference and the Concepts of Treaties and Mutual Relations.* San Francisco: Autin & Winfield, 1994.

Kenney, Sally J., William M. Reisinger, and John Reitz, eds. *Constitutional Dialogues in Comparative Perspective.* New York: St. Martin's Press, 1999.

Kim, Jae-Young. *Sorting out Deregulation: Protecting Free Speech and Internet Access in the United States, Germany, and Japan.* New York: LFB, 2002.

King, Peter. *Crime, Justice, and Discretion in England: 1740–1820.* New York: Oxford University Press, 2000.

Kinkley, Jeffrey C. *Chinese Justice, the Fiction: Law and Literature in Modern China.* Stanford, CA: Stanford University Press, 2000.

Klug, Heinz. *Constituting Democracy: Law, Globalism, and South Africa's Political Reconstruction.* New York: Cambridge University Press, 2000.

Kojeve, Alexandre. *Outline of a Phenomenology of Right.* Translated by Bryan-Paul Frost and Robert Howse. Lanham, MD: Rowman & Littlefield, 2000.

Kommers, Donald P. *Judicial Politics in West Germany.* Beverly Hills: Sage, 1976.

———. *The Constitutional Jurisprudence of the Federal Republic of Germany.* 2d ed. Durham, NC: Duke University Press, 1997.

Koutrakos, Panos. *Trade, Foreign Policy and Defence in EU Constitutional Law.* Oxford: Hart, 2001.

Kramer, Daniel C. *Comparative Civil Rights and Liberties.* Washington, DC: University Press of America, 1982.

Kritz, Neil J., ed. *Transitional Justice: How Emerging Democracies Reckon with Former Regimes.* Washington, DC: United States Institute of Peace Press, 1995.

Kritzer, Herbert M., ed. *Legal Systems of the World: A Political, Social, and Cultural Encyclopedia.* Santa Barbara, CA: ABC-CLIO, 2002.

Ladany, Laszlo. *Law and Legality in China.* Honolulu: University of Honolulu Press, 1992.

Lauren, Paul Gordon. *The Evolution of International Human Rights: Visions Seen.* Philadelphia: University of Pennsylvania Press, 1998.

Layton, Azza Salama. *International Politics and Civil Rights Policies in the United States, 1941–1960.* Cambridge, UK: Cambridge University Press, 2000.

Linden, A. M., ed. *The Canadian Judiciary.* Toronto: Osgood Hall Law School, York University Press, 1976.

Lobban, Michael. *White Man's Justice: South African Political Trials in the Black Consciousness Era.* New York: Oxford University Press, 1996.

Los, Maria, and Andrzej Zybertowicz. *Privatizing the Police State: The Case of Poland.* New York: St. Martin's Press, 2000.

Ludwikowski, Rett R. *Constitution-Making in the Region of Former Soviet Dominance.* Durham, NC and London: Duke University Press, 1996.

MacDougall, Bruce. *Queer Judgements: Homosexuality, Expression, and the Courts in Canada.* Toronto: University of Toronto Press, 2000.

Macklem, Patrick. *Indigenous Difference and the Constitution of Canada.* Toronto: University of Toronto Press, 2001.

Maddex, Robert L. *Constitutions of the World.* 2d ed. Washington, DC: Congressional Quarterly, 2001.

Markesinis, Basil S. *Foreign Law & Comparative Methodology: A Subject and a Thesis.* Oxford: Hart, 1997.

———. *Always The Same Path: Essays On Foreign Law and Comparative Methodology.* Vol. 2. Oxford: Hart, 2001.

Martin, Benjamin. *Crime and Criminal Justice under the Third Republic: The Shame of Marianne.* Baton Rouge: Louisiana State University Press, 1991.

Marx, Tzvi. *Disability in Jewish Law.* New York: Routledge, 2002.

McCormick, Peter. *Canada's Courts.* Toronto: James Lorimer, 1994.

McWhinney, E. *Judicial Review in the English-Speaking World.* 2d ed. Toronto: University of Toronto Press, 1969.

Melone, Albert P. *Creating Parliamentary Government: The Transition to Democracy in Bulgaria.* Columbus: Ohio State University Press, 1998.

Merin, Yuval. *Equality for Same-Sex Couples: The Legal Recognition of Gay Partnerships in Europe and the United States.* Chicago: University of Chicago Press, 2002.

Merrills, J. G. *The Development of International Law by the European Court of Human Rights.* 2d ed. New York: Manchester University Press, 1993.

Merryman, J. H., and D. S. Clark. *Comparative Law: Western European and Latin American Legal Systems.* Indianapolis: Bobbs-Merrill, 1978.

Milne, David. *The New Canadian Constitution.* Toronto: James Lorimer, 1982.

Milton, F. *The English Magistracy.* London, New York, and Toronto: Oxford University Press, 1967.

Ministry of Law, Justice and Company Affairs. *Judges of the Supreme Court and the High Courts.* New Delhi: Government of India Press, 1980.

Mirchandani, G. C. *Subverting the Constitution in India.* Columbia, MO: South Asia Books, 1977.

Mitchell, Richard J. *Political Bribery in Japan.* Honolulu: University of Hawaii Press, 1996.

Monahan, Patrick. *Politics and the Constitution: The Charter, Federalism and The Supreme Court of Canada.* Toronto: Carswell/Methuen, 1987.

Moore, Erin P. *Gender, Law, and Resistance in India.* Tucson: University of Arizona Press, 2002.

Morgan, David Gwynn. *A Judgment Too Far?: Judicial Activism and the Constitution.* Cork, Ireland: Cork University Press, 2001.

Morrison, F. L. *Courts and the Political Process in England.* Beverly Hills and London: Sage, 1973.

Morton, F. L., and Rainer Knopff. *The Charter Revolution and the Court Party.* Peterborough, Ontario: Broadview Press, 2000.

Mueller, Ingo. *Hitler's Justice: The Courts of the Third Reich.* Cambridge: Harvard University Press, 1991.

Murphy, W. F., and J. Tanenhaus. *Comparative Constitutional Law Cases and Commentaries.* New York: St. Martin's Press, 1977.

Nagel, Stuart S., ed. *Handbook of Global Legal Policy.* New York: Marcel Dekker, 2000.

Narain, Vrinda. *Gender and Community: Muslim Women's Rights in India.* Toronto: University of Toronto Press, 2001

Nelken, David, ed. *Comparing Legal Cultures.* Brookfield, VT: Dartmouth, 1997.

————, ed. *Contrasting Criminal Justice: Getting from Here to There.* Burlington, VT: Ashgate, 2000.

Newberg, Paula R. *Judging the State: Courts and Constitutional Politics in Pakistan.* Cambridge: Cambridge University Press, 1995.

Newman, Frank, and David Weissbrodt, eds. *International Human Rights: Law, Politics and Process.* 2d ed. Cincinnati: Anderson, 1996.

Nirmal, Chiranjivi J., ed. *Human Rights in India: Historical, Social and Political Perspectives.* New York: Oxford University Press, 2000.

Nousianinen, Kevat, Asa Gunnarsson, Karin Lundstrom, and Johanna Niemi-Kiesilainen, eds. *Responsible Selves: Women in the Nordic Legal Culture.* Burlington, VT: Ashgate, 2001.

O'Brien, David M., and Yasuo Ohkoshi. *To Dream of Dreams: Religious Freedom and Constitutional Politics in Postwar Japan.* Honolulu: University of Hawaii Press, 1996.

O'Connell, Rory. *Legal Theory in the Crucible of Constitutional Justice: A Study of Judges and Political Morality in Canada, Ireland and Italy.* Burlington, VT: Ashgate, 2000.

Podgorecki, Adam, and Vittorio Olgiati, eds. *Totalitarian and Post-Totalitarian Law.* The Onati International Institute for the Sociology of Law. Aldershot, UK: Dartmouth, 1996.

Politi, Mauro, and Giuseppe Nesi, eds. *The Rome Statute of the International Criminal Court: A Challenge to Impunity.* Burlington, VT: Ashgate, 2001.

Pue, W. Wesley, ed. *Pepper in our Eyes: The APEC Affair.* Vancouver: University of British Columbia Press, 2000.

Reinisch, August. *International Organizations before National Courts.* Cambridge, UK: Cambridge University Press, 2000.

Rendel, M. *The Administrative Function of the French Conseil d'Etat.* London: Weidenfeld and Nicolson, 1970.

Rhyne, C. S., ed. *Law and Judicial Systems of Nations.* 3d ed. Washington, DC: World Peace Through Law Center, 1978.

Riles, Annelise, ed. *Rethinking the Masters of Comparative Law.* Oxford: Hart, 2001.

Roach, Kent. *The Supreme Court on Trial: Judicial Activism or Democratic Dialogue.* Toronto: Irwin Law, 2001.

Rogowski, Ralf, and Thomas Gawron, eds. *Constitutional Courts in Comparison: The U.S. Supreme Court and the German Federal Constitutional Court.* New York: Berghahn Books, 2002.

Ross, Jeffrey Ian. *Making News of Police Violence: A Comparative Study of Toronto and New York City.* Westport, CT: Praeger, 2000.

Rotberg, Robert I., and Dennis Thompson, eds. *Truth v. Justice: The Morality of Truth Commissions.* Princeton, NJ: Princeton University Press, 2000.

Rueschemeyer, Dietrich. *Lawyers and Their Society: A Comparative Study of the Legal Profession in Germany and in the United States.* Cambridge: Harvard University Press, 1973.

Russell, Peter H., and David M. O'Brien, eds. *Judicial Independence in the Age of Democracy*. Charlottesville: University Press of Virginia, 2001.

Sarat, Austin, and Thomas R. Kearns, eds. *Human Rights: Concepts, Contests, Contingencies*. Ann Arbor: University of Michigan Press, 2001.

Sartori, Giovanni. *Comparative Constitutional Engineering: An Inquiry into Structures, Incentives and Outcomes*. 2d ed. New York: New York University Press, 1997.

Sathe, S. P. *Judicial Activism in India: Transgressing Borders and Enforcing Limits*. New Delhi, India: Oxford University Press, 2002.

Schmidhauser, John, ed. *Comparative Judicial Systems: Challenging Frontiers in Conceptual and Empirical Analysis*. London: Butterworths, 1987.

Schmidt, F., and S. Stromholm. *Legal Values in Modern Sweden*. Stockholm: The Bedminster Press, 1964.

Schubert, Glendon. *Political Culture and Judicial Behavior: Political Culture and Judicial Elites*. 2 vols. Lanham, MD: University Press of America, 1985.

Schubert, Glendon, and D. J. Danelski, eds. *Comparative Judicial Behavior: Cross-Cultural Studies of Political Decision-Making in the East and West*. New York: Oxford University Press, 1969.

Schwartz, Herman. *The Struggle for Constitutional Justice in Post-Communist Europe*. Chicago: University of Chicago Press, 2000.

Sciarra, Silvana, ed. *Labour Law in the Courts: National Judges and the European Court of Justice*. Oxford: Hart, 2001.

Shapiro, Martin. *Courts: A Comparative and Political Analysis*. Chicago: University of Chicago Press, 1981.

Shaw, Jo, and Gillian More, eds. *New Legal Dynamics of European Integration*. Oxford: Oxford University Press, 1995.

Shetreet, S. *Judges on Trial: A Study of the Appointment and Accountability of the English Judiciary*. Amsterdam, Oxford, and New York: North-Holland, 1976.

Shoichi, Koseki. *The Birth of Japan's Postwar Constitution*. Translated by Ray A. Moore. Boulder, CO: Westview Press, 1997.

Solomon, Peter H., Jr., and Todd S. Foglesong. *Courts and Transition in Russia: The Challenge of Judicial Reform*. Boulder, CO: Westview Press, 2000.

Solyom, Laszlo, and George Brunner. *Constitutional Judiciary in a New Democracy: The Hungarian Constitutional Court*. Ann Arbor: University of Michigan Press, 2000.

Sossin, Lorne M. *Boundaries of Judicial Review: The Law of Justiciability in Canada*. Scarborough, Ontario: Carswell, 2000.

Stamatoudi, Irini A. *Copyright and Multimedia Works: A Comparative Analysis*. Cambridge, UK: Cambridge University Press, 2002.

Stevens, R. *Law and Politics: The House of Lords as a Judicial Body, 1800–1976*. London: Weidenfield and Nicolson, 1979.

Stevens, Robert. *The English Judges: Their Role in the Changing Constitution*. Oxford and Portland, OR: Hart, 2002.

Stromholm, S. *An Introduction to Swedish Law*. Vol. 1. Devanter, The Netherlands: Kluwer, 1981.

Sunstein, Cass R. *Designing Democracy: What Constitutions Do*. New York: Oxford University Press, 2001.

Sweet, Alec Stone. *Governing with Judges: Constitutional Politics in Europe*. Oxford: Oxford University Press, 2000.

Tanaka, H., and M. D. H. Smith. *The Japanese Legal System: Introductory Cases and Materials*. Tokyo: University of Tokyo Press, 1976.

Tate, C. Neal, and Torbjorn Vallinder, eds. *The Global Expansion of Judicial Power.* New York: New York University Press, 1995.

Terrill, Richard J. *World Criminal Justice Systems: A Survey.* 2d ed. Cincinnati: Anderson, 1992.

The Law Commission of Canada, ed. *Personal Relationships of Dependence and Interdependence in Law.* Vancouver: University of British Columbia Press, 2002.

Tonry, Michael, ed. *Penal Reform in Overcrowded Times.* New York: Oxford University Press, 2001.

Trebilcock, Michael, Ralph A. Winter, Paul Collins, and Edward M. Iacobucci. *The Law and Economics of Canadian Competition Policy.* Toronto: University of Toronto Press, 2002.

Upham, Frank K. *Law and Social Change in Postwar Japan.* Cambridge: Harvard University Press, 1987.

Volcansek, Mary L., and Jacqueline Lucienne Lafon. *Judicial Selection: The Cross-Evolution of French and American Practices.* New York and Westport, CT: Greenwood Press, 1987.

Volcansek, Mary L., Maria Elisabetta de Franciscis, and Jacqueline Lucienne Lafon. *Judicial Misconduct: A Cross-National Comparison.* Gainesville: University Press of Florida, 1996.

Walker, R. J. *The English Legal System.* London: Butterworths, 1976.

Weiler, P. *In The Last Resort: A Critical Study of the Supreme Court of Canada.* Toronto: Carswell/Methuen, 1974.

Welhengama, Gnanapala. *Minorities' Claims: From Autonomy to Secession, International Law and State Practice.* Burlington, VT: Ashgate, 2000.

Weyrauch, Walter O., ed. *Gypsy Law: Romani Legal Traditions and Culture.* Berkeley: University of California Press, 2001.

Widner, Jennifer A. *Building the Rule of Law: Francis Nyalali and the Road to Judicial Independence in Africa.* New York: W. W. Norton, 2001.

Woodhouse, Diana. *The Office of Lord Chancellor.* Oxford: Hart, 2001.

Zemach, Y. S. *Political Questions in the Courts: A Judicial Function in Democracies—Israel and the United States.* Detroit: Wayne State University Press, 1976.

Ziamou, Theodora. *Rulemaking, Participation and the Limits of Public Law in the USA and Europe.* Burlington, VT: Ashgate, 2001.

Zweiger, Konrad, and Hein Kotz. *An Introduction to Comparative Law: The Framework.* Amsterdam: North Holland, 1977.

Law and Society

Abrams, Roger I. *The Money Pitch: Baseball Free Agency and Salary Arbitration.* Philadelphia: Temple University Press, 2000.

Alcock, Anthony E., Brian K. Taylor, and John M. Welton. *The Future of Cultural Minorities.* New York: St. Martin's Press, 1979.

Alix, Ernest Kahlar. *Ransom Kidnapping in America, 1874–1974.* Carbondale: Southern Illinois University Press, 1978.

Ball, Milner S. *Lying Down Together: Law, Metaphor, and Theology.* Madison: University of Wisconsin Press, 1985.

Bayley, David. *Forces of Order: Police Behavior in Japan and in the United States.* Berkeley: University of California Press, 1978.

Beckett, Katherine. *Making Crime Pay: Law and Order in Contemporary American Politics.* New York: Oxford University Press, 1997.

Beckstrom, John H. *Sociobiology and the Law: The Biology of Altruism in the Court of the Future.* Champaign: University of Illinois Press, 1985.

Belknap, Michael, ed. *American Political Trials.* Westport, CT: Greenwood Press, 1981.

Berkman, Ronald. *Opening the Gates: The Rise of the Prisoners' Movement.* Lexington, MA: Lexington Books, 1979.

Berry, Mary Frances. *Why ERA Failed: Politics, Women's Rights and the Amending Process of the Constitution.* Bloomington: Indiana University Press, 1988.

Berry, Robert C., William B. Gould, and Paul D. Standohar. *Labor Relations in Professional Sports.* Dover, MA: Auburn House, 1986.

Biggs, Hazel. *Euthanasia: Death with Dignity and the Law.* Oxford: Hart, 2001.

Bohannan, Paul, ed. *Law and Warfare.* Garden City, NY: Natural History Press, 1967.

Bonsignore, John J., Ethan Katsh, Peter d'Errico, Ronald M. Pipkin, Stephen Arons, and Janet Rifkin. *Before the Law: An Introduction to the Legal Process.* 6th ed. Boston: Houghton Mifflin, 1998.

Bromberg, Walter. *The Uses of Psychiatry in the Law: A Clinical View of Forensic Psychiatry.* Westport, CT: Greenwood, 1979.

Burkhardt, Kathryn. *Women in Prison.* Garden City, NY: Doubleday, 1973.

Burt, Robert A. *Taking Care of Strangers: The Rule of Law in Doctor-Patient Relations.* New York: Free Press, 1979.

Chambliss, William, and Robert Seidman. *Law, Order and Power.* Reading, MA: Addison-Wesley, 1971.

Channels, Noreen L. *Social Science Methods in the Legal Process.* Totowa, NJ: Rowman & Littlefield, 1985.

Cleaver, Eldridge. *Soul On Ice.* New York: McGraw-Hill, 1992.

Cohen, Morris L., Naomi Ronen, and Jan Stepan, comps. *Law and Science.* Cambridge: The MIT Press, 1980.

Cohen, Stanley. *Visions of Social Control: Crime, Punishment and Classification.* Oxford: Polity Press, 1985.

Coser, Lewis. *The Functions of Social Conflict.* New York: Free Press, 1966.

Dahl, Tove Stang. *Child Welfare and Social Defence.* Oslo: Norwegian University Press, 1985.

Davis, Karl. *Discretionary Justice.* Baton Rouge: Louisiana State University Press, 1979.

Deveaux, Monique. *Cultural Pluralism and Dilemmas of Justice.* Ithaca, NY: Cornell University Press, 2000.

Dominguez, Virginia R. *White by Definition: Social Classification in Creole Louisiana.* New Brunswick, NJ: Rutgers University Press, 1994.

Dworkin, Gerald, R. G. Frey, and Sissela Bok. *Euthanasia and Physician-Assisted Suicide.* Cambridge, UK: Cambridge University Press, 1998.

Dwyer, James G. *Vouchers within Reason: A Child-Centered Approach to Education Reform.* Ithaca, NY: Cornell University Press, 2002.

Eckelaar, John, and Mavis Maclean. *Maintenance After Divorce.* Oxford: Clarendon Press, Oxford Socio-Legal Studies, 1986.

Edge, Peter W., and Graham Harvey, eds. *Law and Religion in Contemporary Society: Communities, Individualism, and the State.* Burlington, VT: Ashgate, 2000.

Ehrlich, Eugen. *Fundamental Principles of the Sociology of Law.* Translated by W. Moll. New York: Russell and Russell, 1962.

Ely, James W., Jr. *Railroads and American Law.* Lawrence: University Press of Kansas, 2001.

Epstein, Cynthia. *Women in Law.* 2d ed. Urbana: University of Illinois Press, 1993.

Epstein, Lee, and Joseph F. Kobylka. *The Supreme Court and Legal Change: Abortion and the Death Penalty*. Chapel Hill: University of North Carolina Press, 1992.

Erikson, Kai T. *Wayward Puritans: A Study in the Sociology of Deviance*. New York: John Wiley & Sons, 1986.

Eskridge, William N., Jr. *Gaylaw: Challenging the Apartheid of the Closet*. Cambridge: Harvard University Press, 1999.

Ewick, Patricia, Robert A. Kagan, and Austin Sarat, eds. *Social Science, Social Policy and the Law*. New York: Russell Sage Foundation, 1999.

Faden, Ruth R., Tom L. Beauchamp, and Nancy M. P. King. *A History and Theory of Informed Consent*. Oxford: Oxford University Press, 1986.

Fairchild, Erika S., and Vincent J. Webb, eds. *The Politics of Crime and Criminal Justice*. Beverly Hills: Sage, 1985.

Fairfax, Sally K., and Darla Guenzler. *Conservation Trusts*. Lawrence: University Press of Kansas, 2001.

Feild, Hubert S., and Leigh B. Bienen. *Jurors and Rape: A Study in Psychology and Law*. Lexington, MA: Lexington Books, 1981.

Finkelman, Paul. *The Law of Freedom and Bondage: A Casebook*. New York: Oceana, New York University School of Law: Ingram Documents in American Legal History, 1986.

Fisher, Louis. *Religious Liberty in America: Political Safeguards*. Lawrence: University Press of Kansas, 2002.

Fitzmaurice, Catherine, and Ken Pease. *The Psychology of Judicial Sentencing*. Manchester: Manchester University Press, 1986.

Forsyth, Walter. *History of Trial by Jury*. New York: Burt Franklin, 1971.

Foucault, Michel. *The Birth of the Prison*. New York: Pantheon, 1978.

Foust, Cleon H., and Robert D. Webster. *An Anatomy of Criminal Justice*. Lexington, MA: Lexington Books, 1980.

Fox, Richard L., and Robert W. Van Sickel. *Tabloid Justice: Criminal Justice in an Age of Media Frenzy*. Boulder, CO: Lynne Riener, 2001.

Freeman, Michael. *Children's Rights: A Comparative Perspective*. Aldershot, UK: Dartmouth, 1996.

Freeman, Michael, and Andrew Lewis, eds. *Law and Medicine: Critical Legal Issues 2000*. Vol. 3. New York: Oxford University Press, 2000.

Freidson, Eliot. *Professional Powers: A Study of the Institutionalization of Formal Knowledge*. Chicago: University of Chicago Press, 1986.

Friedlander, Judith, Wiesen Blance Cook, Alice Kessler-Harris, and Carroll Smith-Rosenberg, eds. *Women in Culture and Politics: A Century of Change*. Bloomington: Indiana University Press, 1986.

Friedman, David D. *Law's Order: What Economics has to do with Law and why it Matters*. Princeton, NJ: Princeton University Press, 2000.

Friedrichs, David O. *Law in our Lives: An Introduction*. Los Angeles: Roxbury, 2001.

Gagne, Patricia. *Battered Women's Justice: The Movement for Clemency and the Politics of Self-Defense*. New York: Twayne, 1998.

Gardiner, John A., ed. *Public Law and Public Policy*. New York: Praeger, 1977.

Garland, David. *The Culture of Control: Crime and Social Order in Contemporary Society*. Chicago: University of Chicago Press, 2001.

Gearey, Adam. *Law and Aesthetics*. Oxford and Portland, OR: Hart, 2001.

Geis, Gilbert, and Ezra Stotland. *White-Collar Crime: Theory and Research*. Beverly Hills: Sage, 1980.

Geisler, Charles, and Gail Daneker, eds. *Property and Values: Alternatives to Public and Private Ownership*. Washington, DC: Island Press, 2000.

Geltman, Elizabeth Glass. *Recycling Land: Understanding the Legal Landscape of Brownfield Development*. Ann Arbor: University of Michigan Press, 2000.

Gest, Ted. *Crime and Politics: Big Government's Erratic Campaign for Law and Order*. New York: Oxford University Press, 2001.

Gill, Peter. *Rounding Up the Usual Suspects: Developments in Contemporary Law Enforcement Intelligence*. Burlington, VT: Ashgate, 2000.

Goldberg, David Theo, Michael Musheno, and Lisa C. Bower, eds. *Between Law and Culture: Relocating Legal Studies*. Minneapolis: University of Minnesota Press, 2001.

Goldberg, Stephen B., Eric D. Green, and Frank E. A. Sander, eds. *Dispute Resolution*. Boston: Little, Brown, 1995.

Goldberg, Steven. *Culture Clash: Law and Science in America*. New York: New York University Press, 1994.

Goldstein, Paul J. *Prostitution and Drugs*. Lexington, MA: Lexington Books, 1979.

Gostin, Lawrence O. *Public Health Law: Power, Duty, Restraint*. Berkeley: University of California Press, 2001.

———. *Public Health Law and Ethics: A Reader*. Berkeley: University of California Press, 2002.

Gould, David J. *Law and the Administrative Process: Analytic Frameworks for Understanding Public Policymaking*. Washington, DC: University Press of America, 1979.

Gould, William B. IV. *Labored Relations: Law, Politics, and the NLRB—A Memoir*. Cambridge: The MIT Press, 2000.

Grabosky, Peter, Russell G. Smith, and Gillian Dempsey. *Electronic Theft: Unlawful Acquisition in Cyberspace*. Cambridge, UK: Cambridge University Press, 2001.

Gray, Judge James P. *Why Our Drug Laws Have Failed and What We Can Do About It: A Judicial Indictment of the War on Drugs*. Philadelphia: Temple University Press, 2001.

Gregory, Charles O., and Harold A. Katz. *Labor and the Law*. 3d ed. New York: W. W. Norton, 1979.

Grossman, Joel B., and Mary H. Grossman, eds. *Law and Change in Modern America*. Pacific Palisades, CA: Goodyear, 1971.

Gulliver, P. H. *Disputes and Negotiations: A Cross-Cultural Perspective*. New York: Academic Press, 1979.

Gurr, Ted Robert. *Violence in America: Historical and Comparative Perspectives*. New York: Bantam Books, 1970.

Hamburger, Philip. *Separation of Church and State*. Cambridge: Harvard University Press, 2002.

Haney-López, Ian F. *Racism on Trial: The Chicano Fight for Justice*. Cambridge, MA and London, UK: The Belknap Press of Harvard University Press, 2003.

Hans, Valerie P. *Business on Trial: The Civil Jury and Corporate Responsibility*. New Haven, CT: Yale University Press, 2000.

Hans, Valerie P., and Neil Vidmar. *Judging the Jury*. New York: Plenum, 1986.

Harris, Donald, et. al. *Compensation and Support for Illness and Injury*. Oxford: Clarendon Press, 1984.

Harris, John. *Violence and Responsibility*. Boston: Routledge and Kegan Paul, 1980.

Hartley, Roger E. *Alternative Dispute Resolution in Civil Justice Systems*. New York: LFB Scholarly Publishing, 2002.

Hartog, Hendrik. *Man and Wife in America*. Cambridge: Harvard University Press, 2000.

Heins, Marjorie. *Not in Front of the Children: "Indecency," Censorship, and the Innocence of Youth*. New York: Hill and Wang, 2001.

Hensler, Deborah R., Nicholas M. Page, Bonita Dombey-Moore, Beth Giddens, Jennifer Gross, and Erik K. Moller. *Class Action Dilemmas: Pursuing Public Goals for Private Gain.* Santa Monica, CA: RAND Institute for Civil Justice, 2000.

Herring, Jonathan, ed. *Family Law: Issues, Debates, Policy.* Collompton, UK: Willan, 2001.

Hillyard, Daniel, and John Dombrink. *Dying Right: The Death with Dignity Movement.* New York: Routledge, 2001.

Hilton, N. Zoe. *Legal Responses to Wife Assault.* Newbury Park, CA: Sage, 1993.

Hirsch, Susan F. *Pronouncing and Persevering: Gender and the Discourses of Disputing in an African Islamic Court.* Chicago: University of Chicago Press, 1998.

Hirsch, Werner Z. *Law and Economics: An Introductory Analysis.* 2d ed. New York: Academic Press, 1988.

Hoff-Wilson, Joan, ed. *Rights of Passage: The Past and Future of the ERA.* Bloomington: Indiana University Press, 1986.

Hudson, Joe, and Burt Galaway, eds. *Victims, Offenders, and Alternative Sanctions.* Lexington, MA: Lexington Books, 1980.

Hughes, Gordon, and Adam Edwards, eds. *Crime Control and Community: The New Politics of Public Safety.* Portland, OR: Willan, 2002.

Hull, N. E. H. *Female Felons: Women and Serious Crime in Colonial Massachusetts.* Urbana: University of Illinois Press, 1987.

———, and Peter Charles Hoffer. *Roe v. Wade: The Abortion Rights Controversy in American History.* Lawrence: University Press of Kansas, 2001.

Hurst, James Willard. *The Growth of American Law.* Boston: Little, Brown, 1950.

Jackson, Emily. *Regulating Reproduction: Law, Technology and Autonomy.* Oxford: Hart, 2001.

Jacobs, James B. *Can Gun Control Work?* New York: Oxford University Press, 2002.

Jacobs, James B., and Kimberly Potter. *Hate Crimes: Criminal Law and Identity Politics.* New York: Oxford University Press, 1998.

James, Susan, and Stephanie Palmer, eds. *Visible Women: Essays on Feminist Legal Theory.* Oxford and Portland, OR: Hart, 2002.

Jewkes, Yvonne, ed. *Dot. Cons: Crime, Deviance, and Identity on the Internet.* Cullompton, UK: Willan Press, 2003.

Johnson, Kevin R., ed. *Mixed Race America and the Law: A Reader.* New York and London: New York University Press, 2003.

Kagan, Robert A. *Adversarial Legalism: The American Way of Law.* Cambridge: Harvard University Press, 2003.

———, and Lee Axelrad, eds. *Regulatory Encounters: Multinational Corporations and American Adversarial Legalism.* Berkeley: University of California Press, 2000.

Kalven, Harry, Jr., and Hans Zeisel. *The American Jury.* Boston: Little, Brown, 1966.

Karlen, Delmar. *The Citizen in Court.* New York: Holt, Rinehart and Winston, 1964.

Katsh, M. Ethan. *Law in a Digital World.* New York: Oxford University Press, 1995.

Katz, Michael B. *In the Shadow of the Poorhouse: A Social History of Welfare in America.* New York: Basic Books, 1986.

Kaufman-Osborn, Timothy V. *From Noose to Needle: Capital Punishment and the Late Liberal State.* Ann Arbor: University of Michigan Press, 2003.

Kelly, Kristin A. *Domestic Violence and the Politics of Privacy.* Ithaca, NY: Cornell University Press, 2003.

Keown, John. *Euthanasia, Ethics and Public Policy: An Argument against Legalisation.* Cambridge, UK: Cambridge University Press, 2002.

Kirchheimer, Otto. *Political Justice.* Princeton, NJ: Princeton University Press, 1968.

Kittrie, Nicholas N., and Eldon D. Wedlock, Jr., eds. *The Tree of Liberty: A Documentary History of Rebellion and Political Crime in America*. Baltimore: Johns Hopkins University Press, 1986.

Knutsson, Johannes, ed. *Problem Oriented Policing from Innovation to Mainstream*. Monsey, NY: Criminal Justice Press, 2003.

Koshner, Andrew Jay. *Solving the Puzzle of Interest Group Litigation*. Westport, CT: Greenwood Press, 1998.

Kramnick, Isaac, and Lawrence Moore. *The Godless Constitution: The Case against Religious Correctness*. New York: W. W. Norton, 1996.

Landrine, Hope, and Elizabeth A. Klonoff. *Discrimination against Women: Prevalence, Consequences, Remedies*. Beverly Hills: Sage, 1997.

Lawrence, Frederick M. *Punishing Hate: Bias Crime under American Law*. Cambridge: Harvard University Press, 1999.

Lawrence, Regina G. *The Politics of Force: Media and the Construction of Police Brutality*. Berkeley: University of California Press, 2000.

LeMoncheck, Linda, and Mane Hajdin. *Sexual Harassment: A Debate*. Lanham, MD: Rowman & Littlefield, 1997.

Levine, James P., Michael C. Musheno, and Dennis J. Palumbo. *Criminal Justice: A Public Policy Approach*. New York: Harcourt, Brace and Jovanovich, 1980.

Levit, Nancy. *The Gender Line: Men, Women, and the Law*. New York: New York University Press, 1998.

Lidz, Charles W., Alan Meisel, Eviatar Zerubavel, Mary Carter, Regina M. Sestak, and Loren H. Roth. *Informed Consent: A Study of Decisionmaking in Psychiatry*. New York: Guilford Press, 1984.

Lieberman, Jethro K. *The Litigious Society*. New York: Basic Books, 1983.

Lin, Ann Chih. *Reform in the Making: The Implementation of Social Policy in Prison*. Princeton, NJ: Princeton University Press, 2000.

Llewellyn, Karl, and E. Adamson Hoebel. *The Cheyenne Way*. Norman: University of Oklahoma Press, 1983.

Loewen, James W. *Social Science in the Courtroom: Statistical Techniques and Research Methods for Winning Class-Action Suits*. Lexington, MA: Heath, 1982.

Lopez, Ian F. Haney. *White by Law: The Legal Construction of Race*. New York: New York University Press, 1996.

LoPuck, Lynn M. *Player's Manual for the Debtor-Creditor Game*. St. Paul, MN: West, 1985.

Lukemeyer, Anna. *Courts as Policymakers: School Finance Reform Litigation*. New York: LFB Scholarly Publishing, 2003.

Mackey, Thomas C. *Pornography on Trial*. Santa Barbara, CA: ABC-CLIO, 2002.

Mackinnon, Catharine A. *The Sexual Harassment of Working Women*. New Haven, CT: Yale University Press, 1979.

Macneil, Iran R. *The New Social Contract: An Inquiry into Modern Contractual Relations*. New Haven, CT: Yale University Press, 1980.

Malinchak, Alan A. *Crime and Gerontology*. Englewood Cliffs, NJ: Prentice Hall, 1980.

Markowitz, Michael W., and Delores D. Jones-Brown, eds. *The System in Black and White: Exploring the Connections between Race, Crime, and Justice*. Westport, CT: Praeger, 2000.

Matasar, Ann B. *Corporate PACs and Federal Campaign Financing Laws*. Westport, CT: Quorum Books, 1986.

Matsuda, Mari J., et. al. *Words That Wound: Critical Race Theory, Assaultive Speech, and the First Amendment*. Boulder, CO: Westview Press, 1993.

McCallum, Ronald. *Employer Controls over Private Life.* Sydney, Australia: University of New South Wales Press, 2000.

McDonald, Douglas Carry. *Punishment without Walls: Community Service Sentences in New York City.* New Brunswick, NJ: Rutgers University Press, 1989.

McGlynn, Clare, ed. *Legal Feminisms: Theory and Practice.* Brookfield, VT: Ashgate, 1998.

Meier, Robert F., and Gilbert Geis. *Victimless Crime? Prostitution, Drugs, Homosexuality, Abortion.* Los Angeles: Roxbury, 1997.

Menikoff, Jerry. *Law and Bioethics: An Introduction.* Washington, DC: Georgetown University Press, 2001.

Menninger, Kar. *The Crime of Punishment.* New York: Viking Press, 1977.

Merryman, John Henry, David S. Clark, and Lawrence M. Friedman. *Law and Social Change in Mediterranean Europe and Latin America: A Handbook of Legal and Social Indicators for Comparative Study.* Dobbs Ferry, NY: Oceana, 1979.

Miller, Lisa L. *The Politics of Community Crime Prevention: Implementing Operation Weed and Seed in Seattle.* Burlington, VT: Ashgate, 2001.

Miller, Richard. *The Case for Legalizing Drugs.* New York: Praeger, 1991.

Milovanovic, Dragan. *A Primer in the Sociology of Law.* 2d ed. New York: Harrow & Heston, 1994.

Mink, Gwendolyn. *Hostile Environment: The Political Betrayal of Sexually Harassed Women.* Ithaca, NY: Cornell University Press, 2000.

Mitchell, Charles, and Susan R. Moody, eds. *Foundations of Charity.* Oxford: Hart, 2000.

Mitchell, Lawrence E. *Corporate Irresponsibility: America's Newest Export.* New Haven, CT: Yale University Press, 2001.

Monsma, Stephen V., ed. *Church-State Relations in Crisis: Debating Neutrality.* Lanham, MD: Rowman & Littlefield, 2002.

Mooney, Christopher F. *Boundaries Dimly Perceived: Law, Religion, Education and the Common Good.* Notre Dame, IN: University of Notre Dame Press, 1990.

Moran, Rachel F. *Interracial Intimacy: The Regulation of Race and Romance.* Chicago: University of Chicago Press, 2001.

Morris, Norville. *The Future of Imprisonment.* Chicago: University of Chicago Press, 1977.

Mosley, Albert G., and Nicholas Capaldi. *Affirmative Action: Social Justice or Unfair Preference?* Lanham, MD: Rowman & Littlefield, 1996.

Murrell, Peter, ed. *Assessing the Value of Law in Transition Economies.* Ann Arbor: University of Michigan Press, 2001.

Nader, Laura, ed. *Law in Culture and Society.* Chicago: Aldine, 1969.

Neier, Aryeh. *Only Judgement: The Limits of Litigation in Social Change.* Middletown, CT: Wesleyan University Press, 1985.

Nonet, Philippe, and Philip Selznick. *Law and Society in Transition: Toward Responsive Law.* New Brunswick, NJ: Transaction, 2001.

Novy, Marianne, ed. *Imagining Adoption: Essays on Literature and Culture.* Ann Arbor: University of Michigan Press, 2001.

O'Brien, Ruth. *Crippled Justice: The History of Modern Disability Policy in the Workplace.* Chicago: University of Chicago Press, 2001.

O'Connor, Karen. *No Neutral Ground? Abortion Politics in an Age of Absolutes.* Boulder, CO: Westview Press, 1996.

Osiel, Mark J. *Obeying Orders: Atrocity, Military Discipline & the Law of War.* New Brunswick, NJ: Transaction, 1999.

Palmer, Larry I. *Endings and Beginnings: Law, Medicine, and Society in Assisted Life and Death.* Westport, CT: Praeger, 2000.

Parry, Ruth S., et al., eds. *Custody Disputes: Evaluation and Intervention.* Lexington, MA: Lexington Books, D. C. Heath, 1986.

Patton, Sandra. *Birthmarks: Transracial Adoption in Contemporary America.* New York: New York University Press, 2000.

Pencak, William J., Ralph Lingren, Roberta Kevelson, and Charles N. Yood, eds. *"The Law" v. "The People": Twelfth Roundtable on Law and Semiotics.* New York: Peter Lang, 2000.

Pertman, Adam. *Adoption Nation: How the Adoption Revolution is Transforming America.* New York: Basic Books, 2000.

Pierce, Jennifer L. *Gender Trials: Emotional Lives in Contemporary Law Firms.* Berkeley: University of California Press, 1995.

Posner, Eric A. *Law and Social Norms.* Cambridge: Harvard University Press, 2000.

Pound, Roscoe. *Social Control through Law.* New Haven, CT: Yale University Press, 1968.

Provine, Doris Marie. *Judging Credentials: Nonlawyer Judges and the Politics of Professionalism.* Chicago: University of Chicago Press, 1986.

Rabin, Robert L., and Stephen D. Sugarman, eds. *Regulating Tobacco.* New York: Oxford University Press, 2001.

Reed, Douglas S. *On Equal Terms: The Constitutional Politics of Educational Opportunity.* Princeton, NJ: Princeton University Press, 2001.

Reiss, Albert. *The Police and the Public.* New Haven, CT: Yale University Press, 1971.

Rhode, Deborah L., ed. *The Difference "Difference" Makes: Women and Leadership.* Stanford, CA: Stanford University Press, 2003.

Robbins, Ira P. *Comparative Postconviction Remedies.* Lexington, MA: Lexington Books, 1980.

Roberts, Julian V., and Mike Hough. *Changing Attitudes to Punishment: Public Opinion, Crime and Justice.* Portland, OR: Willan, 2002.

Robinson, Daniel N. *Psychology and Law: Can Justice Survive the Social Sciences?* New York: Oxford University Press, 1980.

Rosenblum, Nancy L., ed. *Obligations of Citizenship and Demands of Faith: Religious Accommodation in Pluralist Democracies.* Princeton, NJ: Princeton University Press, 2000.

Ross, Hamish. *Law as a Social Institution.* Oxford: Hart, 2001.

Ross, Jeffrey Ian, ed. *Varieties of State Crime and its Control.* Monsey, NY: Criminal Justice Press, 2000.

———, and Stephen C. Richards. *Behind Bars: Surviving Prison.* Indianapolis: Alpha Books, 2002.

———. *Convict Criminology.* Belmont, CA: Wadsworth, 2003.

Roth, Rachel. *Making Women Pay: The Hidden Costs of Fetal Rights.* Ithaca, NY: Cornell University Press, 2000.

Rubin, Eva R. *The Supreme Court and the American Family: Ideology and Issues.* Westport, CT: Greenwood Press, Contributions in American Studies 85, 1986.

Rubinowitz, Leonard S., and James E. Rosenbaum. *Crossing the Class and Color Lines: From Public Housing to White Suburbia.* Chicago: University of Chicago Press, 2000.

Ruggiero, Vincenzo. *Crime and Markets: Essays in Anti-Criminology.* New York: Oxford University Press, 2000.

Russell, Katharine K. *The Colour of Crime: Racial Hoaxes, White Fear, Black Protectionism, Police Harassment, and Other Macroaggressions.* New York: New York University Press, 1998.

Sack, Peter, and Jonathan Aleck, eds. *Law and Anthropology.* New York: New York University Press, 1992.

Saks, Michael. *Jury Verdict: The Role of Group Size and Social Decision Rule.* Lexington, MA: Lexington Books, 1977.

Salomone, Rosemary C. *Visions of Schooling: Conscience, Community and Common Education.* New Haven, CT: Yale University Press, 2000.

Sarat, Austin, ed. *Law, Violence, and the Possibility of Justice.* Princeton, NJ: Princeton University Press, 2001.

———, ed. *Pain, Death, and the Law.* Ann Arbor: University of Michigan Press, 2001.

———. *When the State Kills: Capital Punishment and the American Condition.* Princeton, NJ: Princeton University Press, 2001.

Scheingold, Stuart A. *Politics, Crime Control and Culture.* Brookfield, VT: Ashgate, 1997.

Schneider, Elizabeth M. *Battered Women and Feminist Lawmaking.* New Haven, CT: Yale University Press, 2000.

Schuck, Peter H. *The Limits of the Law: Essays on Democratic Governance.* Boulder, CO: Westview Press, 2000.

Schur, Edwin. *Law and Society.* New York: Random House, 1968.

Schwitzgebel, Robert L., and R. Kirland Schwitzgebel. *Law and Psychological Practice.* New York: John Wiley & Sons, 1980.

Sciulli, David. *Corporate Power in Civil Society, an Application of Societal Constitutionalism.* New York: New York University Press, 2001.

Shapiro, Susan P. *Wayward Capitalists: Target of the Securities and Exchange Commission.* New Haven, CT: Yale University Press, Yale Studies on White-Collar Crime, 1984.

Sherwin, Richard K. *When Law Goes Pop: The Vanishing Line between Law and Popular Culture.* Chicago: University of Chicago, 2000.

Shevory, Thomas C. *Body/Politics: Studies in Reproduction, Production, and (Re)Construction.* Westport, CT: Praeger, 2000.

Shichor, David, and Delos H. Kelly, eds. *Critical Issues in Juvenile Delinquency.* Lexington, MA: Lexington Books, 1980.

Shiell, Timothy C. *Campus Hate Speech on Trial.* Lawrence: University Press of Kansas, 1998.

Siegan, Bernard H. *Regulation, Economics, and the Law.* Lexington, MA: Lexington Books, 1979.

Silber, Norman I. *A Corporate Form of Freedom: The Emergence of the Nonprofit Sector.* Boulder, CO: Westview Press, 2001.

Simon, Rita James, ed. *The Sociology of Law: Interdisciplinary Readings.* San Francisco: Chandler, 1968.

Simpson, Sally S. *Corporate Crime, Law, and Social Control.* Cambridge, UK: Cambridge University Press, 2002.

Skolnick, Jerome. *Justice Without Trial: Law Enforcement in a Democratic Society.* 3d ed. New York: John Wiley & Sons, 1994.

Sloan, Frank A., Emily M. Stout, Kathryn Whetten-Goldstein, and Lan Liang. *Drinkers, Drivers and Bartenders: Balancing Private Choices and Public Accountability.* Chicago: University of Chicago Press, 2000.

Smart, Carol. *Feminism and the Power of Law.* New York: Routledge, 1989.

Solinger, Rickie, ed. *Abortion Wars: A Half Century of Struggle, 1950–2000.* Berkeley: University of California Press, 1998.

Spence, Gerry. *Of Murder and Madness: A True Story of Insanity and the Law.* New York: Doubleday, 1983.

Stamatoudi, Irini A. *Copyright and Multimedia Works: A Comparative Analysis.* Cambridge, UK: Cambridge University Press, 2002.

Stein, Laura W. *Sexual Harassment in America: A Documentary History.* Westport, CT: Greenwood Press, 1999.

Steiner, Y. Gilbert. *The Abortion Dispute and the American System.* Washington, DC: Brookings Institution, 1983.

Stenson, Kevin, and Robert P. Sullivan, eds. *Crime, Risk and Justice: The Politics of Crime Control in Liberal Democracies.* Uffculme Cullompten, UK: Willan, 2001.

Suggs, Jon-Christian. *Whispered Consolations: Law and Narrative in African American Life.* Ann Arbor: University of Michigan Press, 2000.

Sullivan, Dennis, and Larry Tifft. *Restorative Justice: Healing the Foundations of our Everyday Lives.* Monsey, NY: Willow Tree Press, 2001.

Sunstein, Cass R., ed. *Behavioral Law and Economics.* New York: Cambridge University Press, 2000.

———. *Republic.Com.* Princeton, NJ: Princeton University Press, 2001.

Susskind, Richard. *Transforming the Law: Essays on Technology, Justice and the Legal Market Place.* New York: Oxford University Press, 2000.

Tata, Cyrus, and Neil Hutton, ed. *Sentencing and Society: International Perspectives.* Burlington, VT: Ashgate, 2002.

Thornes, Barbara, and Jean Collard. *Who Divorces?* Boston: Routledge and Kegan Paul, 1979.

Tonnies, Ferdinand. *Community and Society.* Edited and translated by Charles P. Loomis. New York: Harper and Row, 1963.

Tonry, Michael, and Franklin E. Zimring, eds. *Reform and Punishment: Essays on Criminal Sentencing.* Chicago: University of Chicago Press, Studies in Crime and Justice, 1983.

Tyler, Tom R., and Yuen J. Huo. *Trust in the Law: Encouraging Public Cooperation with the Police and Court.* New York: Russell Sage Foundation, 2002.

Urofsky, Melvin L. *Lethal Judgments: Assisted Suicide and American Law.* Lawrence: University Press of Kansas, 2000.

Walsh, Dermot. *Heavy Business: Commercial Burglary and Robbery.* London: Routledge and Kegan Paul, 1986.

Weber, Max. *On Law in Economy and Society.* Translated with introduction by Max Rheinstein, et al. Cambridge: Harvard University Press, 1954.

Websdale, Neil. *Policing the Poor: From Slave Plantation to Public Housing.* Boston: Northeastern University Press, 2001.

Wechsler, Henry, ed. *Minimum Drinking Age Laws: An Evaluation.* Lexington, MA: Lexington Books, 1980.

Weiler, Paul. *Leveling the Playing Field: How the Law Can Make Sports Better for Fans.* Cambridge: Harvard University Press, 2000.

Weinberg, Lee S., and Judith W. Weinberg. *Law and Society: An Interdisciplinary Introduction.* Washington, DC: University Press of America, 1980.

Weisbrod, Carol. *Emblems of Pluralism: Cultural Differences and the State.* Princeton, NJ: Princeton University Press, 2003.

Weisburd, David, Elin Waring, and Ellen F. Chayet. *White-Collar Crime and Criminal Careers.* New York: Cambridge University Press, 2001.

Weitz, Mark A. *Clergy Malpractice in America: Nally v. Grace Community Church of the Valley.* Lawrence: University Press of Kansas, 2001.

Weizer, Paul I. *Sexual Harassment: Cases, Case Studies, & Commentary.* New York: Peter Lang, 2002.

Welch, Michael. *Detained: Immigration Laws and the Expanding I.N.S. Jail Complex.* Philadelphia: Temple University Press, 2002.

Westley, William A. *Violence and the Police.* Cambridge: The MIT Press, 1971.

White, Susan O., ed. *Handbook of Youth and Justice.* New York: Kluwer/Plenum, 2001.

Wilburn, James R., ed. *Freedom, Order, and the University.* Los Angeles: Pepperdine University Press, 1982.

Wilkinson, David. *Environment and Law.* New York: Routledge, 2002.

Wilson, James Q. *Varieties of Police Behavior.* Cambridge: Harvard University Press, 1968.

Winslade, William J., and Judith W. Ross. *The Insanity Plea: Uses and Abuse.* New York: Charles Scribner's Sons, 1983.

Wood, James E., Jr., ed. *Religion, the State, and Education.* Waco, TX: Baylor University, 1984.

Wright, Eric Olin. *The Politics of Punishment.* New York: Harper Colophon Books, Harper and Row, 1973.

Wunder, John R., ed. *Recent Legal Issues for American Indians, 1968 to the Present.* New York: Garland, 1996.

Yalof, David A., and Kenneth Dautrich. *The First Amendment and the Media in the Court of Public Opinion.* New York: Cambridge University Press, 2002.

Yanney, A. Daniel. *The Psychology of Eyewitness Testimony.* New York: The Free Press, 1979.

Yarbrough, Tinsley E. *Race and Redistricting: The Shaw-Cromartie Cases.* Lawrence: University Press of Kansas, 2002.

Zelizer, Viviana A. *Pricing the Priceless Child: The Changing Social Value of Children.* New York: Basic Books, 1985.

Zimmer, Lynn E. *Women Guarding Men.* Chicago: University of Chicago Press, Studies in Crime and Justice, 1986.

Zimring, Franklin E. *The Contradictions of American Capital Punishment.* New York: Oxford University Press, 2003.

Zimring, Franklin, Gordon Hawkins, and Sam Kamin. *Punishment and Democracy: Three Strikes and You're Out in California.* Oxford: Oxford University Press, 2001.

Legal Profession

Abel, Richard L. *American Lawyers.* New York: Oxford University Press, 1989.

Allegretti, Joseph G. *The Lawyer's Calling: Christian Faith and Legal Practice.* New York: Paulist Press, 1996

Amsterdam, Anthony G., and Jerome Bruner. *Minding the Law.* Cambridge: Harvard University Press, 2000.

Auerbach, Jerome. *Unequal Justice.* New York: Oxford University Press, 1976.

Baxter, Maurice C. *Henry Clay the Lawyer.* Lexington: University Press of Kentucky, 2000.

Bennett, Walter. *The Lawyer's Myth: Reviving Ideals in the Legal Profession.* Chicago: University of Chicago Press, 2001.

Black, Jonathan, ed. *Radical Lawyers.* New York: Avon Books, 1971.

Bloomfield, Maxwell. *American Lawyers in a Changing Society, 1776–1876.* Cambridge: Harvard University Press, 1976.

Brown, Esther L. *Lawyers and the Promotion of Justice.* New York: Russell Sage Foundation, 1938.

Burke, Thomas F. *Lawyers, Lawsuits, and Legal Rights: The Battle over Litigation in American Society.* Berkeley: University of California Press, 2002.

Cain, Maureen, and Christine Harrington. *Lawyers in a Postmodern World: Translation and Transgression.* Buckingham, UK: Open University Press, 1994.

Cain, Patricia A. *Rainbow Rights: The Role of Lawyers and Courts in the Lesbian and Gay Civil Rights Movement.* Boulder, CO: Westview Press, 2000.

Carlin, Jerome E. *Lawyers on Their Own.* New Brunswick, NJ: Rutgers University Press, 1962.

Casper, Jonathan D. *Lawyers Before the Warren Court: Civil Liberties and Civil Rights, 1957–1966.* Urbana: University of Illinois Press, 1990.

Chroust, Anton-Hermann. *The Rise of the Legal Profession in America.* 2 vols. Norman: University of Oklahoma Press, 1965.

Couric, Emily, ed. *Women Lawyers: Perspectives on Success.* New York: Harcourt, Brace, Jovanovich, 1984.

Dieker, Lawrence, Jr. *Letters from Law School: The Life of a Second-Year Law Student.* Lincoln, NE: Writers Club Press, 2000.

Eisenstein, James. *Counsel for the United States: U.S. Attorney in the Political and Legal System.* Baltimore: John Hopkins University Press, 1978.

Fleming, Macklin. *Lawyers, Money and Success: The Consequences of Dollar Obsession.* Westport, CT: Greenwood, 1997.

Flood, John. *The Legal Profession in the United States.* 3d ed. Chicago: American Bar Foundation, 1985.

Galanter, Marc, and Thomas M. Palay. *Tournament of Lawyers: The Transformation of the Big Law Firms.* Chicago: University of Chicago Press, 1991.

Ginger, Ann Fagan. *The Relevant Lawyers.* New York: Simon & Schuster, 1972.

Glendon, Mary Ann. *A Nation under Lawyers: How the Crisis in the Legal Profession is Transforming American Society.* New York: Farrar, Straus and Giroux, 1994.

Goulden, Joseph. *The Super-Lawyers.* New York: Weybright & Talley, 1973.

Granfield, Robert. *Making Elite Lawyers: Visions of Law at Harvard and Beyond.* New York: Routledge, Chapman and Hall, 1992.

Green, Mark J. *The Other Government: The Unseen Power of Washington Lawyers.* Rev. ed. New York: W. W. Norton, 1978.

Grossman, Joel B. *Lawyers and Judges: The ABA and the Politics of Judicial Selection.* New York: John Wiley & Sons, 1965.

Gruzenberg, O. *Yesterday: Memoirs of a Russian-Jewish Lawyer.* Lexington, MA: Lexington Books, 1981.

Hagan, John, and Fiona Kay. *Gender in Practice: A Study of Lawyers' Lives.* New York: Oxford University Press, 1995.

Halliday, Terence, and Lucien Karpik, eds. *Lawyers and the Rise of Western Political Liberalism: Legal Professions and the Constitution of Modern Politics.* Oxford: Oxford University Press, 1997.

Handler, Joel. *The Lawyer and His Community.* Madison: University of Wisconsin Press, 1967.

Harriger, Katy J. *The Special Prosecutor in American Politics.* 2d ed., revised. Lawrence: University Press of Kansas, 2000.

Heinz, John P., and Edward O. Laumann. *Chicago Lawyers: The Social Structure of the Bar.* New York: Basic Books, 1994.

Hoy, Jerry Van, ed. *Legal Professions: Work, Structure and Organization.* New York: JAI-Elsevier Science, 2001.

Hutchinson, Dennis J., and David J. Garrow, eds. *The Forgotten Memoir of John Knox: A Year in the Life of a Supreme Court Clerk in FDR's Washington.* Chicago: University of Chicago Press, 2002.

Irons, Peter. *The New Deal Lawyers.* New York: Princeton University Press, 1993.

Katz, Jack. *Poor People's Lawyers in Transition.* New Brunswick, NJ: Rutgers University Press, 1982.

Kelly, Michael J. *Lives of Lawyers: Journeys in the Organizations of Practice.* Ann Arbor: University of Michigan Press, 1994.

Kinoy, Arthur. *Rights on Trial: The Odyssey of a People's Lawyer.* Cambridge: Harvard University Press, 1994.

Koenig, Thomas H., and Michael L. Rustad. *In Defense of Tort Law.* New York: New York University Press, 2001.

Kressel, Neil J., and Dorit F. Kressel. *Stack and Sway: The New Science of Jury Consulting.* Cambridge: Westview Press, 2002.

Kritzer, Herbert M. *Lawyers and Nonlawyers at Work.* Ann Arbor: University of Michigan Press, 1999.

Kronman, Anthony. *The Lost Lawyer: Failing Ideals of the Legal Profession.* Cambridge: The Belknap Press of Harvard University Press, 1993.

Landon, Donald D. *Country Lawyers: The Impact of Context on Professional Practice.* New York: Praeger, 1990.

Langum, David J. *William M. Kunstler: The Most Hated Lawyer in America.* New York: New York University Press, 1999.

Lefcourt, Robert. *Law Against the People.* New York: Vintage Books, 1971.

Linowitz, Sol. *The Betrayed Profession: Lawyering at the End of the Twentieth Century.* New York: Charles Scribner's Sons, 1994.

Luban, David. *Lawyers and Justice: An Ethical Study.* Princeton, NJ: Princeton University Press, 1988.

MacDowell, Laurel Sefton. *Renegade Lawyer: The Life of J. L. Cohen.* Toronto: Published for the Osgoode Society for Canadian Legal History by University of Toronto Press, 2001.

Mather, Lynn, Craig A. McEwen, and Richard J. Maiman. *Divorce Lawyers at Work: Varieties of Professionalism in Practice.* New York: Oxford University Press, 2001.

Mayer, Martin. *The Lawyers.* New York: Dell, 1980.

McIntyre, Lisa J. *The Public Defender: The Practice of Law in the Shadows of Repute.* Chicago: University of Chicago Press, 1987.

Medcalf, Linda. *Law and Identity: Lawyers, Native Americans, and Legal Practice.* Beverly Hills: Sage, 1978.

Melone, Albert P. *Lawyers, Public Policy and Interest Group Politics.* Washington, DC: University Press of America, 1977/1979.

Nader, Ralph, and Wesley J. Smith. *No Contest: Corporate Lawyers and the Perversion of Justice in America.* New York: Random House, 1996.

Pound, Roscoe. *The Lawyer from Antiquity to Modern Times.* St. Paul, MN: West, 1953.

Prest, Wilfrid R. *The Rise of the Barristers: A Social History of the English Bar, 1590–1640.* Oxford: Clarendon Press, 1986.

Rhode, Deborah L. *In The Interests of Justice: Reforming the Legal Profession.* New York: Oxford University Press, 2000.

Rosenthal, Douglas. *Lawyer and Client: Who's in Charge?* New Brunswick, NJ: Transaction Books, 1977.

Ross, Peggy A. *The Constitutionality of State Bar Residency Requirements.* Chicago: American Bar Association, 1982.

Roth, Andrew, and Jonathan Roth. *Devil's Advocates: The Unnatural History of Lawyers.* Berkeley, CA: Nolo Press, 1989.

Rueschemeyer, Dietrich. *Lawyers and Their Society: A Comparative Study of the Legal Profession in Germany and in the United States*. Cambridge: Harvard University Press, 1973.

Sarat, Austin, and William F. Felstiner. *Divorce Lawyers and their Clients: Power and Meaning in the Legal Process*. New York: Oxford University Press, 1995.

Sarat, Austin, and Stuart Scheingold, eds. *Cause Lawyering: Political Commitments and Professional Responsibilities*. New York: Oxford University Press, 1998.

Shaffer, Thomas, and Robert Redmount. *Lawyers, Law Students and People*. Indianapolis: Sheppard's, 1977.

Shamir, Ronen. *Managing Legal Uncertainty: Elite Lawyers in the New Deal*. Durham, NC: Duke University Press, 1995.

Smigel, Erwin O. *The Wall Street Lawyer*. New York: The Free Press, 1964.

Spangler, Eve. *Lawyers for Hire: Salaried Professionals at Work*. New Haven, CT: Yale University Press, 1986.

Stevens, Robert. *Law School: Legal Education in America from the 1850s to the 1980s*. Chapel Hill: University of North Carolina Press, 1983.

Stumpf, Harry P. *Community Politics and Legal Services*. Beverly Hills: Sage, 1975.

Turow, Scott. *One L*. New York: G. P. Putnam's Sons, 1977.

Twiss, Benjamin. *Lawyers and the Constitution*. Princeton, NJ: Princeton University Press, 1942.

Van Hoy, Jerry. *Franchise Legal Firms and the Transformation of Personal Legal Services*. Westport, CT: Quorum Books, 1997.

———, ed. *Legal Professions: Work, Structure and Organization*. New York: JAI-Elsevier Science, 2001.

Vile, John R., ed. *Great American Lawyers: An Encyclopedia*. Santa Barbara, CA: ABC-CLIO, 2001.

Warren, Charles. *A History of the American Bar*. Boston: Little, Brown, 1911.

Wice, Paul B. *Criminal Lawyer: An Endangered Species*. Beverly Hills: Sage, 1978.

Wood, Arthur Lewis. *Criminal Lawyer*. New Haven, CT: College & University Press, 1967.

Zemans, Frances K., and Victor Rosenblum. *The Making of a Public Profession*. Chicago: American Bar Foundation Press, 1981.

INDEX